JUMOKE MALUMI

CIMA

Certificate Paper C4

FUNDAMENTALS OF BUSINESS ECONOMICS

For assessments under the 2006 new syllabus in 2006 and 2007

Study Text

In this June 2006 new edition

- A **user-friendly format** for easy navigation
- Regular **fast forward** summaries emphasising the key points in each chapter
- **Assessment focus points** showing you what the assessor will want you to do
- **Questions** and **quick quizzes** to test your understanding
- **Question bank** containing objective test questions with answers
- **A full index**

BPP's **i-Pass** product also supports this paper.

FOR ASSESSMENTS UNDER THE 2006 NEW SYLLABUS IN 2006 AND 2007

First edition June 2006
Reprinted with amendments November 2006

ISBN 0 7517 2650 8

British Library Cataloguing-in-Publication Data
A catalogue record for this book
is available from the British Library

Published by

BPP Professional Education
Aldine House, Aldine Place
London W12 8AW

www.bpp.com

Printed in Great Britain by
Ashford Colour Press Ltd
Unit 600
Fareham Reach
Fareham Road
Gosport
Hampshire
PO13 0FW

We are grateful to the Chartered Institute of Management Accountants for permission to reproduce past examination questions. The suggested solutions in the Answer bank have been prepared by BPP Professional Education.

Contents

INTRODUCTION

T, FN, S, S
3-5. 6-9 10-13 14,15

Computer-based learning products from BPP

If you want to reinforce your studies by **interactive** learning, try BPP's **i-Learn** product, covering major syllabus areas in an interactive format. For **self-testing**, try **i-Pass,** which offers a large number of **objective test questions**, particularly useful where objective test questions form part of the exam.

See the order form at the back of this text for details of these innovative learning tools.

Learn Online

Learn Online uses BPP's wealth of teaching experience to produce a fully **interactive** e-learning resource **delivered via the Internet**. The site offers comprehensive **tutor support** and features areas such as **study**, **practice**, **email service**, **revision** and **useful resources**.

Visit our website www.bpp.com/cima/learnonline to sample aspects of Learn Online free of charge.

Learning to Learn Accountancy

BPP's ground-breaking **Learning to Learn Accountancy** book is designed to be used both at the outset of your CIMA studies and throughout the process of learning accountancy. It challenges you to consider how you study and gives you helpful hints about how to approach the various types of paper which you will encounter. It can help you **focus your studies on the subject and exam**, enabling you to **acquire knowledge**, **practise and revise efficiently and effectively**.

The BPP Study Text

Aims of this Study Text

To provide you with the knowledge and understanding, skills and application techniques that you need if you are to be successful in your exams

This Study Text has been written around the **Fundamentals of Business Economics** syllabus.

- It is **comprehensive**. It covers the syllabus content. No more, no less.
- It is written at the **right level**. Each chapter is written with CIMA's precise learning outcomes in mind.
- It is targeted to the **exam**. We have taken account of the pilot paper, guidance the examiner has given and the assessment methodology.

To allow you to study in the way that best suits your learning style and the time you have available, by following your personal Study Plan (see page (viii))

You may be studying at home on your own until the date of the exam, or you may be attending a full-time course. You may like to (and have time to) read every word, or you may prefer to (or only have time to) skim-read and devote the remainder of your time to question practice. Wherever you fall in the spectrum, you will find the BPP Study Text meets your needs in designing and following your personal Study Plan.

To tie in with the other components of the BPP Effective Study Package to ensure you have the best possible chance of passing the exam (see page (vi))

The BPP Effective Study Package

Recommended period of use	The BPP Effective Study Package
From the outset and throughout	**Learning to Learn Accountancy** Read this invaluable book as you begin your studies and refer to it as you work through the various elements of the BPP Effective Study Package. It will help you to acquire knowledge, practise and revise, efficiently and effectively.
Three to twelve months before the exam	**Study Text and i-Learn** Use the Study Text to acquire knowledge, understanding, skills and the ability to apply techniques. Use BPP's **i-Learn** product to reinforce your learning.
Throughout	**Learn Online** Study, practise, revise and take advantage of other useful resources with BPP's fully interactive e-learning site with comprehensive tutor support.
Throughout	**i-Pass** **i-Pass**, our computer-based testing package, provides objective test questions in a variety of formats and is ideal for self-assessment.
One to six months before the exam	**Practice & Revision Kit** Try the numerous examination-format questions, for which there are realistic suggested solutions prepared by BPP's own authors. Then attempt the two mock exams.
From three months before the exam until the last minute	**Passcards** Work through these short, memorable notes which are focused on what is most likely to come up in the exam you will be sitting.
One to six months before the exam	**Success CDs** The CDs cover the vital elements of your syllabus in less than 90 minutes per subject. They also contain exam hints to help you fine tune your strategy.

Help yourself study for your CIMA assessments

Assessments for professional bodies such as CIMA are very different from those you have taken at college or university. You will be under **greater time pressure before** the exam – as you may be combining your study with work. There are many different ways of learning and so the BPP Study Text offers you a number of different tools to help you through. Here are some hints and tips: they are not plucked out of the air, but **based on research and experience**. (You don't need to know that long-term memory is in the same part of the brain as emotions and feelings - but it's a fact anyway.)

The right approach

1 **The right attitude**

Believe in yourself	Yes, there is a lot to learn. Yes, it is a challenge. But thousands have succeeded before and you can too.
Remember why you're doing it	Studying might seem a grind at times, but you are doing it for a reason: to advance your career.

2 **The right focus**

Read through the Syllabus and learning outcomes	These tell you what you are expected to know and are supplemented by Assessment focus points in the text.
Study the Exam Paper section	The pilot paper is likely to be a good guide to what you should expect in the assessment.

3 **The right method**

The whole picture	You need to grasp the detail - but keeping in mind how everything fits into the whole picture will help you understand better. • The **Introduction** of each chapter puts the material in context. • The **Syllabus content, Learning outcomes** and **Assessment focus points** show you what you need to **grasp**.
In your own words	To absorb the information (and to practise your written communication skills), it helps to **put it into your own words**. • **Take notes.** • Answer the **questions** in each chapter. You will practise your written communication skills, which become increasingly important as you progress through your CIMA exams. • Draw **mindmaps**. • Try **'teaching' a subject** to a colleague or friend.
Give yourself cues to jog your memory	The BPP Study Text uses **bold** to **highlight key points**. • Try **colour coding** with a highlighter pen. • Write **key points** on cards.

4 **The right review**

Review, review, review	It is a **fact** that regularly reviewing a topic in summary form can **fix it in your memory**. Because **review** is so important, the BPP Study Text helps you to do so in many ways. • **Chapter roundups** summarise the 'fast forward' key points in each chapter. Use them to recap each study session. • The **Quick quiz** is another review technique you can use to ensure that you have grasped the essentials. • Go through the **Examples** in each chapter a second or third time.

Developing your personal Study Plan

BPP's **Learning to Learn Accountancy** book emphasises the need to prepare (and use) a study plan. Planning and sticking to the plan are key elements of learning success.
There are four steps you should work through.

Step 1 How do you learn?

First you need to be aware of your style of learning. The BPP **Learning to Learn Accountancy** book commits a chapter to this **self-discovery**. What types of intelligence do you display when learning? You might be advised to brush up on certain study skills before launching into this Study Text.

BPP's **Learning to Learn Accountancy** book helps you to identify what intelligences you show more strongly and then details how you can tailor your study process to your preferences. It also includes handy hints on how to develop intelligences you exhibit less strongly, but which might be needed as you study accountancy.

Are you a **theorist** or are you more **practical**? If you would rather get to grips with a theory before trying to apply it in practice, you should follow the study sequence on page (ix). If the reverse is true (you like to know why you are learning theory before you do so), you might be advised to flick through Study Text chapters and look at examples, case studies and questions (Steps 8, 9 and 10 in the **suggested study sequence**) before reading through the detailed theory.

Step 2 How much time do you have?

Work out the time you have available per week, given the following.

- The standard you have set yourself
- The time you need to set aside later for work on the Practice & Revision Kit and Passcards
- The other exam(s) you are sitting
- Very importantly, practical matters such as work, travel, exercise, sleep and social life

		Hours
Note your time available in box A.	A	

Step 3 **Allocate your time**

- Take the time you have available per week for this Study Text shown in box A, multiply it by the number of weeks available and insert the result in box B. B [ ]
- Divide the figure in box B by the number of chapters in this text and insert the result in box C. C [ ]

Remember that this is only a rough guide. Some of the chapters in this book are longer and more complicated than others, and you will find some subjects easier to understand than others.

Step 4 **Implement**

Set about studying each chapter in the time shown in box C, following the key study steps in the order suggested by your particular learning style.

This is your personal **Study Plan**. You should try and combine it with the study sequence outlined below. You may want to modify the sequence a little (as has been suggested above) to adapt it to your **personal style**.

BPP's **Learning to Learn Accountancy** gives further guidance on developing a study plan, and deciding where and when to study.

Suggested study sequence

It is likely that the best way to approach this Study Text is to tackle the chapters in the order in which you find them. Taking into account your individual learning style, you could follow this sequence.

Key study steps	Activity
Step 1 **Topic list**	Each numbered topic is a numbered section in the chapter.
Step 2 **Introduction**	This gives you the big picture in terms of the context of the chapter, the learning outcomes the chapter covers, and the content you will read. In other words, it sets your objectives for study.
Step 3 **Knowledge brought forward boxes**	In these we highlight information and techniques that it is assumed you have 'brought forward' with you from your earlier studies. If there are topics which have changed recently due to legislation for example, these topics are explained in more detail.
Step 4 **Fast forward**	Fast forward boxes give you a quick summary of the content of each of the main chapter sections. They are listed together in the roundup at the end of each chapter to provide you with an overview of the contents of the whole chapter.
Step 5 **Explanations**	Proceed methodically through the chapter, reading each section thoroughly and making sure you understand.
Step 6 **Key terms and Exam focus points**	• Key terms can often earn you *easy marks* if you state them clearly and correctly in an appropriate exam answer (and they are highlighted in the index at the back of the text). • Exam focus points state how we think the examiner intends to examine certain topics.
Step 7 **Note taking**	Take brief notes, if you wish. Avoid the temptation to copy out too much. Remember that being able to put something into your own words is a sign of being able to understand it. If you find you cannot explain something you have read, read it again before you make the notes.

Key study steps	Activity
Step 8 **Examples**	Follow each through to its solution very carefully.
Step 9 **Case studies**	Study each one, and try to add flesh to them from your own experience. They are designed to show how the topics you are studying come alive (and often come unstuck) in the real world.
Step 10 **Questions**	Make a very good attempt at each one.
Step 11 **Answers**	Check yours against ours, and make sure you understand any discrepancies.
Step 12 **Chapter roundup**	Work through it carefully, to make sure you have grasped the significance of all the fast forward points.
Step 13 **Quick quiz**	When you are happy that you have covered the chapter, use the Quick quiz to check how much you have remembered of the topics covered and to practise questions in a variety of formats.
Step 14 **Question(s) in the Exam question bank**	Either at this point, or later when you are thinking about revising, make a full attempt at the Question(s) suggested at the very end of the chapter. You can find these at the end of the Study Text, along with the Answers so you can see how you did.
Step 15 **Objective test questions**	Use the bank of OTs at the back of this Study Text to practise, and to determine how much of the Study Text you have absorbed. If you have bought i-Pass, use this too.

Short of time: Skim study technique?

You may find you simply do not have the time available to follow all the key study steps for each chapter, however you adapt them for your particular learning style. If this is the case, follow the **skim study** technique below.

- Study the chapters in the order you find them in the Study Text.
- For each chapter:
  - Follow the key study steps 1-3
  - Skim-read through step 5, looking out for the points highlighted in the fast forward boxes (step 4)
  - Jump to step 12
  - Go back to step 6
  - Follow through steps 8 and 9
  - Prepare outline answers to questions (steps 10/11)
  - Try the Quick quiz (step 13), following up any items you can't answer
  - Do a plan for the Question (step 14), comparing it against our answers
  - You should probably still follow step 7 (note-taking), although you may decide simply to rely on the BPP Passcards for this.

Moving on...

However you study, when you are ready to embark on the practice and revision phase of the BPP Effective Study Package, you should still refer back to this Study Text, both as a source of **reference** (you should find the index particularly helpful for this) and as a way to **review** (the Fast forwards, Exam focus points, Chapter roundups and Quick quizzes help you here).

And remember to keep careful hold of this Study Text – you will find it invaluable in your work.

More advice on Study Skills can be found in BPP's **Learning to Learn Accountancy** book.

Learning outcomes and Syllabus

Paper C4 Fundamentals of Business Economics

Syllabus overview

This syllabus provides students with a knowledge of the economic and financial concepts necessary for conducting the role of a management accountant and underpins their studies towards attainment of the award of Chartered Management Accountant.

Assessment

There will be a computer based assessment of 2 hours duration comprising of 75 compulsory questions, each with one or more parts.

Aims

This syllabus aims to test student's ability to:

- Distinguish the differing goals of organisations and identify how these differing goals affect the decisions made by managers
- Illustrate how market economies function and identify the reasons for and impacts of government involvement in economic activities
- Identify the role of financial institutions and markets in the provision of short and long term finance to individuals, businesses and governmental organisations
- Identify how macroeconomic variables and government economic policies affect the organisation.

Learning outcomes and syllabus content

C4 A - The goals and decisions of organisations – weighting 20%

Learning outcomes

On completion of their studies students should be able to:

(i) Distinguish the goals of profit seeking organisations, not-for-profit organisations and governmental organisations;

(ii) Identify and compute the point of profit maximisation for a single product firm in the short run;

(iii) Distinguish the likely behaviour of a firm's unit costs in the short run and long run and illustrate the effects of long run cost behaviour on prices, the size of the organisation, and the number of competitors in the industry;

(iv) Illustrate shareholder wealth, the variables affecting shareholder wealth, and its application in management decision making;

(v) Identify stakeholders and their likely impact on the goals of not-for-profit organisations and the decisions of the management of not-for-profit organisations;

(vi) Distinguish between the potential objectives of management and those of shareholders and illustrate the effects of this principal-agent problem on decisions concerning price, output and growth of the firm.

(vii) Describe the main mechanisms to improve corporate governance in profit seeking organisations.

Syllabus content		Covered in chapter
(1)	The forms of ownership of organisations by which we mean public, private and mutual, and their goals	1
(2)	Graphical treatment of short run cost and revenue behaviour as output increases (revenue and cost curves) and identification of point of short-run profit maximisation using graphical techniques and from data.	2
(3)	Long run cost behaviour and the impact of economies and diseconomies of scale	2
(4)	Concept of returns to shareholder investment in the short run (ROCE and EPS) and long run (NPV of free cash flows) leading to need for firms to provide rates of return to shareholders at least equal to the firm's cost of capital.	1
(5)	Calculation of impact on the value of shares of a change to a company's forecast cash flows or required rate. Calculations required will be either perpetual annuity valuations with constant annual free cash flows, or NPV calculations with variable cash flows over three years.	1
(6)	Types of not-for-profit organisations (NPOs) and the status of economic considerations as constraints rather than primary objectives in the long run.	1
(7)	Role of stakeholders in setting goals and influencing decisions in NPOs and potential ways of resolving differing stakeholder demands.	1
(8)	The principal-agent problem, its likely effect on decision-making in profit seeking and NPO organisations, and the concepts of scrutiny and corporate governance.	1

C4 B - The market system and the competitive process – weighting 30%

Learning Outcomes

On completion of their studies students should be able to:

(i) Identify the equilibrium price in a product or factor markets likely to result from specified changes in conditions of demand or supply;

(ii) Calculate the price elasticity of demand and the price elasticity of supply and identify the effects of price elasticity of demand on a firm's revenues following a change in prices;

(iii) Define market concentration and describe the factors giving rise to differing levels of concentration between markets;

(iv) Describe market failures, their effects on prices, efficiency of market operation and economic welfare and illustrate the likely responses of government to these;

(v) Distinguish the nature of competition in different market structures and identify the impacts of the different forms of competition on prices and profitability.

Syllabus content		Covered in chapter
(1)	The price mechanism: determinants of supply and demand and their interaction to form and change equilibrium price.	3
(2)	The price elasticity of demand and its effect on firms' revenues and pricing decisions.	4
(3)	The price elasticity of supply and its impact on prices, supply and buyers' expenditure.	4
(4)	Business integration: mergers, vertical integration and conglomerates.	2
(5)	Calculation of market concentration and its impact on efficiency, innovation and competitive behaviour.	7
(6)	Impact of monopolies and collusive practices on prices and output and role of competition policy in regulating this.	6, 7, 8
(7)	Factors causing instability of prices in primary goods markets (ie periodic and short run inelasticity of supply, the cobweb or hog cycle) and the implications of this for producer incomes, industry stability and supply and government policies to combat this (eg deficiency payments, set-aside, subsidies)	4
(8)	Impact of minimum price (minimum wages) and maximum price policies in goods and factor markets.	3
(9)	Positive and negative externalities in goods markets and government policies to deal with these (including indirect taxes, subsidies, polluter pays policies and regulation).	5
(10)	Public assurance of access to public goods, healthcare, education and housing.	5
(11)	Public versus private provision of services (nationalisation, privatisation, contracting out, public private partnerships).	8

C4 C - The Financial System – weighting 20%

Learning outcomes

On completion of their studies students should be able to:

(i) Identify the factors leading to liquidity surpluses and deficits in the short, medium and long run in households, firms and governments;

(ii) Explain the role of various financial assets, markets and institutions in assisting organisations to manage their liquidity position and to provide an economic return to holders of liquidity;

(iii) Identify the role of insurance markets in the facilitation of the economic transfer and bearing of risk for households, firms and governments;

(iv) Identify the role of the foreign exchange market and the factors influencing it, in setting exchange rates and in helping organisations finance international trade and investment;

(v) Explain the role of national and international governmental organisations in regulating and influencing the financial system and identify the likely impact of their policy instruments on businesses.

Syllabus content		Covered in chapter
(1)	The causes of short-term, medium term and long term lack of synchronisation between payments and receipts in households (ie month to month cash flow, short-term saving and borrowing, and longer term property purchases and pensions provision).	9
(2)	The causes of short-term, medium term and long term lack of synchronisation between payments and receipts in firms (ie month to month cash flow management, finance of working capital and short-term assets and long term permanent capital).	9
(3)	The causes of short-term, medium term and long term lack of synchronisation between payments and receipts in governmental organisations (ie month to month cash flow management, finance of public projects and long term management of the national debt).	9
(4)	The principal contracts and assets issued by financial institutions and borrowers to attract liquidity in the short, medium and long term (eg credit agreements, mortgages, bills of exchange, bonds, certificates of deposit and equities)	9
(5)	The roles and functions of financial intermediaries and the principal institutions and markets in the financial system.	9
(6)	The influence of commercial banks on the supply of liquidity to the financial system through their activities in credit creation.	10
(7)	Yield on financial instruments (ie bill rate, running yield on bonds, net dividend yield on equity), relation between rates, role of risk, the yield curve.	10
(8)	Influence of central banks on yield rates through market activity and as providers of liquidity to the financial system.	10
(9)	Principal insurance contracts available, and basic operation of insurance markets including terminology (eg broking, underwriting, reinsurance).	9
(10)	The role of foreign exchange markets in facilitating international trade and in determining the exchange rate.	11
(11)	Effect of exchange rates on the international competitiveness of firms (including elementary foreign exchange translation calculations).	11
(12)	Credit and foreign exchange risks of international trading firms and the use of letters of credit, export credit guarantees and exchange rate hedging to manage these risks.	11
(13)	Influences on exchange rates (interest rates, inflation rates, trade balance, currency speculation).	11
(14)	Governmental and international policies on exchange rates (ie exchange rate management, fixed and floating rate systems, single currency zones) and the implications of these policies for international business.	11

C4 D - The macroeconomic context of business – weighting 30%

Learning outcomes

On completion of their studies students should be able to:

(i) Explain macroeconomic phenomena (ie growth, inflation, unemployment, demand management and supply-side policies) using circular flow of income and aggregate demand and supply analysis;

(ii) Explain the main measures and indicators of a country's economic performance and the problems of using these to assess the wealth and commercial potential of a country;

(iii) Identify the stages of the trade cycle, its causes and consequences, and discuss the business impacts of potential policy responses of government to each stage;

(iv) Explain the main principles of public finance (ie deficit financing, forms of taxation) and macroeconomic policy (fiscal, monetary and supply side policies);

(v) Explain the concept of the balance of payments and its implications for business and for government policy;

(vi) Identify the main elements of national policy with respect to trade including protectionism, trade agreements and trading blocks;

(vii) Identify the conditions and policies necessary for economic growth in traditional, industrial and post-industrial societies and discuss the potential consequences of such growth;

(viii) Discuss the concept and consequences of globalisation for businesses and national economies;

(ix) Identify the major institutions promoting global trade and development and explain their respective roles.

	Syllabus content	Covered in chapter
(1)	National Income Accounting identity and the three approaches to calculation and presentation of national income (Output, Expenditure and Income).	12
(2)	Interpretation of national income accounting information for purposes of time series or cross sectional evaluation of economic performance.	12
(3)	The circular flow of income and the main injections and withdrawals.	12
(4)	Illustration of changes to equilibrium level of national income using aggregate demand and supply analysis.	13
(5)	Government macroeconomic policy goals (low unemployment, inflation, external equilibrium and growth) and the effects on business of the government's pursuit of these.	14
(6)	Types and consequences of unemployment, inflation and balance of payments deficits.	13, 15
(7)	The trade cycle and the implications for unemployment, inflation and trade balance of each stage (recession, depression, recovery, boom).	13
(8)	Government policy for each stage of the business cycle and the implications of each policy for business.	13
(9)	The central government budget and forms of direct and indirect taxation. Incidence of taxation (progressive, regressive) and potential impact of high taxation on incentives and avoidance.	14

Syllabus content		Covered in chapter
(10)	Fiscal, monetary and supply side policies, including relative merits of each.	14
(11)	Layout of balance of payments accounts and the causes and effects of fundamental imbalances in the balance of payments.	15
(12)	Arguments for and against free trade and policies to encourage free trade (eg bi-lateral trade agreements, multi-lateral agreements, free trade areas, economic communities and economic unions). And protectionist instruments (tariffs, quotas, administrative controls, embargoes)	15
(13)	Principal institutions encouraging international trade (eg WTO/GATT, EU, G8)	15
(14)	Nature of globalisation and factors driving it (eg improved communications, political realignments, growth of global industries and institutions, cost differentials).	15
(15)	Impacts of globalisation (eg industrial relocation, emergence of growth markets, enhanced competition, cross-national business alliances and mergers, widening economic divisions between countries)	15
(16)	Role of World Bank, International Monetary Fund, European Bank etc in fostering international development and economic stabilisation.	15

The assessment

Format of computer-based assessment (CBA)

The CBA will not be divided into sections. There is likely to be a total of seventy-five objective test questions with one or more parts and you will need to answer them in the time allowed of two hours.

Frequently asked questions about CBA

Q What are the main advantages of CBA?

A
- Assessments can be offered on a continuing basis rather than at six-monthly intervals
- Instant feedback is provided for candidates by displaying their results on the computer screen

Q Where can I take CBA?

A
- CBA must be taken at a 'CIMA Accredited CBA Centre'. For further information on CBA, you can email CIMA at cba@cimaglobal.com.

Q How does CBA work?

A
- Questions are displayed on a monitor
- Candidates enter their answers directly onto a computer
- Candidates have 2 hours to complete the Fundamentals of Business Economics examination
- The computer automatically marks the candidate's answers when the candidate has completed the examination
- Candidates are provided with some indicative feedback on areas of weakness if the candidate is unsuccessful

Q What sort of questions can I expect to find in CBA?

Your assessment will consist entirely of a number of different types of **objective test question**. Here are some possible examples.

- **MCQs.** Read through the information on page (xx) about MCQs and how to tackle them.
- **Data entry.** This type of OT requires you to provide figures such as the correct figure for creditors in a balance sheet.
- **Hot spots.** This question format might ask you to identify which cell on a spreadsheet contains a particular formula or where on a graph marginal revenue equals marginal cost.
- **Multiple response.** These questions provide you with a number of options and you have to identify those which fulfil certain criteria.
- **Matching.** This OT question format could ask you to classify particular costs into one of a range of cost classifications provided, to match descriptions of variances with one of a number of variances listed, and so on.

This text provides you with **plenty of opportunities to practise** these various question types. You will find OTs **within each chapter** in the text and the **Quick quizzes** at the end of each chapter are full of them. The Question Bank contains fifty objective test questions similar to the ones that you are likely to meet in your CBA.

Further information relating to OTs is given on page (xxi).

The **Practice and Revision Kit** for this paper was published in **June 2006** and is **full of OTs**, providing you with vital revision opportunities for the fundamental techniques and skills you will require in the assessment.

Tackling multiple choice questions

In a multiple choice question on your paper, you are given how many **incorrect** options?

A Two
B Three
C Four
D Five

The correct answer is B.

The MCQs in your exam contain four possible answers. You have to **choose the option that best answers the question**. The three incorrect options are called distracters. There is a skill in answering MCQs quickly and correctly. By practising MCQs you can develop this skill, giving you a better chance of passing the exam.

You may wish to follow the approach outlined below, or you may prefer to adapt it.

Step 1 **Skim read** all the MCQs and **identify** what appear to be the easier questions.

Step 2 Attempt each question – **starting with the easier questions** identified in Step 1. Read the question thoroughly. You may prefer to work out the answer before looking at the options, or you may prefer to look at the options at the beginning. Adopt the method that works best for you.

Step 3 Read the four options and see if one matches your own answer. **Be careful with numerical questions**, as the distracters are designed to match answers that incorporate common errors. Check that your calculation is correct. Have you followed the requirement exactly? Have you included every stage of the calculation?

Step 4 You may **find that none of the options matches your answer**.

- Re-read the question to ensure that you understand it and are answering the requirement.
- Eliminate any obviously wrong answers.
- Consider which of the remaining answers is the most likely to be correct and select the option.

Step 5 If you are still **unsure** make a note **and continue to the next question**.

Step 6 **Revisit unanswered** questions. When you come back to a question after a break you often find you are able to answer it correctly straight away. If you are still unsure have a guess. You are not penalised for incorrect answers, so **never leave a question unanswered!**

Exam focus. After extensive practice and revision of MCQs, you may find that you recognise a question when you sit the exam. Be aware that the detail and/or requirement may be different. If the question seems familiar read the requirement and options carefully – do not assume that it is identical.

BPP's i-Pass for this paper provides you with plenty of opportunity for further practice of MCQs.

Tackling objective test questions

Between 20% and 50% of the questions in the assessment will be objective test questions, the remainder will be MCQs. Questions will be worth between 2 to 4 marks, the total marks available in the assessment being more than 100.

What is an objective test question?

An **OT** is made up of some form of **stimulus**, usually a question, and a **requirement** to do something.

(a) Multiple choice questions
(b) Filling in blanks or completing a sentence
(c) Listing items, in any order or a specified order such as rank order
(d) Stating a definition
(e) Identifying a key issue, term, figure or item
(f) Calculating a specific figure
(g) Completing gaps in a set of data where the relevant numbers can be calculated from the information given
(h) Identifying points/zones/ranges/areas on graphs or diagrams, labelling graphs or filling in lines on a graph
(i) Matching items or statements
(j) Stating whether statements are true or false
(k) Writing brief (in a specified number of words) explanations
(l) Deleting incorrect items
(m) Choosing right words from a number of options
(n) Complete an equation, or define what the symbols used in an equation mean

OT questions in CIMA exams

CIMA has offered the following **guidance** about OT questions in the exam.

- Credit may be given for **workings** where you are asked to calculate a specific figure.
- If you **exceed a specified limit on the number of words** you can use in an answer, you will **not be awarded any marks**.
- If you make **more than one attempt** at a question, clearly **cross through** any answers that you do not want to submit. If you don't do this, only your first answer will be marked.

Examples of OTs are included within each chapter, in the **quick quizzes** at the end of each chapter and in the **objective test question bank**.

BPP's i-Pass for this paper provides you with plenty of opportunity for further practice of OTs.

Part A

The goals and decisions of organisations

1 Organisations in a mixed economy

Introduction

Most major industrialised countries have mixed economies, with both a large private sector and also a substantial public (or government) sector. In Section 1 of this chapter we will set out some basic economic ideas that help us to understand how all economic activity is conducted.

In subsequent sections we will look more carefully at the kinds of organisations that undertake economic activity, their objectives and some ideas about the way in which they should be run.

We conclude the chapter with an a discussion of the role of shareholders and the methods used to compute their interest in the firms they invest in.

Topic list	Learning outcomes	Syllabus references	Ability required
1 Fundamental economic ideas	–	–	–
2 Organisations	A (i)	A (1), A (6)	Comprehension
3 The objectives of firms	A (i), A (vi)	A (1)	Comprehension
4 Corporate governance	A (v), A (vii)	A (7), A (8)	Comprehension
5 Shareholders' interest	A (iv)	A (1)	Comprehension
6 Measuring shareholder wealth	A (iv)	A (4), A (5)	Comprehension

1 Fundamental economic ideas

FAST FORWARD Economics is concerned with how choices are made about the use of resources: what shall be produced and who shall consume it. The need to make such decisions arises because economic resources are scarce. Making decisions involves the sacrifice of benefits that could have been obtained from using resources in an alternative course of action.

1.1 Economics as a social science

Economics studies the ways in which society decides what to produce, how to produce it and who to produce it for. We are all economic agents and economic activity is what we do to make a living. Economists assume that people behave rationally at all times and always seek to improve their circumstances. This assumption leads to more specific assumptions.

- Producers will seek to maximise their profits.
- Consumers will seek to maximise the benefits (their 'utility') from their income.
- Governments will seek to maximise the welfare of their populations.

Both the basic assumption of rationality and the more detailed assumptions may be challenged. In particular, we will look again later at the assumption that businesses seek always to maximise their profits. A further complication is that concepts such as utility and welfare are not only open to interpretation, but that the interpretation will change over time.

The way in which the resource allocation choices are made, the way value is measured and the forms of ownership of economic wealth will vary according to the type of **economic system** that exists in a society.

(a) In a **centrally planned** or **command economy**, the decisions and choices about resource allocation are made by the government. Money values are attached to resources and to goods and services, but it is the government that decides what resources should be used, how much should be paid for them, what goods should be made and what their price should be. This approach is based on the theory that only the government can make fair and proper provision for all members of society.

(b) In a **market economy**, the decisions and choices about resource allocation are left to **market forces of supply and demand**, and the workings of the price mechanism. This approach is based on the observable fact that it generates more wealth in total than the command approach.

(c) In a **mixed economy** the decisions and choices are made partly by free market forces of supply and demand, and partly by government decisions. Economic wealth is divided between the private sector and the public sector. This approach attempts to combine the efficiency of the market system with the centrally planned system's approach to fair and proper distribution.

In practice, all modern national economies are mixed economies, although with differing proportions of free market and centrally planned decision-making from one country to the next. In such economies, the government influences economic activity in a variety of ways and for a variety of purposes.

(a) Direct control over macroeconomic forces can be exercised through policy on tax, spending and interest rates.

(b) Taxes, subsidies and direct controls can affect the relative prices of goods and services.

(c) Government-owned institutions such as the UK's National Health Service (NHS) can provide goods and services direct at low or nil cost.

(d) Regulation can be used to restrict or prevent the supply of goods and services.

(e) Incomes can be influenced through the tax and welfare systems.

Key terms

Microeconomics is the study of individual economic units; these are called **households** and **firms**.
Macroeconomics is the study of the aggregated effects of the decisions of economic units. It looks at a complete national economy or the international economic system as a whole.

1.2 Scarcity of resources

It is a fact of life that there are limits to available resources.

(a) For the individual **consumer** the scarcity of goods and services might seem obvious enough. Most people would like to have more: perhaps a car, or more clothes, or a house of their own. Examples of services include live theatre performances, public passenger transport and child-minding.

(b) For the world as a whole, resources available to serve human consumption are limited. For example, as we all know, the supply of non-renewable energy resources is, by definition, limited. The amount of many minerals which it is feasible to extract from the earth (for example, metals of various kinds) is also limited.

(c) Some resources are not scarce. Air to breathe is not normally scarce unless, perhaps, you are trapped underwater or underground. Ice is not scarce in Antarctica, and sand is plentiful in the Sahara desert.

In the case of producers, we can identify four types of resource, which are also called **factors of production.**

(a) **Land** is rewarded with **rent**. Although it is easy to think of land as property, the economic definition of land is not quite what you might suppose. Land consists not only of property (the land element only: buildings are capital) but also the natural resources that grow on the land or that are extracted from it, such as timber and coal.

(b) **Labour** is rewarded with **wages** (including salaries). Labour consists of both the mental and the physical resources of human beings.

(c) **Capital** is rewarded with **interest**. It is easy to think of capital as financial resources, and the rate of interest is the price mechanism in balancing the supply and demand for money. However, capital in an economic sense is not 'money in the bank'. Rather, it refers to man-made items such as plant, machinery and tools which are made and used not for their own sake, but to aid the production of other goods and services. The cost of using machinery and plant and so on is **interest**.

(d) **Enterprise**, or entrepreneurship, is a fourth of factor of production. An entrepreneur is someone who undertakes the task of organising the other three factors of production in a business enterprise, and in doing so, bears the risk of the venture. He creates new business ventures and the reward for the risk he takes is **profit**.

Key terms

Scarcity is the excess of human wants over what can actually be produced. A **scarce resource** is a resource for which the quantity demanded at a nil price would exceed the available supply.

Since resources for production are scarce and there are not enough goods and services to satisfy the total potential demand, choices must be made. Choice is only necessary because resources are scarce.

(a) Consumers must choose what goods and services they will have.
(b) Producers must choose how to use their available resources, and what to produce with them.

Economics studies the nature of these choices.

(a) What will be produced?
(b) What will be consumed?
(c) And who will benefit from the consumption?

Making choices about the use to be made of scarce resources is the fundamental problem of economics.

1.3 The production possibility curve

We can approach the central questions of economics by looking first at the possibilities of production. Suppose, to take a simple example, that an imaginary society can use its available resources to produce two products, A and B. The society's resources are limited. Therefore there are restrictions on the amounts of A and B that can be made. The possible combinations of A and B can be shown by a **production possibility curve** (or frontier).

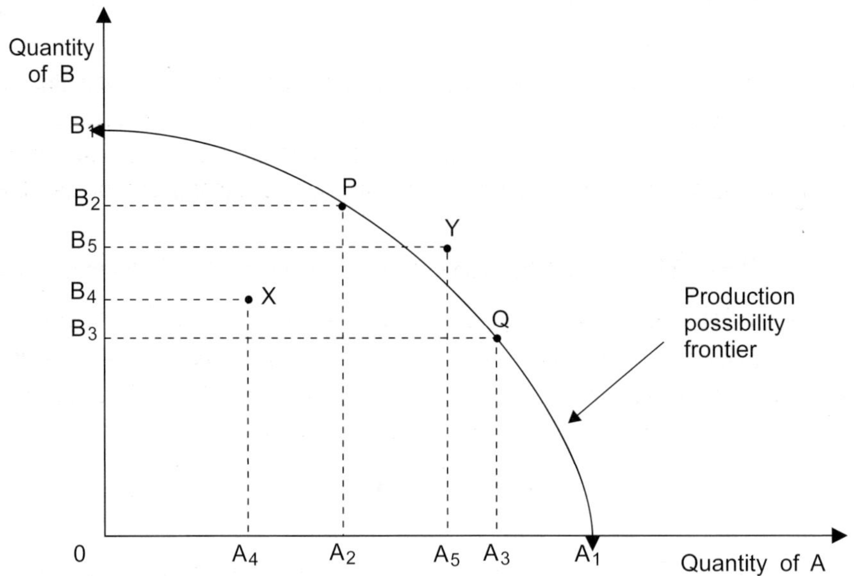

Figure 1 Production possibility curve

The curve from A_1 round to B_1 in Figure 1 shows the various combinations of A and B that a society can make, if it uses its limited resources efficiently.

(a) The society can choose to make up to:

- A_1 units of A and no B
- B_1 units of B and no A
- A_2 units of A and B_2 of B (point P on the curve)
- A_3 units of A and B_3 of B (point Q on the curve)

(b) The combination of A_4 units of A and B_4 units of B plotted at point X is within the production possibility curve. More than these quantities can be made of either or both of A and B. Point X is therefore an inefficient production point for the economy, and if the society were to make only A_4 of A and B_4 of B, it would be using its limited resources inefficiently.

(c) Note that the production possibility curve is just what it says: it defines what is achievable if **all** productive resources are fully employed. It follows that changes in the level of unemployment have no effect upon it. Similarly, changes in price levels will affect the **monetary value** of what can be produced, but not the **volume**.

Production possibility curve

What can you say about the combination of A and B indicated by point Y in Figure 1?

Answer

Point Y lies outside the production possibility curve. Even with efficient use of resources it is impossible to produce this combination of A and B. To reach point Y either current resources must be increased or production methods must be improved – perhaps by developments in technology.

The production possibility curve is an important idea in economics: it illustrates **the need to make choices** about what to produce because it is not possible to have everything. Although we have characterised the products of our hypothetical economy as A and B, we can generalise the production possibility curve to show the production possibilities for different types of good, and also for some 'good X' on one axis and 'all other goods' on the other axis.

1.4 Opportunity cost: the cost of one use for resources rather than another

Choice involves sacrifice. If there is a choice between having A and having B, and a country chooses to have A, it will be giving up B to have A. The cost of having a certain amount of A can therefore be regarded as the sacrifice of not being able to have a certain amount of B. There is a sacrifice involved in the choices of consumers and firms (producers), as well as the choices of governments at the level of national economy.

Key terms

The cost of an item measured in terms of the alternatives forgone is called its **opportunity cost**.

A production possibility curve illustrates opportunity costs. For example, if in Figure 1 it is decided to switch from making A_3 units of A and B_3 units of B (point Q) to making A_2 units of A and B_2 units of B (point P), then **the opportunity cost of making ($B_2 - B_3$) more units of B would be the lost production of ($A_3 - A_2$) units of A**.

The production possibility line is a **curve** and not a straight line because some resources are more useful for making A than for making B and *vice versa*. As a result, opportunity costs change as we move away from a situation in which production is wholly devoted to either A or B. Thus, as we move away from point A_1, and introduce an increasing level of production of B, the amount of B that we gain from losing each unit of A progressively diminishes.

At the level of the firm, the production possibility curve can be seen as showing the maximum output of different goods the firm can produce when all of its resources are fully used – for example, a firm might operate production lines capable of producing washing machines or refrigerators. Producing more washing machines bears the opportunity cost of a lower level of production of refrigerators.

2 Organisations

Various types of organisation are found in the mixed economy. The economy can be divided into the **public and private sectors**. The public sector contains a range of organisations that **provide public services** and may also include some state-owned businesses. The private sector includes both **profit-seeking businesses** and **non-profit-making organisations** such as charities, and mutuals.

2.1 The public and private sectors

The economy of a developed country can usually be divided into two sectors: public and private. Private sector organisations, also called businesses, are owned and operated by private individuals or institutions, while organisations in the public sector are owned by the state.

2.2 Private sector organisations

Private sector organisations are of two main types: those that **seek profit** for their owners and those that have **other objectives**. The latter are known as non-profit making or not-for-profit organisations.

2.2.1 Non-profit organisations

This terminology is a little misleading, in that 'non-profit' organisations often engage in profitable trade and they are not able to run consistently at a loss. The essence of their status as 'non-profit' organisations is not that they seek to avoid generating a surplus of funds, but that the generation of wealth for their owners is **not the primary purpose** of their existence. Non-profit seeking organisations include co-operatives and mutual organisations; charities; and unincorporated clubs, societies and associations.

Non-profit making organisations use the surplus they generate to further their other objectives. Clubs and associations exist to provide some kind of benefit to their members. **Charities** generally exist to provide some kind of benefit to society at large, though UK law allows the potential **beneficiaries** of a charity to be restricted to a defined group, such as the victims of a particular disaster.

Mutual organisations are a special case in the private sector. The essence of their nature is that they are commercial operations **owned by their customers** rather than having capital – providing shareholders for whom they have to earn profit. This means that their customers benefit both from the **services** the mutuals provide to them and from the **trading surplus** they make by doing so. It is also possible for the managers of mutuals to pursue **purposes other than profit**. These can include a high level of charitable giving, the promotion of community interests and a high quality of service; such pursuits may well provide a high degree of intangible benefit to members. Mutuals thus resemble both non-profit making organisations and profit-seeking companies.

2.2.2 Profit seeking organisations

The economy is mostly driven by the profit-seeking part of the private sector. It is businesses that undertake the most enterprising aspects of economic activity; provide the bulk of employment opportunities and tax revenue; and create the growth needed to enhance economic welfare. Businesses are of two main types, distinguished by the extent to which the owners are liable for the debts of the undertaking.

(a) An individual may set up business on his own account as a **sole trader** or in **partnership** with others. In either case, the law will not distinguish between the private assets and liabilities of the owners and those of the enterprise. The owners have **unlimited liability** for the debts of their businesses.

(b) This degree of risk is unattractive to many potential investors, so to enable them to invest and thus release more funds for wealth-producing enterprise, the legal systems of most countries provide for some form of **limited liability** enterprise. Such businesses are referred to as corporations or **companies**.

In the UK, there are two forms of limited liability company. They both limit the liability of investors to the nominal value of their share holdings; they differ in the extent to which they are permitted to solicit investment from the general public. **Private limited companies** may not offer their securities to the public; a **public limited company** (plc) may. When the shares of plcs are regularly bought and sold on a stock exchange, they may be referred to as **quoted companies**, because the current price of their shares will be quoted in a journal of record.

Assessment focus point

> Remember that not all public limited companies are quoted companies.

Note carefully this further example of rather confusing terminology: **public limited companies** are owned by **private** investors; they are **not** part of the **public sector**.

2.3 Public sector organisations

We used to divide public sector organisations into **two main groups**: those that **provide public services**, such as hospitals, schools, the police and the armed forces; and **state owned industries**. This distinction has become less clear over the last quarter-century as governments have privatised state-owned industries and sought to **reform the public sector** by involving private companies in the provision of public services. The objective has been to **curb waste** of public money and **improve efficiency** by importing the disciplined cost control that is required if profit is to be created.

In the UK, many providers of public services such as hospitals and schools and formerly state owned industries such as London Underground are now involved in different forms of **public-private partnership**. In such partnerships, the private sector provides funds for public sector purposes such as education . For example the Private Funding Initiative (PFI) for schools seeks private partners to fund and manage school buildings in return for an agreed fee. Some services in the UK NHS are provided by self-governing trusts. These trusts sell their services to the NHS.

Public sector bodies are all, ultimately, **responsible to government** for their activities and their purposes are defined in the laws that establish them. They have a range of possible aims and objectives: rarely will they set out to trade at a profit. Nevertheless, their managers will be expected to exercise **good stewardship** and **prevent waste of resources**. Public sector bodies' objectives will usually be defined in terms of the **provision of a service** that is deemed to be beneficial to society.

It is an important feature of public sector bodies that (unless they engage in trade of some kind) they have little control over their incomes; they depend upon government for the funds they need to operate. The funds they receive will be influenced by a large number of forces, including current public opinion, government aspirations, the skill of their leaders in negotiation, the current state of the public finances overall and the current economic climate.

2.4 Primary, secondary and tertiary sectors

A distinction can be made between the **primary**, **secondary** and **tertiary** sectors of the economy.

2.4.1 The primary sector

The primary sector of the economy produces **raw materials** such as crops and minerals. Agriculture, forestry, fisheries, mining and quarrying are the main industries in this sector. Over the long term, the trend for the UK is one of decline in this sector when measured in terms of its share of gross domestic product (GDP). Viewed against the process of economic growth, this declining share reflects **the rising absolute level** of output of other industries.

2.4.2 The secondary sector

The secondary sector consists of industries that **process raw materials** in order to **manufacture** goods. This sector is therefore also known as the **manufacturing** sector. Manufacturing in the UK is in a state of decline, mainly because of competition from developing, low-wage countries.

2.4.3 The tertiary sector

The tertiary sector provides services and is therefore also known as the **service** sector. This sector has become the predominant provider of employment and output in the UK economy in recent decades. A major reason for the continuing growth in this sector has been the rapid expansion in the banking, finance and insurance sectors.

3 The objectives of firms

FAST FORWARD

Although it is convenient for economists to assume that **profit maximisation** is the central objective of firms, we should not overlook the fact that in reality the motives of managers may operate to serve **alternative goals**.

3.1 The firm

Key terms

Firm is the term used in economics for any organisation that carries on a business.

We will use the rest of this Chapter to examine firms and profit.

3.2 Profit maximisation and other objectives

Profit maximisation is assumed to be the goal of the firm in most economic textbooks and in a great deal of economic theory. This is not universally accepted: the great management thinker *Peter Drucker* said that a business exists 'to create a customer', by which he meant that its activities were best explained in terms of marketing activity. Other writers have suggested that **survival** is the main long-term aim. We discuss some other ideas later in this section.

Where the entrepreneur is in full managerial control of the firm, as in the case of a small owner-managed company or partnership, the profit maximisation assumption would seem to be very reasonable. However, some companies have considerations that constrain their ability to maximise profits. These include the demands of ethics in pharmaceutical and medical companies, the requirement to provide a public service where specific subsidies are received, and the demands of safety in shipping and airline companies. The process of incorporating UK companies may define its particular **type of business**, though it is possible to incorporate as a 'general commercial company', which makes it legal for the company to undertake any kind of legal business activity.

3.3 Agency theory

FAST FORWARD

Where the management of a business is separated from its ownership by the employment of professional managers, the managers may be considered to be the agents of the owners. **Agency theory** is concerned to analyse the way agents may be expected to behave and how they can be motivated to promote their principals' interest.

In fact, few large businesses are managed by their owners. In the case of larger companies, the shareholders are numerous and unlikely to wish to take part in the management of the company, viewing it simply as a vehicle for investment. Even where ownership is concentrated, large companies tend to be managed mostly by professional managers who have little ownership interest, if any. This **separation of ownership from control** has arisen for several reasons.

(a) Limited liability structure does not give shareholders power to manage the company (unless they are also managers); their influence normally extends only to proposing and voting on resolutions at company meetings.

(b) It is impracticable for a large number of shareholders to exercise managerial powers jointly; to be effective, power must be concentrated.

(c) Many shareholders are not interested in being managers, and are content to employ professional managers so long as their investment prospers.

(d) Many organisations are so large or complex or deal with such advanced technology that they can only be managed effectively by well-qualified professionals

Separation of ownership from control has been a feature of business for over a century and brings with it a recurring problem: the business should be managed so as to promote the economic interest of the shareholders as a body, but the power to manage lies in the hands of people who may use it to promote their own interests. How can the managers be made to favour the interest of the owners rather than their own?

This problem is not confined to the management of companies: it is the general problem of the **agency relationship** and occurs whenever one person (the **principal**) gives another (the **agent**) power to deal with his affairs.

3.3.1 Resolving the agency problem

A common approach to ensuring that company managers act in the owners interest is to offer them **reward incentives** that depend on the achievement of ownership goals. Thus, it is common for Chief Executives' remuneration to depend, at least in part, on satisfactory achievement in such matters as profit and share price. At lower levels, **bonus schemes** can be based on achievement of targets that support good overall performance, such as improved sales or reduced costs. **Profit sharing schemes** that provide shares to large numbers of employees are intended to align their interests with those of the wider body of shareholders.

Unfortunately, these types of approach can be flawed in that they have to be designed – and the designers themselves are in an agency relationship with the owners. Thus executive remuneration schemes have been criticised for emphasising the wrong targets or for setting the targets too low.

3.4 Alternative managerial goals

Under the conditions of the agency relationship between owners and managers , the goal of profit maximisation might not fully explain management behaviour, because managers have interests of their own.

Managers will not necessarily make decisions that will maximise profits.

(a) They may have no **personal interests** at stake in the size of profits earned, except in so far as they are accountable to shareholders for the profits they make.

(b) There may be a **lack of competitive pressure** in the market to be efficient, minimise costs and maximise profits, for example where there are few firms in the market.

It has been suggested that price and output decisions will be taken by managers with **managerial objectives** in mind. Rather than seeking to **maximise** profits, managers may choose to achieve a **satisfactory** profit for a firm: this is called **satisficing**. Satisficing is also a common managerial response when there are multiple objectives, such as boosting share price, and achieving revenue growth. Similarly, if directors' remuneration schemes are based on criteria such as growth or corporate social responsibility, then they are unlikely to make the maximisation of profit their sole objective.

3.5 Baumol's sales maximisation model

One managerial model of the firm – *Baumol's* **sales maximisation model** – assumes that the firm acts to **maximise sales revenue** rather than profits. The management of a firm might opt for sales revenue maximisation in order to maintain or increase its market share, ensure survival, and discourage competition. Managers benefit personally because of the prestige of running a large and successful company, and also because salaries and other perks are likely to be higher in bigger companies than in smaller ones.

3.6 Williamson's management discretion model

Another managerial model – *Williamson's* **management discretion model** – assumes that managers act to further their own interests and so **maximise** their own **utility** (or satisfaction), subject to a minimum profit requirement. Utility may be thought of in terms of prestige, influence and other personal satisfactions. The profit aimed for will not be maximum profit, because of management's wish for expenditure on themselves, their staff and the perquisites of management.

3.7 A behavioural theory of the firm

Cyert and March suggested that a firm is an **organisational coalition** of shareholders, managers, employees and customers, with each group having different goals, and so there is a need for **political compromise** in establishing the goals of the firm. Each group must settle for less than it would ideally want to have. Shareholders must settle for less than maximum profits, and managers for less than maximum utility, and so on.

3.8 Business objectives and management discretion

There are differing views about the extent to which external pressures modify business objectives and form boundaries to the exercise of management discretion.

Ansoff suggested that a company has a number of **different levels of objectives**.

(a) A **primary economic objective**, aimed at optimising the efficiency and effectiveness of the firm's 'total resource-conversion process'.

(b) **Non-economic, social objectives**, which are secondary and modify management behaviour. These social objectives are the result of interaction among the individual objectives of the differing groups of stakeholders.

(c) **Responsibilities** are obligations which a company undertakes, but which do not form a part of its 'internal guidance or control mechanism'. Responsibilities would include charitable donations and contributions to the life of local communities.

(d) **Boundaries** are rules that restrict management's freedom of action, and include government legislation (on, for instance, pollution levels, health and safety at work, employment protection, redundancy and monopolies) and agreements with trade unions.

4 Corporate governance

Key term

Corporate governance is the system by which organisations are directed and controlled. CIMA *Official Terminology*

4.1 Management accountability

FAST FORWARD

Organisations are not autonomous; they exist to serve some external purpose, usually manifested in a group such as shareholders in a company or trustees of a charity. All managers have a **duty of faithful service** to the external purpose of the organisation.

As the agents of its owners, a company's managers are **collectively responsible** for the conduct of its affairs. This is true of organisations generally, whatever their nature and whether or not they seek profit. There is a **chain of authority and accountability** that runs hierarchically up and down the organisation. Junior managers are accountable to more senior ones and so on up the chain until the most senior managers are reached. The question then arises: to whom are

these accountable for the activities of the organisation as a whole? As a matter of principle, we can say that there should be some **external entity** on behalf of which the most senior managers control the organisation and to which they are accountable.

Question

Accountability

Learning outcome A(v)

Who are the senior managers of the following organisations and to whom are they accountable?

(a) A charity
(b) The government of a democracy
(c) A trade union

Answer

(a) The senior management of a charity is likely to be similar in nature to the board of a company, consisting of heads of departments, such as fundraising and operations, together with some non-executive directors. Their collective responsibility is likely to be to subscription-paying members of the institution assembled in a general meeting, where these exist, or possibly to a supervisory board, or even to a court of law. In any event, the actions of the managers in dealing with the interests of **those the charity is intended to benefit** will be the main concern.

(b) The senior management of a democratic government is called the Cabinet and, again, consists of senior politicians with functional and advisory roles. The external body to which it is responsible is the electorate, which has the power collectively to expel it from office and install a completely different government.

(c) The senior management of a trade union will consist of senior executives and, depending on its constitution, is likely to be responsible to the membership of the union. The extent of this responsibility will depend on local law and tradition and may be discharged for example, through postal ballots or, less satisfactorily, through mass meetings.

4.2 Fiduciary responsibility

The essence of all these examples of **external accountability** is that organisations are **not autonomous**: that is to say, they do not exist to serve their own purposes or those of their senior managers. They exist to serve some external purpose and their managers have a duty to run them in a way that serves that purpose, whether it be to relieve distress (a charity), to keep the peace and manage the economy (a government), to promote the interests of its members (a trade union) or to make a profit (a business). Managers have a **fiduciary responsibility** (or duty of faithful service) in this respect and their behaviour must always reflect it.

4.3 The objectives of commercial organisations

We implied above that the objective of a commercial organisation is to make a profit. It is possible to argue that wider objectives should be acknowledged and that the interests of people other than the owners should be served. This is the 'stakeholder view' and is discussed further below. Nevertheless, whatever an organisation's objectives may be, it is the duty of its managers to seek to attain them. Many senior figures in the world of business have given the impression that the organisations they run exist to serve their own personal purposes. This is not the case and managers at all levels must be aware of this.

4.4 Personal motivation and corruption

We shall have something more to say about corrupt practices later on in this chapter, but for now, we must emphasise that managers need not be actually corrupt in order to fail in their fiduciary duty. The CEO who sets in motion a takeover bid that will enhance his prestige; the head of department who 'empire builds'; and the IT manager who buys an unnecessarily sophisticated enterprise resource management system are all failing in their fiduciary duty even though they receive no material benefit themselves.

4.5 Stakeholders

FAST FORWARD

The stakeholder view holds that there are many groups in society with an **interest in the organisation's activities**. Stakeholders can be divided into internal, connected and external groups. The organisation's response to their priorities can be analysed according to their **power** (or influence) and their **interest**.

Stakeholders are persons or groups (other than the owners of a firm) that have a **legitimate interest in a business's conduct** and whose concerns should be addressed as a matter of principle. Many stakeholder groups have influence over they way in which organisations are managed and operate. They can therefore be fundamental to corporate governance.

Key terms

Stakeholders are those persons and organisations that have an interest in the strategy of an organisation.

CIMA *Official Terminology*

There are three broad types, or **constituencies**, of stakeholder in an organisation.

- **Internal** stakeholders such as employees and management
- **Connected** stakeholders such as shareholders, customers, suppliers and financiers
- **External** stakeholders such as the community, government and pressure groups

The extent to which external stakeholders are recognised is linked to the size of the organisation, in that the policies and actions of **larger organisations** are more likely to be of interest to **national governments** and even **international bodies** than are those of smaller organisations.

Stakeholders may also be analysed into those who have a formal contractual relationship with the organisation and those who do not. These two groups are called **primary** and **secondary** stakeholders. Internal and connected stakeholders fall into the primary category, therefore, while external stakeholders equate to secondary stakeholders.

Mendelow classifies stakeholders on a matrix whose axes are **power** (or influence) and degree of **interest** in the organisation's activities. These factors will help define the type of relationship the organisation should seek with its stakeholders.

		Level of interest: Low	Level of interest: High
Power	Low	A	B
	High	C	D

(a) **Key players** are found in segment D: strategy must be *acceptable* to them, at least. An example would be a major customer. These stakeholders may **participate** in decision-making.

(b) Stakeholders in segment C must be **treated with care**. While often passive, they are capable of moving to segment D. They should, therefore be **kept satisfied.** Large institutional shareholders might fall into segment C.

(c) Stakeholders in segment B do not have great ability to influence strategy, but their views can be important in **influencing more powerful stakeholders**, perhaps by lobbying. They should therefore be **kept informed.** Community representatives and charities might fall into segment B.

(d) **Minimal effort** is expended on segment A. An example might be a contractor's labour force.

Internal stakeholder groups are likely to have both more influence and more interest than external groups. Coalitions of stakeholder groups are likely to have more influence than single stakeholders or small uniform groups.

4.6 Stakeholder influence

Stakeholders are particularly important to understanding the **policies and actions of non-profit organisations**. Such bodies do not have an over-riding responsibility to promote the interests of the owners: instead, they are subject to significant influence from more than one stakeholder group. The concept of the **behavioural coalition** is particularly relevant here, since there is often a clear need for the organisation's managers both to recognise and to manage the **expectations** of the various stakeholder groups.

A **charity** is a good example. There will be a class of **beneficiaries** whose requirements are the reason the organisation exists. However, there are also likely to be at least two other **important constituencies** whose views and requirements must be carefully considered.

(a) **Donors** are likely to be very interested in the way the funds they have supplied are used. It will be hoped that they will continue to provide funds in the future.

(b) **Employees**, particularly those working directly with beneficiaries, are likely to be highly motivated and to have high ideals about the role of the charity. They may accept low rates of pay because they feel that their work is important to society.

These two stakeholder groups are likely to be very vocal if disappointed. They are fundamental to operations and are able to disrupt them if they wish to, simply by walking away. It is important that they are not disappointed or aggrieved.

In general we may discern three areas in which stakeholders exercise influence in non-profit organisations.

(a) **Objectives and goals** are not based on profit, so there is scope for stakeholders to influence what the organisation sets out to do.

(b) **Strategies** cannot be aimed simply at profitability, so it can be developed to achieve other ends, such as effectiveness and economy. Many non-profit organisations will demand a particularly high standard of conduct in **ethical terms**.

(c) **Management style and practices**, particularly those elements that relate to the **management of people**, are highly likely to be of interest to some stakeholder groups.

4.7 Stakeholder conflicts

Since their interests may be widely different, **conflict between stakeholders** can be quite common. Managers must take the potential for such conflict into account when setting policy and be prepared to deal with it if it arises in a form that affects the organisation.

Hunt identifies five different initial management responses to the handling of conflict.

(a) **Denial/withdrawal**. *Torrington and Hall* say that 'to some extent conflict can be handled by ignoring it.' If the conflict is very trivial, it may indeed 'blow over' without an issue being made of it, but if the causes are not identified, the conflict may grow to unmanageable proportions.

(b) **Suppression/accommodation.** One party suppresses its own interest and accommodates the other in order to preserve working relationships despite minor conflicts. As Hunt remarks, however: 'Some cracks cannot be papered over'.

(c) **Dominance**: the dominant group may be able to apply power or influence to settle the conflict. The disadvantage of this is that it creates all the lingering resentment and hostility of 'win-lose' situations.

(d) **Compromise**: a consensus may be reached by bargaining and negotiating. However, individuals tend to exaggerate their positions to allow for compromise, and compromise itself is seen to weaken the value of the decision, perhaps reducing commitment.

(e) **Integration and collaboration**: it may be most appropriate to confront the issue on which the parties differ and work towards an accommodation of the differences. This may lead to a better overall solution than simply splitting the difference. Emphasis must be put on the task, individuals must accept the need to modify their views for its sake, and group effort must be seen to be superior to individual effort.

4.8 Failures of corporate governance

FAST FORWARD

A number of reports have been produced in various countries aiming to address the risk and problems posed by poor corporate governance.

There were three significant corporate governance reports in the United Kingdom during the 1990s. The **Cadbury and Hampel reports** covered general corporate governance issues, whilst the **Greenbury report** concentrated on remuneration of directors.

The recommendations of these three reports were merged into a **Combined Code** in 1998, with subsequent updates, with which companies listed on the London Stock Exchange are required to comply.

Though mostly discussed in relation to large quoted companies, governance is an issue for all bodies corporate; commercial and not for profit.

An increasing number of **high profile corporate scandals** and collapses, including Polly Peck International, BCCI, and Maxwell Communications Corporation prompted the development of governance codes in the early 1990s. However, scandals since then, such as Parmalat and Enron, have raised questions about further measures that may be necessary. The scandals over the last 25 years have highlighted the need for guidance to tackle the various **risks and problems** that can arise in organisations' systems of governance.

4.8.1 Domination by a single individual

A feature of many corporate governance scandals has been boards dominated by a single senior executive with other board members merely acting as a rubber stamp. Sometimes the single individual may bypass the board to action his own interests. The report on the UK *Guinness* case suggested that the Chief Executive, *Ernest Saunders* paid himself a £3 million reward without consulting the other directors. The presence of non-executive directors on the board is felt to be an important safeguard against domination by a single individual.

4.8.2 Lack of involvement of board

Boards that meet irregularly or fail to consider systematically the organisation's activities and risks are clearly weak. Sometimes the failure to carry out proper oversight is due to a **lack of information** being provided.

4.8.3 Lack of adequate control function

An obvious weakness is a **lack of internal audit,** since this is one of the most important aspects of internal control.

Another important control is **lack of adequate technical knowledge** in key roles, for example in the audit committee or in senior compliance positions. A rapid turnover of staff involved in accounting or control may suggest inadequate resourcing, and will make control more difficult because of lack of continuity.

4.8.4 Lack of supervision

Employees who are not properly supervised can create large losses for the organisation through their own incompetence, negligence or fraudulent activity. The behaviour of *Nick Leeson*, the employee who caused the collapse of *Barings* bank was not challenged because he appeared to be successful, whereas he was using unauthorised accounts to cover up his large trading losses. Leeson was able to do this because he was in charge of both dealing and settlement, a systems weakness or **lack of segregation of key roles** that featured in other financial frauds.

4.8.5 Lack of independent scrutiny

External auditors may not carry out the necessary questioning of senior management because of fears of losing the audit, and internal audit do not ask awkward questions because the chief financial officer determines their employment prospects. Often corporate collapses are followed by criticisms of external auditors, such as the *Barlow Clowes* affair, where poorly planned and focused audit work failed to identify illegal use of client monies.

4.8.6 Lack of contact with shareholders

Often board members may have grown up with the company but lose touch with the **interests and views** of shareholders. One possible symptom of this is the payment of remuneration packages that do not appear to be warranted by results.

4.8.7 Emphasis on short-term profitability

Emphasis on short-term results can lead to the **concealment** of problems or errors, or **manipulation** of accounts to achieve desired results.

4.8.8 Misleading accounts and information

Often misleading figures are symptomatic of other problems (or are designed to conceal other problems) but in many cases, poor quality accounting information is a major problem if markets are trying to make a fair assessment of the company's value. Giving out misleading information was a major issue in the UK's *Equitable Life* scandal where the company gave contradictory information to savers, independent advisers, media and regulators.

4.9 Benefits of improving corporate governance

4.9.1 Risk reduction

Clearly, the ultimate risk is of the organisation **making such large losses** that **bankruptcy** becomes inevitable. The organisation may also be closed down as a result of **serious regulatory breaches,** for example misapplying investors' monies. Proper corporate governance reduces such risks by aligning directors' interests with the company's strategic objectives and by providing for measures to reduce fraud.

4.9.2 Performance

Performance should improve if accountabilities are made clear and directors' motivation is enhanced by performance-related remuneration. Also, the extra breadth of experience brought by non-executive directors and measures to prevent domination by a single powerful figure should improve the quality of decision-making at board level.

4.9.3 External support

External perceptions of the company should be enhanced. This can have wide-ranging benefits.

- Improved ability to raise finance
- Improved corporate image with public and government
- Improved relations with stakeholders such as customers and employees

4.10 Reports on corporate governance

There have been a number of important reports on corporate governance, in the UK and elsewhere: these have dealt primarily with companies, but many of the principles are applicable to non-profit organisations.

4.11 Cadbury report

The Cadbury Committee created a Code of Best Practice, based on **openness**, **integrity** and **accountability**.

4.12 Greenbury report

The Greenbury Committee considered the problem of rewarding performance in an appropriate fashion and made recommendations to improve accountability, transparency and the improvement of performance.

4.13 The Hampel report

The major recommendations of the committee were that shareholders should be able to **vote separately** on each **substantially separate issue**; and that the practice of 'bundling' unrelated proposals in a single resolution should cease.

4.14 Stock Exchange Combined Code

The recommendations of the various reports have been consolidated into the Stock Exchange Combined Code.

The board

Every director should use **independent judgement** when making decisions. Every director should receive appropriate **training**. There should also be a strong and independent body of **non-executive directors** with a recognised senior member other than the chairman.

Chairman and Chief Executive

There are two leading management roles; running the board (chairman) and running the company (chief executive). A **clear division of responsibilities** should exist so that there is a balance of power, and no-one person has unfettered powers of decision. Combination of the roles of chairman and chief executive should be justified publicly.

Remuneration

Companies should establish a formal and clear procedure for **developing policy** on **executive remuneration** and for fixing the remuneration package of individual directors. **Directors should not be involved** in **setting their own remuneration**. A **remuneration committee**, staffed by independent non-executive directors, should make **recommendations** about the framework of executive remuneration, and should determine specific remuneration packages. The board should determine the remuneration of non-executive directors

Audit committees and auditors

There should be **formal and clear arrangements** with the **company's auditors**, and for applying the financial reporting and internal control principles. Companies should have an **audit committee** consisting of non-executive directors, the majority of whom should be independent. The audit committee should review the audit, and the independence and objectivity of the auditors. In particular the committee should keep matters under review if the auditors supply significant non-audit services.

5 Shareholders' interest

FAST FORWARD

Investors invest in companies by buying their shares. The companies are expected to maximise the wealth of their shareholders by generating **profit** from trading operations. Investors will only provide funds if they believe that the prospective returns are adequate.

5.1 Shares and share prices

A **company** is one of the commonest vehicles for carrying out a business. Funds are raised for the business activity by dividing up the ownership of the company into equal parts called **shares** that are then sold to investors for cash. The shares are **ordinary shares** if they have no additional rights attached to them such as prriority rights to receive payments from the company. The money paid for the shares, together with loans and retained profits, is used to finance the activities of the company.

A **shareholder** is someone who owns shares in a company. The number of shares held by a shareholder represents his proportional ownership of the profits, losses and assets of the company. Any ownership interest is generally known as **equity**. Thus, if your house is worth more than your outstanding mortgage, the difference is your equity in the property. Ownership of shares represents ownership of equity in the company concerned: the term '**equities**' is often used to mean shares in companies. This is by contrast with **bonds**, which represent a formal loan to the company, rather than an ownership interest.

Preference shares are a special class of shares that you will learn more about in your financial accounting studies. For now, we may simply say that not all companies have them and we will not include them in the category of equity shares.

We discussed the objectives of companies earlier in this chapter. We will work on the basis that the main financial objective of a company is to **maximise the wealth of its shareholders**. It does this by **trading at a profit**. Profits can then be paid to the shareholders as **dividends**, which are an immediate cash benefit, or they can be retained and re-invested in the company, which should **increase the value of the shareholders' equity**.

Shares in quoted companies are usually bought and sold *via* an official **stock exchange market,** such as the London Stock Exchange. Buying and selling prices for each share are quoted by the exchange's dealers. If a company's shares are traded on a stock market, the wealth of the shareholder is increased when the share price goes up.

The ordinary shares of UK companies have a **nominal value**, typically £1, 50p or 10p. Outside the UK it is not uncommon for a company's shares to have no nominal value. The **market value** of a quoted company's shares bears no relation to their nominal value, except when the company issues new ordinary shares for cash: then the issue price must be at least equal to the nominal value of the shares.

5.2 Return on investment

Money is required for all forms of business activity and, of course, it is not freely available. If you wish to borrow money to buy a car, the finance company will expect you to pay interest. A similar principle applies when companies raise funds by issuing shares: the investors **expect to see a return on their investment**. Shareholders are assumed to have a firm idea of the **return they require** from their investments: this will be based in part on the performance of other similar investments. Generally, the source of this return will be the company's profits. As already discussed, these can either be used to fund the payment of **dividends** or they can be **retained and reinvested** in the business. In either case, the shareholders' wealth increases.

Income, in the form of profit, and **capital**, in the form of the market value of equities, are very much equivalent when considering a **quoted company**, because cash and shares are easily converted into one another by appropriate dealings on the relevant stock exchange. Also, any increase in value would be easily apparent in the case of a quoted company, since the market value of its shares would be public knowledge. It is far less obvious (and possibly difficult to establish and measure) in the case of a private company, since the shares of private companies are not actively traded. Most of what we will have to say in the rest of this Chapter will relate to quoted companies and their shareholders, therefore.

Two very important considerations when deciding whether to buy shares in a company are its current **share price** and its **prospects for the future**. Investors will ask themselves whether they can reasonably expect to receive a proper **return on their investment**, either in dividends or in the form of an increase in the value of their shares. This will be generally true whether they are taking up an initial issue of shares or buying existing shares on a stock exchange.

A further important consideration in deciding just what would be a proper return is the **risk** associated with the investment. A high degree of risk means that returns are likely to accrue at **irregular intervals** and that they are likely to be **variable in amount**. Therefore, the higher the risk, the higher the overall return the shareholder will require. This is an important principle that you will return to later in your CIMA studies.

The market price of a firm's shares is thus subject to a number of influences connected with the investment's likely effect on shareholder wealth. **Good profit performance** will tend to push the price up, as will **enhanced prospects for the future**, such as better trading conditions; an **increase in risk** will tend to push it down, as will **reduced prospects for future profit**. These influences on share price themselves result from the interplay of a large number of factors; these factors can be divided into those **internal to the firm** and those **external** to it.

(a) **Internal factors** are heavily influenced by management policy and action and include such things as rate of new product development, marketing activity, financial management and control of costs.

(b) **External factors** include wider developments such as economic recession and demographic change; and events and forces specific to the industry concerned, such as the degree of competition in the market and the behaviour of suppliers and customers.

The management of a quoted company is under pressure to maintain and, if possible, to improve **current profit performance**, while, at the same time, continuing to **invest for the future**. Shareholders are assumed to monitor the performance of the companies they invest in and are likely to **sell their shares** in companies that **under-perform** in order to invest in companies that seem to be performing more satisfactorily. If a large number of shareholders decide to dispose of their shares, the market forces of supply and demand (which are dealt with later in this Study Text) will cause the share price to **fall to a level that reflects its performance and prospects**. Conversely, the same forces will tend to **drive up the price** of shares in a company that is seen to be **outperforming its rivals**.

6 Measuring shareholder wealth

FAST FORWARD

Shareholders need **objective measures of company performance** if they are to make sensible investment decisions. Short-term measures include **ROCE**, **EPS** and **P/E** number. ROCE and EPS are straightforward measures of current achievement; P/E number, however, reflects the market's view of the share's future prospects.

Shareholders need some objective measures of company performance so that they can make informed investment decisions. These measures can be divided into those suitable for the shorter term and those suitable for the longer term. In this context, the limit of the shorter term may be taken to be the issue of the next set of financial statements.

6.1 Short-term measures

6.1.1 Return on capital employed

Return on capital employed (ROCE) is a simple measure of a company's current success in using the money invested in it to generate a return. The *amount* of profit is not in itself an adequate measure: it must be related to the **value of the resources** employed in generating it, so that it reflects the efficiency with which they have been used. ROCE does this for us.

In the simplest terms, ROCE is calculated as **profit divided by capital employed**: for most companies, this will produce an answer that can be expressed as a percentage between zero and, say, 50%. Clearly if the company makes a loss, the ROCE figure will be negative; ROCE figures above 50% are not impossible, but would be considered unusual (and possibly too good to be true). A very high return might well indicate a rather speculative and therefore risky investment.

We would hope that a company's ROCE would be higher than the minimum level its shareholders have decided is acceptable to them as a return on their investment. The greater the margin of safety between this **required return** and ROCE, the better.

Unfortunately both profit and capital employed are **accounting concepts** and can be defined in a number of different ways. The principle employed here is that ROCE is of interest to all parties with a claim on the company's profits, including both **shareholders** and **lenders**, so it is best to compute both capital and profit in terms that relate to all categories of providers of capital. As result, the figure for profit is most usually taken **before the payment of tax and interest** to lenders (PBIT), while capital employed is defined as **total assets less current liabilities**. (Calculating capital in this way leads to an alternative name for this measure: **return on net assets**).

Return on capital employed (ROCE)

$$\text{ROCE} = \frac{\text{PBIT}}{\text{Capital employed}}\% = \frac{\text{Profit from operations}}{\text{Total assets less current liabilities}}\%$$

Profit before interest and tax, or profit from operations, is profit available for all holders of capital (shares and loans).

Note that interest is deducted as a cost when accounts are prepared so, to calculate PBIT from a set of accounts, you would have to **add back to profit before tax the amount of any interest paid**. Total assets and current liabilities are shown as such on balance sheets prepared in accordance with international standards, so you should have no difficulty in arriving at the figure for capital employed. This sum should be equal to equity plus the nominal value of any outstanding loans.

6.1.2 Example: ROCE

In 20X7, Snoxall plc paid bank interest of £ 21,909 and had profit before tax of £225, 102. Total assets less current liabilities were £751,969. The corresponding figures for 20X8 were £ 18,115, £342,130 and £988,899.

Calculate ROCE for both years.

	20X8	*20X7*
	£	£
Profit on ordinary activities before tax	342,130	225,102
Interest payable	18,115	21,909
PBIT	360,245	247,011

Solution

	20X8	*20X7*
ROCE =	$\frac{360{,}245}{988{,}899}$	$\frac{247{,}011}{751{,}969}$
=	36.4%	32.8%

This exercise illustrates a common use of measures such as ROCE: the making of comparisons between one year and another. We cannot really comment on the size of Snoxall plc's ROCE unless we know something about what is normal for its industry, but we can definitely say that it has improved between 20X7 and 20X8.

6.1.3 Earnings per share

Earnings per share (EPS) is usually regarded as a measure of how well the company has performed for its equity shareholders specifically, rather than providers of capital generally. It is usually calculated as the profit available to equity shareholders divided by the number of equity shares in issue. Note that a company is likely to have far more shares **authorised** than **issued**; it is the number of shares **actually issued to shareholders** that we are interested in here. The total number of shares in the authorised share capital is of limited interest.

Earnings per share

$$\text{EPS} = \frac{\text{Profit after tax and preference dividends}}{\text{Number of equity shares in issue}}$$

Here, because we are interested in the equity shareholders' point of view, we take the profit after interest and tax payments and we also deduct any dividends due to **preference shareholders**, who are regarded for this purpose as having more in common with lenders than with equity shareholders.

6.1.4 Example: EPS

Here is an extract from Monocular plc's income statement for 20X6.

	£
Profit before interest and tax	120,000
Interest	(20,000)
Profit before tax	100,000
Taxation	(40,000)
Profit after tax	60,000
Preference dividend	(1,000)
Profit available for ordinary shareholders (= earnings)	59,000
Ordinary dividend	(49,000)
Retained profits	10,000

The company has 80,000 ordinary shares and 20,000 preference shares.

Calculate earnings per share in 20X4.

Solution

EPS is $\frac{£59,000}{80,000}$ = 73.75 pence

In practice there are usually further complications in calculating the EPS, but fortunately these are outside your syllabus for this subject.

6.1.5 P/E number

P/E number (or ratio or multiple) is calculated by dividing the market price of a share by the EPS.

Key term

Price earnings (P/E) number = $\frac{\text{Market price per share}}{\text{Earnings per share}}$

ROCE and EPS are simple measures of current performance. We have included P/E number in this section since it makes use of EPS. However, it differs in concept from ROCE and EPS in that it looks into the future. P/E number is interesting in that **it reflects shareholder opinion about company prospects**. A high P/E number indicates that investors are content with a relatively low current return from the share. This is usually because they anticipate that their return will improve substantially in the future, possibly as a result of emerging opportunities or new and impressive products.

6.2 A longer-term measure: the dividend valuation model

FAST FORWARD

The **dividend valuation model** discounts expected future dividends to relate the cost of equity to market share price.

ROCE and EPS are both based on **historical accounting information**. As a result, their usefulness is greatest as measures of how a company has performed in the recent past. We can expect that they will also give us a reasonable idea of how the company is doing in the current accounting period, but their relevance to the more distant future is limited. P/E number incorporates some information about investors' view of the future, but, again, is most relevant to the nearer term.

Unfortunately, no-one has the ability to predict the future with any great degree of accuracy, so thinking about longer-term investment takes a different course. For the past, we could reasonably ask whether the company has **actually satisfied its shareholder's requirements**; for the future, we ask **what it will have to do in order to satisfy them in the longer term**. The requirements themselves are neatly encapsulated in the phrase '**cost of capital**'.

Key term

Cost of capital is the minimum acceptable return on an investment. *CIMA Official Terminology*

Capital overall includes shares of all kinds and borrowings, and establishing a valid overall cost of capital is a difficult task that will form part of your continuing CIMA studies all the way to the Strategic level. Here we are only concerned with equity capital and thus with the rather simpler concept of the **cost of equity**. This represents the equity shareholders' requirements for the performance of their investments.

It is widely accepted that the current price of a quoted company's shares reflects the future income to which shareholders are entitled to. There are two ways to measure this

(a) The first is to base future income on **expected future dividends**, these being the actual cash disbursements that a company makes to its shareholders

(b) The second concept which is more complex and will be covered in 6.4 is to base the valuation on the **free cash flow to equity**.

We will look first at a model based on **expected future dividends**, which allows for the way that companies tend to use their reserves to smooth dividend payments over time, averaging out the good years with the bad. We assume that a **constant dividend** will be paid each year into the indefinite future. This **dividend valuation model** shows the relationship between the current share price, the cost of equity (the shareholders' required return, remember) and the size of the dividend expected each year. If we assume that **dividends are constant** throughout the life of the company then the share price is expressed by the formula shown below

$$P_0 = \frac{d}{(1+k_e)} + \frac{d}{(1+k_e)^2} + \frac{d}{(1+k_e)^3} + ... = \frac{d}{k_e}, \text{ so } k_e = \frac{d}{P_0}$$

where k_e is the shareholders' required return

d is the annual dividend per share, starting at year 1 and then continuing annually in perpetuity.

P_0 is the ex-dividend share price (the price of a share where the share's new owner is **not** entitled to the dividend that is soon to be paid).

A more realistic assumption is that dividends, rather than being the same throughout the life of the company, will actually grow at a constant rate. In this case the share price is $P_0 = \frac{d}{k_e - g}$

Key terms

Cum dividend or cum div means the purchaser of shares is entitled to receive the next dividend payment.

Ex dividend or ex div means that the purchaser of shares is not entitled to receive the next dividend payment

If you have already studied the Business Mathematics syllabus (as recommended by CIMA), you will recognise this formula as being based on the process of **discounting** and very similar to that for the **present value of a perpetuity**. If you have not already studied basic discounting, **you should break off from economics now and do so.**

Formulae

Cost of equity share capital, paying an annual dividend d in perpetuity, and having a current ex div price P_0:

$$k_e = \frac{d}{P_0}$$

Where dividends grow at a constant rate g, the cost of equity capital $k_e = \frac{d}{P_0} + g$

6.3 Example: dividend valuation model

Tekel plc pays out 25% of its earnings as a dividend and expects zero future growth in dividends. The company has one million £1 ordinary shares in issue and the market value of the company is £50 million. After-tax profits for future years are expected to be £20 million.

What is the expected rate of return from the ordinary shares?

Solution

With earnings of £20 million and a 25% payout rate, total dividends = 20 million/4 = £5 million

With one million shares in issue, dividend per share = £5 million/1 million = £5

and market price per share = £50 million/1 million = £50

Therefore, using the formula $k_e = \frac{d}{P_0}$

k_e = 5/50 = 10% = the rate of return to ordinary shareholders

6.4 Free cash flow valuation

ST FORWARD

The valuations based on **discounting forecast free cash flows** also relate the cost of equity to market share price.

Some companies do not pay dividends: *Microsoft*, for example, paid no dividends until 2003. When this is the case, models based on earnings may be used. There are several such models: we are interested for the purposes of your syllabus in a simple model based on **discounting the free cash flows**. Once again, it is important for your consideration of this model that you are familiar with the basic process of discounting as explained in your BPP Business Mathematics Study Text.

Key term

The **free cash flow to the firm (FCFF)** is the after tax cash generated by the business and available for distribution to the **equity holders** and **debt holders** of the company.

It is calculated in its simplest form from the Profit before interest and tax (PBIT) by adding back non-cash items such as depreciation and subtracting taxes and capital expenditure, ie

FCFF = PBIT + DEPRECIATION – TAX – CAPITAL EXPENDITURE.

Key term

The **free cash flow to equity (FCFE)** represents the potential income that could be distributed to the **equity holders** of a company, as opposed to dividends which measures the actual cash disbursements to shareholders.

The free cash flow to equity (FCTE) is calculated in the same way as free cash flow to the firm (ECFF) except that interest payments due to debt holders have to be deducted as

FCFE = FCFF – INTEREST PAYMENTS TO DEBT HOLDERS.

6.4.1 Example

The following information is available on a company.

PBIT	5,000,000
Interest Expenses	500,000
Taxes	1,000,000
Capital Expenditure	300,000

The free cash flow to the firm (FCFF) is

FCFF = PBIT – Taxes – Capital Expenditure
= 5,000,000 – 1,000,000 – 300,000 = 3,700,000

The free cash flow to equity (FCFE) is

FCFE = FCFF – Interest Expenses
= 3,700,000 – 500,000 = 3,200,000

If we know what the equity shareholders' required rate of return is, we can use it as a **discount rate** to find the value of the company. Conversely, in principle, if we know the current market value of the company's shares and its **forecast free cash flows**, we can use this information to estimate the shareholders' required rate of return. However, this computation is outside your syllabus.

6.5 Example: discounting free cash flows

Upharsin plc's directors have forecast the company's expected levels of earnings in their medium term strategic plan. The earnings figures for the next three years are given below.

Time	£
Year 1	7,530,000
Year 2	7,980,000
Year 4	8,240,000

The company has 2,400,000 ordinary shares in issue. The equity shareholders require a rate of return on their investment of 17%. What should the company's current market value and ordinary share price be?

Solution

Year	*Cash flow*	*Discount factors*	*Present value*
	£	17%	£
1	7,530,000	0.855	6,438,150
2	7,980,000	0.731	5,833,380
3	8,240,000	0.624	5,141,760
			17,413,290

The current market value on this basis is the sum of the present value column above, which is £17, 413,290. Dividing this figure by 2,400,000 will give us the current ordinary share price: this is £7.26.

Assessment focus point

Your syllabus requires you to be able to carry out both types of valuation calculation illustrated above.

6.6 The interaction between cash flows, required return and market value

FAST FORWARD

An **increase** in forecast dividends or free cash flows will lead to an **increase** in current market price, as will a **reduction** in the cost of equity.

In both the dividend valuation and free cash flow models, we have a relationship between three quantities.

(a) The investors' required rate of return (the cost of equity)
(b) Expected future cash flows (either FCFE or dividends payable)
(c) The current market value of the company's shares

It is important that you appreciate this simple relationship: the **current market value is determined by the other two factors**. The dynamics of the relationship are simple.

(a) If the expected cash flows **increase**, predictably enough, the current market value will **increase** and *vice versa*. Changes in the immediate future will have a larger effect than those in the more distant future.

(b) An **increase** in the **cost of equity** will **reduce** the current market value and *vice versa*. We can demonstrate this effect by recomputing Upharsin plc's current value assuming that investors have increased their required return to 20%.

Year	*Cash flow*	*Discount factors*	*Present value*
	£	20%	£
1	7,530,000	0.833	6,272,490
2	7,980,000	0.694	5,538,120
3	8,240,000	0.579	4,770,960

The current market value is now £16,581,570. Actually, examination of the discount factors themselves will demonstrate the basic principle involved. The higher the discount rate is, the smaller the discount factors are and so, logically, the smaller are the present values of the discounted cash flows.

As a result of the relationship outlined above, we can forecast with confidence that if either the **forecast future cash flows change or the cost of equity changes, current market value must change in consequence**. Current market value is, by definition, something that exists in the present; however, the cash flows are, again by definition, things that do not yet exist: they are expected future events. The rate of return required by investors is a feature of the present but is determined by investors' assessments of both current and expected future factors such as **risk** and the **returns likely to be available elsewhere**.

Question

Changing cash flows

Tekel plc's directors have increased their after tax profit forecast from £20 million to £24 million each year.

Required

Explain the effect this is likely to have on the market value of the company's shares.

Answer

The profit forecast has increased by one fifth. If the directors retain their 25% dividend policy, cash payments to shareholders should also increase by one fifth. Current investors' desired rate of return is 10%: the forecast increase in profits is unlikely to alter this immediately, so their perception of the market value of the company is also likely to increase by one fifth.

Using the formula $k_e = \frac{d}{P_0}$, if k_e remains the same and d increases by 20%, P_0 must also increase by 20%.

In practical terms, Tekel plc's shares will become more attractive to investors with capital to invest and demand for them will increase. Existing investors, knowing that the profit forecast has been increased, will only sell at a price that reflects the company's improved prospects.

Question

Changing the cost of equity

Upharsin plc has for many years been involved in dangerous and speculative activities involving prospecting for radio-active ores in politically unstable parts of the world. The company's directors have stated that the company effectively ceased its participation in these activities at the end of the end of the last accounting period; the funds released have been invested in a portfolio of commercial properties in European capital cities. Remarkably, the net effect of this change on forecast profits is zero.

Required

Explain the effect this change is likely to have on the market value of the company's shares.

Answer

The effect of this change in business focus is a significant reduction in the riskiness of Upharsin plc's activities overall. This should have the effect of reducing the cost of equity, since investors no longer need high returns to compensate them for a high level of risk. Since the forecast cash flows are unchanged, but the cost of equity has fallen, we would expect the market value of Upharsin plc's shares to rise.

In practical market terms, Upharsin plc has become a much more attractive investment, offering high returns at low risk. Demand will increase, but the current owners of the shares will be reluctant to sell at the existing market price. Increased demand will drive the price up to a point at which the current investors are prepared to sell.

Chapter roundup

- Economics is concerned with how choices are made about the use of resources: what shall be produced and who shall consume it. The need to make such decisions arises because economic resources are scarce. Making decisions involves the sacrifice of benefits that could have been obtained from using resources in an alternative course of action.
- Various types of organisation are found in the mixed economy. The economy can be divided into the **public and private sectors**. The public sector contains a range of organisations that **provide public services** and may also include some state-owned businesses. The private sector includes both **profit-seeking businesses** and **non-profit-making organisations** such as charities, and mutuals.
- Although it is convenient for economists to assume that **profit maximisation** is the central objective of firms, we should not overlook the fact that in reality the motives of managers may operate to serve **alternative goals**.
- Where the management of a business is separated from its ownership by the employment of professional managers, the managers may be considered to be the agents of the owners. **Agency theory** is concerned to analyse the way agents may be expected to behave and how they can be motivated to promote their principals' interest.
- Organisations are not autonomous; they exist to serve some external purpose, usually manifested in a group such as shareholders in a company or trustees of a charity. All managers have a **duty of faithful service** to the external purpose of the organisation.
- The stakeholder view holds that there are many groups in society with an **interest in the organisation's activities**. Stakeholders can be divided into internal, connected and external groups. The organisation's response to their priorities can be analysed according to their **power** (or influence) and their **interest**.
- A number of reports have been produced in various countries aiming to address the risk and problems posed by poor corporate governance.

  There were three significant corporate governance reports in the United Kingdom during the 1990s. The **Cadbury and Hampel reports** covered general corporate governance issues, whilst the **Greenbury report** concentrated on remuneration of directors.

  The recommendations of these three reports were merged into a **Combined Code** in 1998, with which companies listed on the London Stock Exchange are required to comply.
- Investors invest in companies by buying their shares. The companies are expected to maximise the wealth of their shareholders by generating **profit** from trading operations. Investors will only provide funds if they believe that the prospective returns are adequate.
- Shareholders need **objective measures of company performance** if they are to make sensible investment decisions. Short-term measures include **ROCE**, **EPS** and **P/E** number. ROCE and EPS are straightforward measures of current achievement; P/E number, however, reflects the market's view of the share's future prospects.
- The **dividend valuation model** discounts expected future dividends to relate the cost of equity to market share price.
- The valuations based on **discounting forecast free cash flows** discounts also relate the cost of equity to market share price.
- An **increase** in forecast dividends or free cash flows will lead to an **increase** in current market price, as will a **reduction** in the cost of equity.

Quick quiz

1 What is the essential feature of a command economy?

2 Macroeconomics is the study of economic units such as households and firms. True or false?

3 Which of the following is not recognised as a factor of production?

A Capital
B Management
C Land
D Labour

4 The cost of an item measured in terms of the resources used is called its opportunity cost. True or false?

5 Who proposed a model of business based on the objective of maximising sales?

A Drucker
B Williamson
C Ansoff
D Baumol

6 Which of the following is not used as a name for a group of stakeholders?

A Coalition
B Connected
C External
D Primary

7 What is the formula for return on capital employed?

8 What is the formula for earnings per share?

9 Megalith plc has authorised share capital of 25,000,000 preference shares and 100,000,000 ordinary shares. Profit before tax was £27, 800,000. Tax payable is £6,900,000 and preference dividend payable is £1,900,000. The company has 95,000,000 ordinary shares in issue, with a market price of £2.85 and 24,500,000 preference shares in issue, with a market price of £1.15. What is Megalith plc's P/E number?

A 12.95
B 14.25
C 15.00
D 13.64

10 The present value of Megalith's forecast future free cash flows is now £267 million. What will happen to this value if Megalith plc's cost of equity rises?

A It will rise
B It will fall
C It will remain the same
D It is impossible to say

Answers to quick quiz

1 Decisions about resources, production and prices are made by the government.

2 False. The study of individual economic units is called microeconomics. Macroeconomics is the study of a complete national economy.

3 B The fourth factor is enterprise or entrepreneurship.

4 False. Opportunity cost is defined as the cost of an item in terms of the alternatives forgone. Cost in terms of resources used is a reasonable definition of the accounting concept of 'full cost'.

5 D Baumol

6 A Coalition

7 ROCE $= \dfrac{\text{PBIT}}{\text{Capital employed}}\,\% = \dfrac{\text{Profit from operations}}{\text{Total assets less current liabilities}}\,\%$

8 EPS $= \dfrac{\text{Profit after tax and preference dividends}}{\text{Number of equity shares in issue}}$

9 B Profit after tax and preference dividend is £19,000,000. If we divide this by 95,000,000, the number of shares in issue, we have an EPS of 20 pence. Dividing this into £2.85 gives us a P/E number of 14.25. If you thought the answer was 15.00, you have used the authorised number of shares rather than the issued number. If you thought the answer was 12.95, you have included the preference dividend in your earnings figure. If you thought the answer was 13.64, you have made both of these mistakes.

10 B An increase in the discount rate used for a present value calculation will inevitably produce a fall in the present value computed.

Now try the questions below from the Exam Question Bank

Question numbers	Page
1 – 5	363

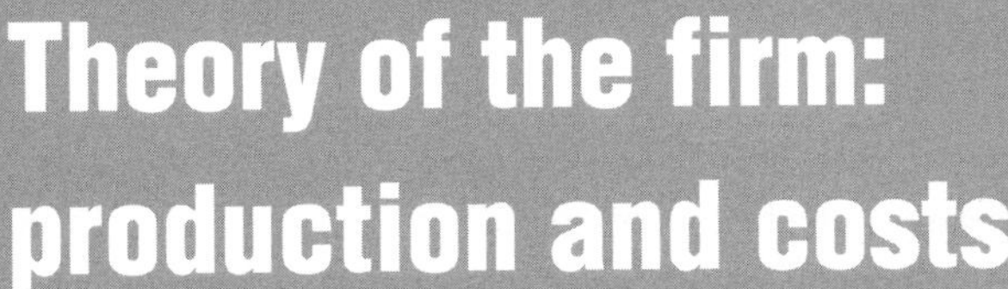

Theory of the firm: production and costs

Introduction

In this chapter we shall be looking at the costs and output decisions of an *individual* firm. In other words, we shall look at what the costs of production are for a single firm, and how these are affected by both short run and long run factors.

We contrast the concept of *opportunity cost*, which was introduced in Chapter 1, with financial cost as seen from the accountant's point of view.

We also consider how much output a firm will produce at a given market price.

The aggregate amount of goods supplied by every individual firm adds up to the market supply. By studying an individual firm we are looking at the 'building blocks' of market supply.

Topic list	Learning outcomes	Syllabus references	Ability required
1 Costs of production	A (iii)	A (2)	Comprehension
2 Average costs, marginal costs and diminishing returns	A (iii)	A (2)	Comprehension
3 The firm's output decision	A (ii)	A (2)	Comprehension
4 Economies of scale and long run costs	A (iii)	A (3)	Comprehension
5 Growth of firms	B (iii)	B (4)	Knowledge

1 Costs of production

Having considered other possible objectives for firms, let us return to profit: it is widely accepted that this will enable us to give a usefully accurate explanation of the way firms behave. The basic condition for profitability is very simple: **overall revenues must exceed overall costs**.

Key terms

Profit is equal to total revenue minus total cost of any level of output.

In order to understand how firms go about seeking profit, therefore, we must examine the ways in which costs and revenues arise. We will start by considering the costs incurred by a firm that makes and sells goods.

1.1 Short run and long run costs

FAST FORWARD

A firm's output decisions can be examined in the **short run**, when some factors of production are fixed and in the **long run**, when all factors of production can be varied. Total costs can be divided into fixed and variable elements. These elements have different effects on total cost as output is increased.

Assessment focus point

The theory of costs and revenue is of importance in later stages of the CIMA programme, as well as in the *Fundamentals of Business Economics* assessment.

Production is carried out by firms using the factors of production which must be paid or rewarded for their use. The cost of production is the cost of the factors used.

Factor of production	Its cost
Land	Rent
Labour	Wages
Capital	Interest
Enterprise	Normal profit

Notice that normal profit is viewed as a cost. This may seem odd to an accountant, who thinks of profit as the difference between revenue and cost – a point we shall return to later. Any profit earned in excess of the profit needed to reward the entrepreneur (in other words, the **opportunity cost** of keeping the entrepreneur from **going elsewhere**) is called **supernormal, abnormal or excess profit.**

Key term

The **short run** is a time period in which the amount of at least one input is fixed. The **long run** is a period sufficiently long to allow full flexibility in all the inputs used.

1.2 Fixed costs and variable costs

In the **short run**, certain costs are fixed because the availability of resources is restricted. Decisions must therefore be taken for the short run within the restriction of having some resources in fixed supply. In the **longer run**, however, most costs are **variable**, because the supply of skilled labour, machinery, buildings and so on can be increased or decreased. Decisions in the long run are therefore subject to fewer restrictions about resource availability.

Inputs are variable at the decision of management. For example, management might decide to buy more raw materials, hire more labour, start overtime working and so on.

(a) **Labour is usually considered to be variable** in the short run. Inputs which are treated as **fixed** in the short run will include **capital items**, such as buildings and machinery, for which a significant lead time might be needed before their quantities are changed.

(b) All inputs are variable in the long run. A decision to change the quantity of an input variable which is fixed in the short run will involve a change in the **scale of production**.

1.3 Short run costs: total costs, average costs and marginal costs

Let us now turn our attention to short run costs: the costs of output during a time period in which only some resources of production are variable in availability and the remaining resources of production are fixed in quantity.

Figure 1 shows how the various elements of cost vary as output changes.

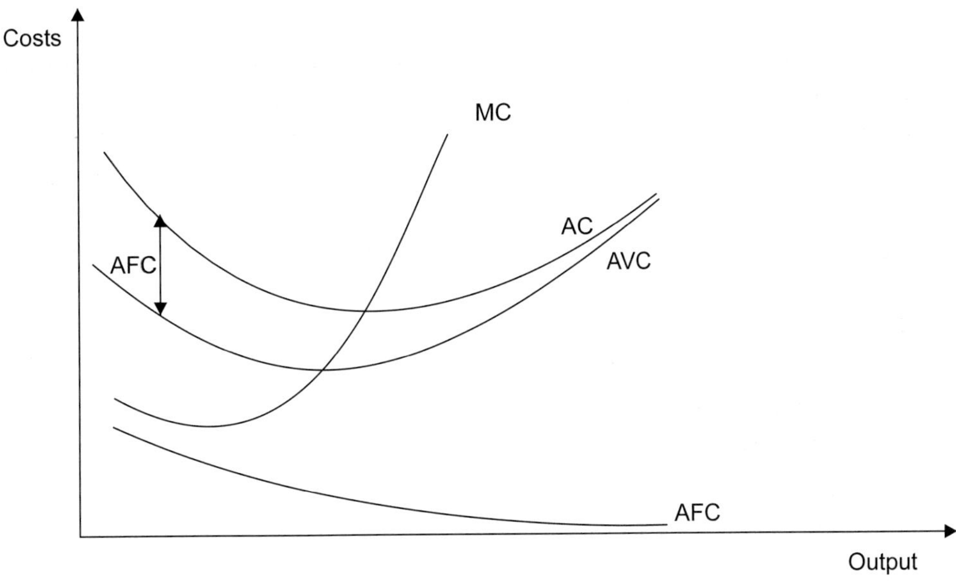

Figure 1 Components of a firm's short run costs

Key term

- **Total cost** (TC). Total cost for a given level of output comprises total fixed cost (TFC) and total variable cost (TVC)
- **Average cost** (AC). Average cost for a given level of output is simply the total cost divided by the total quantity produced.

  Average cost is made up of an average fixed cost per unit plus an average variable cost per unit.

  $$AC = \frac{TC}{N} = \frac{TFC}{N} + \frac{TVC}{N}$$

  AC = AFC + AVC

  Average fixed cost per unit (AFC) will get smaller as more units (N) are produced. This is because TFC is the same amount regardless of the volume of output, so as N gets bigger, AFC must get smaller.

  Average variable costs per unit (AVC) will change as output volume increases.
- **Marginal cost** (MC). This is the addition to total cost of producing one more unit of output. For example, the marginal cost for a firm of producing the 50th unit of output is the total cost of making the first 50 units minus the total cost of making the first 49 units.

Question

Costs

To test your understanding of these concepts, look at the three definitions given below. Which one(s) of them, if any, correctly describes the marginal cost of producing one extra unit of output?

(a) MC = increase in total cost of production
(b) MC = increase in variable cost of production
(c) MC = increase in average cost of production

Answer

(a) and (b) are correct; (c) is incorrect. An example might help. Suppose a firm has made 100 units of output, and now goes on to produce one more. The costs might be as follows.

	Cost of 100 units	*Cost of 101 units*
	£	£
Total variable cost	200	202
Total fixed cost	100	100
Total cost	300	302
Average cost	£3.00	£2.99

Marginal cost = 302p – 300p = 2p.

1.4 Numerical illustration

Let us suppose that a firm employs a given amount of capital which is a fixed (invariable) input in the short run: in other words, it is not possible to obtain extra amounts of capital quickly. The firm may combine with this capital different amounts of labour, which we assume to be an input which is variable in the short term. Thus fixed capital and variable labour can be combined to produce different levels of output.

Here is an illustration of the relationship between the different definitions of the firm's costs. (The figures used are hypothetical.)

Units of output	*Total cost*	*Average cost*	*Marginal cost*	
n	*TC*	*AC*	*MC*	
	£	£	£	
1	1.10	1.10	1.10	
2	1.60	0.80	0.50	(1.60 – 1.10)
3	1.75	0.58	0.15	(1.75 – 1.60)
4	2.00	0.50	0.25	(2.00 – 1.75)
5	2.50	0.50	0.50	(2.50 – 2.00)
6	3.12	0.52	0.62	(3.12 – 2.50)
7	3.99	0.57	0.87	(3.99 – 3.12)
8	5.12	0.64	1.13	(5.12 – 3.99)
9	6.30	0.70	1.18	(6.30 – 5.12)
10	8.00	0.80	1.70	(8.00 – 6.30)

(a) **Total cost** is the sum of labour costs plus capital costs, since these are by assumption the only two inputs.

(b) **Average cost** is the cost per unit of output, ie AC = $\frac{\text{TC}}{\text{output}} = \frac{\text{TC}}{\text{n}}$

(c) **Marginal cost** is the total cost of producing n units minus the total cost of producing one less unit, ie (n – 1) units.

Note the following points on this set of figures.

(a) **Total cost.** Total costs of production carry on rising as more and more units are produced.

(b) **Average cost.** AC changes as output increases. It starts by falling, reaches a lowest level, and then starts rising again.

(c) **Marginal cost.** The MC of each extra unit of output also changes with each unit produced. It too starts by falling, fairly quickly reaches a lowest level, and then starts rising.

(d) **AC and MC compared.** At lowest levels of output, MC is less than AC. At highest levels of output, though, MC is higher than AC. There is a 'cross-over' point, where MC is exactly equal to AC. In this example, it is at 5 units of output.

1.5 Economists' and accountants' concepts of cost

AST FORWARD

Economic costs are different from **accounting costs**, and represent the **opportunity costs of the factors of production** that are used.

As we have already mentioned, to an economist, cost includes an amount for normal profit which is the reward for entrepreneurship. **Normal profit is the opportunity cost of entrepreneurship**, because it is the amount of profit that an entrepreneur could earn elsewhere, and so it is the profit that he must earn to persuade him to keep on with his investment in his current enterprise.

A further feature of **cost accounting** is that costs can be divided into fixed costs and variable costs. Total fixed costs per period are a given amount, regardless of the volume of production and sales. Cost accountants usually assume that the variable cost per unit is a **constant amount,** so that the total **variable cost** of sales is directly proportional to the **volume** of sales.

Economists do not take this approach. In the short run, there are **fixed costs** and **variable costs**, but the variable cost of making an extra unit of output need not be the same for each extra unit that is made. As a result, the **marginal cost** of **each extra unit** is not constant, either.

Accounting profits consist of sales revenue minus the **explicit costs** of the business. Explicit costs are those which are clearly stated and recorded, for example:

- Materials costs – prices paid to suppliers
- Labour costs – wages paid
- Depreciation costs on fixed assets
- Other expenses, such as rates and building rental

Economic profit consists of sales revenue minus both the explicit costs and the **implicit costs** of the business. Implicit costs are benefits forgone by not using the factors of production in their next most profitable way.

It is a well established principle in accounting and economics that relevant costs for decision-making purposes are **future costs incurred as a consequence of the decision**. Past or 'sunk' costs are not relevant to our decisions now, because we cannot change them: they have already been incurred. Relevant future costs are the **opportunity costs** of the input resources to be used.

1.6 Example: economic profits and opportunity costs

Suppose that a sole trader in 19X7 sells goods worth £200,000. He incurs materials costs of £70,000, hired labour costs of £85,000, and other expenses of £20,000. He has no fixed assets other than the building, on which depreciation is not charged. In accounting terms, his profit would be as follows.

	£	£
Sales		200,000
Materials	70,000	
Labour	85,000	
Other expenses	20,000	
		(175,000)
Profit		25,000

But suppose the buildings he uses in his business could have been put to another use to earn £15,000, and his own labour as business manager could get him a job with a salary of £20,000. The position of the business in economic terms would be as follows.

	£
Sales less explicit costs	25,000
Implicit costs	(35,000)
Loss	(10,000)

In economic terms, the business has made a loss. It would pay the trader to put his buildings and capital to their alternative uses, and employ his own labour another way, working for someone else at a salary of £20,000.

Question

Accounting profit and economic profit

Wilbur Proffit set up his business one year ago. In that time, his firm has earned total revenue of £160,000, and incurred costs of £125,000, including his own salary of £12,000. Before, he had been a salaried employee of Dead End Ventures Ltd, earning an annual salary of £20,000.

To finance the business, Wilbur had to sell his investment of £200,000 in government securities which earned interest of 10% pa. He used £80,000 of this to buy a warehouse, whose annual commercial rental value would be £11,000 pa. The remaining £120,000 has been used to finance business operations.

Required

Calculate:

- The accounting profit earned by Wilbur in the last year
- The economic profit or loss earned

Answer

Accounting profit

	£
Revenue	160,000
Costs	125,000
Profit	35,000

Economic profit

	£	£
Revenue		160,000
Accounting costs	125,000	
Opportunity cost of owner's time – extra salary forgone From alternative employment (20,000 – 12,000)	8,000	
Rental of factory (opportunity cost of £80,000)	11,000	
Opportunity cost of other capital tied up in the business (10% of £120,000)	12,000	
		156,000
Economic profit		4,000

2 Average costs, marginal costs and diminishing returns

2.1 The relationship between AC and MC

The relationships between average and marginal costs are important.

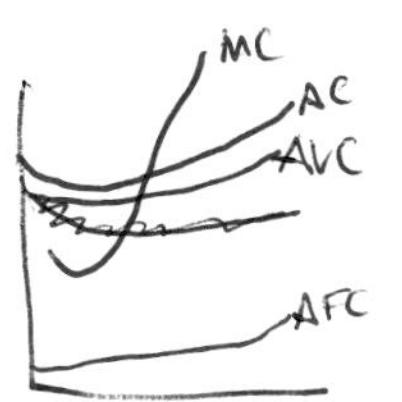

(a) **When the average cost schedule is rising, the marginal cost will always be higher than the average cost**. If the cost of making one extra unit of output exceeds the average cost of making all the previous units, then making the extra unit will clearly cause an increase in the average unit cost.

(b) In our example in Section 1.4 of this chapter, the average cost schedule rises from six units of output onwards and MC is bigger than AC at all these levels of output (6 – 10 units).

(c) **When the average cost curve is falling, marginal cost lies below it**. This follows similar logic. If the cost of making an extra unit is less than the average cost of making all the previous units, the effect of making the extra unit must be a reduction in average unit cost. In our example, this happens between production of one and four units.

(d) **When the average cost curve is horizontal, marginal cost is equal to it**. In our example in Section 1.4, when there are five units of output, the average cost stays at £0.50 and the marginal cost of the fifth unit is also £0.50.

Question — **Cost curves**

(a) It is possible for the average total cost curve to be falling while the average variable cost curve is rising. True or false?

(b) Marginal fixed costs per unit will fall as output increases. True or false?

Answer

(a) True. Average total cost (AC) comprises average fixed cost (AFC) and average variable cost (AVC). AFC falls as output rises, and the fall may be sufficient to outweigh a possible increase in AVC. In such a case, AC will fall while AVC rises.

(b) False. It is *average* fixed costs per unit that fall as output increases. *Marginal* fixed costs = 0.

The marginal cost curve always cuts through the average cost curve at the lowest point of the average cost curve (see Figure 1 earlier).

2.2 U-shaped short run average cost curve

FAST FORWARD

In the short run, a firm's average cost (SRAC) curve is U shaped, due to **diminishing returns** beyond a certain output level. In the short run, a firm will maximise its profits where MR = MC.

The short run average cost curve (AC in Figure 1) **is U shaped**. We now consider why.

Fixed costs per unit of output, ie average fixed costs, will fall as the level of output rises. Thus if fixed costs are £10,000 and we make 10,000 units, the average fixed cost (AFC) will be £1 per unit. If output increases to 12,500 units the AFC will fall to 80p (10,000 ÷ 12,500) and if output increases to 15,000 units, the AFC will fall again to 67p (10,000 ÷ 15,000), and so on. Spreading fixed costs over a larger amount of output is a major reason why short run average costs per unit fall as output increases.

Variable costs are made up from the cost of the factors of production whose use can be varied in the short run – for example wages, fuel bills and raw material purchases. **Total variable costs therefore vary with output in the short run as well as in the long run.**

(a) The accountant's assumption about short run variable costs is that **up to a certain level of output, the variable cost per unit is more or less constant** (eg wages costs and materials costs per unit of output are unchanged). If the average fixed cost per unit is falling as output rises and the average variable cost per unit is constant, it follows that the average total cost per unit will be falling too as output increases.

(b) However, there are other reasons for the initial fall in average total cost. The first are the effects of the **division of labour** and **specialisation**. Imagine a small but fully equipped factory, with a variety of machinery and equipment and a workforce of, say, ten. If each person attempts to perform all the operations on a single item, production is likely to be low.

    (i) They will be unable to develop a high level of skill at every one of the jobs

    (ii) Time will be lost as they move from machine to machine

    (iii) Individual variability will produce a high rate of defects, perhaps with each person tending to produce different faults

    (iv) Individuals will work at different rates on different operations: as a result, queues will form at some machines and others will be under-utilised

    If there is a degree of specialisation, expertise and speed will rise, machines will be run at optimum rates and output will rise. Average costs will therefore fall.

(c) **The second reason is the utilisation of indivisibilities.** If a machine has an output capacity of 100 units per day but is only used to produce 50 units per day, the machinery cost of each of those 50 units will be twice the level it would be if the machine was used to capacity. Operation of a plant below normal output is uneconomical, so there are cost savings as production is increased up to capacity level.

2.3 The law of diminishing returns

Key term

Eventually, as output increases, average costs will tend to rise. The **law of diminishing returns** says that if one or more factors of production are fixed, but the input of another is increased, the extra output generated by each extra unit of input will eventually begin to fall. In our factory, as we add staff, we start to see queues forming at machines; it becomes more difficult to co-ordinate work; machinery starts to break down through over-use and there simply is not enough space to work efficiently.

The law of diminishing returns states that, given the present state of technology, as more units of a variable input factor are added to input factors that are fixed in supply in the short run, the resulting increments to total production will eventually and progressively decline. In other words, as more units of a variable factor (eg labour) are added to a quantity of a fixed factor (eg a hectare of land), there may be some **increasing returns** or **constant returns** as more units of the variable factor (eg labour) are added, but eventually, **diminishing returns** will set in. Putting more people to work on a hectare of land will increase the yield up to a point, but eventually it will be costing more to employ additional labour than is being earned in additional yield. Observation of agriculture is the origin of the law of diminishing returns.

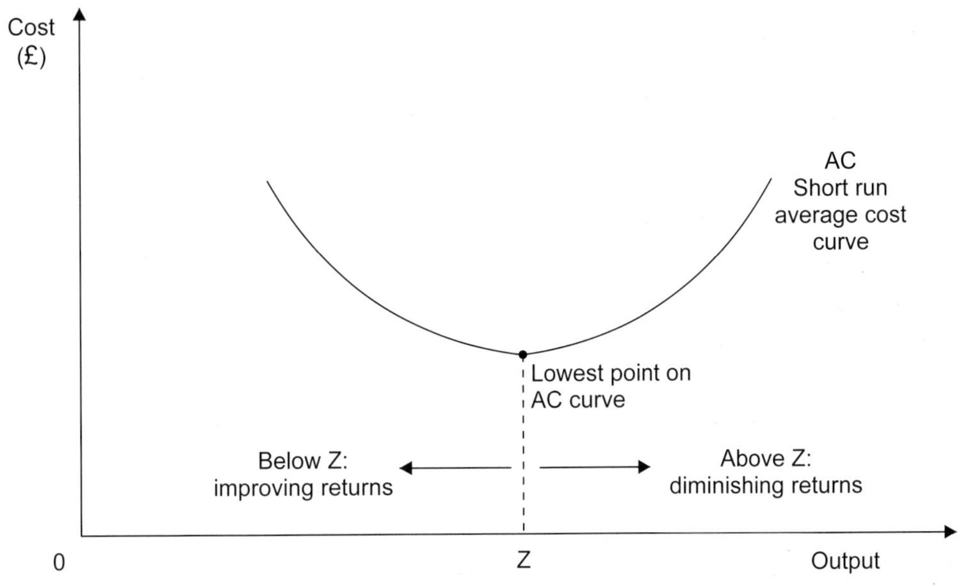

Figure 2 U shaped short run cost curve and diminishing returns

Assessment focus point

Remember that this is a **short run** phenomenon; at least one factor of production is fixed.

The law of diminishing returns is expressed in production quantities, but it obviously has direct implications for short run average and marginal **costs**. Resources cost money, and the average and marginal costs of output will depend on the quantities of resources needed to produce the given output.

Question **Diminishing returns**

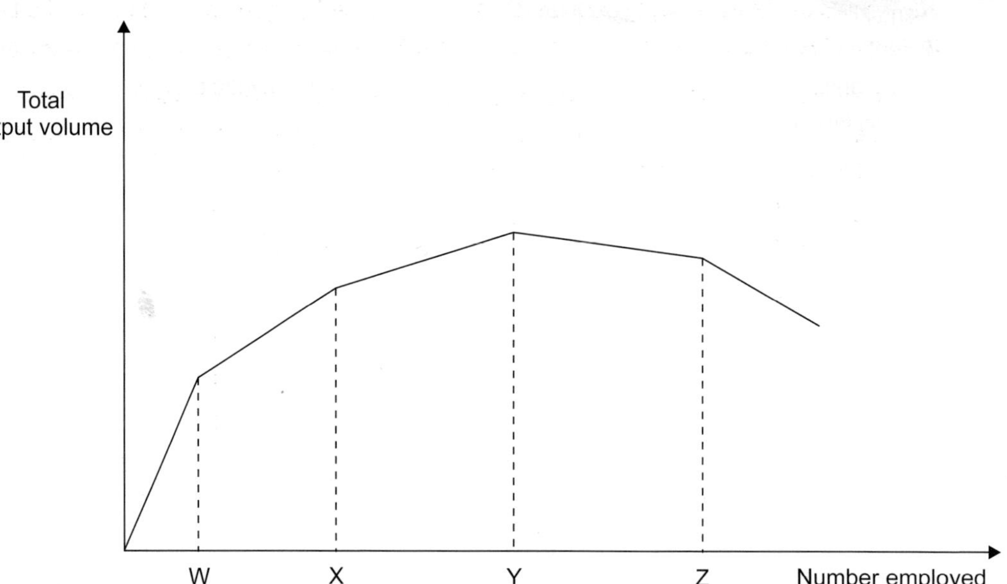

In the diagram above, from what level of employment do diminishing returns start to occur?

Answer

Diminishing returns occur when the marginal physical product of extra units of labour starts to decline. This begins to happen at output W, when the rate of increase in total output starts to decline as numbers employed continue to increase.

3 The firm's output decision

FAST FORWARD

The assumption of **profit maximisation** provides a basis for beginning to look at the output decisions of individual firms.

Key term

Profit is equal to total revenue minus total cost of any level of output.

3.1 Total revenue, average revenue and marginal revenue

There are three aspects of revenue to consider.

(a) **Total revenue** (TR) is the total income obtained from selling a given quantity of output. We can think of this as quantity sold multiplied by the price per unit.

(b) **Average revenue** (AR) we can think of as the price per unit sold.

(c) **Marginal revenue** (MR) is the addition to total revenue earned from the sale of one extra unit of output.

3.2 The average revenue curve

When a firm can sell all its extra output at the same price, the AR 'curve' will be a straight horizontal line on a graph. The **marginal revenue** per unit from selling extra units at a fixed price must be the same as the **average revenue** (see Figure 4).

If the price per unit must be cut in order to sell more units, then the **marginal revenue** per unit obtained from selling extra units will be less than the previous price per unit (see Figure 5). In other words, when the AR is falling as more units are sold, the MR must be less than the AR.

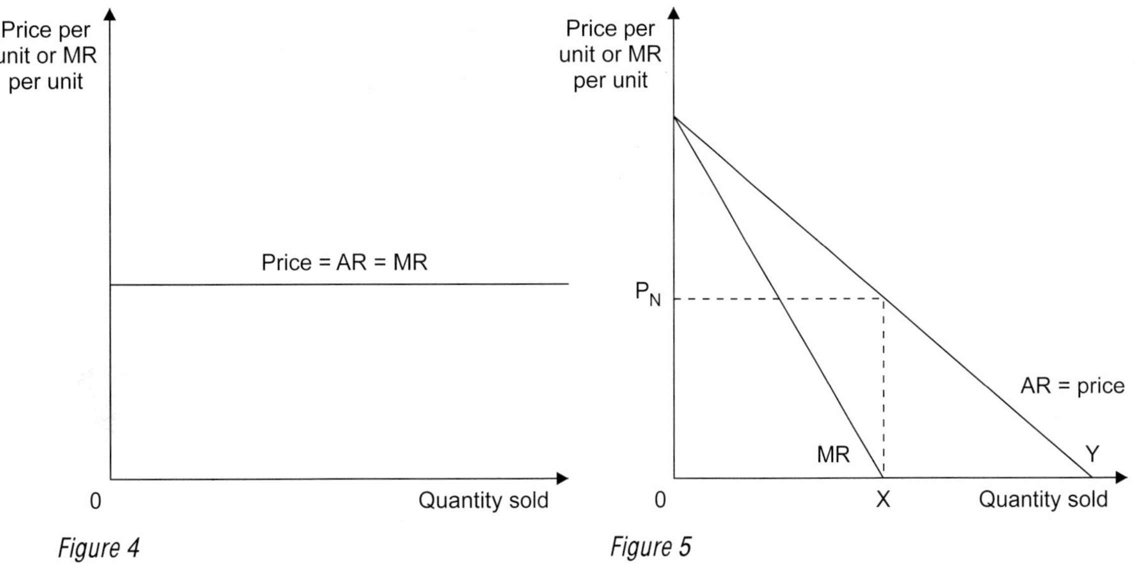

Figure 4

Figure 5

In Figure 5, with straight line MR and AR curves, the length 0X is exactly half of the length 0Y.

ssessment ocus point

Figure 5 is another important diagram and forms the basis of other more detailed illustrations.

Note that in Figure 5, at any given level of sales, **all units are sold at the same price**. The firm has to reduce its price to sell more, but the price must be reduced for *all* units sold, not just for the extra units. This is because we are assuming that all output is produced for a single market, where a single price will prevail.

When the price per unit has to be reduced in order to increase the firm's sales the marginal revenue can become negative. This happens in Figure 5 at price P_N when a reduction in price does not increase output sufficiently to earn the same total revenue as before. In this situation, demand would be price inelastic.

3.3 Profit

We have defined profit as TR minus TC.

(a) Figure 6 shows, in simplified form, how TR and TC vary with output. As you might expect, TC increases as output rises. The effect of increasing marginal cost (caused by diminishing returns) is that the rise in TC accelerates as output increases and so the TC curve becomes steeper.

(b) Conversely, the gradient of the TR curve reduces as output and sales increase. This is because most firms operate under the conditions illustrated in Figure 5. That is to say, they must reduce their prices in order to sell more. The rate of growth of TR therefore declines.

(c) Notice carefully that the vertical axis of Figure 6 shows total values whereas in Figures 4 and 5, it shows value per unit.

(d) Profits are at a maximum where the vertical distance AB between the TC and TR curves is greatest.

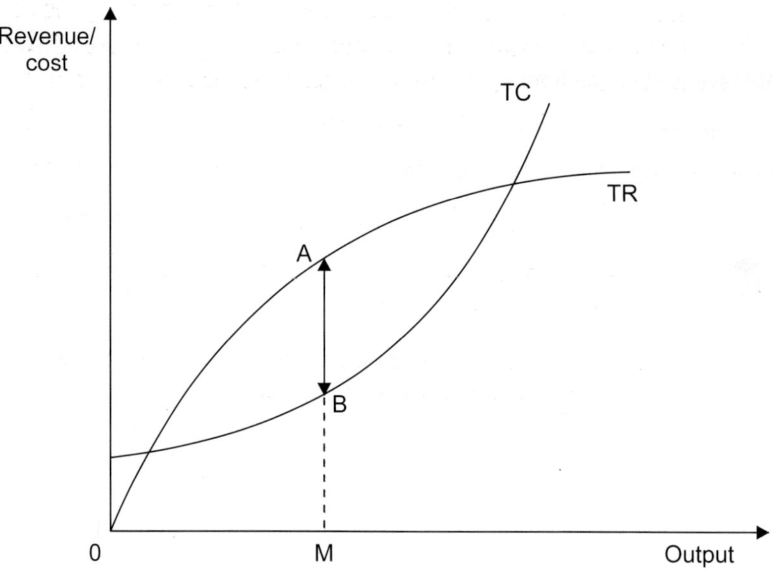

Figure 6 Profit maximisation

3.4 Marginal cost equals marginal revenue

As a firm produces and sells more units, its total costs will increase and its total revenues will also increase (unless demand is price inelastic and MR has become negative).

(a) Provided that the extra cost of making an extra unit is **less than** the extra revenue obtained from selling it, the firm will increase its profits by making and selling the extra unit.

(b) If the extra cost of making an extra unit of output **exceeds** the extra revenue obtainable from selling it, the firm's profits would be reduced by making and selling the extra unit.

(c) If the extra cost of making an extra unit of output is **exactly equal** to the extra revenue obtainable from selling it, bearing in mind that economic cost includes an amount for normal profit, it will be worth the firm's while to make and sell the extra unit. And since the extra cost of yet another unit would be higher (the law of diminishing returns applies) whereas extra revenue per unit from selling extra units is never higher, the profit-maximising output is reached at this point where MC = MR.

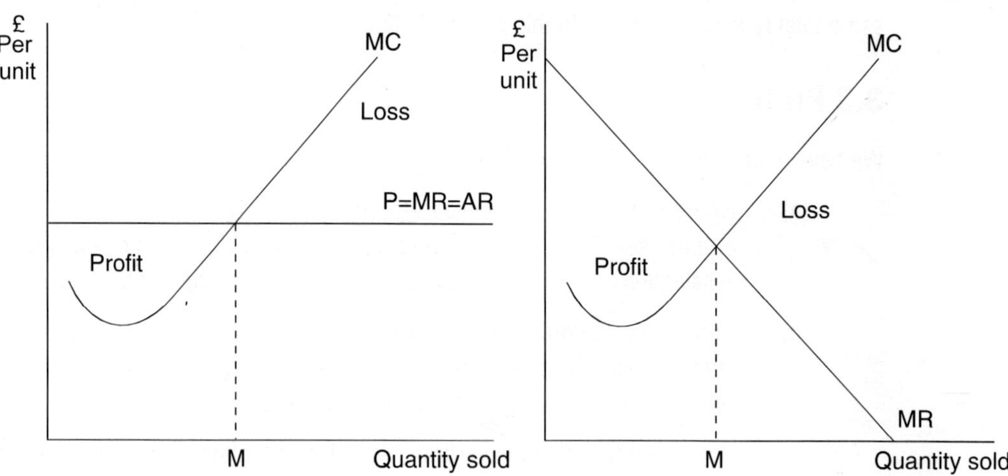

Figure 7

Figure 8

(d) Figures 7 and 8 show the profit maximising output quantity M for the 2 types of firm shown in Figures 4 and 5. In both cases, the marginal cost function is as discussed earlier in this chapter. The firm makes a profit on each extra item it produces, albeit a smaller one, until output M is reached. At this level of output the MC and MR curves cross. The addition to total revenue from the next unit is less than the increase in total cost which it causes. This level of output corresponds to the level M shown in Figure 6.

In other words, given the objective of profit maximisation there are **three possibilities**.

(a) If MC is less than MR, profits will be increased by making and selling more.

(b) If MC is greater than MR, profits will fall if more units are made and sold, and a profit-maximising firm would not make the extra output.

(c) If MC = MR, the profit-maximising output has been reached, and so this is the output quantity that a profit-maximising firm will decide to supply.

Question

Revenue and costs

The following data refer to the revenue and costs of a firm.

Output	*Total revenue* £	*Total costs* £
0	-	110
1	50	140
2	100	162
3	150	175
4	200	180
5	250	185
6	300	194
7	350	229
8	400	269
9	450	325
10	500	425

Required

(a) Calculate the marginal revenue for the firm and state which sort of market it is operating in.
(b) Calculate the firm's fixed costs and the marginal cost at each level of output.
(c) What level of output will the firm aim to produce and what amount of profit will it make at this level?

Answer

Output	Total revenue (TR) £	(a) Marginal revenue $TR_n - TR_{(n-1)}$ £	Total costs (TC) £	(b) Marginal costs $TC_n - TC_{(n-1)}$ £	Total profit TR - TC £
0	-	-	110	-	(110)
1	50	50	140	30	(90)
2	100	50	162	22	(62)
3	150	50	175	13	(25)
4	200	50	180	5	20
5	250	50	185	5	65
6	300	50	194	9	106
7	350	50	229	35	122
8	400	50	269	40	131(max)
9	450	50	325	56	125
10	500	50	425	100	75

(a) Marginal revenue is the additional revenue which results from the sale of the last unit of output.

The figures in the table above show that marginal revenue is a constant £50 at all levels of output given. This means that average revenue (price) must also be a constant £50. The firm's demand curve is perfectly elastic, indicating that the firm is operating in a perfectly competitive market.

(b) The fixed costs of the firm are those costs which do not vary with output. The level of fixed costs are therefore the total costs of £110 at the output level of zero.

Marginal cost is the change in total cost arising from the production of the last unit of output. The marginal cost for each level of output is shown in the table.

(c) As stated in (a) above, the firm is operating in a perfectly competitive market. The firm will seek to maximise profits by producing at a level of output at which marginal cost equals marginal revenue. It can be seen from the table that this occurs at output level 8 (marginal cost: £40) and output level 9 (marginal cost: £56). Whether the firm can produce output between the values 8 and 9 will depend on the nature of the product. For whole units of output, total profit (total revenues minus total costs) is maximised at an output of 8, where total profit is £131.

4 Economies of scale and long run costs

FAST FORWARD

In the long run, a firm's SRAC curve can be shifted, and a firm's minimum achievable average costs at any level of output can be depicted by a **long run average cost (LRAC) curve**.

4.1 Costs in the long run

We have not yet considered a firm's long run costs of output. In the long run, all inputs are variable, so the problems associated with the diminishing returns to variable factors do not arise; in other words, the law of diminishing returns applies only to short run costs and not to long run costs. Whereas short run output decisions are concerned with diminishing returns given fixed factors of production, **long run output decisions** are concerned with **economies of scale** when all factor inputs are variable.

Output will vary with variations in inputs, such as labour and capital.

(a) If output increases in the **same proportion** as inputs (for example doubling all inputs doubles output) there are **constant returns to scale**.

(b) If output increases **more than in proportion** to inputs (for example doubling all inputs trebles output) there are **economies of scale** and in the long run average costs of production will continue to fall as output volume rises.

(c) If output increases **less than in proportion** to inputs (for example trebling all inputs only doubles output) there are **diseconomies of scale** and in the long run average costs of production will rise as output volume rises.

Returns to scale are, for example, concerned with improvements or declines in productivity **by increasing the scale of production**, for example by mass-producing instead of producing in small batch quantities.

4.2 Constant returns to scale

A feature of constant returns to scale is that **long run** average costs and marginal costs per unit remain constant. For example:

Output	*Total cost (with constant returns)*	*Average cost per unit*	*Marginal cost per unit*
	£	£	£
1	6	6	6
2	12 (2 × 6)	6	6
3	18 (3 × 6)	6	6
4	24 (4 × 6)	6	6

In the real world, the duplication of all inputs might be impossible if one incorporates qualitative as well as quantitative characteristics in inputs. One such input is entrepreneurship. Doubling the size of the firm does not necessarily double the inputs of organisational and managerial skills, even if the firm does hire extra managers and directors. The input of entrepreneurship might be intangible and indivisible.

4.3 Economies of scale

Key term

> **Economies of scale**: factors which cause average cost to decline in the long run as output increases.

The effect of economies of scale is to shift the whole cost structure downwards and to the right on the graph. A **long run average cost curve (LRAC)** can be drawn as the 'envelope' of all the short run average cost curves (SRAC) of firms producing on different scales of output. The LRAC is tangential to each of the SRAC curves. Figure 9 shows the shape of such a long run average cost curve if there are increasing returns to scale – economies of scale – up to a certain output volume and then constant returns to scale thereafter.

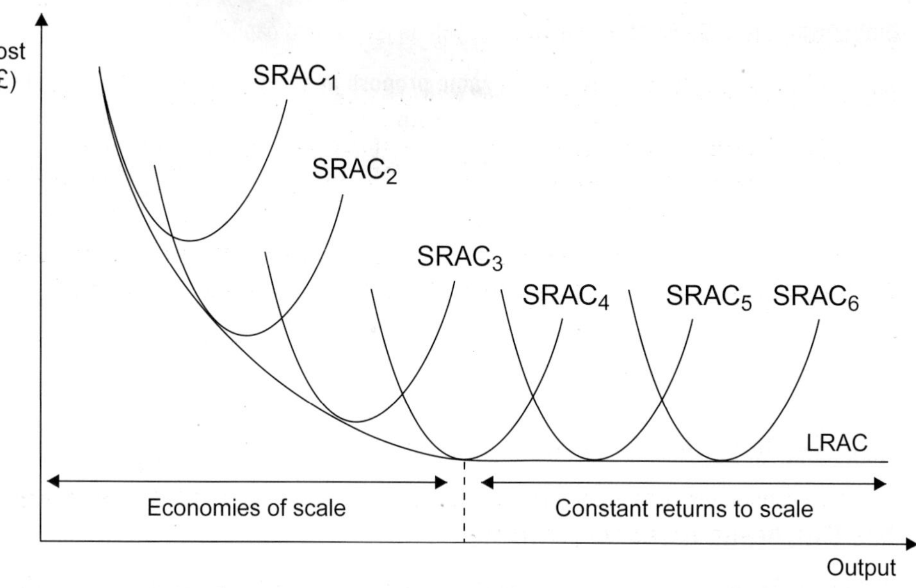

Figure 9 Economies of scale

FAST FORWARD

The shape of the LRAC depends on whether there are **increasing**, **constant** or **decreasing returns to scale**. Even if increasing returns to scale are not achievable indefinitely as output rises, up to a certain **minimum efficient scale of production** (MES) there will be **increasing returns to scale**. Firms will reduce their average costs by producing on a larger scale up to the MES.

4.4 Diseconomies of scale

It may be that the flat part of the LRAC curve is never reached, or it may be that diseconomies of scale are encountered. Diseconomies of scale might arise when a firm gets so large that it cannot operate efficiently or it is too large to manage efficiently, so that average costs begin to rise.

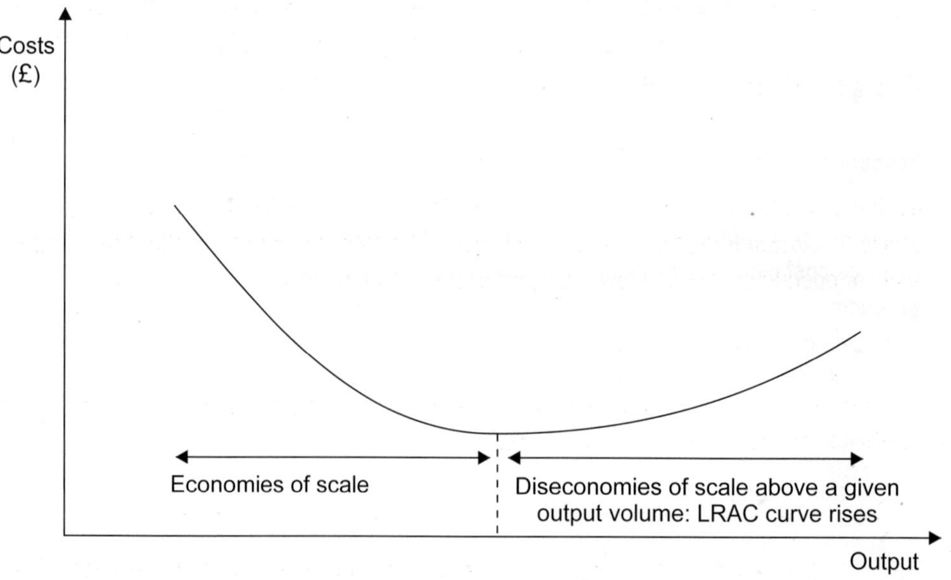

Figure 10 Diseconomies of scale

A firm should try to minimise its average costs in the long run, and to do this it ought to try to produce output on a scale where the LRAC curve is at its lowest point. While there are economies of scale, a firm should always be trying to grow.

4.5 Reasons for economies of scale

The economies of scale attainable from large scale production fall into two categories.

(a) **Internal economies**: economies **arising within** the firm from the organisation of production
(b) **External economies**: economies attainable by the firm because of the growth of the industry as a whole

ST FORWARD

Whether there are constant or decreasing returns to scale beyond the MES will **vary** between **industries** and **firms**. Similarly, whether economies of scale are significant will vary between industries.

4.6 Internal economies of scale

4.6.1 Technical economies

Technical economies arise in the production process. They are also called **plant economies of scale** because they depend on the size of the factory or piece of equipment.

Large undertakings can make use of **larger and more specialised machinery**. If smaller undertakings tried to use similar machinery, the costs would be excessive because the machines would become obsolete before their physical life ends (ie their economic life would be shorter than their physical life). Obsolescence is caused by falling demand for the product made on the machine, or by the development of newer and better machines.

Indivisibility of operations

(a) There are operations which must be carried out at the same cost, regardless of whether the business is small or large; these are fixed costs and **average fixed costs always decline as production increases**.

(b) Similarly, other operations' costs vary a little, but not proportionately, with size (ie having 'semi-fixed' costs).

(c) Some operations are not worth considering below a certain level of output (eg advertising campaigns).

Dimensional economies of scale arise from the relationship between the volume of output and the size of equipment (eg storage tanks) needed to hold or process the output. The cost of a container for 10,000 gallons of product will be much less than ten times the cost of a container for just 1,000 gallons.

4.6.2 Commercial or marketing economies

Buying economies may be available, reducing the cost of material purchases through bulk purchase discounts. Similarly, **stockholding** becomes more efficient. The most economic quantities of inventory to hold increase with the scale of operations, but at a lower proportionate rate of increase.

4.6.3 Organisational economies

When the firm is large, centralisation of functions such as administration, R&D and marketing may reduce the burden of overheads on individual operating locations.

4.6.4 Financial economies

Large firms may find it easier to obtain loan finance at attractive rates of interest. It is also feasible for them to sell shares to the public via a stock exchange.

Question **Economies of scale**

The above list is not exhaustive. Can you add to it?

Answer

(a) Large firms attract *better quality employees* if the employees see better career prospects than in a small firm.

(b) Specialisation of labour applies to management, and there are thus *managerial economies*; the cost per unit of management will fall as output rises.

(c) *Marketing economies* are available, because a firm can make more effective use of advertising, specialist salesmen, and specialised channels of distribution.

(d) Large companies are able to devote more resources to *research and development* (R & D). In an industry where R & D is essential for survival, large companies are more likely to prosper.

(e) Large companies find raising finance easier and can often do so more cheaply. Quoted public limited companies have access to the Stock Exchange for new share issues. They are also able to borrow money more readily.

4.7 External economies of scale

External economies of scale occur as an **industry** grows in size. Here are two examples.

(a) **A large skilled labour force is created** and educational services can be geared towards training new entrants.

(b) **Specialised ancillary industries will develop** to provide components, transport finished goods, trade in by-products, provide special services and so on. For instance, law firms may be set up to specialise in the affairs of the industry.

4.8 The effect of size

FAST FORWARD

If **economies of scale** are significant, there is a strong argument in favour of **growth** by firms, which might occur either through organic growth (building up the firm's own resources) or through mergers and takeovers.

The extent to which both internal and external economies of scale can be achieved will vary from industry to industry, depending on the conditions in that industry. In other words, big-sized firms are better suited to some industries than others.

(a) **Internal economies of scale** are potentially more significant than external economies to a supplier of a product or service for which there is a large consumer market. It may be necessary for a firm in such an industry to grow to a certain size in order to benefit fully from potential economies of scale, and thereby be cost-competitive and capable of making profits and surviving (see Section 4.9 below).

(b) **External economies of scale** are potentially significant to smaller firms who specialise in the ancillary services to a larger industry. For example, the development of a large world-wide industry in drilling for oil and natural gas off-shore has led to the creation of many new specialist supplier firms, making drilling rigs, and various types of equipment. Thus, a specialist firm may benefit more from the market demand created by a large customer industry than from its own internal economies of scale.

4.9 Diseconomies of scale

Economic theory predicts that there will be **diseconomies of scale** in the long run costs of a firm, once the firm gets beyond an ideal size. The main reasons for possible diseconomies of scale are human and behavioural problems of managing a large firm. In a large firm employing many people, with many levels in the hierarchy of management, there may be a number of undesirable effects.

(a) Communicating information and instructions may become difficult.

(b) Chains of command may become excessively long.

(c) Morale and motivation amongst staff may deteriorate.

(d) Senior management may have difficulty in assimilating all the information they need in sufficient detail to make good quality decisions.

There will not usually be **technical** factors producing diseconomies of scale. The technology of higher volume equipment, on the contrary, is more likely to create further economies of scale.

The implication of diseconomies of scale is that companies should achieve a certain size to benefit fully from scale economies, but should not become too big, when cost controls might slacken and organisational inefficiency is likely to develop.

4.10 Minimum efficient scale

Key term

Given the idea of economies of scale, it is generally accepted that in any industry, there is a **minimum efficient scale** of production which is necessary for a firm to achieve the full potential economies of scale.

Just what this **minimum efficient scale** (MES) is will vary from industry to industry. In the paint manufacturing industry, for example, it might be necessary to have a 15% share of the market in order to achieve maximum scale economies, whereas in frozen food production, a 25% share of the market might be necessary, and so on. If a firm has a production capacity below the minimum economic scale, its unit costs of production will be higher than the unit costs of its bigger competitors, and so it will not compete successfully and it will make lower profits, or even losses. A profit maximising firm should be attempting to minimise its unit costs, and this means striving to achieve maximum scale economies, which in turn may mean having to grow bigger.

Question — **Economies of scale and diminishing returns**

Explain in detail the difference between economies of scale and diminishing returns to a factor.

Answer

Diminishing returns. In the short run, some factors of production are fixed, and some are variable. This means that a firm can increase the volume of its output in the short run, but only within the constraint of having some fixed factors. As a result, the short run average cost curve is U shaped, because of increasing and then diminishing marginal returns. Diminishing marginal returns occur within a given production capacity limit.

Economies of scale. In the long run, all factors of production are variable and so a firm can increase the scale of its output in the long run without any constraints of fixed factors. By increasing output capacity in this way, a firm might be able to reduce its unit costs, for example by mass-producing with bigger and more efficient machines or more specialised machines. These cost reductions are economies of scale.

If economies of scale are sufficiently great, average costs and more particularly marginal unit costs will fall to the point where suppliers are able to reduce their selling prices and still maximise profits at the lower selling price. MC has fallen, and so MR will fall too, at the profit-maximising output level.

Economies of scale explain the L shape of a firm's long run average cost curve.

5 Growth of firms

FAST FORWARD

Firms seek to grow in order to improve their relationship with their owners and to achieve **economies of scale**. The two methods of growth are **organic** and by **mergers and takeovers**. Growth may take the form of **vertical** or **horizontal integration** or **conglomerate diversification**.

5.1 Forms of growth

The possibility of achieving economies of scale through expansion should encourage firms to try to grow in size. There are two broad methods of obtaining growth in sales and output volumes, and growth in profits.

(a) **Organic growth,** which is growth through a gradual build-up of the firm's own resources, developing new products, acquiring more plant and machinery, hiring extra labour and so on. Organic growth is often a slow but steady process.

(b) **Growth through mergers and takeovers,** which is the combination of two or more firms into one.

5.2 Mergers and takeovers

The nature of a merger or takeover can be categorised according to which firms are coming together: are they in exactly the same line of business? Are they in very similar businesses? Are they in related businesses, but operating in different stages of the production and selling process? Are they in unrelated lines of business?

Key term

Horizontal integration. When two firms in the same business merge, there is horizontal integration. Horizontal integration tends to create monopolies, so that if, for example, All-England Chocolate plc with a 15% share of the UK chocolate market were to merge with British Choc plc which has a 20% share of the UK market, the enlarged company might expect to hold a 35% share of the market.

Vertical integration. Two firms operating at different stages in the production and selling process might merge. When they do, vertical integration occurs. For example a company which operates exclusively in oil refining might take over an oil shipping company, and perhaps an oil extraction company too. This would be backward vertical integration, back through stages in production towards the raw material growing/ extracting stage. The same company might take over a company with a distribution fleet of petrol tanker lorries, and perhaps a chain of petrol stations too. This would be forward vertical integration, forward through stages in production and selling towards the end consumer sales stage.

Conglomerate diversification. A company might take over or merge with another company in a different business altogether. This form of merger is diversification, and a group of diversified companies is referred to as a conglomerate organisation.

The advantages and disadvantages of these different types of business expansion are summarised in the table below.

Horizontal expansion or integration	
Advantages • Economies of scale from larger production quantities, ie lower costs. – Technical economies (use of larger machines or more specialised machines) – Managerial economies (greater specialisation of middle managers) – Commercial economies (bulk buying and selling) – Financial economies (ability to borrow money more cheaply) – Risk-bearing economies (some greater spread of products made within the same general market should help the firm to spread its risks) • Possibility of achieving monopoly or oligopoly status, and so having greater influence in the market and chance to earn superprofits and raise prices.	**Disadvantages** • Top management might be unable to handle the running of a large firm efficiently, ie there might be management diseconomies of scale. • The creation of a monopoly will be unacceptable to government.
Vertical integration	
Advantages • Gives the firm greater control over its sources of supply (backward vertical integration) or over its end markets (forward vertical integration). • Financial economies of scale and possibly some commercial economies. Otherwise few economies of scale unless production now becomes better co-ordinated through its various stages.	**Disadvantages** • Possible management diseconomies of scale, owing to lack of familiarity with businesses acquired.
Diversification	
Advantages • Risks are spread by operating in several industries. If one industry declines, others may thrive.	**Disadvantages** • No economies of scale apart from financial economies. • Possible management diseconomies of scale, owing to lack of familiarity with businesses acquired.

5.3 Advantages of small firms

If there are economies of scale, it is reasonable to ask why small firms continue to prosper. In some industries and professions, small firms predominate (eg building, the legal profession) and in some, small and large firms co-exist. The number of small firms in the UK has grown in recent years. The reasons for the survival of the small firm may be divided into three categories.

(a) **Diseconomies of scale in large firms**, meaning that small firms face lower costs, and the other disadvantages of large firms

(b) **Economic advantages of small firms**

(c) **Financial and managerial challenges of expansion**. Entrepreneurs may be unwilling to use outside capital as this erodes their autonomy, while their business may not generate enough funds to pay for expansion. Also, they may be temperamentally unsuited to management by delegation, preferring to make all decisions themselves; this will place a limit on their firms' expansion.

Small firms have certain advantages over large firms which may outweigh economies of scale.

(a) Since they are small, they are more likely to operate in **competitive markets**, in which prices will tend to be lower and the most efficient firms will survive at the expense of the inefficient.

(b) They are more likely to be **risk takers**, investing 'venture capital' in projects which might yield high rewards. Innovation and entrepreneurial activity are important ingredients for economic recovery or growth.

(c) **Management-employee relations** are more likely to be **co-operative**, with direct personal contacts between managers at the top and all their employees.

(d) Small firms tend to **specialise**, and so **contribute efficiently** towards the division of labour in an economy.

(e) The structure of a small firm may allow for **greater flexibility** (eg an employee or manager can switch from one task to another much more readily).

(f) Small firms often sell to a **local market**; large firms need wider markets, and may incur relatively higher costs of transport.

(g) **Managerial economies** can be obtained by hiring expert consultants, possibly at a cheaper cost than permanent management specialists.

(h) Some small firms act as **suppliers** or **sub-contractors** to larger firms. Market demand may be insufficient to justify large scale production.

Chapter roundup

- A firm's output decisions can be examined in the **short run**, when some factors of production are fixed and in the **long run**, when all factors of production can be varied. Total costs can be divided into fixed and variable elements. These elements have different effects on total cost as output is increased.
- **Economic costs** are different from **accounting costs**, and represent the **opportunity costs of the factors of production** that are used.
- In the short run, a firm's average cost (SRAC) curve is U shaped, due to **diminishing returns** beyond a certain output level. In the short run, a firm will maximise its profits where MR = MC.
- The assumption of **profit maximisation** provides a basis for beginning to look at the output decisions of individual firms.
- In the long run, a firm's SRAC curve can be shifted, and a firm's minimum achievable average costs at any level of output can be depicted by a **long run average cost (LRAC) curve**.
- The shape of the LRAC depends on whether there are **increasing**, **constant** or **decreasing returns to scale**. Even if increasing returns to scale are not achievable indefinitely as output rises, up to a certain **minimum efficient scale of production** (MES) there will be **increasing returns to scale**. Firms will reduce their average costs by producing on a larger scale up to the MES.
- Whether there are constant or decreasing returns to scale beyond the MES will **vary** between **industries** and **firms**. Similarly, whether economies of scale are significant will vary between industries.
- If **economies of scale** are significant, there is a strong argument in favour of **growth** by firms, which might occur either through organic growth (building up the firm's own resources) or through mergers and takeovers.
- Firms seek to grow in order to improve their relationship with their owners and to achieve **economies of scale**. The main methods of growth are **organic** and by **mergers and takeovers**. Growth may take the form of **vertical** or **horizontal integration** or **conglomerate diversification**.

Quick quiz

1 Explain the distinction between long run and short run costs.

2 What is the law of diminishing returns?

3 At what point is the firm's profit maximised?

4 Why might there be diseconomies of scale?

5 Which of the following is an example of an external economy of scale?

A Increased wage costs due to falling unemployment in the region.
B The employment of specialist managers by a firm to cope with higher output levels.
C The extension of low-cost telecommunication links to an area of the country not previously served by such links.
D Cheaper finance in recognition of the firm's increased share of the market and therefore its stability.

6 Which of the following cannot be true? In the short run as output falls:

A Average variable costs falls
B Average total cost falls
C Average fixed cost falls
D Marginal costs falls

7 The tendency for unit costs to fall as output increases in the short run is due to the operation of:

A Economies of scale
B The experience of diminishing marginal returns
C Falling marginal revenue
D Increasing marginal returns

8 Which of the following cannot be true in the short run as output rises:

A Average variable cost rises
B Average total cost rises
C Average fixed cost rises
D Marginal cost rises

9 Harold Ippoli employs 30 people in his factory which manufactures sweets and puddings. He pays them £5 per hour and they all work maximum hours. To employ one more person he would have to raise the wage rate to £5.50 per hour. If all other costs remain constant, the marginal cost of labour is:

A £20.50
B £15.00
C £5.50
D £0.50

10 Which of the statements below best defines the difference between the short run and the long run?

A Labour costs are fixed in the short run and variable in the long run.
B Economies of scale are present in the long run but not in the short run.
C At least one factor of production is fixed in the short run but in the long run it is possible to vary them all.
D None of the factors of production is fixed in the short run

Answers to quick quiz

1 The distinction between the short run and the long run is that in the long run, all resource inputs are variable. In the short run, probably only the amount of labour input is variable.

2 If one or more factors of production are fixed, but the input of another is increased, the extra output generated by each extra unit of input will eventually begin to fall.

3 At the level of output at which marginal cost equals marginal revenue

4 Diseconomies of scale are problems of size and tend to arise when the firm grows so large that it cannot be managed efficiently. Communications may become difficult, motivation may deteriorate because of alienation and senior management may find it difficult to identify the information they need in the vast volumes available.

5 C This is an external economy of scale.

A is a diseconomy of scale.
B is an internal economy of scale.
D is an internal economy of scale.

6 C Factual knowledge. The key to this question is to draw a diagram of the cost curves.

7 D The benefits of specialisation and the division of labour
Economies of scale only operate in the long run.
B results in rising unit costs in the short run.
C is nothing to do with costs.

8 C Average fixed cost must continue to fall as output rises in the short term. This is a mathematical fact.

9 A

	£
Cost of 31 people (at £5.50 per hour)	170.50
Cost of 30 people (at £5.00 per hour)	150.00
Marginal cost	20.50

10 C

Now try the questions below from the Exam Question Bank

Question numbers	Page
6 – 8	364

Part B

The market system and the competitive process

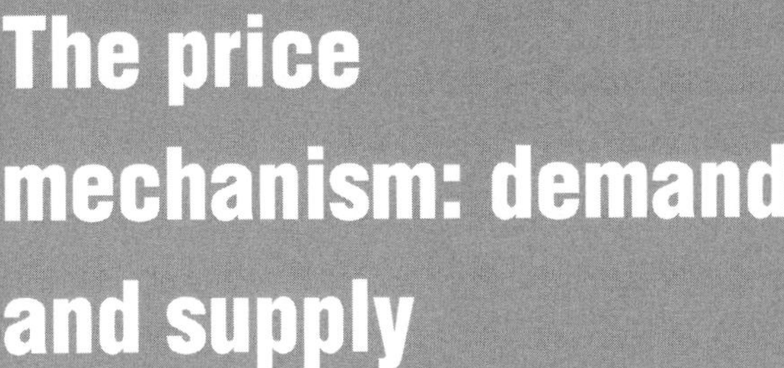

The price mechanism: demand and supply

3

Introduction

The distinction between the microeconomic level and the macroeconomic level was mentioned in Chapter 1.

In this chapter, we look in more depth at the microeconomic level of the individual firm, individual markets and consumers (or households). This means analysing how price and output are determined through the interaction of demand and supply.

We start by examining the concept of a market which in economics goes beyond the idea of a single geographical place where people meet to buy and sell goods.

Topic list	Learning outcomes	Syllabus references	Ability required
1 The concept of a market	B (i)	B (1)	Comprehension
2 The demand schedule	B (i)	B (1)	Comprehension
3 The supply schedule	B (i)	B (1)	Comprehension
4 The equilibrium price	B (i)	B (1)	Comprehension
5 Demand and supply analysis	B (i)	B (1)	Comprehension
6 Maximum and minimum prices	B (iv)	B (8)	Comprehension

1 The concept of a market

In a free market, the **price mechanism** signals demand and supply conditions to producers and consumers. It therefore determines the activities of both producers and consumers, influencing the levels of demand for and the supply of goods.

1.1 What is a market?

A market involves **the buyers and sellers of a good who influence its price**. Markets can be worldwide, as in the case of oil, wheat, cotton and copper for example. Others are more localised, such as the housing market or the market for second-hand cars.

Key terms

A **market** can be defined as a situation in which potential buyers and potential sellers (*suppliers*) of a good or service come together for the purpose of exchange.

Suppliers and potential suppliers are referred to in economics as **firms**. The potential purchasers of consumer goods are known as **households**.

Some markets have buyers who are other firms or government authorities. For example, a manufacturing firm buys raw materials and components to go into the products that it makes. Service industries and government departments must similarly buy in supplies in order to do their own work. The demand for goods by firms and government authorities is a **derived demand** in that it depends on the demand from households for the goods and services that they produce and provide.

Markets for different goods or commodities are often inter-related. All commodities compete for households' income so that if more is spent in one market, there will be less to spend in other markets. Further, if markets for similar goods are separated geographically, there will be some price differential at which it will be worthwhile for the consumer to buy in the lower price market and pay shipping costs, rather than buy in a geographically nearer market.

1.2 Price theory and the market

Price theory is concerned with how market prices for goods are arrived at, through the interaction of demand and supply.

A good or service has a **price** if it is **useful** as well as **scarce**. Its usefulness is shown by the fact that consumers demand it. In a world populated entirely by vegetarians, meat would not command a price, no matter how few cows or sheep there were.

1.3 Utility

Utility is the word used to describe the pleasure or satisfaction or benefit derived by a person from the consumption of goods. **Total utility** is then the total satisfaction that people derive from spending their income and consuming goods.

Marginal utility is the **satisfaction gained** from consuming one **additional** unit of a good or the **satisfaction forgone** by consuming one unit **less**. If someone eats six apples and then eats a seventh, total utility refers to the satisfaction he derives from all seven apples together, while marginal utility refers to the additional satisfaction from eating the seventh apple, having already eaten six.

1.4 Assumptions about consumer rationality

The following assumptions are made.

(a) Generally the consumer prefers more goods to less.

(b) Generally the consumer is willing to substitute one good for another provided its price is right.

(c) **Choices are transitive**. This means that if at a given time a commodity A is preferred to B and B is preferred to C then we can conclude that commodity A is preferred to commodity C.

Acting rationally means that the consumer attempts to **maximise the total utility** attainable with a limited income. When the consumer decides to buy another unit of a good he is deciding that its marginal utility exceeds the marginal utility that would be yielded by any **alternative** use of the price he pays.

If a person has maximised his total utility, it follows that he has allocated his expenditure in such a way that the utility gained from spending the last penny spent on each good will be equal.

We shall now look at demand and supply in turn, and then consider how demand and supply interact through the price mechanism.

2 The demand schedule

The position of the **demand curve** is determined by the demand conditions, which include consumers' tastes and preferences, and consumers' incomes.

2.1 The concept of demand

Key term

Demand for a good is the quantity of that good that potential purchasers would buy, or attempt to buy, if the price of the good were at a certain level.

Demand might be satisfied, and so actual quantities bought would equal demand. On the other hand, some demand might be unsatisfied, with more would-be purchasers trying to buy a good that is in insufficient supply, and so there are then not enough units of the good to go around.

Demand does not mean the quantity that potential purchasers **wish** they could buy. For example, a million households might wish that they owned a luxury yacht, but there might only be actual attempts to buy one hundred luxury yachts at a given price.

2.2 The demand schedule and the demand curve

The relationship between demand and price can be shown graphically as a **demand curve**. The demand curve of a single consumer or household is derived by estimating how much of the good the consumer or household would demand at various hypothetical market prices. Suppose that the following **demand schedule** shows demand for biscuits by one household over a period of one month.

Price per kg	*Quantity demanded*
£	kg
1	9.75
2	8
3	6.25
4	4.5
5	2.75
6	1

Notice that we show demand falling off as price increases. This is what normally happens with most goods. This is because purchasers have a limited amount of money to spend and must choose between goods that compete for their attention. When the price of one good rises, it is likely that other goods will seem relatively more attractive and so demand will switch away from the more expensive good.

We can show this schedule graphically, with **price on the y axis** and **quantity demanded on the x axis.** If we assume that there is complete divisibility, so that price and quantity can both change in infinitely small steps, we can draw a demand curve by joining the points represented in the schedule by a continuous line (Figure 1). This is the household's demand curve for biscuits in the particular market we are looking at.

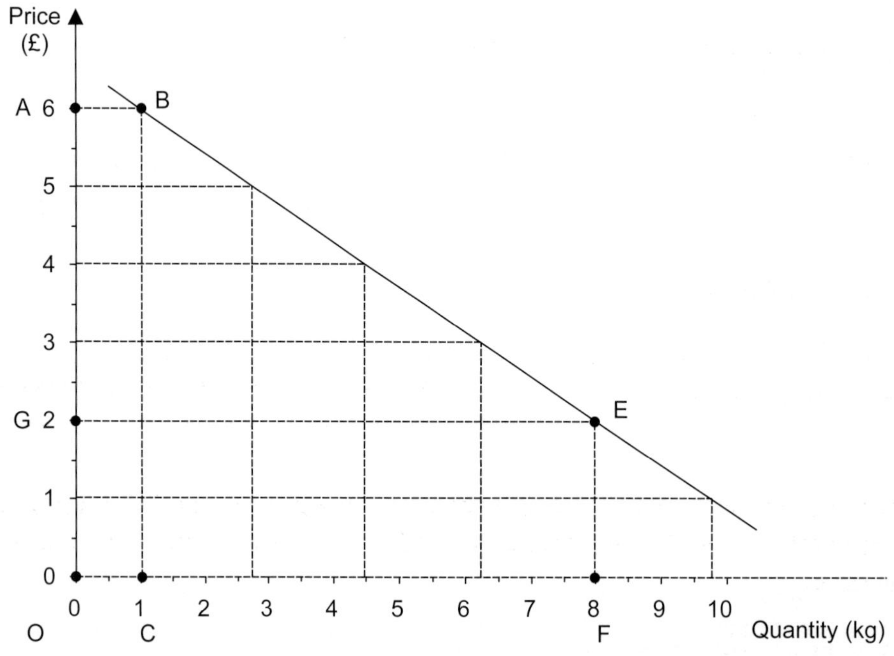

Figure 1 Graph of a demand schedule

The area of each rectangle in Figure 1 represents consumers' total money outlay at the price in question. For example, at a price of £6, demand would be 1 kilogram and total spending would be £6, represented by rectangle ABCO. Similarly, at a price of £2, demand would be 8 kilograms and the total spending of £16 is represented by rectangle GEFO.

Assessment focus point

> Sketching demand and/or supply curves may be a useful way of analysing an assessment question.

In Figure 1, the demand curve happens to be a straight line. Straight line demand curves are often used as an illustration in economics because it is convenient to draw them this way. In reality, a demand curve is more likely to be a curved line convex to the origin. As you will be able to appreciate, such a demand curve means that there are progressively larger increases in quantity demanded as price falls (Figure 2).This happens because of the fall in marginal utility experienced as consumption of a good increases.

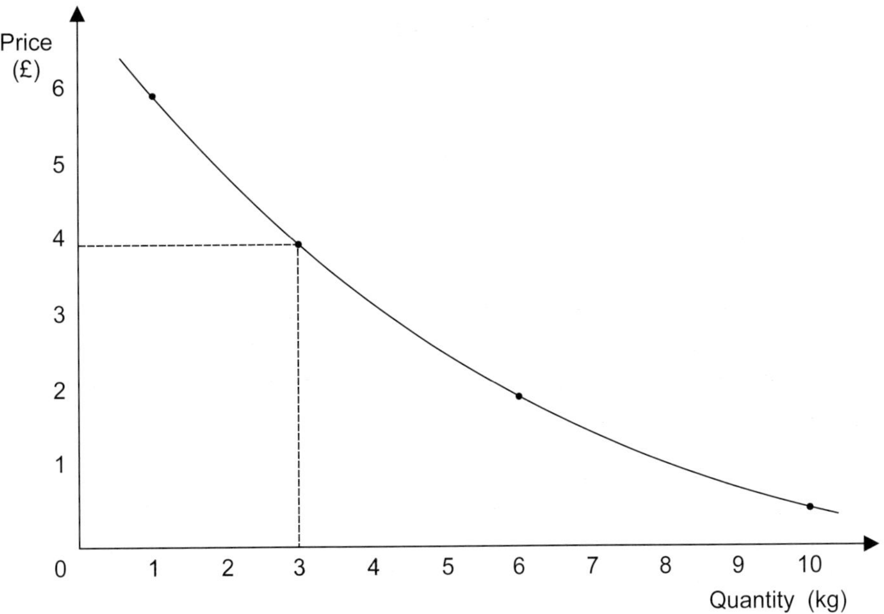

Figure 2 Demand curve convex to the origin

Question

Demand curve

Refer to Figure 2. Suppose the price of the commodity is £3. What would be the (approximate) demand for the commodity? And if the price fell to £2?

Answer

Demand is about 4.2 kilos at a price of £3 per kilo, rising to 6 kilos at the reduced price of £2 per kilo.

Note that changes in demand caused by changes in price are represented by movements **along the demand curve,** from one point to another. The price has changed, and the quantity demanded changes, but **the demand curve itself remains the same**.

2.3 The market demand curve

In the example above, we have been looking at the demand schedule of a single household. A **market demand curve** is a similar curve, drawn from a demand schedule, expressing the expected total quantity of the good that would be demanded by **all consumers together**, at any given price.

Market demand is the total quantity of a product that **all** purchasers would want to buy at each price level. A market demand schedule and a market demand curve are therefore simply the sum of all the individual demand schedules and demand curves put together. Market demand curves would be similar to those in Figures 1 and 2, but with quantities demanded (total market demand) being higher at each price level.

A **demand curve generally slopes down from left to right**.

(a) As we saw earlier, the curve is downward sloping curve because progressively larger quantities are demanded as price falls.

(b) A fall in the good's price means that households with lower incomes will also be able to afford it. The overall size of the market for the good increases. The converse argument applies to an increase in prices; as a price goes up, consumers with lower incomes will no longer be able to afford the good, or will buy something else whose price is relatively cheaper, and the size of the market will shrink.

Several factors influence the total market demand for a good. One of these factors is obviously its price, but there are other factors too, and to help you to appreciate some of these other factors, you need to recognise that households buy not just one good with their money but a whole range of goods and services.

Factors determining demand for a good

- The **price** of the good
- The price of other goods (products and services)
- The size of households' income
- Tastes and fashion
- Expectations of future price changes
- The distribution of income among households.

A demand curve shows how the quantity demanded will change in response to a change in price **provided that all other conditions affecting demand are unchanged** – that is, provided that there is no change in the prices of other goods, tastes, expectations or the distribution of household income. *(Ceteris paribus*, remember, is the assumption that all other things remain equal.)

2.4 Substitutes and complements

Key term

Substitute goods are goods that are alternatives to each other, so that an **increase** in the demand for one is likely to cause a **decrease** in the demand for another. Switching demand from one good to another 'rival' good is **substitution**

Complements are goods that tend to be bought and used together, so that an **increase** in the demand for one is likely to cause an **increase** in the demand for the other.

A change in the price of one good will not necessarily change the demand for another good. For example, we would not expect an increase in the price of cocoa to affect the demand for motor cars. However, there are goods for which the market demand is inter-connected. These inter-related goods are referred to as either **substitutes** or **complements**.

Examples of substitute goods and services

- Rival brands of the same commodity, like Coca-Cola and Pepsi-Cola
- Tea and coffee
- Some different forms of entertainment

Substitution takes place when the price of one good rises relative to a substitute good.

Examples of complements

- Cups and saucers
- Bread and butter
- Motor cars and the components and raw materials that go into their manufacture

Substitutes and complements

What might be the effect of an increase in the ownership of domestic deep freezers on the demand for perishable food products?

Answer

(a) Domestic deep freezers and perishable products are complements because people buy deep freezers to store perishable products.

(b) Perishable products are supplied either as fresh produce (for example, fresh meat and fresh vegetables) or as frozen produce, which can be kept for a short time in a refrigerator but for longer in a freezer. The demand for frozen produce will rise, while the demand for fresh produce will fall.

(c) Wider ownership of deep freezers is likely to increase bulk buying of perishable products. Suppliers can save some packaging costs, and can therefore offer lower prices for bulk purchases.

2.5 Household income and demand: normal goods and inferior goods

As you might imagine, more income will give households more to spend, and they will want to buy more goods at existing prices. However, a rise in household income will not increase market demand for all goods and services. The effect of a rise in income on demand for an individual good will depend on the nature of the good.

Demand and the level of income may be related in different ways.

(a) A rise in household income may increase demand for a good. This is what we might normally expect to happen, and goods for which demand rises as household income increases are called **normal goods**.

(b) Demand may rise with income up to a certain point but then fall as income rises beyond that point. Goods whose demand eventually falls as income rises are called **inferior goods**: examples might include tripe and cheap wine. The reason for falling demand is that as incomes rise, demand switches to superior products, for example beef instead of tripe; better quality wines instead of a cheaper variety.

2.6 Demand, fashion and expectations

A change in fashion will alter the demand for a product. For example, if it becomes fashionable for middle class households in the UK to drink wine with their meals, expenditure on wine will increase. There may be passing 'crazes', such as roller blades or skateboards.

If consumers believe that prices will rise, or that shortages will occur, they may attempt to stock up on the product, thereby creating excess demand in the short term which will increase prices. This can then lead to panic buying. Examples of things producing this effect include fear of war, the budget, the effect of strikes or a rumour.

2.7 Market demand and the distribution of income

Market demand for a good is influenced by the way in which the national income is shared among households.

In a country with many rich and many poor households and few middle income ones, we might expect a relatively large demand for luxury cars and yachts and also for bread and potatoes. In a country with many middle-income households, we might expect high demand for medium-sized cars and TV sets, and other middle income goods.

Question

Income distribution

What do you think might be the demand for swimming pools amongst a population of five households enjoying total annual income of £1m, if the distribution of income is either as under assumption 1 or as under assumption 2.

	Annual income	
	Assumption 1	*Assumption 2*
	£	£
Household 1	950,000	200,000
Household 2	12,500	200,000
Household 3	12,500	200,000
Household 4	12,500	200,000
Household 5	12,500	200,000

Answer

Under assumption 1, the demand for swimming pools will be confined to household 1. Even if this household owns three or four properties, the demand for swimming pools is likely to be less than under assumption 2, where potentially all five households might want one.

2.8 Changes in demand

If the price of a good goes up or down, given no changes in the other factors that affect demand, then there will be a change in the quantity demanded, depicted as a movement **along** the demand curve.

2.9 Shifts of the demand curve

When there is a **change in other factors that affect demand**, the relationship between demand quantity and price will also change, and there will be a different price/quantity demand schedule and so **a different demand curve**. We refer to such a change as a **shift of the demand curve**.

Figure 3 depicts a rise in demand at each price level, with the demand curve shifting to the right, from D_0 to D_1. For example, at price P_1, demand for the good would rise from X to Y. This shift could be caused by any of the following factors.

- A rise in household income
- A rise in the price of substitutes
- A fall in the price of complements
- A change in tastes towards this product
- An expected rise in the price of the product.

It should be easy for you to appreciate that a fall in demand at each price level would be represented by a shift in the opposite direction: to the **left** of the demand curve. Such a shift may be caused by the opposite of the changes described in the previous paragraph.

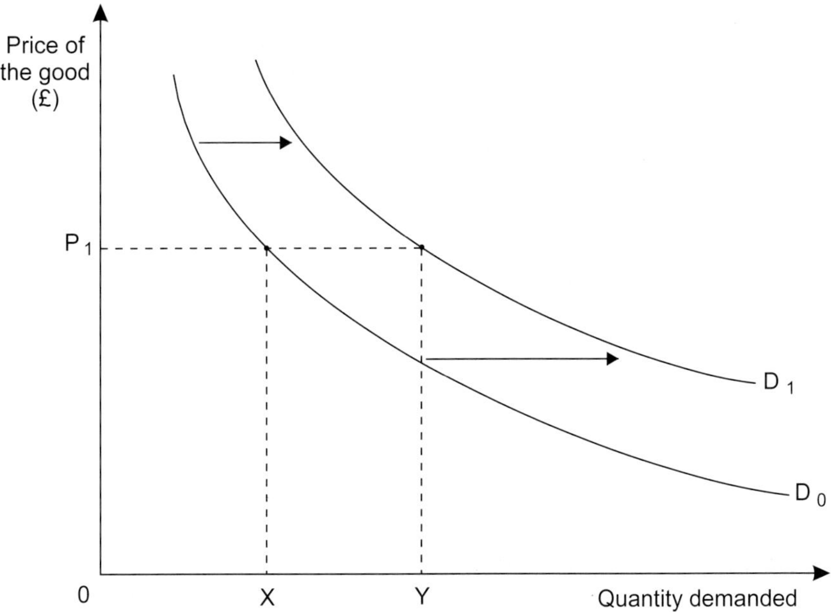

Figure 3 Outward shift of the demand curve

ssessment ocus point

The difference between a change in demand and a shift of the demand curve is of fundamental importance. Remember:

(a) Movements along a demand curve for a good are caused by changes in its price

(b) Shifts in the demand curve for a good are caused by any of the other factors which affect demand for a good, other than its price

3 The supply schedule

The **supply curve** shows the quantity of a good which would be supplied by producers at a given price.

3.1 The concept of supply

Key term

Supply refers to the quantity of a good that existing suppliers or would-be suppliers would want to produce for the market at a given price.

As with demand, supply relates to a period of time – for example, we might refer to an annual rate of supply or to a monthly rate.

The quantity of a good supplied to a market varies up or down for two reasons.

(a) Existing suppliers may increase or reduce their output quantities.

(b) Firms may stop production altogether and leave the market, or new firms may enter the market and start to produce the good.

If the quantity that firms want to produce at a given price exceeds the quantity that purchasers would demand, there will be an **excess of supply**, with firms competing to win what sales demand there is. Over-supply and competition would then be expected to result in price-competitiveness and **a fall in prices**.

As with demand, a distinction needs to be made.

(a) Market supply is the total quantity of the good that all firms in the market would want to supply at a given price.

(b) An individual firm's supply schedule is the quantity of the good that the individual firm would want to supply to the market at any given price.

3.2 The supply curve

A **supply schedule** and **supply curve** can be created both for an individual supplier and for all firms which produce the good.

A supply curve is constructed in a similar manner to a demand curve (from a schedule of supply quantities at different prices) but shows the quantity suppliers are willing to produce at different price levels. It is an **upward sloping curve from left to right**, because greater quantities will be supplied at higher prices.

Suppose, for example, that the supply schedule for product Y is as follows.

Price per unit	*Quantity that suppliers would supply at this price*
£	Units
100	10,000
150	16,000
300	30,000
500	40,000

The relationship between output and price is shown as a supply curve in Figure 4.

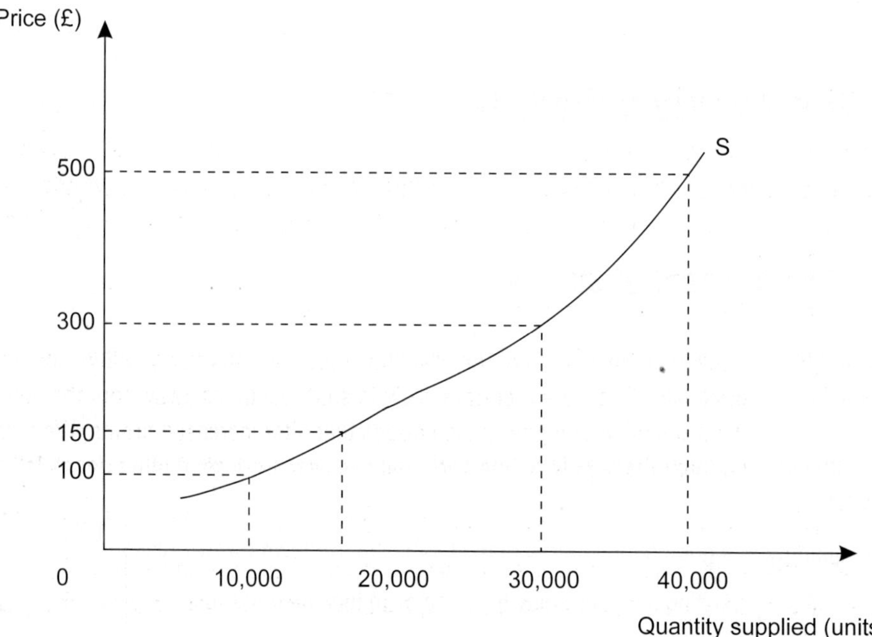

Figure 4 Supply curve

3.3 Factors influencing the supply quantity

The quantity supplied of a good depends, as you might expect, on prices and costs. More specifically, it depends on the following factors.

(a) **Expectations of price changes**.

(b) The **prices of other goods**. When a supplier can switch readily from supplying one good to another, the goods concerned are called **substitutes in supply**. An increase in the price of one such good would make the supply of a good whose price does not rise less attractive to suppliers. When a production process has two or more distinct and separate outputs, the goods produced are known as **goods in joint supply** or **complements in production**. Goods in joint supply include, for example, meat and hides. If the price of beef rises, more will be supplied and there will be an accompanying increase in the supply of cow hide.

(c) The **costs of making the good**. These include raw materials costs, which ultimately depend on the prices of factors of production (wages, interest rates, land rents and profit expectations)

(d) **Changes in technology**. Technological developments which reduce costs of production (and increase productivity) will raise the quantity of supply of a good at a given price

(e) **Other factors**, such as changes in the weather (for example, in the case of agricultural goods), natural disasters or industrial disruption

The supply curve shows how the quantity supplied will change in response to a change in price. If **supply conditions** alter, a different supply curve must be drawn. In other words, a change in price will cause a shift in supply along the supply curve. A change in other supply conditions will cause a shift in the supply curve itself.

ssessment ocus point

This distinction is just as important as the similar distinction relating to demand.

3.4 Shifts of the market supply curve

The **market supply curve** is the aggregate of the supply curves of individual firms in the market. A shift of the market supply curve occurs when supply conditions (other than the price of the good itself) change. Figure 5 shows a shift in the supply curve from S_0 to S_1. A rightward shift of the curve shows an expansion of supply and may be caused by the factors below.

(a) A fall in the cost of factors of production

(b) A fall in the price of other goods. The production of other goods becomes relatively less attractive as their price falls. Firms are therefore likely to shift resources away from the goods whose price is falling and into the production of higher priced goods that offer increased profits. We therefore expect that (ceteris paribus) the supply of one good will rise as the prices of other goods fall (and vice versa)

(c) Technological progress, which reduces unit costs and also increases production capabilities

A shift of the supply curve is the result of changes in costs, either in absolute terms or relative to the costs of other goods (Figure 5). If the price of the good is P_1, suppliers would be willing to increase supply from Q_0 to Q_1 under the new supply conditions.

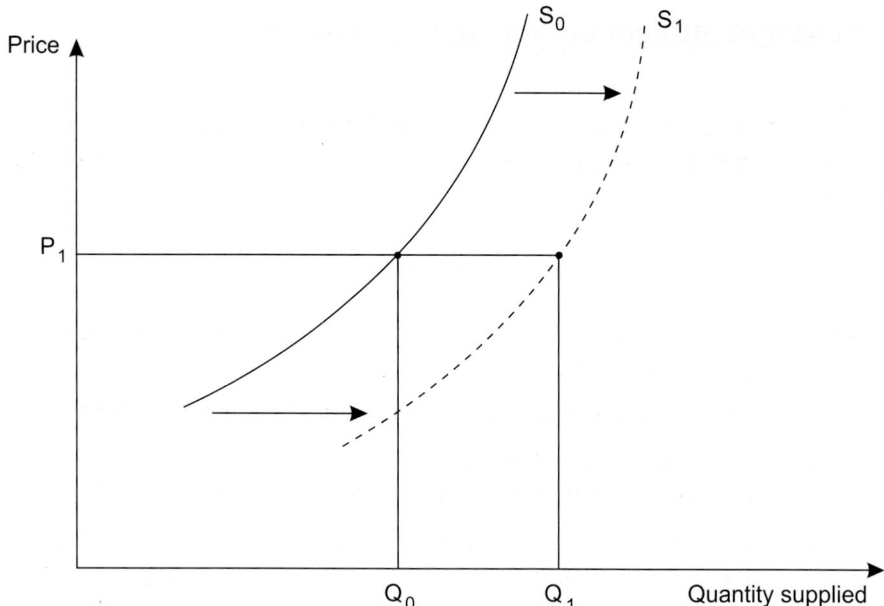

Figure 5 Outward shift of the supply curve

We need to distinguish between short run and long run responses of both supply and demand. **In the short run** both supply and demand are **relatively unresponsive** to changes in price, as compared to the **long run**.

(a) **In the case of supply**, changes in the quantity of a good supplied often require the laying off or hiring of new workers, or the installation of new machinery. All of these changes, brought about by management decisions, must take some time to implement.

(b) **In the case of demand**, it takes time for consumers to adjust their buying patterns, although demand will often respond more rapidly than supply to changes in price or other demand conditions.

In some markets, responses to changes in price are relatively rapid. In others, response times are much longer. In stock markets for example, the supply and demand for company shares respond very rapidly to price changes, whereas in the markets for fuel oils or agrichemicals response times are much longer.

Question

Supply and demand

In a stock market the 'products' bought and sold include shares in companies. What can you say about the supply of and demand for these 'products', and how quickly does their price change in response to changes in supply and demand factors?

Answer

The supply of shares in a particular company comes from sellers of secondhand shares, although new shares will also be issued from time to time. Demand for a company's shares will depend largely on how well the company is seen as performing, with broader market sentiment also often being influential. The price mechanism responds very rapidly – a share price may fluctuate up and down at very short intervals, sometimes undergoing several changes in the course of a single day.

4 The equilibrium price

The competitive market process results in an **equilibrium price**, which is the price at which market supply and market demand quantities are in balance. In any market, the equilibrium price will change if market demand or supply conditions change.

4.1 Functions of the price mechanism

People only have a limited income and they must decide what to buy with the money they have. The prices of the goods they want will affect their buying decisions.

Firms' output decisions will be influenced by both demand and supply considerations.

(a) Market demand conditions influence the price that a firm will get for its output. Prices act as **signals** to producers, and changes in prices should stimulate a response from a firm to change its production quantities.

(b) Supply is influenced by production costs and profits. The objective of maximising profits provides the **incentive** for firms to respond to changes in price or cost by changing their production quantities.

(c) When a firm operates efficiently, responding to changes in market prices and controlling its costs it is **rewarded** with profit.

Decisions by firms about what industry to operate in and what markets to produce goods for will be influenced by prices obtainable. Although some firms have been established in one industry for many years, others are continually opening up, closing down or switching to new industries and new markets. Over time, firms in an industry might also increase or reduce the volume of goods they sell.

4.2 The equilibrium price

Key term

The price mechanism brings demand and supply into equilibrium and the **equilibrium price** for a good is the price at which the volume demanded by consumers and the volume that firms would be willing to supply are the same. This is also known as the **market clearing price** since at this price there will be neither surplus nor shortage in the market.

This can be illustrated by drawing the market demand curve and the market supply curve on the same graph (Figure 6).

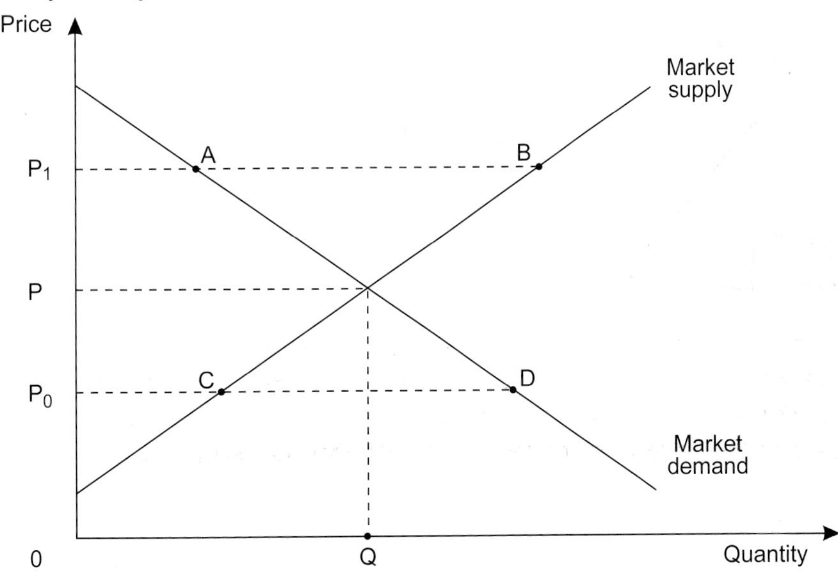

Figure 6 Market equilibrium

At price P_1 in Figure 6, there is an excess quantity that suppliers want to produce over the quantity demanded at that price, equal to the distance AB. Suppliers would react as unsold stocks accumulate.

(a) They would cut down the current level of production in order to sell unwanted stocks (de-stock).
(b) They would also reduce prices in order to encourage sales.

The opposite will happen at price P_0 where there is an excess of demand over supply shown by the distance CD. Output and price would increase. Faced with an excess of demand, manufacturers would be able to raise their prices. This would make supplying the good more profitable and supply would increase.

At price P the amount that sellers are willing to supply is equal to the amount that customers are willing to buy. Consumers will be willing to spend a total of (P × Q) on buying Q units of the product, and suppliers will be willing to supply Q units to earn revenue of (P × Q). P is the **equilibrium price**.

The forces of supply and demand push a market to its equilibrium price and quantity. Note carefully the following key points.

(a) If there is no change in conditions of supply or demand, the **equilibrium price will prevail** in the market and will remain stable.

(b) If price is not at the equilibrium, the market is in **disequilibrium** and supply and demand will push prices towards the equilibrium price.

(c) Shifts in the supply curve or demand curve will change the equilibrium price (and the quantity traded).

4.3 Consumer surplus and producer surplus

The **marginal utility** derived by different consumers from consumption of a unit quantity of a good will vary and so, therefore, will the price they would offer. Because of this, consumers may be able to buy the good at a prevailing market price **lower than the price they were prepared to pay**: you will be familiar with this idea from your own experience. This is called a **consumer surplus**, which can be represented as shown in Figure 7.

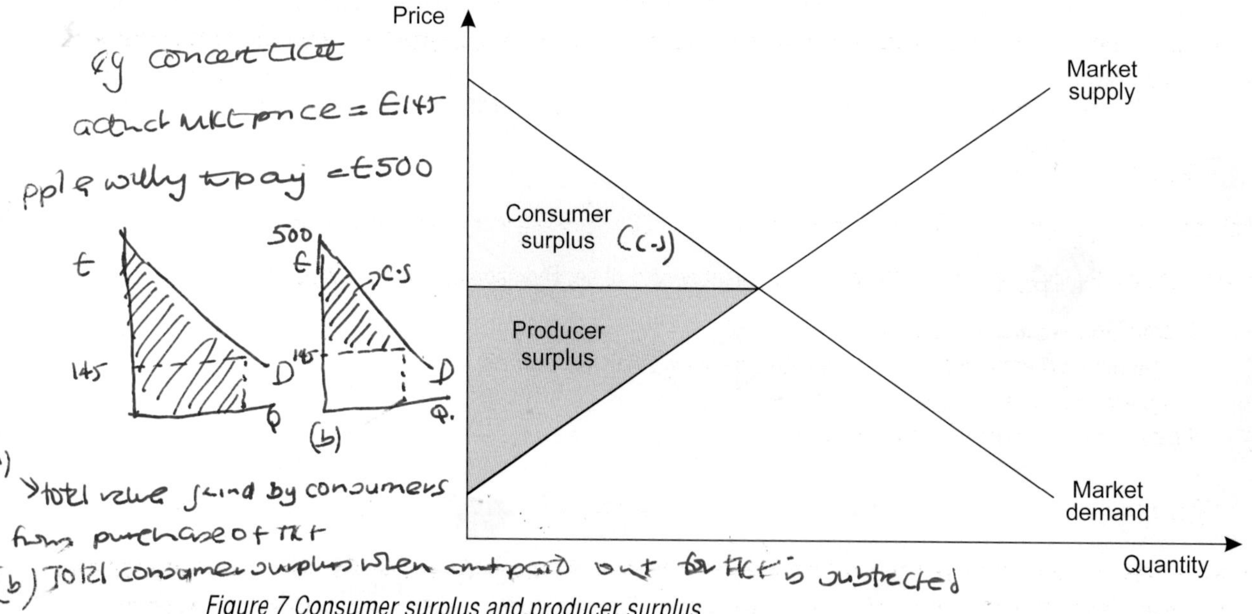

Figure 7 Consumer surplus and producer surplus

The **producer surplus** shown in Figure 7 arises because there will be suppliers in the market who will be prepared to sell quantities of the good at **less than the market price**.

Question — **Consumer surplus**

The diagram shows an individual's demand for fresh pasta. A special offer coupon makes it possible for this person to buy fresh pasta at a reduced price P_R rather than at the normal price P.

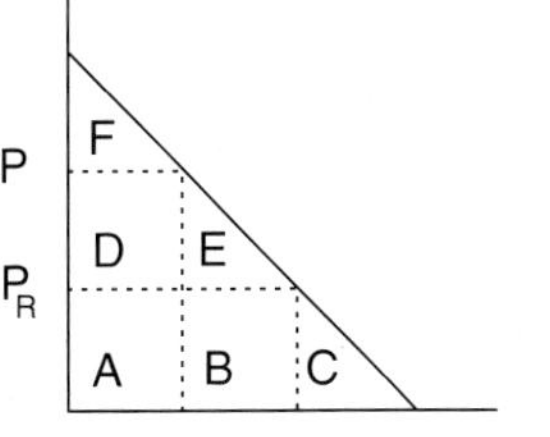

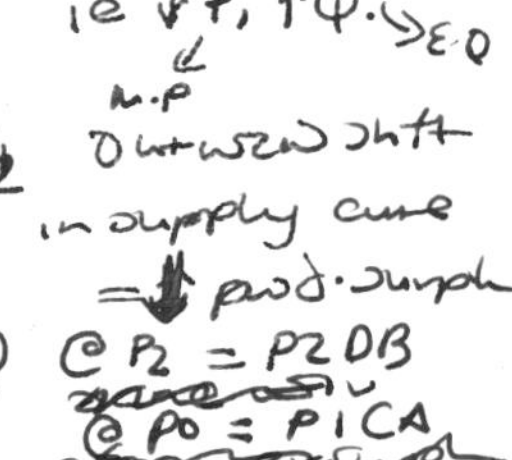

Which area shows the addition to the person's consumer surplus?

A D + E
B F + E + D
C F
D E + B

Answer

A F + E + D is the *total* consumer surplus with the coupon. F is the consumer surplus *without* the coupon. E + B has no significance.

5 Demand and supply analysis

AST FORWARD

The effects of **demand and supply conditions** on markets can be analysed by studying the behaviour of both demand and supply curves.

5.1 Case example

In this section we look at a Case Example involving the analysis of demand and supply conditions.

We will examine the likely effects on the price and quantity sold of second hand cars in the event of:

(a) A large increase in petrol prices
(b) A legal requirement that all cars fitted with expensive emission controls
(c) A big increase in the price of new cars
(d) A massive investment in public transport

5.2 Analysis

Petrol and cars are **complementary** products; hence, any change in the market for petrol (part (a) of this Case Example) would be expected to affect the market for second-hand cars. The demand for petrol, however, is likely to be **price inelastic** so that a major change in its price will be necessary to affect the demand for any complementary product. Figure 8 assumes that there is a large increase in the price of fuel (petrol) as stated above.

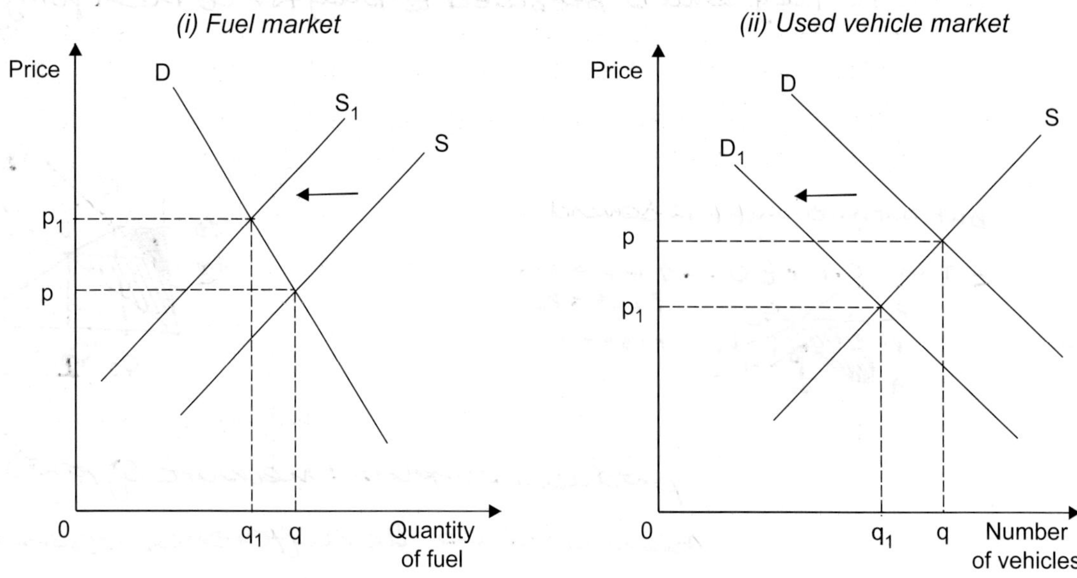

Figure 8

In this instance, the rise in the price of fuel results from a change in the conditions of supply. This is the basis of the new supply curve S_1 to the left of the existing one (Figure 8 (i)). A rise in the price of fuel is a rise in the cost of owning and running a car. There will thus be a fall in the demand for second-hand cars and a fall in the price and quantity sold (Figure 8 (ii)).

The requirement to have expensive emission controls fitted would raise the supply price of second-hand vehicles and result in a fall in the numbers sold (Case Example part (b)). Consequently the **supply curve** would move **to the left**, representing an increase in price at each level of output.

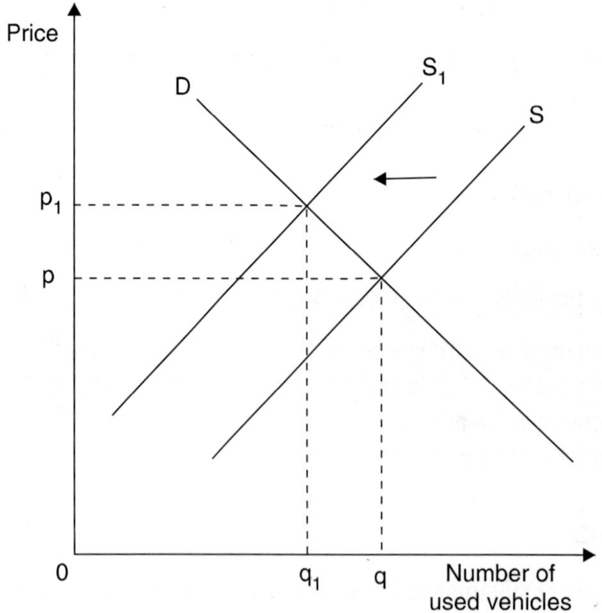

Figure 9

Expensive emission controls could well involve an outlay which is large in relation to the market value of many second-hand cars. Such controls fitted in the factory to new vehicles could make only a relatively small difference in their price.

This could result in an increased preference for new cars as against second-hand cars. The supply curve shifts to the left (from S to S_1 in Figure 9) and the quantity of vehicles traded falls (from q to q_1). Any fall in the demand for second-hand vehicles would then depress the price, offsetting in part the increase resulting from the new requirements.

Part (c) of this Case Example involves new vehicles and used vehicles as **substitute** products, touched upon in the answer to part (b) of the example.

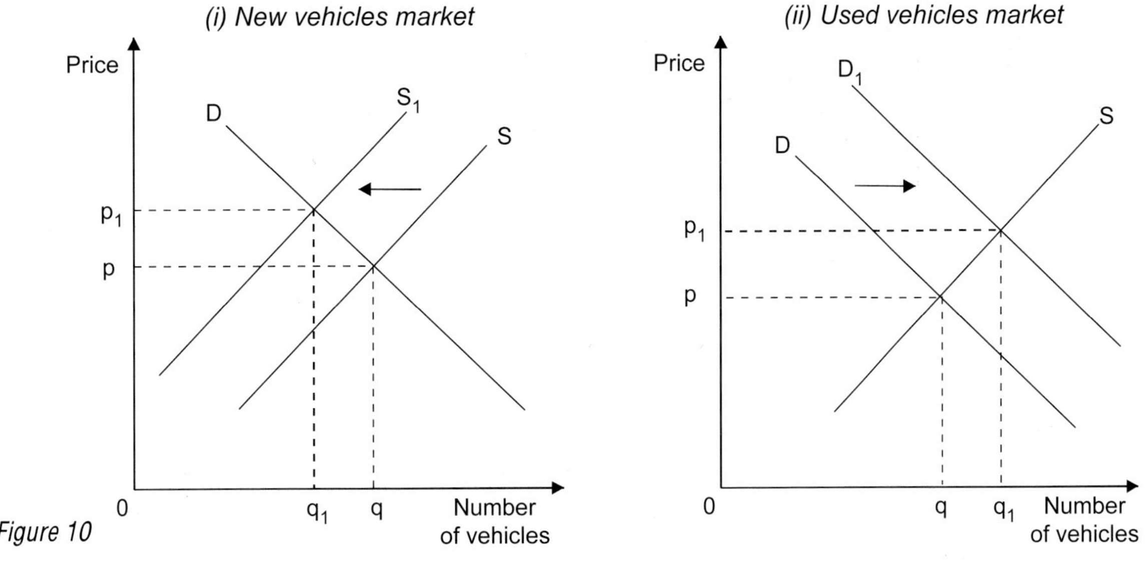

Figure 10

It is assumed that the increase in the price of new cars is the result of a major increase in supply costs. The rise in price causes a switch of demand into second-hand vehicles, so pushing up their price and leading to an increase in the number sold (Figure 10(ii)).

The increased price of new vehicles could alternatively result from an increase in the demand for them.

Case Example, part (c) involves another 'product' which is in competition with second-hand cars. If there is a reduction in the price of public transport services, the following could be the result (Figure 11).

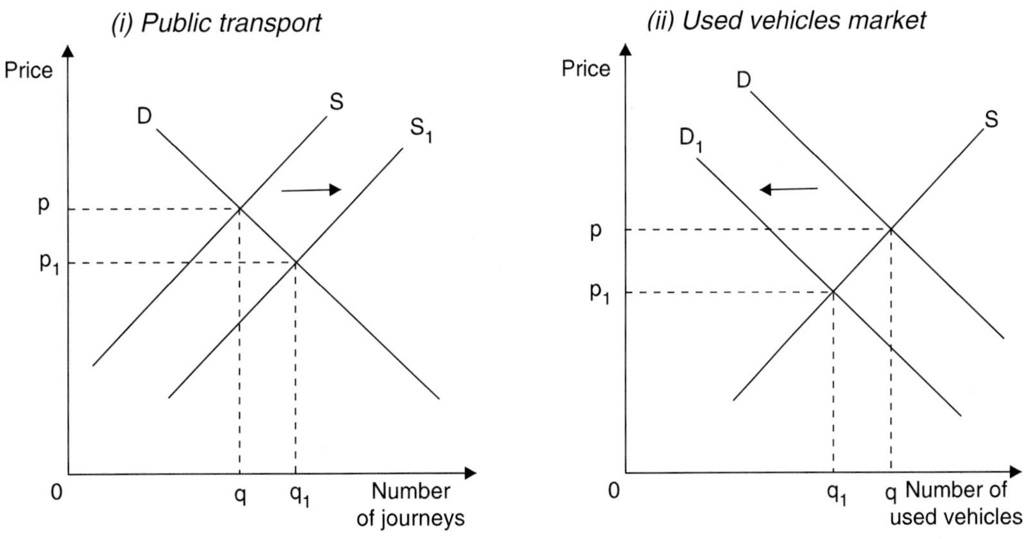

Figure 11

In part (d) of our Case Example, the fall in public transport prices leads to an expansion in demand for public transport (Figure 11(i)) while the demand for second-hand cars falls (with a new demand line D_1 in Figure 11(ii)) together with a fall in price. However, the relationship between public transport and the market for second-hand cars is likely to be a highly complex and indeterminate one. Thus, people might make greater use of public transport while the ownership of cars (including second-hand cars) could continue to increase.

6 Maximum and minimum prices

FAST FORWARD

Where **maximum prices** are imposed, there will be **excess demand**: rationing may be necessary, and black marketeers may seek to operate. Where **minimum prices** are imposed, producers will make **excess supply**.

6.1 Price regulation

The regulation of prices provides an illustration of how demand and supply analysis can be applied. Governments might try to control prices in two ways.

(a) They might set a **maximum** price for a good, perhaps as part of an anti-inflationary economic policy (such as a prices and incomes policy).

(b) They might set a **minimum** price for a good. The EU Common Agricultural Policy (CAP) aims to ensure that farmers receive at least the minimum prices for their produce.

6.2 Maximum prices

The government may try to prevent prices of goods rising by establishing a price ceiling. If the price ceiling is higher than the equilibrium price, setting a price ceiling will have no effect at all on the operation of market forces. Make sure that you can see why this is so.

If the maximum price M is lower than what the equilibrium price would be, there will be an excess of demand over supply (Figure 12). The low price attracts customers, but deters suppliers. Because the price ceiling M is below the equilibrium price P, producers will reduce the quantity of goods supplied to the market place from Q to A. The quantity demanded will increase from Q to B because of the fall in price. The excess quantity demanded is AB.

To prevent an unfair allocation of the A units of the good that are available, the government might have to introduce **rationing** (as with petrol coupons) or a **waiting list** (as for local authority housing). Rationing and **black marketeers** tend to go together. In Figure 12 consumers demand quantity B but can only get A. However, for quantity A they are prepared to pay price Z, which is well above the official price M. The black marketeers step in to exploit the gap. The commodity may be sold on ration at the official price M, but black marketeers may sell illicit production at price Z.

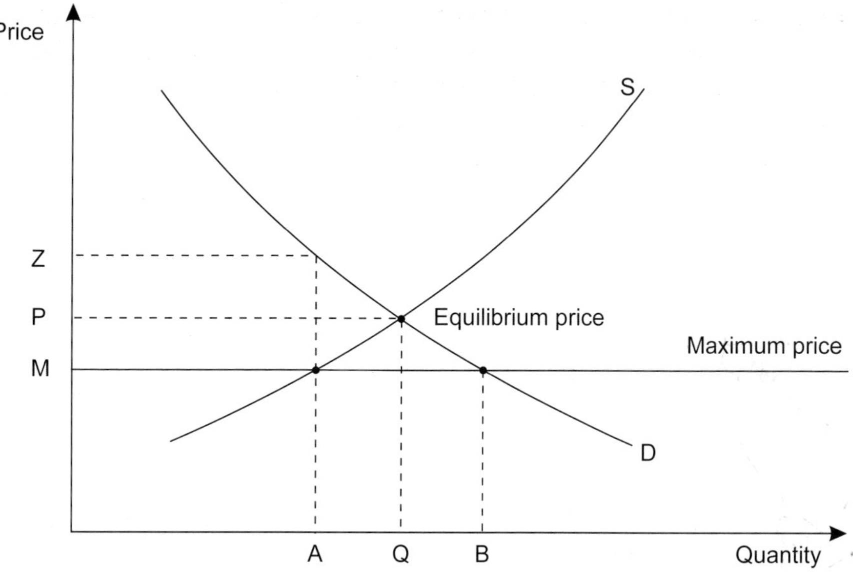

Figure 12 Maximum price below equilibrium price

Question

Equilibrium

Supply of and demand for good Q are initially in equilibrium as shown in the diagram below.

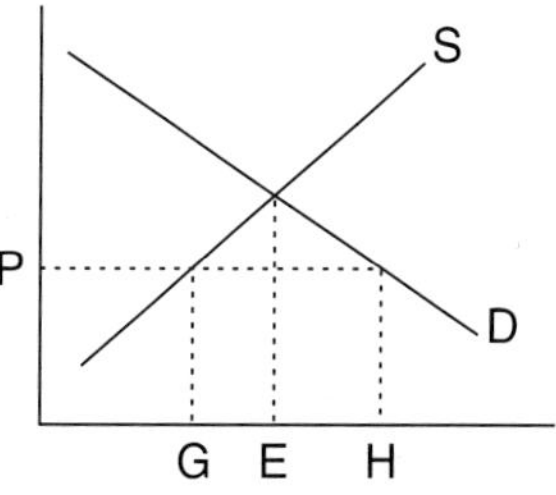

The government introduces a maximum price P. What effect will this have on the quantity of good Q purchased?

A It will rise from G to E
B It will rise from E to H
C It will fall from H to G
D It will fall from E to G

Answer

D Quantity demanded at the controlled price P will be H. However, only quantity G will be supplied and purchases will therefore be limited to this amount.

6.3 Minimum prices

Minimum price legislation aims to ensure that suppliers earn at least the minimum price for each unit of output they sell.

If the minimum price is set below the market equilibrium there is no effect. But if it is set above the market price, it will cause an excess supply of AB (as in Figure 9). This has been a recurring problem in Europe, resulting in the 'butter mountains' and 'wine lakes' of past years.

In Figure 13, the minimum price M is set above the equilibrium price P. The quantity demanded falls from Q to A but the quantity supplied increases to B. There is excess supply equal to the quantity AB.

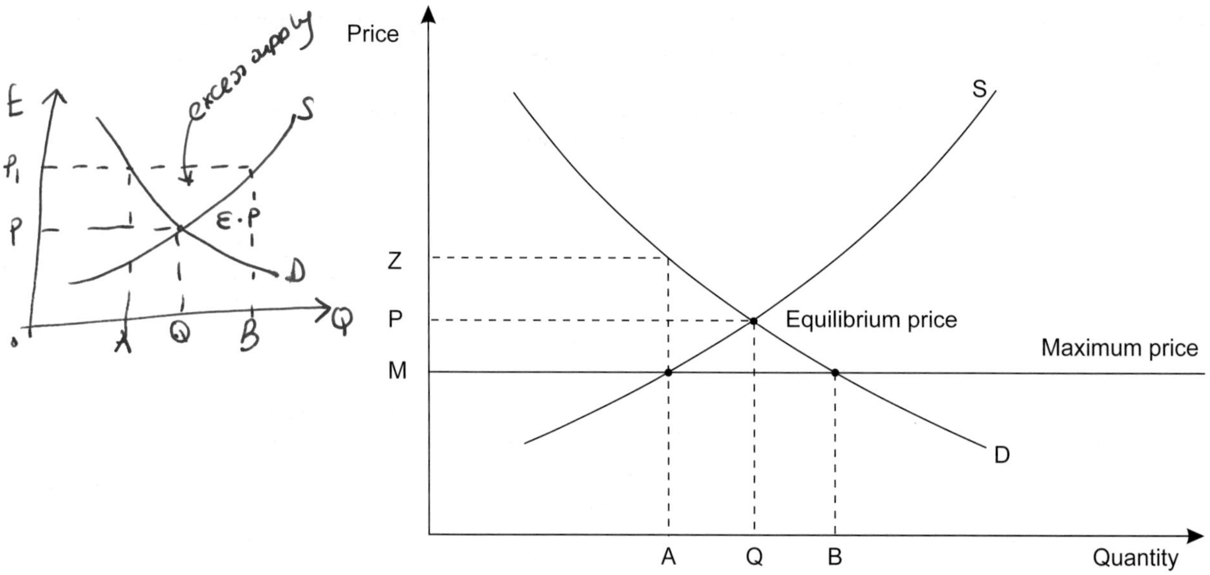

Figure 13 Minimum price above equilibrium price

When there is an excess of supply over demand, there is a danger that more of the good will be produced than can be sold at the minimum price, and so surplus quantities will build up, which suppliers might sell off at low prices just to get rid of them.

To try to prevent over-supply and 'dumping' of excess supply at low prices, a system of **production quotas** might be introduced whereby each supplier is allowed to produce up to a maximum quantity and no more. For some types of produce, the EU tried to overcome the problem of excess supply by imposing quotas on farmers. From 1992, the EU Common Agricultural Policy started to oblige farmers to take land out of production: this is called 'set-aside'.

Question

Government controls

Many governments impose controls on the rents of private property with the object of assisting lower-paid workers. What are the likely consequences of such policies?

Answer

You should see this question as a variation of maximum price legislation, which can be answered accordingly by supply and demand analysis. In addition, you could add points about:

(a) the deteriorating quality of rented accommodation if rents are held down, with landlords reluctant to pay for repairs and maintenance

(b) the creation of a black market in rented property

(c) discouraging new investment in building rented property.

6.4 Minimum wages

The UK now has minimum wage legislation. The purpose of a minimum wage is to ensure that low-paid workers earn enough to have an acceptable standard of living. If a minimum wage is enforced by legislation (a **statutory minimum wage**) or negotiated nationally for an industry by a trade union the minimum wage will probably be above the current wage level for the jobs concerned. This would have two consequences.

- To raise wage levels for workers employed to a level above the 'equilibrium' wage rate
- To reduce the demand for labour and so cause job losses

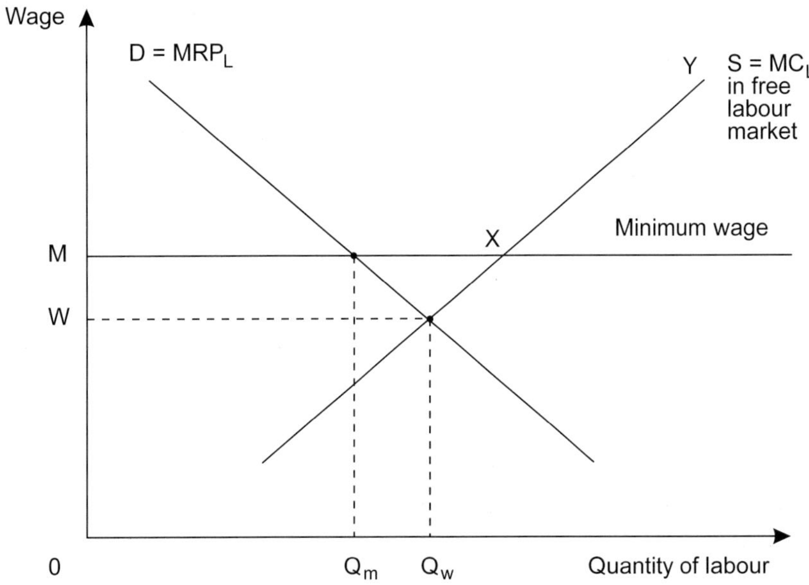

Figure 6 Minimum wage

Without a minimum wage, OQ_w workers would be employed at wage rate W (Figure 6).

Question — **Minimum wage**

By reference to Figure 6, work out what happens when a minimum wage M, higher than the existing rate W, is imposed.

Answer

The supply curve for labour is now the line MXY.

Demand for labour from employers will fall to OQ_m, but OQ_m workers will at least earn a higher wage.

Despite this commonsense result, there is some evidence that the imposition of a minimum wage can actually **increase** the numbers employed. This can occur where there is effectively a single purchaser of labour and is particularly apparent in markets for lower grade labour. Where such employers hold wages to a low level, they will generally have vacancies since employment with them is unattractive. Where a higher wage is imposed by law, they will find it easier to recruit and their numbers on payroll may actually rise. Their need for labour outweighs the market forces that would otherwise lead to reductions in numbers employed.

6.5 Case example

The extract below gives an account of conditions in the markets for hazelnuts, almonds and pistachio nuts in the run-up to Christmas. As you read it, note down the different influences on the prices of each type of nut which are described in the extract.

'Revellers may have to shell out more for nuts'

'Consumers had better get cracking if they want to make sure of a crunchy Christmas. A looming shortage has pushed up prices of almonds and pistachios, while the cost of hazelnuts has jumped by 35 per cent since August after the Turkish government intervened to bolster prices.

Good-quality almonds are almost sold out and prices are up 20 per cent in the past six weeks following a poor Californian crop for the second year running.

Pistachio prices are also 20 per cent higher after bad weather affected almost half of this year's Iranian crop ...

Californian almond prices have more than doubled over the past two years as cold and windy weather during the important growing periods caused a decline in the harvest and poor-quality nuts. After a disastrous crop in 1995 there were no stocks to carry over to this season.

Pistachio prices have risen from $3,200 a tonne in July to $4,000 (£2,400), and [it is believed that] there will be a further rise of $50-$100 before next summer when supplies will run out. The new season's crop comes to market in November.

The Turkish government's farm co-operative has so far bought 25 per cent of this year's hazelnut harvest at almost $1,000 a tonne higher than the free market price in an effort to push up prices from their low base of recent years.

"It will encourage a lot more farmers to plant nuts and in five years when those trees produce, there will be a whole spate of deliveries," said a nut buyer for a leading UK confectioner.

Free market prices have risen to $3,800 a tonne, but remain below the $4,100 a tonne which the Turkish co-operative is believed to be paying farmers.'

(*Financial Times*, 5 December 1996)

Chapter roundup

- In a free market, the **price mechanism** signals demand and supply conditions to producers and consumers. It therefore determines the activities of both producers and consumers, influencing the levels of demand for and the supply of goods.
- The position of the **demand curve** is determined by the demand conditions, which include consumers' tastes and preferences, and consumers' incomes.
- The **supply curve** shows the quantity of a good which would be supplied by producers at a given price.
- The competitive market process results in an **equilibrium price**, which is the price at which market supply and market demand quantities are in balance. In any market, the equilibrium price will change if market demand or supply conditions change.
- The effects of **demand and supply** conditions on markets can be analysed by studying the behaviour of both demand and supply curves.
- Where **maximum prices** are imposed, there will be **excess demand**: rationing may be necessary, and black marketeers may seek to operate. Where **minimum prices** are imposed, producers will make **excess supply**.

Quick quiz

1 What factors influence demand for a good?

2 What are (a) substitutes and (b) complements?

3 What factors affect the supply quantity?

4 What is meant by equilibrium price?

5 A demand curve is drawn on all *except* which of the following assumptions?

A Incomes do not change.
B Prices of substitutes are fixed.
C Price of the good is constant.
D There are no changes in tastes and preferences.

6 The diagram shown relates to the demand for and supply of Scotch. The market is initially in equilibrium at point X. The government imposes a specific tax on Scotch whilst at the same time, the price of Irish Whiskey (a substitute for Scotch Whisky) rises. Which point, A, B, C or D represents the new market equilibrium?

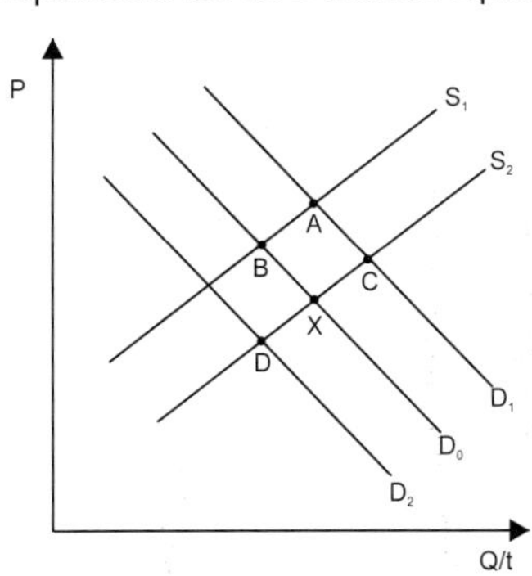

7 A price ceiling set above the equilibrium market price will result in:

A Market failure
B A perpetual surplus
C Market equilibrium
D An alternative (to price) rationing system

8 Which one of the following would normally cause a rightward shift in the demand curve for a product?

A A fall in the price of a substitute product
B A reduction in direct taxation on incomes
C A reduction in price of the product
D An increase in the price of a complementary product

9 What is an inferior good?

A A good of such poor quality that demand for it is very weak
B A good of lesser quality than a substitute good, so that the price of the substitute is higher
C A good for which the cross elasticity of demand with a substitute product is greater than 1
D A good for which demand will fall as household income rises

Answers to quick quiz

1 The price of the good
The price of other goods
Household income
Taste and fashion

2 Substitutes are goods that are alternatives to each other
Complements are goods which are bought and used together

3 The price obtainable for the good
The prices obtainable for other goods, particularly goods in joint supply
The costs of making the good
Disruptions such as bad weather and strikes

4 The price at which the volume of demand and the volume of supply are equal; there is neither surplus nor shortage.

5 C Demand curves express the quantity demanded at each given market price. Non-price determinants such as income must be held constant when looking at the effect of price movements in isolation.

6 A Supply shifts from S_2 to S_1, reflecting the per-unit tax. Demand shifts from D_0 to D_1 as the price of a substitute (Irish whiskey) rises.

7 C If the price ceiling is above the equilibrium market price, it will not interfere with the working of the price mechanism. The market will not be forced from its current equilibrium.

8 B A reduction in income tax will increase 'real' household income, and so demand for normal products will shift to the right, ie quantity demanded will be greater at any given price.

A fall in the price of a substitute good would entice consumers away from the original good. This would cause a leftward shift in the demand curve.

A change in the price of the good itself does not cause a shift in the curve but a movement along it.

Complementary products tend to be bought and used together, so an increase in the price of one will lead to a reduction in demand for the other, reflected in a leftward shift in the demand curve.

9 D Inferior goods are defined in terms of the relationship between quantity demanded and income. The issue of substitutes is not relevant.

Now try the questions below from the Exam Question Bank

Question numbers	Page
9 – 12	365

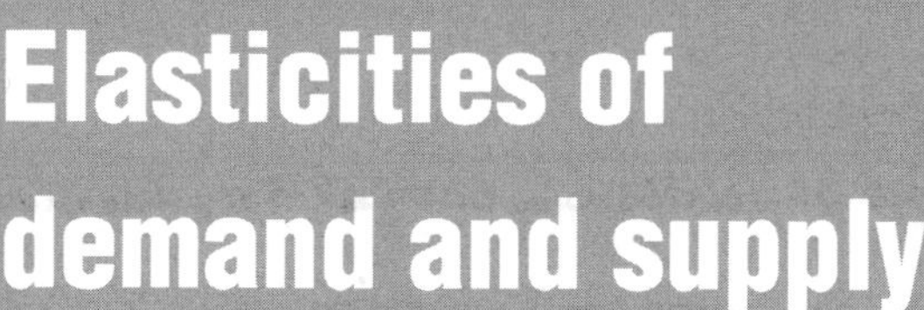
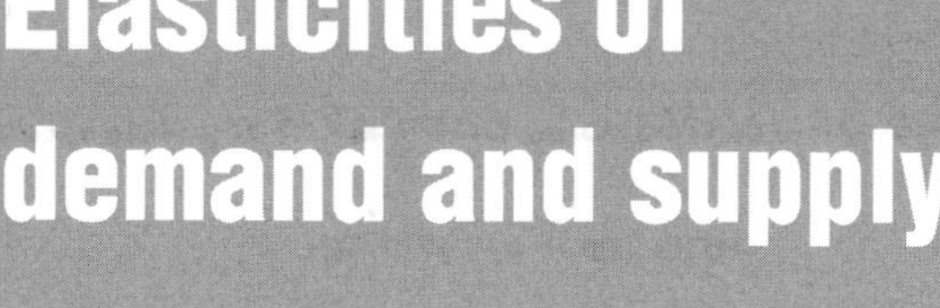

Elasticities of demand and supply

4

Introduction

We have discussed in the previous chapter the direction of changes in demand and supply when prices change. When price goes up, the quantity demanded will fall, and the quantity suppliers will be willing to produce will go up.

If prices are increased or reduced, how much will this affect the amount of revenue from selling a good?

How much will supply of a good change if the price changes?

How do changes in household income affect the market for a good?

In this chapter, we consider such questions, bringing in the concept of elasticity. You need to have a good understanding of this concept, which could be relevant in a number of different contexts in assessment questions.

Topic list	Learning outcomes	Syllabus references	Ability required
1 Elasticity of demand	B (ii)	B (2)	Application
2 Elasticity of supply	B (ii)	B (3)	Application
3 Primary markets	B (iv), (v)	B (7)	Comprehension

1 Elasticity of demand

FAST FORWARD

Demand for a good depends largely on **price**, **household income** and the relative **price of substitutes or complementary goods**. Changes in any of these will cause either a movement along the demand curve or a shift in the demand curve. **Price elasticity of demand** indicates the responsiveness of total expenditure in a market for a good to price changes.

1.1 The price elasticity of demand

Assessment focus point

Elasticity is a common assessment topic. It is also of great practical importance in the real world of business.

If prices went **up** by 10%, would the quantity demanded **fall** by the same percentage?

Key terms

Price elasticity of demand (PED) is a measure of the extent of change in market demand for a good in response to a change in its price.

PED is measured as:

$$\frac{\text{The change in quantity demanded, as a \% of demand}}{\text{The change in price, as a \% of the price}}$$

Since demand usually increases when the price falls, and decreases when the price rises, elasticity has a negative value. **However, it is usual to ignore the minus sign.**

This can be expressed as:

$$\frac{\frac{\Delta Q}{Q}\times 100}{\frac{\Delta P}{P}\times 100}, \quad \text{which is equivalent to } \frac{\Delta Q}{Q}\times\frac{P}{\Delta P} \text{ and to } \frac{\Delta Q}{\Delta P}\times\frac{P}{Q}$$

where Δ is the symbol for 'change in'
Q is the quantity demanded of the good
P is the price of the good

If we are measuring the responsiveness of demand to a large change in price, we can measure elasticity between two points on the demand curve, and the resulting measure is called the **arc elasticity of demand**. We calculate the arc elasticity of demand from the percentage change in quantity relative to **average** quantity for the relevant range of output and from the percentage price change relative to the **average** of the corresponding price range.

If we wish to measure the responsiveness of demand at a particular point in the demand curve, we can calculate a **point elasticity of demand**, without averaging price and quantity over a range. In doing so, it is convenient to assume that the demand curve is a straight line unless told otherwise.

1.2 Example: arc elasticity of demand

The price of a good is £1.20 per unit and annual demand is 800,000 units. Market research indicates that an increase in price of 10 pence per unit will result in a fall in annual demand of 70,000 units.

What is the price elasticity of demand measuring the responsiveness of demand over this range of price increase?

Solution

Annual demand at £1.20 per unit is 800,000 units.
Annual demand at £1.30 per unit is 730,000 units.

Average quantity over the range is 765,000 units.
Average price is £1.25.

% change in demand $\frac{70{,}000}{765{,}000} \times 100\% = 9.15\%$

% change in price $\frac{10p}{125p} \times 100\% = 8\%$

Price elasticity of demand = $\frac{-9.15}{8} = -1.14$

Ignoring the minus sign, the arc elasticity is 1.14.

The demand for this good, over the range of annual demand 730,000 to 800,000 units, is elastic because the price elasticity of demand is greater than 1. Now try the following exercise yourself.

Question

Arc price elasticity of demand

If the price per unit of X rises from £1.40 to £1.60, it is expected that monthly demand will fall from 220,000 units to 200,000 units.

What is the arc price elasticity of demand over these ranges of price and output?

Answer

Monthly demand at £1.40 per unit = 220,000 units

Monthly demand at £1.60 per unit = 200,000 units

Average quantity = 210,000 units

Average price = £1.50

% change in demand $\frac{20{,}000}{210{,}000} \times 100\% = 9.52\%$

% change in price $\frac{20}{150} \times 100\% = 13.33\%$

Arc price elasticity of demand = $\frac{-9.52}{13.33} = -0.71\%$

Demand is inelastic over the demand range considered, because the price elasticity of demand (ignoring the minus sign) is less than 1.

1.3 Example: point elasticity of demand

Refer to the details in the example in Paragraph 1.2.

Required

Calculate the elasticity of demand when the price is £1.20.

Solution

We are asked to calculate the elasticity at a particular price. We assume that the demand curve is a straight line.

At a price of £1.20, annual demand is 800,000 units. For a price rise:

% change in demand $\frac{70{,}000}{800{,}000} \times 100\% = 8.75\%$ (fall)

% change in price $\frac{10p}{120p} \times 100\% = 8.33\%$ (rise)

Price elasticity of demand at price £1.20 = $\frac{-8.75}{8.33} = -1.05$

Ignoring the minus sign, the price elasticity at this point is 1.05. Demand is **elastic** at this point, because the elasticity is greater than unity.

Question **Point price elasticity of demand**

Using the same details as in Paragraph 1.2 above, calculate the elasticity of demand when the price is £1.30.

Answer

We can use the same price/quantity change data, assuming that the demand curve is a straight line, although we are now looking at a different point on the curve.

At a price of £1.30, annual demand is 730,000 units.

For a price fall from £1.30 of 10 pence:

% change in demand $\frac{70{,}000}{730{,}000} \times 100\% = 9.59\%$ (rise)

% change in price $\frac{10p}{130p} \times 100\% = 7.69\%$ (fall)

Price elasticity of demand = $\frac{9.59}{-7.69} = -1.25$,

or 1.25 ignoring the minus sign.

Demand is **elastic** at this point.

If it is not clear from the details of an assessment question whether you need to calculate arc or point elasticity, then calculate the **point** elasticity.

Question

Range of elasticity

A shop sells 100 shirts each month at a price of £20. When the price is increased to £24, the total sales revenue rises by 14%. Within which range does the price elasticity of demand lie?

A Under 0.15
B Greater than 0.15 and less than 0.8
C Greater than 0.8 and less than 1.5
D Greater than 1.5

Answer

B Total revenue of £20 = 100 × £20 = £2,000
Total revenue at £24 = £2,000 × 1.14 = £2,280
Number sold at £24 = £2,280 ÷ 24 = 95

Price elasticity of demand

Point method

$$\frac{\frac{5}{100} \times 100}{\frac{4}{20} \times 100} = \frac{5\%}{20\%} = 0.25$$

Arc method

$$\frac{\frac{5}{97\frac{1}{2}} \times 100}{\frac{4}{22} \times 100} = \frac{5.13\%}{18.2\%} = 0.28$$

1.4 Elastic and inelastic demand

The value of demand elasticity may be anything from zero to infinity.

- Demand is **inelastic** if the absolute value is less than 1
- Demand is **elastic** if the absolute value is greater than 1

Think about what this means if there is a price reduction. Where demand is **inelastic**, the quantity demanded falls by a smaller percentage than the fall in price. Where demand is elastic, demand falls by a larger percentage than the rise in price.

1.5 Price elasticity and the slope of the demand curve

Generally, demand curves slope downwards. Consumers are willing to buy more at lower prices than at higher prices. Except in certain special cases (which we look at below), **elasticity will vary in value along the length of a demand curve**.

It is therefore not possible merely by looking at the slopes of any two curves to state their comparative elasticities over different price ranges. However, it is possible to say that if a downward sloping demand curve shifts to become **steeper** over a particular range of quantity, then demand is becoming more **inelastic**. Conversely, a demand curve becoming **shallower** over a particular range indicates more **elastic** demand.

The ranges of price elasticity (η) at different points on a downward sloping straight line demand curve are illustrated in Figure 1. Check the arithmetic yourself and make sure you understand this.

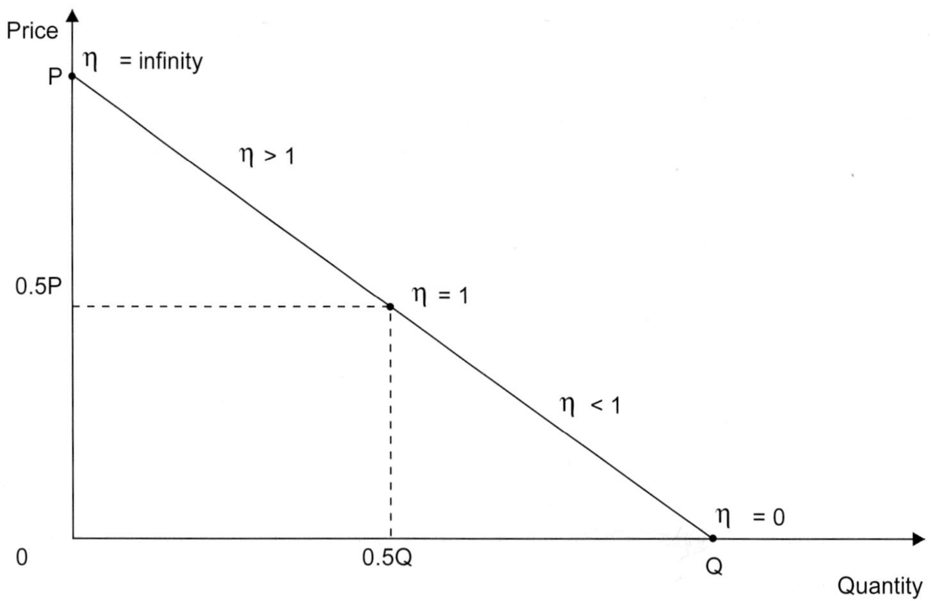

Figure 1 Ranges of price elasticity

At higher prices on a straight line demand curve (the top of the demand curve), **small** percentage price reductions can bring **large** percentage increases in quantity demanded. This means that demand is **elastic** over these ranges.

At lower prices on a straight line demand curve (the bottom of the demand curve), large percentage price reductions can bring small percentage increases in quantity. This means that demand is **inelastic** over these price ranges.

1.6 Special values of price elasticity of demand

There are three special values of price elasticity of demand: 0, 1 and infinity.

(a) **Demand is perfectly inelastic**: $\eta = 0$. There is no change in quantity demanded, regardless of the change in price. This is the case where the demand curve is a **vertical straight line**.

(b) **Perfectly elastic demand**: $\eta = \infty$ (infinitely elastic). Consumers will want to buy an infinite amount, but only up to a particular price level. Any price increase above this level will reduce demand to zero. This is the case where the demand curve is a **horizontal straight line.**

(c) **Unit elasticity of demand**: $\eta = 1$. Total revenue for suppliers (which is the same as total spending on the product by households) does not change when the price changes. The demand curve of a good whose price elasticity of demand is 1 over its entire range is a **rectangular hyperbola** (Figure 2).

(d) This means that in Figure 2, rectangles OABC, ODEF and OGHJ all have the same area, since the areas of these rectangles represent total spending by customers at each price.

   (i) If the selling price were D, total demand would be F and total spending on the product would be D $\times$ F (rectangle ODEF).

   (ii) If the selling price were A, total demand would be C, and total spending on the product would be A $\times$ C (rectangle OABC).

   (iii) If the selling price were G, total demand would be J and total spending on the product would be G $\times$ J (rectangle OGHJ).

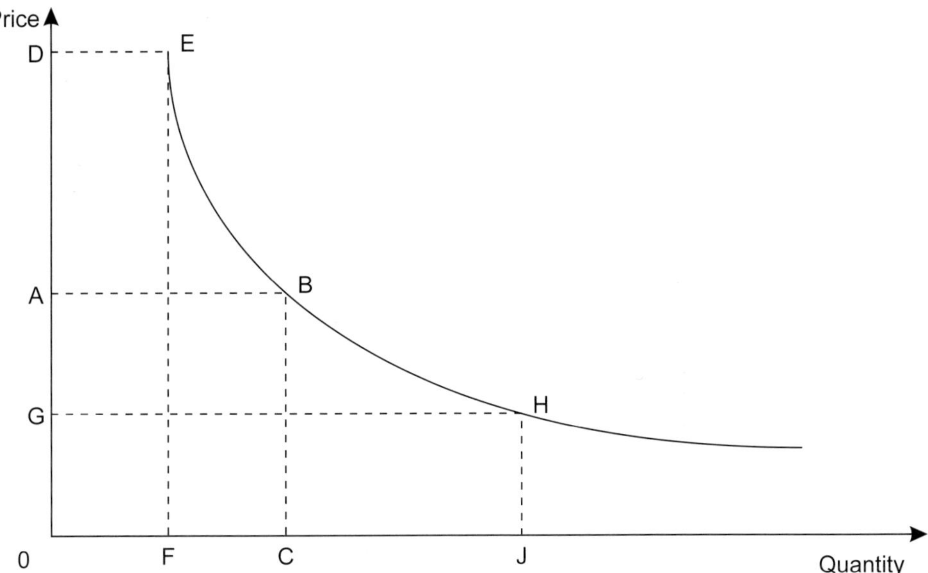

Figure 2 Unit elasticity of demand

1.7 The significance of price elasticity of demand

FAST FORWARD

For the assessment, you need to be able:

- To distinguish between the **factors influencing elasticity**
- To **measure** price elasticity from given price and demand data, and to draw appropriate conclusions from such information
- To draw the correct implications for the **total revenue** of the producer of changes in the price of the product

The price elasticity of demand is relevant to total spending on a good or service. Total expenditure is a matter of interest to both suppliers, to whom sales revenue accrues, and to government, who may receive a proportion of total expenditure in the form of taxation.

When demand is **elastic,** an increase in price will result in a fall in the quantity demanded, and **total expenditure will fall**. In Figure 3, total expenditure at price P_A is represented by the area OP_AAQ_A and total expenditure at price P_B is represented by the area OP_BBQ_B. Area OP_AAQ_A is greater than area OP_BBQ_B: this can be seen by observing that area Y (expenditure lost on a rise in price from A to B) is greater than area X (expenditure gained).

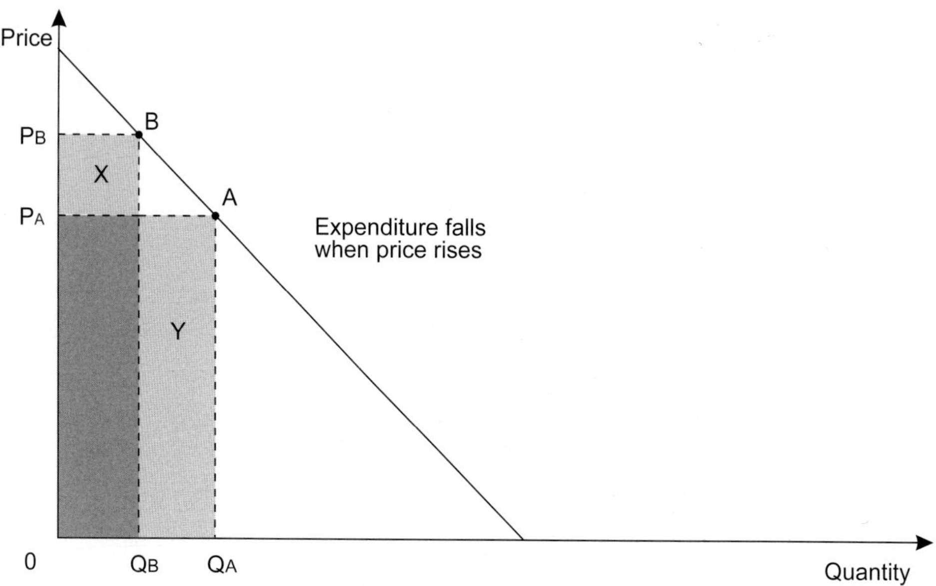

Figure 3 Elastic demand

When demand is **inelastic,** an increase in price will still result in a fall in quantity demanded, but **total expenditure will rise**. In Figure 4, area X (expenditure gained) is greater than area Y (expenditure lost).

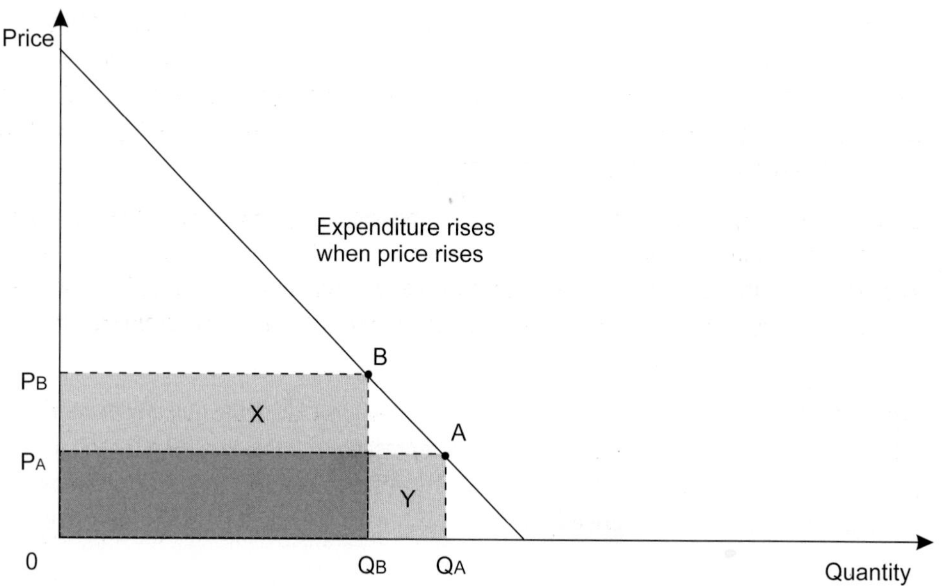

Figure 4 Inelastic demand

With **unit elasticity, expenditure will stay constant** on a change in price. In Figure 5, area X and area Y are the same.

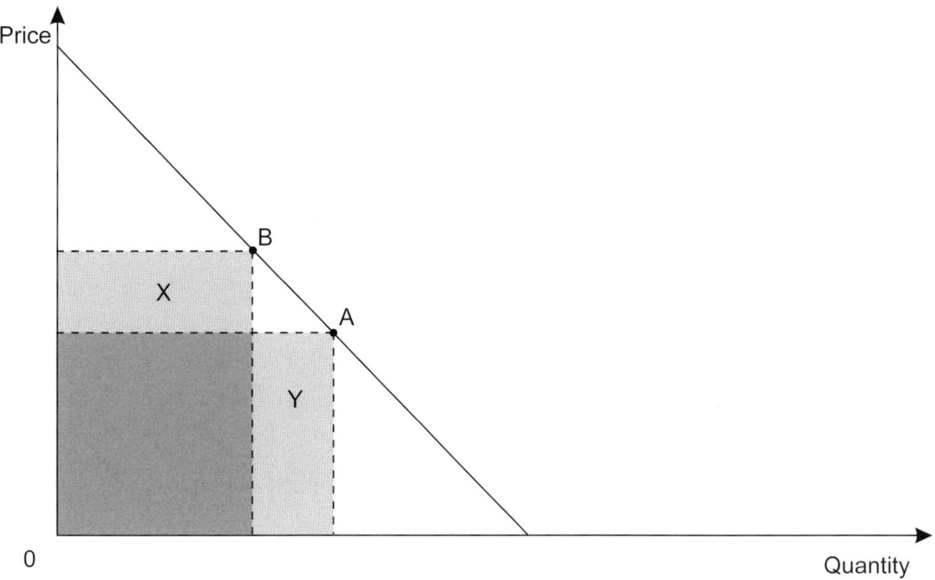

Figure 5 Unit elasticity

1.8 Information on price elasticity of demand

Information on price elasticity of demand indicates how **consumers can be expected to respond to different prices**. Business people can make use of information on how consumers will react to pricing decisions as it is possible to trace the effect of different prices on total revenue and profits. Information on price elasticities of demand will be useful to a business which needs to know the price decrease necessary to clear a surplus (excess supply) or the price increase necessary to eliminate a shortage (excess demand).

Government policy makers can also use information about elasticity, for example when making decisions about indirect taxation. Items with a low price elasticity of demand such as cigarettes and alcohol tend to be useful targets for taxation since by increasing taxes on these, total revenue can be increased. If demand for cigarettes was price elastic, increases in taxation would be counter-productive as they would result in lower government revenue.

Question **Elasticity and total revenue**

Suppose that there are two products, A and B.

Product A currently sells for £5, and demand at this price is 1,700 units. If the price fell to £4.60, demand would increase to 2,000 units.

Product B currently sells for £8 and demand at this price is 9,500 units. if the price fell to £7.50, demand would increase to 10,000 units.

In each of these cases, calculate:

(a) The price elasticity of demand (PED) for the price changes given

(b) The effect on total revenue, if demand is met in full at both the old and the new prices, of the change in price.

Answer

(a) Product A

At price £5:

Change in quantity $\frac{300}{1,700} = 17.7\%$

Change in price $\frac{40p}{£5} = 8\%$

PED $= -\frac{17.7\%}{8\%} = -2.2$

Demand is elastic and a fall in price should result in such a large increase in quantity demanded that total revenue will rise.

	£
Revenue at old price of £5 (× 1,700)	8,500
Revenue at new price of £4.60 (× 2,000)	9,200
Increase in total revenue	700

(b) Product B

At price £8:

Change in quantity $\frac{500}{9,,500} = 5.3\%$

Change in price $\frac{50p}{£8} = 6.25\%$

PED $= -\frac{5.3\%}{6.25\%} = -0.85$

Demand is inelastic and a fall in price should result in only a relatively small increase in quantity demanded. Total revenue falls.

	£
Revenue at old price of £8 (× 9,500)	76,000
Revenue at new price of £7.50 (× 10,000)	75,000
Fall in total revenue	1,000

1.9 Positive price elasticities of demand. Giffen goods

When the price of a good rises, there will be a **substitution effect**: consumers will buy other goods instead because they are now relatively cheaper. But there will also be an **income effect** in that the rise in price will reduce consumers' real incomes, and will therefore affect their ability to buy goods and services. The 19th century economist Sir Robert Giffen observed that this **income effect could be so great** for certain goods (called **Giffen goods**) that the demand curve would be **upward sloping**. The price elasticity of demand in such a case would be positive. Giffen observed that among the labouring classes of his day, consumption of bread rose when its price rose. This could happen because the increase in price of a commodity which made up a high proportion of individuals' consumption could have a significant effect on real incomes. People would have to increase their consumption of bread because they were no longer able to afford more expensive foods.

The demand curve for a good might also slope upwards if it is bought **for purposes of ostentation**, so that having a higher price tag makes the good more desirable to consumers and thus increases demand.

1.10 Factors influencing price elasticity of demand for a good

Factors that determine price elasticity of demand are similar to the factors other than price that affect the volume of demand. The PED is really a measure of the strength of these other influences on demand.

Main factors affecting PED

- Availability of substitutes
- The time horizon
- Pricing policies of competitors

1.11 Availability of substitutes

The more substitutes there are for a good, especially close substitutes, the more elastic will be the price elasticity of demand for the good. For example, in a greengrocer's shop, a rise in the price of one vegetable such as carrots or cucumbers is likely to result in a switch of customer demand to other vegetables, many vegetables being fairly close substitutes for each other. To give a second example, the elasticity of demand for a particular brand of breakfast cereals will be much greater than the elasticity of demand for breakfast cereals as a whole, because the former have much closer substitutes. **Availability of substitutes is probably the most important influence on price elasticity of demand.**

1.12 The time horizon

Over time, consumers' demand patterns are likely to change and so, if the price of a good is increased, initially, there might be very little change in demand. Then, as consumers adjust their buying habits in response to the price increase, demand might fall substantially. The time horizon influences elasticity largely because the longer the period of time which we consider, the greater the **knowledge** of substitution possibilities by consumers and the **provision** of substitutes by producers.

1.13 Competitor pricing

If the response of competitors to a price increase by one firm is to keep their prices unchanged, the firm raising its prices is likely to face elastic demand for its goods at higher prices. If the response of competitors to a reduction in price by one firm is to match the price reduction themselves, the firm is likely to face inelastic demand at lower prices. This is a situation which probably faces many large firms with one or two major competitors (ie oligopolies).

1.14 Income elasticity of demand

FAST FORWARD

Income elasticity of demand measures the responsiveness of demand to changes in household income. **Cross elasticity of demand** is determined by the availability of substitute (competitors') products.

It is possible to construct other elasticity measures, and an important one which you need to know about is the **income elasticity of demand**. The income elasticity of demand for a good indicates the responsiveness of demand to changes in **household incomes.**

$$\text{Income elasticity of demand} = \frac{\text{\% change in quantity demanded}}{\text{\% change in household income}}$$

(a) Demand for a good is **income elastic** if income elasticity is greater than 1 so that quantity demanded rises by a larger percentage than the rise in income. For example, if the demand for compact discs will rise by 10% if household income rises by 7%, we would say that the demand for compact discs is income elastic.

(b) Demand for a good is **income inelastic** if income elasticity is between 0 and 1 and the quantity demanded rises less than the proportionate increase in income. For example, if the demand for books will rise by 6% if household income rises by 10%, we would say that the demand for books is income inelastic.

The change in quantity demanded takes the form of a **shift in the position of the demand curve**, not a movement along it, since it is **not** stimulated by a change in price.

Goods whose income elasticity of demand is positive are said to be **normal goods**, meaning that demand for them will rise when household income rises. If income elasticity is negative, the commodity is called an **inferior good** since demand for it falls as income rises.

For most commodities, an increase in income will increase demand. The exact effect on demand will depend on the type of product. For example the demand for some products like bread will not increase much as income rises. Therefore, bread has a low income elasticity of demand. In contrast, the demand for luxuries increases rapidly as income rises and luxury goods therefore have a high income elasticity of demand.

Question

Income tax

What will be the effect on price and quantity demanded and supplied of sailing boats, given a significant reduction in income tax?

Answer

The demand curve for sailing boats will shift to the right. Both price and quantity demanded/supplied will go up. The effect of a cut in income tax is to leave households with more to spend. Sailing boats are a luxury good, and the income elasticity of demand is likely to be quite high. The percentage increase in demand for boats is therefore likely to be greater than the percentage increase in after-tax household income.

1.15 Cross elasticity of demand

Key term

Cross elasticity of demand is the responsiveness of demand for one good to changes in the price of another good.

$$\text{Cross elasticity of demand} = \frac{\text{\% change in quantity of good A demanded*}}{\text{\% change in the price of good B}}$$

*(given no change in the price of A)

The cross elasticity depends upon the degree to which goods are **substitutes or complements**.

(a) If the two goods are **substitutes, cross elasticity will be positive** and a fall in the price of one will reduce the amount demanded of the other.

(b) If the goods are **complements, cross elasticity will be negative** and a fall in the price of one will raise demand for the other.

Cross elasticity involves a comparison between two products. The concept is a useful one in the context of considering substitutes and complementary products.

2 Elasticity of supply

FAST FORWARD

As a measure of the responsiveness of supply to changes in price, the **elasticity of supply** is an indicator of the readiness of an industry to respond following a shift in the demand curve.

2.1 Price elasticity of supply

Key term

The **price elasticity of supply** indicates the responsiveness of supply to a change in price.

$$\text{Elasticity of supply} = \frac{\%\text{ change in quantity supplied}}{\%\text{ change in price}}$$

Where the supply of goods is **fixed** whatever price is offered, for example in the case of antiques, vintage wines and land, supply is **perfectly inelastic** and the elasticity of supply is **zero. The supply curve is a vertical straight line.**

Where the supply of goods varies proportionately with the price, elasticity of supply equals one and the supply curve is a straight line passing through the origin. (Note that a demand curve with unit elasticity along all of its length is **not** a straight line, but a supply curve with unit elasticity **is** a straight line.)

Where the producers will **supply any amount at a given price** but none at all at a slightly lower price, elasticity of supply is infinite, or **perfectly elastic. The supply curve is a horizontal straight line.**

Perfectly inelastic supply, unit elastic supply and perfectly elastic supply are illustrated in Figure 6.

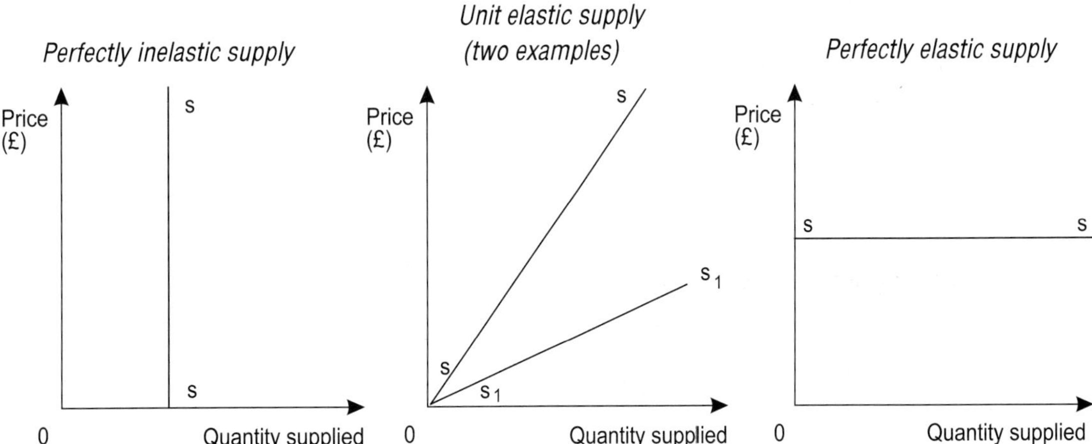

Figure 6 Elasticity of supply

Supply is **elastic** (greater than 1) when the percentage change in the amount producers want to supply exceeds the percentage change in price. Supply is **inelastic** (less than 1) when the amount producers want to supply changes by a smaller percentage than the percentage change in price.

2.2 Factors affecting elasticity of supply

Elasticity of supply is a measure of firms' ability to adjust the quantity of goods they supply. This depends on a number of constraints.

(a) **Existence of stocks of finished goods**: perishability or shelf life are important considerations.

(b) **Availability of labour**: when unemployment is low it may be difficult to find workpeople with the appropriate skills.

(c) **Availability of raw materials and components**. The existence and location of stocks is important, as is perishability, just as for finished goods.

(d) **Barriers to entry** are covered in more detail later in this study text. Here it is sufficient to point out that if firms can move into the market easily and start supplying elasticity of supply will be increased.

(e) The **time scale** is dealt with in the next paragraph.

2.3 Elasticity of supply and time

As with elasticity of demand, **the elasticity of supply of a product varies according to the time period over which it is measured**. For analytical purposes, four lengths of time period may be considered.

(a) **The market period** is so short that supplies of the commodity in question are limited to existing stocks. In effect, supply is fixed.

(b) **The short run** is a period long enough for supplies of the commodity to be altered by increases or decreases in current output, but not long enough for the fixed equipment (plant, machinery and so on) used in production to be altered. This means that suppliers can produce larger quantities only if they are not already operating at full capacity; they can reduce output fairly quickly by means of lay-offs and redundancies.

(c) **The long run** is a period sufficiently long to allow firms' fixed equipment to be altered. There is time to build new factories and machines, and time for old ones to be closed down. New firms can enter the industry in the long run.

(d) **The secular period** is so long that underlying economic factors such as population growth, supplies of raw materials (such as oil) and the general conditions of capital supply may alter. ('Secular' is derived from the Latin word 'saecula' meaning 'centuries'.) The secular period is ignored by economists except in the theory of economic growth.

2.4 Response to changes in demand

The price elasticity of supply can be seen as a measure of the readiness with which an industry responds following a shift in the demand curve.

Suppose that there is an increase in the demand for restaurant meals in a city, shown by the rightward shift in the demand curve in Figure 7 from D_1 to D_2. The capacity of the industry is limited in the short run by the number of restaurants in operation. The restaurants can be used more **intensively** to a certain extent, and so supply (S_1) is not perfectly inelastic, but there is a limit to this process. As a result, in the short run there is a large increase in the price from P_1 to P_2.

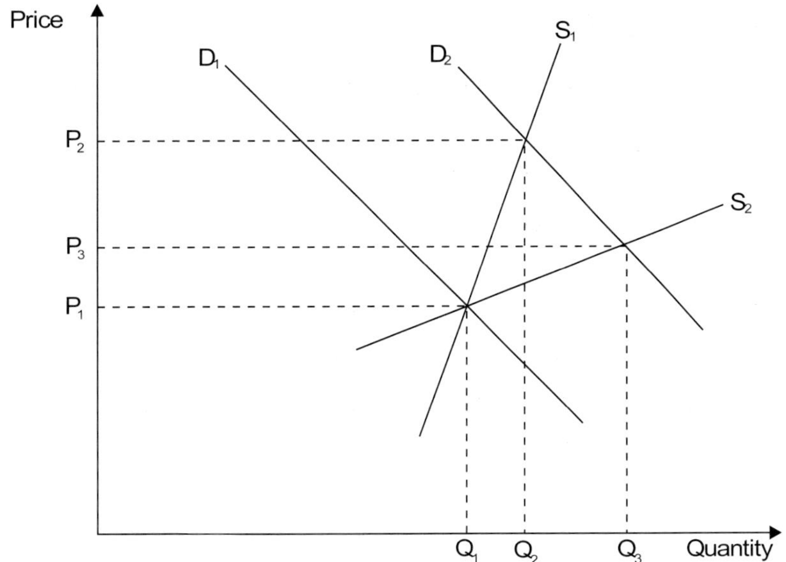

Figure 7 Response to a shift in the demand curve

The rise in price in the **short run** will encourage entrepreneurs to open new restaurants to take advantage of the profits to be earned. In the **long run**, supply is consequently **more elastic** and is shown by supply curve S_2. The expanded output in the industry leads to a new equilibrium at a lower price P_3 with the new level of output being Q_3.

Question

Perfectly elastic demand

Which diagram shows perfectly elastic demand?

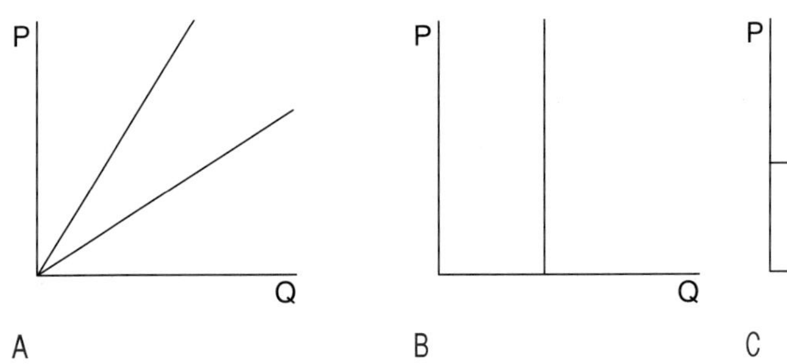

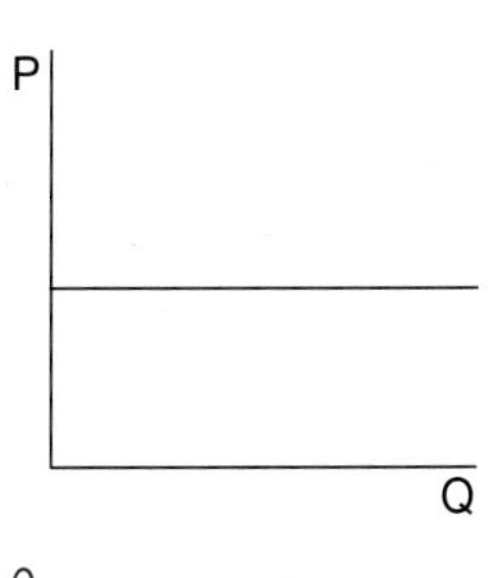

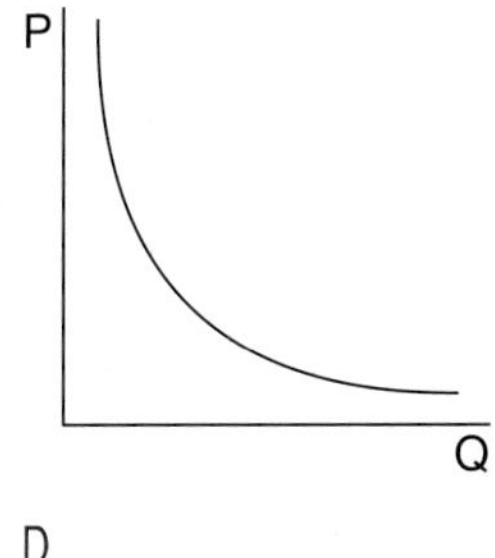

A B C D

Answer

C A is unit elastic supply (two examples). B is perfectly inelastic demand (or supply), D is unit elastic demand. C also shows perfectly elastic supply.

3 Primary markets

FAST FORWARD

Inelasticity of both **supply** and **demand** is an important feature of some markets, particularly in the primary sector. Agricultural markets illustrate two important effects especially well: these are the **cyclic variation** in supply and the paradox that farmers' incomes tend to vary inversely with levels of production.

3.1 Cyclic variation in supply

The characteristics of some goods are such that adjustments to levels of production take **significant periods** to have effect. This is particularly true of agricultural products, many of which are subject to long delays between the decision to produce and eventual delivery to market. In temperate climates, for example, many crops can only be grown on an annual cycle.

3.1.1 The 'hog cycle'

The effect of such long time lags in adjusting supply is to create **linked cyclic variations in both price and output**.

A very good example of this cyclic variation is found in the production of pork. In the USA, the production of 'hogs', as pigs are known there, has been observed to be highly cyclic, with a complete cycle taking, on average, about four years. The reproductive biology of pigs is such that there is a time lag of about 10 months between the decision to increase output and the delivery of increased numbers of animals to market. This delay drives the cycle.

The 'hog cycle' is illustrated in Figure 8.

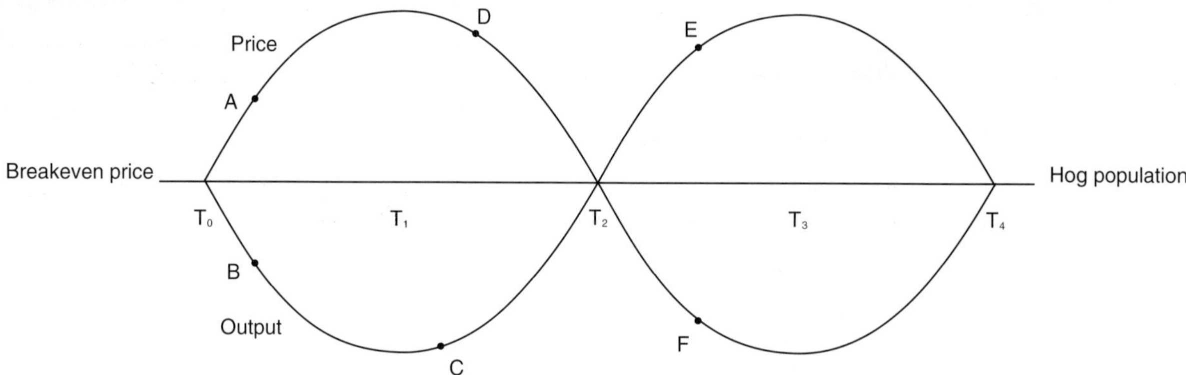

Figure 8 The Hog Cycle

In the diagram, the horizontal axis represents both the break-even price and the average national total number of hogs. The cycle begins with a small rise in price that takes it above the break-even level. As the price rises towards point A, producers decide to **increase output**. To do this, they need more breeding stock, so they **send fewer animals to market**. This is, effectively, a *reduction* in output towards point B, so prices continue to rise. Approximately a year later, the decision to increase breeding stock starts to have effect and output rises past point C. As a result, **price starts to fall** past point D.

At about the end of year 2, price has fallen to the break-even level and farmers decide to **reduce production**. This cannot be done immediately and, in the short term, the decision leads to an *increase* in the number of animals sent to market as breeding stock numbers are run down. The production curve rises towards point E, while **price falls** towards point F. Production then actually declines during year 4, while price rises back to the break-even point and the cycle begins again.

A similar cycle has been observed in the production of potatoes.

3.1.2 The cobweb effect

The implications of a delayed supply response to changing prices can be explored further using the kind of supply and demand diagrams you have become familiar with. These particular illustrations are known as **cobweb diagrams**, for reasons that will become obvious if you extrapolate the trajectory of market price in the diagrams below.

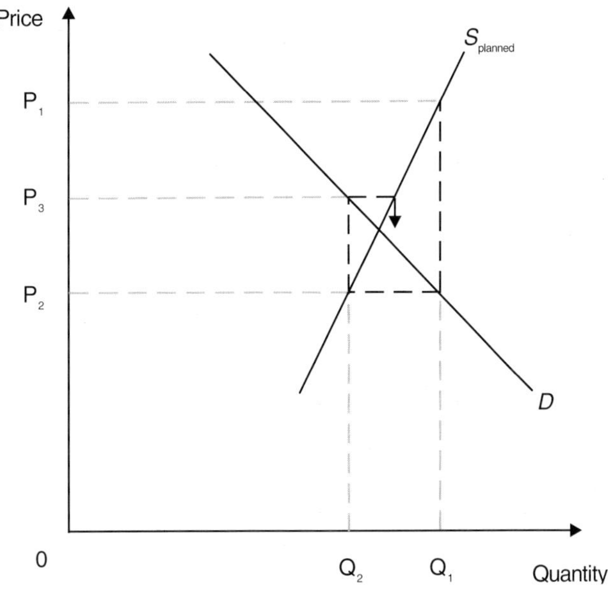

Figure 9 Convergent cobweb

Figure 9 shows a situation that starts in the same way as the hog cycle: the market in the first time period is in **disequilibrium** because the current price is P_1, not the market clearing price. This price leads producers to plan to supply Q_1 in the second time period. When this amount of the good eventually reaches the market, the producers are disappointed to find that price falls to P_2. They decide that they will only produce quantity Q_2 in the third time period. This restriction in supply inevitably leads to a rise in price to P_3.

It is easy to see what will happen in subsequent time periods: price and quantity will continue to **oscillate**, though, in this case, the market will approach equilibrium at the market clearing price.

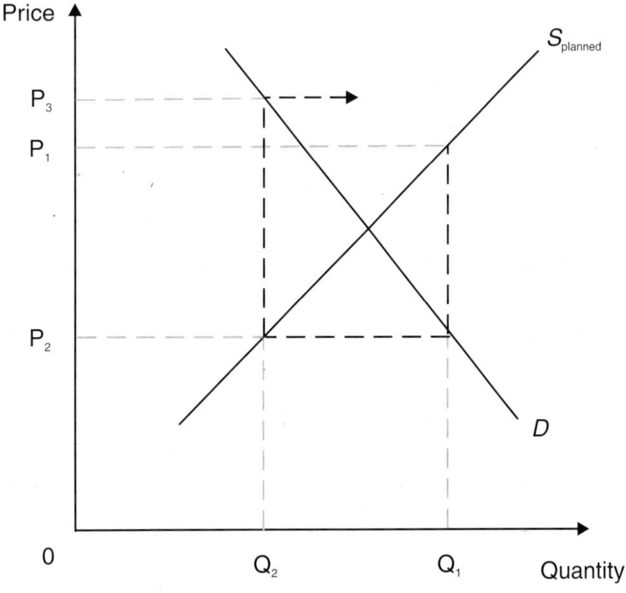

Figure 10 Divergent cobweb

Figure 10 shows a rather different situation. Here the **oscillations diverge** and equilibrium is never attained. Such a market would produce alternating surpluses and shortages of increasing size. Fortunately, this is an entirely theoretical situation.

The nature of the **market oscillations** depends on the relationship between the gradients of the **supply** and **demand** curves. If the supply curve is steeper than the demand curve, the oscillations will decay towards equilibrium, as in Figure 9. If the demand curve is steeper than the supply curve, the oscillations will expand, as shown in Figure 10. There is also the intermediate case, of course, where the gradients are identical: in this case the oscillations will continue at the same magnitude indefinitely.

3.1.3 Weather and agricultural output

Agriculture is particularly subject to the influence of the weather. In temperate climates, levels of production can vary quite markedly from year to year. Paradoxically, a good growing season does not usually mean a good trading year for farmers and *vice versa*. This is because demand for agricultural produce is quite **inelastic** overall: people's choices of individual foodstuffs are affected by their relative prices, but their total consumption does not vary very much.

Earlier in this chapter we discussed **the effect of a rise in price when demand is inelastic** and we showed that total revenue would rise. This is the situation farmers find themselves in when harvests generally are bad: the supply curve moves to the left, with less being offered at any price, and **prices go up**.

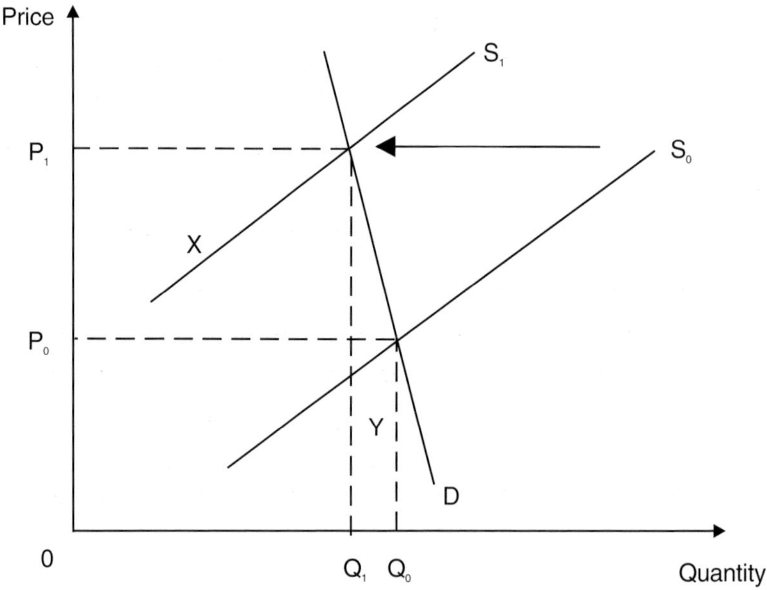

Figure 11 The effect of a poor harvest

Figure 11 shows the effect of the overall shift in the supply curve resulting from a poor harvest. At time 0, supply was at S_0 and price was at P_0. The next harvest was poor and by time 1, the supply curve has moved to the left. The quantity sold, Q_1, is not very much reduced below Q_0, but there has been a marked increase in price from P_0 to P_1. Total revenue equal to area Y has been lost, but this is more than compensated for by extra revenue equal to area X.

It is easy to see that in years when harvests generally are good, the opposite effect will be apparent: the supply curve will shift to the right, prices will fall and more total revenue will be lost than will be gained from the extra quantity sold.

So, when harvests generally have been good and there is an abundance of supply, farmers find their incomes falling. Conversely, when harvests are poor and prices rise, farmers will have higher incomes. There is thus considerable potential for instability and insecurity of supply in agriculture, in that a series of good harvests can lead to lack of investment, exit from the industry and even financial failure among farmers.

3.1.4 Case example

The report below illustrates the immediate and damaging effect of a glut of natural products.

The report goes on to describe the way that this problem has been exacerbated by a huge influx of similar crabs imported from the Far East. The US blue crab market thus illustrates both the effect of the weather on primary sector markets dealing in fresh food and the basic relationship between supply, demand and market price.

'Blue Crabs'

'As warm weather returns to Chesapeake Bay, so too does one of its delicacies: blue crabs. Seasoned and steamed, breaded and lightly fried, or picked clean for crab cakes, few crustaceans are more delicious.

The first crab catch this year was the biggest in more than a decade. Yet the glut, attributed to the mild winter and an increase in the number of juvenile crabs, is bringing anything but profits for the watermen, some of whom still speak with the Elizabethan lilt of their 17th- and 18th-century British ancestors. Prices at the dock are running at $8-10 a bushel (60-80 crabs), down from $30 in April. Last year, the price ranged from $40 to $85.'

(*The Economist*, 27 May 2006)

3.1.5 Government response to agricultural price instability

Historically, governments have been willing to intervene in agricultural markets. The current extent of such intervention in the USA and EU is now a matter of political controversy, but there is a fairly strong case to be made for intervention aimed at stabilising the market. Such intervention can take several forms, including **direct payments** to producers, **subsidies** for producing particular crops and **government purchase of surpluses.**

Unfortunately, there are disadvantages to all forms of intervention and there is therefore a strong case to be made against it.

(a) It is extremely difficult to decide the price at which the market should be stabilised.

(b) Intervention has costs, to public funds, to consumers or to both.

(c) Intervention tends to protect inefficient producers against efficient ones and domestic producers against foreign ones: the effects on less-developed countries are particularly harmful.

(d) Purchase of surpluses represents a shift of the demand curve to the right: as a result, production expands, tending to produce very large surpluses. The EU has a bad record for dumping its surpluses on the world market, further depressing the prospects of producers in less developed countries.

Chapter roundup

- Demand for a good depends largely on **price**, **household income** and the relative **price of substitutes or complementary goods**. Changes in any of these will cause either a movement along the demand curve or a shift in the demand curve. **Price elasticity of demand** indicates the responsiveness of total expenditure in a market for a good to price changes.
- For the assessment, you need to be able:
  - To distinguish between the **factors influencing elasticity**
  - To **measure** price elasticity from given price and demand data, and to draw appropriate conclusions from such information
  - To draw the correct implications for the **total revenue** of the producer of changes in the price of the product
- **Income elasticity of demand** measures the responsiveness of demand to changes in household income. **Cross elasticity of demand** is determined by the availability of substitute (competitors') products.
- As a measure of the responsiveness of supply to changes in price, the **elasticity of supply** is an indicator of the readiness of an industry to respond following a shift in the demand curve.
- **Inelasticity** of both **supply** and **demand** is an important feature of some markets, particularly in the primary sector. Agricultural markets illustrate two important effects especially well: these are the **cyclic variation** in supply and the paradox that farmers' incomes tend to vary inversely with levels of production.

Quick quiz

1 What is meant by the price elasticity of demand (PED) for a commodity?

2 What is the significance of PED to:

(a) A manufacturer?
(b) The Chancellor of the Exchequer?

3 What determines the cross elasticity of demand between two goods?

4 If the absolute value of the price elasticity of demand for dry white wine is greater than one, a decrease in the price of all wine would result in:

A A more than proportional decrease in the quantity of dry white wine purchased
B A less than proportional decrease in the quantity of dry white wine purchased
C A less than proportional increase in the quantity of dry white wine purchased
D A more than proportional increase in the quantity of dry white wine purchased

5 Which combination of demand and supply curves would be appropriate for a firm attempting to increase its profits by increasing its market share?

A Inelastic demand, inelastic supply
B Elastic demand, elastic supply
C Inelastic demand, elastic supply
D Elastic demand, inelastic supply

6 Which of the statements given about the goods X, Y and Z is correct?

A 5% increase in the price of:	*Leads to the following % changes in purchases due to price change* X	Y	Z
X	-3	-3	-2
Y	-2	-10	+3
Z	-1	+5	-1

A X and Y are substitutes, X and Z have inelastic demand
B X and Z are substitutes, X and Y have elastic demand
C X and Z are complements, X and Z have inelastic demand
D An increase in the price of Z leads to a fall in Z's revenue

7 Using the point method, what is the price elasticity of demand of product X as price falls from £20 to £15?

	X	*X*
Price	20	15
Quantity	10	15

A 0.5
B 1
C 1.5
D 2

8 Which of the following statements is true? 1. If the price elasticity of demand is more than 1, a fall in price will result in a fall in total expenditure on the good; 2. The income elasticity of demand will only be zero in the case of inferior goods; 3. The cross-elasticity of demand for complementary goods will always be positive.

A None of them is true
B Statement 1 only is true
C Statement 2 only is true
D Statement 3 only is true

9 Elasticity is not constant along a straight line demand curve.

Put the correct values for elasticity in the boxes on this diagram.

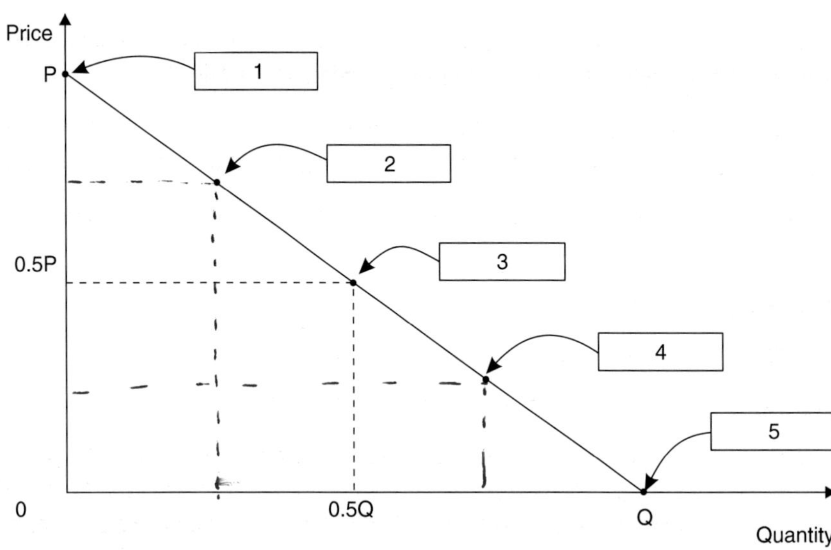

A 1
B Less than 1
C Greater than 1
D Zero
E Infinity

10 Which diagram shows perfectly inelastic supply?

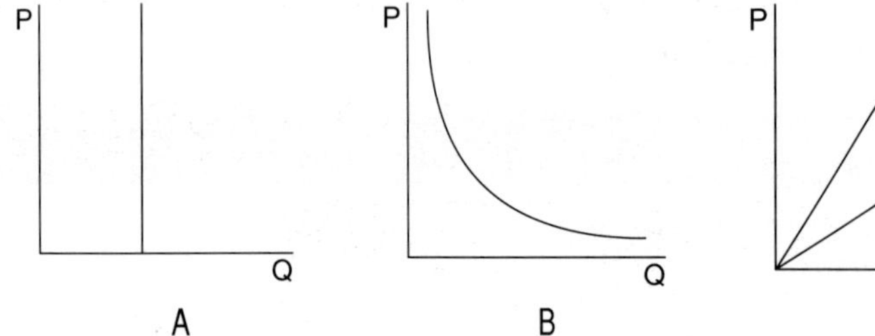

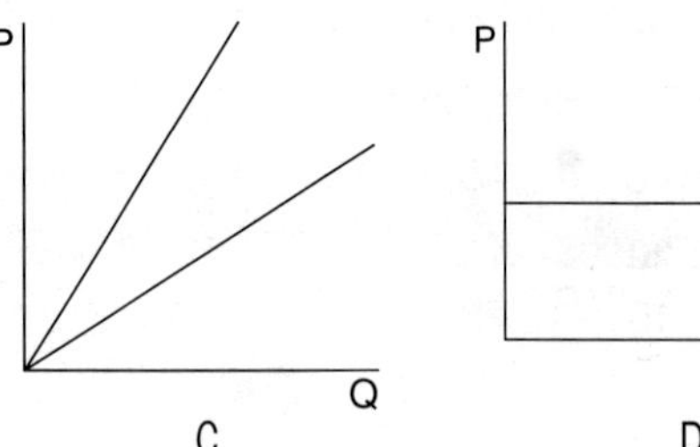

Answers to quick quiz

1 A measure of the extent to which market demand changes proportionately in response to a change in price.

2 If a good has low elasticity of demand, the manufacturer can increase the price without losing much sales revenue, and the Chancellor can impose a tax on it and expect to collect revenue. People will buy almost the same amount of the good even if its price goes up.

3 Cross elasticity of demand is the responsiveness of demand for one good to changes in the price of another. It is determined by the extent that the goods are substitutes or complements. Substitutes display positive cross elasticity and complements, negative cross elasticity.

4 D Assuming a normal good, a decrease in price results in a greater quantity being demanded. Given that demand is price elastic, the increase in quantity will be proportionally greater than the price fall.

5 B To increase market share requires greater quantities both demanded and supplied. To sell more, a firm needs to lower price. For this to be profitable, demand must be elastic. To produce more, supply must also be elastic.

6 C Demand moves in the same direction for X and Y in response to changes in their price. Therefore they are not substitutes.

X and Z are complements. Also X has inelastic demand.

Z is price inelastic, therefore revenue would rise if price rises.

7 D Percentage change in quantity = 50%. Percentage change in price = 25%.

8 A Statement 1 is incorrect. When demand is price elastic, a fall in price will increase total spending on the good. Statement 2 is incorrect, because when household income rises, demand for an inferior good will fall: income elasticity of demand will be negative, not zero. Statement 3 is incorrect. If goods A and B are complements, a rise in the price of B will cause a fall in the demand for A, and so cross elasticity of demand is negative.

9
1 E Change in quantity from or to zero is infinitely large.
2 C % change in quantity is larger than % change in price.
3 A % change in quantity and price are identical.
4 B % change in price is larger than % change in quantity.
5 D Change in price from or to zero is infinitely large.

10 A B could show unit elastic demand, C is unit elastic supply (two examples), D is perfectly elastic supply or demand. A also shows perfectly inelastic demand.

Now try the questions below from the Exam Question Bank

Question numbers	Page
13 – 15	366

Market failure, externalities and intervention

5

Introduction

In this chapter, we are concerned with why a free market would result in an allocation of resources that is not optimal – that is, not the best possible.

A **market imperfection** is any situation where actual behaviour in the market differs from what it would be if there were perfect competition in the market (which we discuss in more detail in a later chapter).

Trading goods and services, and economic activity in general, may have effects beyond the participants in the market. We are all affected by pollution from private cars for example, even if we do not have a car ourselves. Such effects are called 'externalities'.

Government actions and **governmental controls** affect all economies, and we examine some aspects of these actions and controls in this chapter.

Topic list	Learning outcomes	Syllabus references	Ability required
1 Market failure	B (iv)	B (9)	Comprehension
2 Externalities and government intervention	B (iv)	B (9), B (10)	Comprehension
3 Indirect taxes and subsidies	B (iv)	B (9)	Comprehension

1 Market failure

Free markets may not lead to an ideal allocation of resources, and there are various methods of **regulating** markets.

1.1 The case for a free market

What is the general case for allowing market forces to set prices? The following arguments are put forward by advocates of the free market.

(a) Free markets are **efficient**. Suppliers and consumers react fairly quickly to changes in market conditions in making their output and purchasing decisions; **resource allocation** within the economy is quick to adapt to the new conditions.

(b) The market is **impersonal**. Prices and levels of output are arrived at as a result of numerous decisions of consumers and suppliers, and not as the result of bureaucratic or political regulation.

Advocates of a free market economy argue that the market forces of supply and demand will result in an **efficient allocation of economic resources**.

(a) Consumers will want lower prices and producers will want higher prices; a balance of supply and demand is struck in the market through the price mechanism.

(b) Producers will decide what goods to produce, and in what quantities, by relating their prices to the costs of production (and the costs of the scarce resources needed to produce them).

(c) If the price of a product is too high, consumers will want to buy less of it. If the price is too low, producers will make less of it and switch their production resources into making something different.

However, the arguments in favour of a free market are based on the assumption that there is **perfect competition**. Perfect competition has a number of prerequisites.

(a) Markets each have a large number of competing firms, each producing a homogeneous product and each having only a small share of the market.

(b) Consumers and producers have perfect information about markets and prices.

(c) There is perfect mobility of factors of production, which can be switched easily from making one type of good into making another, and free entry and exit of firms into and out of the market.

In reality, these assumptions are not often completely valid. However, the markets for many goods approximate to conditions of perfect competition.

1.2 The concept of market failure

Key term

Market failure occurs when a free market mechanism fails to produce the most efficient allocation of resources.

Market failure is caused by a number of factors.

- Imperfections in a market
- Divergence between private costs and social costs (externalities)
- The need to provide public goods
- The need to consider non-market goals, such as the consumption of merit goods

The following are examples of market imperfections.

(a) If a monopoly firm controls a market, it might prevent other firms from entering the market (for example by claiming patent rights, or launching a strong marketing campaign with the intention of keeping customers away from the new firms). By restricting supply in this way, the monopolist may keep prices higher than they would be in a competitive market. (Monopoly is a subject of a later chapter.)

(b) Just as monopolies are firms which dominate supply to a market, monopsony buyers are large individual buyers who dominate demand in a market. Monopsonists may exert control over the market, exacting low prices or other favourable conditions from suppliers.

(c) Consumers may make bad purchasing decisions because they do not have complete and accurate information about all goods and services that are available.

(d) It takes time for the price mechanism to work. Firms cannot suddenly enter a new market or shut down operations. The slow response of the price mechanism to changes in demand creates some short term inefficiency in resource allocation.

ssessment focus point

A question on the price mechanism may also ask you to describe why this mechanism can sometimes 'fail'.

2 Externalities and government intervention

AST FORWARD

Note the following concepts.

- **Market failure**: the failure of a market to produce a satisfactory allocation of resources.
- **Social costs**: the total costs to society of using economic resources.
- **Social benefits**: the total gains to society as a whole flowing from an economic decision.
- **Externalities**: the differences between private and social costs.
- **Public goods**: goods which cannot be provided privately because if they are provided, all will benefit from them: as a result, individuals would have no incentive to pay for them.
- **Merit goods**: goods which need to be provided in the long-term public interest.

2.1 Social costs and private costs

In a free market, suppliers and households make their output and buying decisions for their own private benefit, and these decisions determine how the economy's scarce resources will be allocated to production and consumption. Private costs and private benefits therefore determine what goods are made and bought in a free market.

- **Private cost** measures the cost **to the firm** of the resources it uses to produce a good.
- **Social cost** measures the cost **to society as a whole** of the resources that a firm uses.
- **Private benefit** measures the benefit obtained directly by a supplier or by a consumer.
- **Social benefit** measures the total benefit to society from a transaction.

It can be argued that a free market system would result in a satisfactory allocation of resources, **provided that** private costs are the same as social costs and private benefits are the same as social benefits. In this situation, suppliers will maximise profits by supplying goods and services that benefit customers, and that customers want to buy. By producing their goods and services, suppliers are giving benefit to both themselves and the community.

However, there are other possibilities.

(a) Members of the economy (suppliers or households) may do things which give benefit to others, but no reward to themselves.

(b) Members of the economy may do things which are harmful to others, but at no cost to themselves.

When private benefit is **not** the same as social benefit, or when private cost is **not** the same as social cost, an allocation of resources which reflects private costs and benefits only **may not be socially acceptable**.

Here are some examples of situations where **private cost and social cost differ**.

(a) A firm produces a good and, during the production process, pollution is discharged into the air. The private cost to the firm is the cost of the resources needed to make the good. The social cost consists of the private cost plus the additional 'costs' incurred by other members of society, who suffer from the pollution.

(b) The private cost of transporting goods by road is the cost to the haulage firm of the resources to provide the transport. The social cost of road haulage would consist of the private cost plus the cost of repairs and maintenance of the road system (which sustains serious damage from heavy goods vehicles) plus any environmental costs, such as harm to wildlife habitats from road building.

2.2 Private benefit and social benefit

Here are some examples of situations where **private benefit and social benefit differ**.

(a) Customers at a café in a piazza benefit from the entertainment provided by professional musicians, who are hired by the café. The customers of the café are paying for the service in the prices they pay, and they obtain a private benefit from it. At the same time, other people in the piazza, who are not customers of the café, might stop and listen to the music. They will obtain a benefit, but at no cost to themselves. They are **free riders**, taking advantage of the service without contributing to its cost. The social benefit from the musicians' service is greater than the private benefit to the café's customers.

(b) Suppose that a large firm pays for the training of employees as accountants, expecting a certain proportion of these employees to leave the firm in search of a better job once they have qualified. The private benefits to the firm are the benefits of the training of those employees who continue to work for it. The total social benefit includes the enhanced economic output resulting from the training of those employees who go to work for other firms.

Question — **Private and public costs and benefits**

Think of some situations other than those mentioned above in which private costs differ from social costs and private benefits differ from social benefits. How might these differences be prevented or compensated for in each situation?

2.3 Externalities

Key term

> **Externalities** are effects of a transaction which extend beyond the parties to the transaction. The differences between the private and the social costs, or benefits, arising from an activity are externalities.

Less formally, an 'externality' is a cost or benefit which the market mechanism fails to take into account because the market responds to purely private signals. One activity might produce both harmful and beneficial externalities.

We can use demand and supply analysis to illustrate the consequences of externalities. If an adverse externality exists, so that the social cost of supplying a good is greater than the private cost to the supplier firm, then a supply curve which reflects total social costs will be above the (private cost) market supply curve.

Figure 1 shows two possibilities.

(a) If a free market exists, the amount of the good produced will be determined by the interaction of demand (curve D) and supply curve S. Here, output would be Y, at price P_y

(b) If social costs are taken into account, and the market operated successfully, the amount of the good produced should be X, at price P_X.

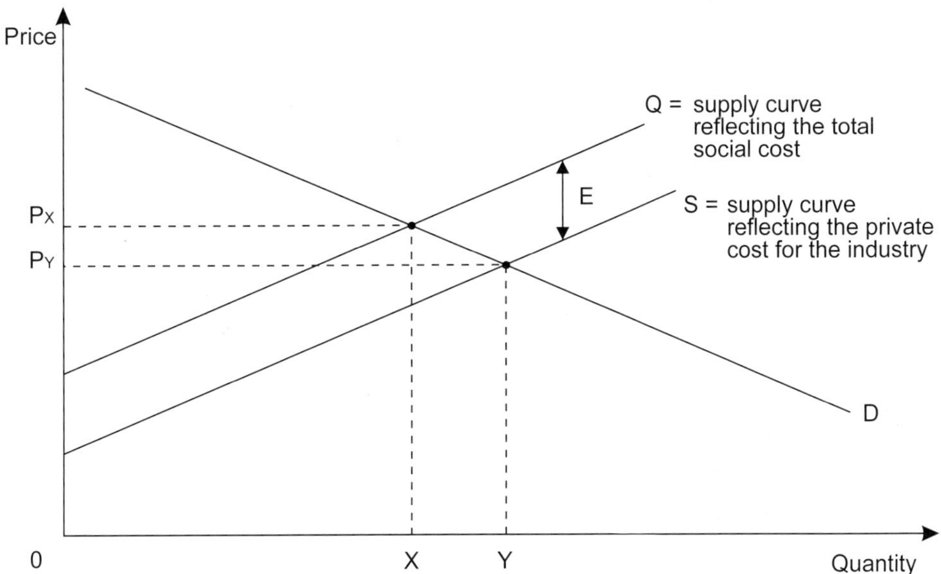

Figure 1 Externalities

Given a free market, output of the good will exceed what it ideally should be, and so resources will have been over-allocated to production of this particular good.

2.4 Public goods

Key term

> Some goods, by their very nature, involve so much 'spill-over' of externalities that they are difficult to provide except as **public goods** whose production is organised by the government.

In the case of public goods, the consumption of the good by one individual or group **does not significantly reduce the amount available for others**. Furthermore, it is often difficult or impossible to **exclude** anyone from its benefits, once the good has been provided. As a result, in a free market, individuals benefiting from the good would have no economic incentive to pay for them, since they might as well be **free riders** if they can, enjoying the good while others pay for it.

National defence is perhaps the most obvious examples of a public good. It is clearly not practicable for individuals to buy their own defence systems. Policing is sometimes cited as another example of a public good, although the growth of private security firms in the private sector illustrates how some areas of policing are now becoming privatised.

2.5 Merit goods

The existence of market failure and of externalities suggests the need for intervention in markets by the government, in order to improve the allocation of resources. Another possible reason for intervention is to **increase** the consumption of **merit goods**.

Key term

Merit goods are considered to be worth providing in greater volume than would be purchased in a free market, because higher consumption is in the long-term public interest. Education is one of the chief examples of a merit good.

On the other hand, many governments want to see **less** consumption of certain **demerit goods**, such as tobacco.

Apart from **providing** public goods and merit goods, a government might choose to intervene in the workings of markets by other methods.

(a) **Controlling the means of production** (for example, through state ownership of industries)

(b) **Influencing markets** through legislation and regulation (regulation of monopolies, bans on dangerous drugs, enforcement of the use of some goods such as car seat belts, laws on pollution control and so on) or by persuasion (for example, using anti-tobacco advertising)

(c) **Redistributing wealth**, perhaps by taxing relatively wealthy members of society and redistributing this tax income so as to benefit the poorer members

(d) **Influencing market supply and demand** through:

- Price legislation
- Indirect taxation
- Subsidies

(e) **Creating a demand for output that creates employment**. A free market system would match supply with demand. Demand would thus lead to **employment** because of the needs of suppliers, but the level of demand might not be high enough to ensure **full employment**. Government might therefore wish to intervene to create a demand for output in order to create more jobs.

Some externalities, particularly the problems of pollution and the environment, appear to call for co-operation between governments. The UN Conference on the Environment and Development held in Rio de Janeiro in 1992 led to a convention on climate change which included commitments about emission reduction. The Kyoto Protocol of 1997 was also directed at climate change.

Question **Pollution**

An industrial company alters its production methods to reduce the amount of waste discharged from its factory into the local river. What will be the effect (increase or decrease) on:

(a) Private costs
(b) External benefits
(c) Social costs

Answer

(a) Private costs of the company will presumably increase: the anti-pollution measures will have involved a financial outlay.

(b) External benefits will presumably increase: the public will benefit from a cleaner river.

(c) Social costs may stay the same: the increase in private costs may be balanced by the reduction the external costs to society.

2.6 Pollution policy

One area often discussed in relation to externalities is that of pollution. If polluters take little or no account of their actions on others, this generally results in the output of polluting industries being greater than is optimal. If polluters were forced to pay for any externalities they impose on society, producers would almost certainly change their production techniques so as to minimise pollution and consumers would choose to consume less of those goods which cause pollution.

One solution is to levy a tax on polluters equal to the cost of removing the effect of the externality they generate: this is called the 'polluter pays' principle. This approach is generally held to be preferable to regulation, as this can be difficult to enforce and provides less incentive to reduce pollution levels permanently.

Apart from the imposition of a tax, there are a number of other measures open to the government in attempting to reduce pollution. One of the main measures available is the application of subsidies which may be used either to persuade polluters to reduce output and hence pollution, or to assist with expenditure on production processes, such as new machinery and air cleaning equipment, which reduce levels of pollution.

A problem with using subsidies is that, unlike taxes, they do not provide an incentive to reduce pollution any further: indeed, profits are increased under subsidies which may have the perverse effect of encouraging more pollution to be generated in order to qualify for a subsidy. In addition, this is likely to be an expensive option for the government whereas imposing a tax actually provides the government with additional revenue.

An example of a subsidy to encourage a specific environmental alternative is that provided to a garbage burning power station opened in Lewisham, South London in 1994. The station receives a guaranteed high price for its power, which is effectively subsidised by electricity consumers. The subsidy thus actually encourages the plant to burn garbage wastefully.

3 Indirect taxes and subsidies

Demand and supply analysis can be used to examine the effects on a market of imposing an **indirect tax** or a **subsidy**.

3.1 Indirect taxes

Key term

Indirect taxes are levied on expenditure on goods or services as opposed to direct taxation which is applied to incomes. A **selective** indirect tax is imposed on some goods but not on others (or which is imposed at a higher rate).

We looked at the effects of one form of government intervention in markets – price regulation – earlier. An alternative form of price and output regulation is **indirect taxation**.

If an indirect tax is imposed on one good, the tax will shift the supply curve **upwards** by the amount the tax adds to the price of each item. This is because the price to **consumers** includes the tax, but the suppliers still only receive the **net-of-tax price**. For example, in Figure 2:

- The supply curve net of tax is S_0
- The supply curve including the cost of the tax is S_1
- The tax is equal to $P_1 - P_2$ or the distance A – B.

So if demand is for X_1 units the price to suppliers will be P_2 (or B) but the price with tax to the consumer would be P_1 (or A) – and the tax would be $(P_1 - P_2)$ or distance AB.

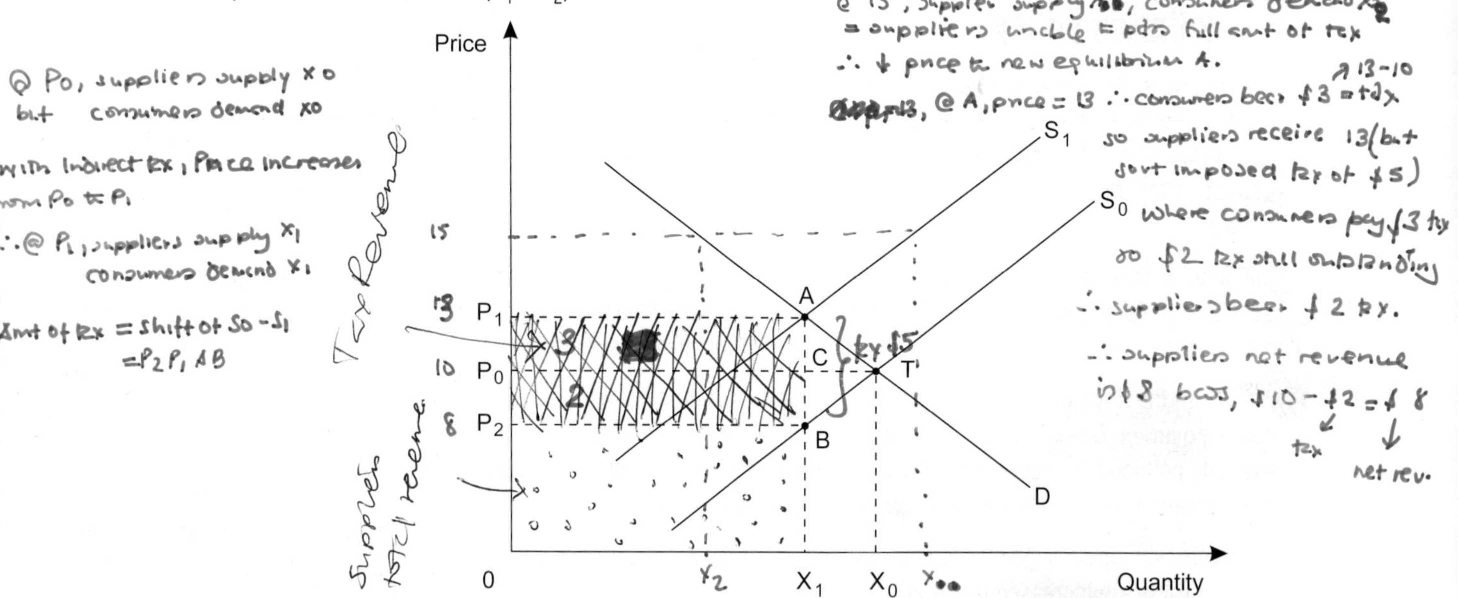

Figure 2 Selective indirect tax

Without the tax, output would be X_0 and price P_0. Total expenditure is shown by the rectangle OP_0TX_0.

(a) After the tax has been imposed, output falls to X_1 and price with tax rises to P_1. Total expenditure is OP_1AX_1, of which P_2P_1AB is tax revenue and OP_2BX_1 is producers' total revenue.

(b) A new equilibrium arises at point A.

 (i) Price to the customer has risen from P_0 to P_1.

 (ii) Average revenue received by producers has fallen from P_0 to P_2.

 (iii) The tax burden is therefore shared between the producers and consumers, with CB borne by the supplier and AC borne by consumers.

Consumers pay P_0P_1AC of total tax revenue and producers pay P_2P_0CB.

3.2 Elasticity effects

The proportion of the tax which is passed on to the consumer rather than being borne by the supplier depends upon the elasticities of demand and supply in the market.

Figures 3(a) and 3(b) illustrate the extreme cases of perfectly elastic demand and perfectly inelastic demand respectively.

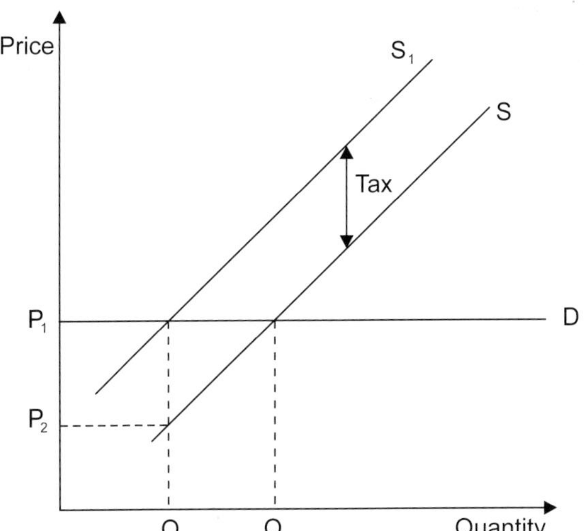

(b) Perfectly inelastic demand

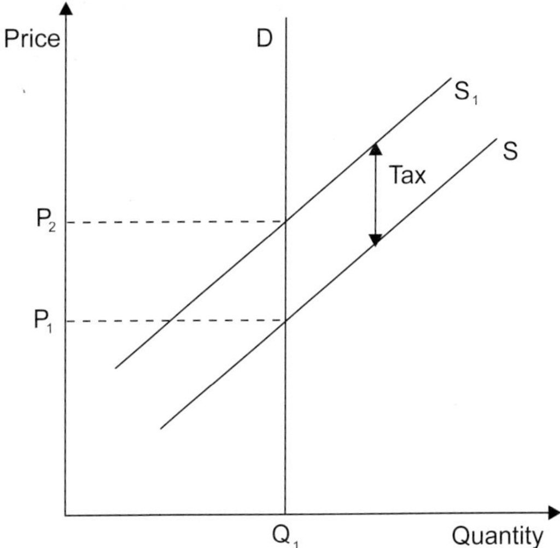

Figure 3 Elasticity of demand

Question

Burden of taxation

Try to work out yourself (from general principles, or from study of Figure 3) who bears the burden of taxation in each of these extreme cases.

Answer

In Figure 3(a), with perfectly elastic demand, demand falls to zero if the price is raised. Consequently, the supplier must bear the full burden of the tax. In spite of the imposition of the tax, the market price remains the same but there is a fall in the quantity supplied from Q_1 to Q_2. The supplier only receives P_2.

In the case of perfectly inelastic demand (Figure 3(b)), the supplier can pass on the full amount of the tax to the consumer by increasing the price from P_1 to P_2 by the full amount of the tax. The quantity supplied remains unchanged.

The elasticity of supply is also relevant. Figure 4 shows that for a given demand curve, the more inelastic is the supply curve, the greater is the proportion of the tax that is borne by the supplier.

(a) Figure 4(a) shows a relatively inelastic supply curve S. Imposition of the tax shifts the supply curve vertically upwards to S1 and the equilibrium price rises from P1 to P2. The price to the consumer rises by AB per unit, while the supply price to the producer falls by BC per unit. Thus, the greater burden is borne by the supplier.

(b) Figure 4(b) in contrast shows a relatively elastic supply curve S. With the imposition of the tax, the supply curve shifts to S1 and the equilibrium price rises to P2. The price to the consumer rises by AB per unit, and the supply price to the producer falls by BC per unit.

It can be appreciated from Figure 4 that the consumer bears a greater proportion of the tax burden the more elastic is the supply curve. Figure 4 also shows that, for a given demand curve, the price rise and the fall in the equilibrium quantity will both be greater when the supply curve is more elastic.

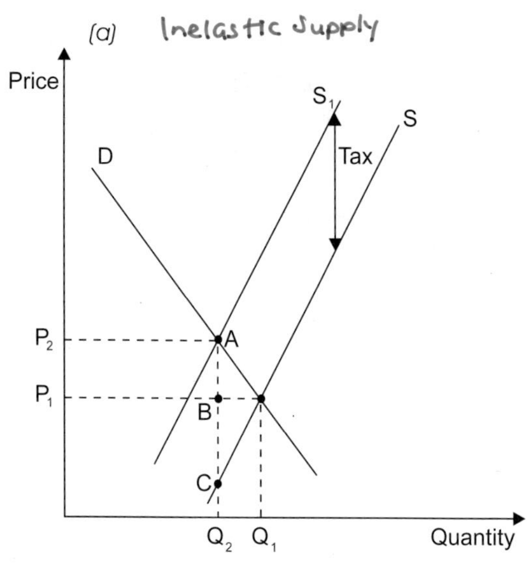

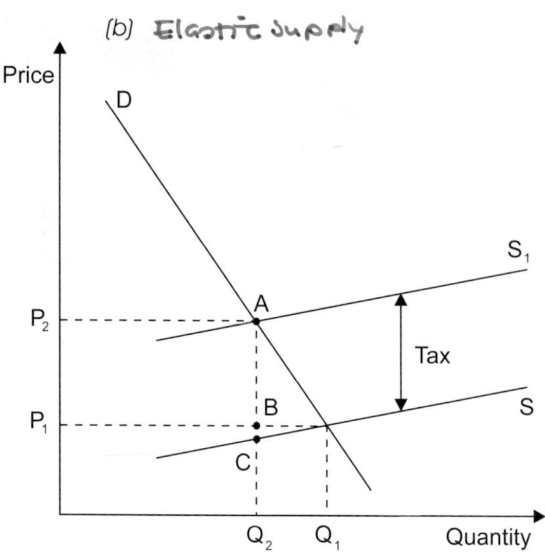

Figure 4 The effect of elasticity illustrated

In general, the greater the elasticities of demand and supply, the greater will be the effect of a tax in reducing the quantity sold in and therefore produced for the market.

It can be shown that:

$$\frac{\text{Consumers' share of tax}}{\text{Producers' share of tax}} = \frac{\text{Elasticity of supply}}{\text{Elasticity of demand}}$$

(though proof is omitted here).

Thus if a selective indirect tax of 10p is placed on a product where supply elasticity is 1.2 and demand elasticity is 0.8, the consumer would pay 6p and the supplier would pay 4p of the tax of 10p per unit and the price of the good would rise by 6p.

Further points to note

(a) **Since such a tax reduces output, it may be harmful to an industry**. For some companies, the reduction in quantities produced may lead to significant rises in the unit costs of production. This could have adverse consequences on the competitive position of the firm if it competes in domestic or overseas markets with foreign firms which are not subject to the same tax.

(b) Indirect taxation may be used to create an improvement in the **allocation of resources** when there are damaging externalities.

3.3 Subsidies

A subsidy is a payment to the supplier of a good by the government. The payment may be made for a variety of reasons.

(a) **To encourage more production of the good**, by offering a further incentive to suppliers

(b) **To keep prices lower for socially desirable goods** whose production the government wishes to encourage

(c) **To protect a vital industry** such as agriculture, when demand in the short term is low and threatening to cause an excessive contraction of the industry.

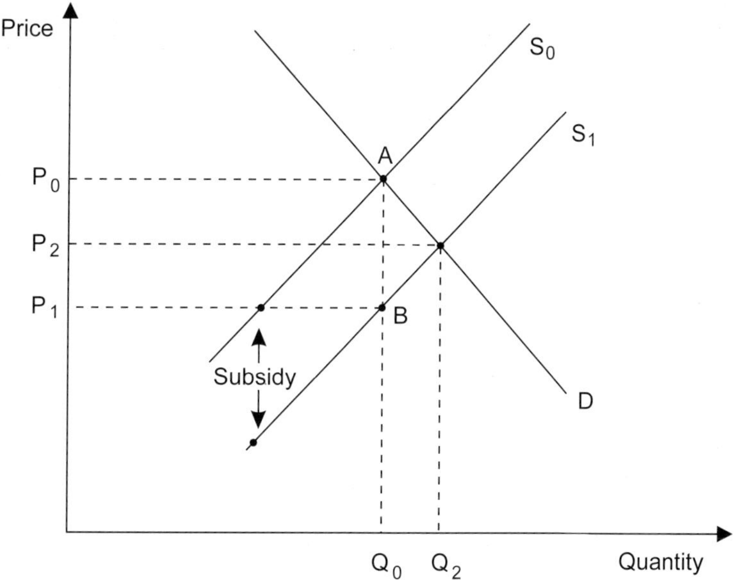

Figure 5 Subsidy

A subsidy is rather like indirect taxation in reverse.

- In Figure 5, supply curve S_0 is what the supply curve would be if no subsidy existed
- Payment of the subsidy moves the supply curve downwards to S_1.

If there was no subsidy, the free market equilibrium price would be P_0, and output Q_0. A subsidy per unit equivalent to AB is introduced so that suppliers would now be willing to produce Q_0 at a lower price (P_1 rather than at P_0). In other words, the supply curve shifts from S_0 to S_1. But there will be a shift in the equilibrium quantity produced to Q_2, which can be sold on the market for P_2. Thus, the subsidy will have two effects.

- The amount supplied in equilibrium will increase.
- The price will fall, but the decrease in price will be less than the value of the subsidy itself.

Question

Subsidy

By reference to Figure 5, analyse the extent to which the benefit of the subsidy falls to:

(a) The consumer
(b) The supplier

Who bears the cost of the subsidy?

Answer

The benefit of the subsidy will be shared between the consumer and the supplier.

(a) Consumers benefit by the lowering of prices from P_0 to P_2.
(b) Suppliers benefit because although they receive a lower price, P_2, they receive the subsidy AB per unit.
(c) The cost of the subsidy is borne by the government (in effect, the taxpayer).

Chapter roundup

- **Free markets** may not lead to an ideal allocation of resources, and there are various methods of **regulating** markets.
- Note the following concepts.
  - **Market failure**: the failure of a market to produce a satisfactory allocation of resources.
  - **Social costs**: the total costs to society of using economic resources.
  - **Social benefits**: the total gains to society as a whole flowing from an economic decision.
  - **Externalities**: the differences between private and social costs.
  - **Public goods**: goods which cannot be provided privately because if they are provided, all will benefit from them: as a result, individuals would have no incentive to pay for them.
  - **Merit goods**: goods which need to be provided in the long-term public interest.
- **Demand and supply analysis** can be used to examine the effects on a market of imposing an **indirect tax** or a **subsidy**.

Quick quiz

1 What is the general case in favour of allowing a free market to operate?

2 What is market failure, and what are its main causes?

3 What is an externality?

4 List the various forms of government intervention in markets.

5 Which of the following are imperfections in a market? 1. Consumer brand loyalty to a firm's branded goods, regardless of price; 2. The lack of completely accurate information for consumers about all goods and services available; 3. The slow response of firms to price changes and the relatively inelastic supply of a good in the short run.

A Items 1 and 2 only
B Items 2 and 3 only
C Items 1 and 3 only
D Items 1, 2 and 3

6 Which of the following are weaknesses of a completely free-enterprise economic system? 1. It only reflects private costs and private benefits; 2. It may lead to serious inequalities in the distribution of income and wealth; 3. It may lead to production inefficiencies and a wastage of resources.

A 1 and 2 only
B 2 and 3 only
C 1 and 3 only
D 1, 2 and 3

7 Muddy Waters Ltd is an industrial company which has altered its production methods so that it has reduced the amount of waste discharged from its factory into the local river. Which of the following is most likely to be reduced?

A Total private costs
B Social costs
C External benefit
D Variable costs

8 Much Wapping is a small town in Hampshire where a municipal swimming pool and sports centre have just been built by a private firm Hands Nielsen Bumpsydaisy Ltd. Which of the following is an external benefit of the project?

A The increased trade of local shops
B The increased traffic in the neighbourhood
C The increased profits for the sports firm
D The increased building on previous open land

9 The Chancellor increases the tax on tobacco. Assuming that the demand for cigarettes is completely inelastic, who pays the tax?

A It is shared between supplier and consumer in proportions equal to the relative prices before and after the increase.

B The supplier

C The consumer

D It is shared between supplier and consumer in proportions equal to the relative quantities sold before and after the increase.

10 In Ruritania, the government has recently introduced minimum price legislation for agricultural products, whereby the government buys up surplus produce which is not purchased by consumers at the minimum price. The minimum price for most agricultural products is well in excess of the free market price that has been obtained in the markets in recent years.

Which of the following statements is untrue?

A The supply of agricultural produce will increase, because more resources will be put into production

B Demand for agricultural produce will be unaffected, because the government will buy up all surplus food supplies

C The minimum price legislation will encourage some farmers to be less efficient, and to produce at high unit costs of output

D There will not be any black market in the sale of agricultural produce at free market prices

Quick quiz answers

1 Free markets are efficient in that they adjust quickly to changing demand and supply and they operate automatically, without need for direction or control.

2 Market failure occurs when a free market mechanism produces an allocation of resources which can be criticised on efficiency, social or political grounds.

3 An externality is an effect caused by an economic transaction which extends beyond the parties to the transaction.

4 Controlling the means of production
Legal regulation of products and prices
Indirect taxation
Subsidies
Redistributing income via taxation and welfare payments

5 D Brand loyalty can make consumers pay more for a good, without getting any greater total satisfaction from consuming it. Lack of information to consumers will result in 'bad' purchasing decisions. The slowness to price changes is a further market imperfection.

6 D The need to limit or avoid these weaknesses is the chief argument in favour of some government involvement in the allocation of economic resources – ie in favour of a mixed economy or even a command economy.

7 B Social cost is the sum of the private cost to a firm *plus* the external cost to society as a whole. Here, social cost is the sum of production costs (private costs) plus the cost of pollution (external cost). The firm's private costs might have been increased by the measures to reduce pollution, but the external costs will have fallen, so that total social costs should have fallen too.

8 A This is correct because the benefits to local shops are additional to the private benefits of the sports firm and as such are external benefits.

B is an external *cost* of the project, since increased volumes of traffic are harmful to the environment.

C is a private benefit for the firm.

D would only be an external benefit if a building is better for society than the use of open land, which is unlikely.

9 C As the consumer's consumption is not altered by the price rise, the supplier can pass it on in full.

10 B

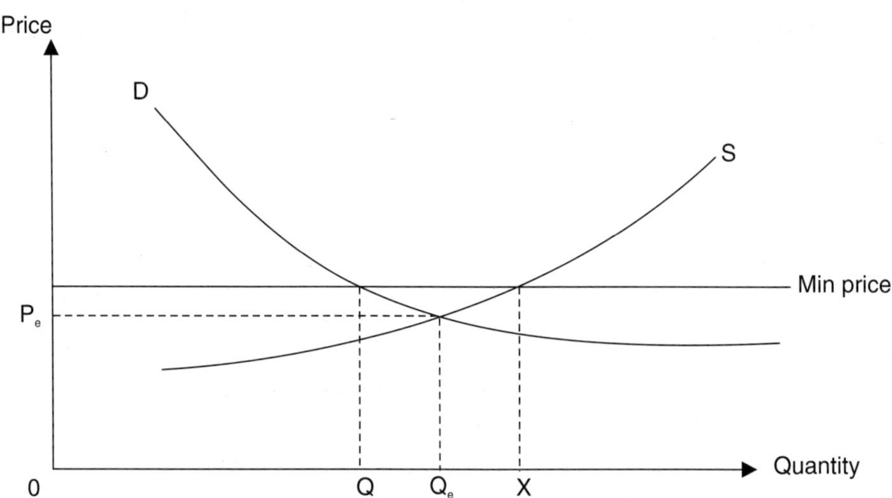

Statement B is incorrect because demand will fall for Q_e to Q, although the government *will* have to buy up the surplus production, which is (X – Q) in the diagram above. *Statement A* is correct, since supply will increase from Qe to X. *Statement C* is correct, because farmers can still make profits even when they incur higher costs – this is likely to create some production inefficiencies. *Statement D* is correct – although the negative statement might have confused you. Black markets are associated with maximum price legislation, not minimum prices.

Now try the questions below from the Exam Question Bank

Question numbers	Page
16 – 18	367

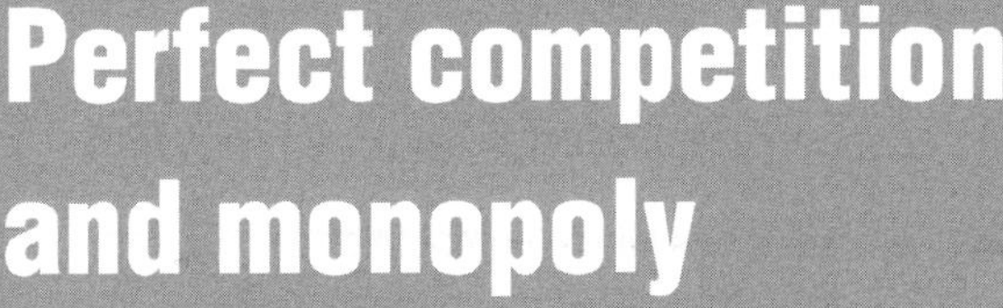

Perfect competition and monopoly

Introduction

Businesses operate in two sets of markets, one for inputs, such as labour, and one for output.

The objectives of businesses may vary, as may the structure and nature of the markets in which they operate. To understand the immediate environment within which a business operates, you need to be aware of the implications of these variations. We look at these implications in this part of the Study Text.

The purpose of this chapter is to consider output decisions by firms which operate with the different forms of market structure characterised as **perfect competition** and **monopoly**.

In the next Chapter, we will go on to look at two other forms of 'imperfect' market structure: **oligopoly** and **monopolistic competition**.

You should have a full understanding of each of these four models of market structure.

Topic list	Learning outcomes	Syllabus references	Ability required
1 Equilibrium under perfect competition	B (v)	–	Comprehension
2 Equilibrium for a monopoly	B (v)	B (6)	Comprehension
3 More about monopoly	B (v)	B (6)	Comprehension

1 Equilibrium under perfect competition

FAST FORWARD

In **perfectly competitive markets**, firms are **price takers**, and so their decisions are concerned with what output level will maximise profits. In imperfect competition, firms can influence the market price, and so their decisions are about what price to set as well as what volumes of output to produce. **Pure monopoly** is an extreme form of **imperfect competition**.

1.1 Perfect competition

Key term

Perfect competition: a theoretical market structure in which no supplier has an advantage over another.

Perfect competition acts as a useful theoretical benchmark.

(a) We can use it to **judge or predict what firms might do** in markets where competition shows some or most of the characteristics of being perfect

(b) We can also **contrast the behaviour of firms in less perfect markets**. We shall be looking in this chapter and the next at imperfect types of market structure – namely, monopoly, monopolistic competition and oligopoly.

Characteristics of perfect competition

- There is a large number of buyers and sellers in the market.
- Firms are 'price takers', unable to influence the market price individually.
- Producers and consumers act rationally and have the same information.
- The product is homogeneous: one unit of the product is the same as any other unit.
- There is free entry of firms into and free exit of firms out of the market.
- There are no transport costs or information gathering costs.

Assessment focus point

You should be familiar with the above assumptions of the 'perfect competition' model for your assessment.

Question **Perfect market**

Think about the market for a particular product – say motor cars. To what extent is this market 'perfect', as defined by the six criteria above?

Answer

(a) There is a huge number of buyers, and many sellers too. For any given model of car, a particular dealer is likely to be a price taker.

(b) Communication is generally good. Product features are well known and list prices are freely available. And discount levels too are widely commented on, in the press and by word of mouth.

(c) Consumers don't always act rationally. Some might be attracted to a car with a higher price, even if it is no better than other cheaper cars. Some may not shop around at different dealers even though it could save them money.

(d) The product is very far from homogeneous.

(e) Entry to the market is not easy, whether we are talking about manufacturers of motor cars (very high start-up costs), or dealers.

(f) Transport costs are *not* absent. On the contrary, significant geographical price differentiation is possible because of the high transport costs involved.

1.2 Equilibrium in the short run

How are price and output determined in the case of the profit-maximising firm operating under conditions of perfect competition in the short run?

The short run is a period in which the number of firms in the market is **temporarily fixed**. In these circumstances it is possible for firms to make supernormal profits or losses.

1.3 Diagrammatic explanation

Figure 1 shows the cost and demand curves of a firm in the short run making supernormal profits. The demand curve is the horizontal line D_1 at price P_1. The curve is a horizontal line indicating that **the firm has to accept the price that the market as a whole fixes** for it. If the firm were to charge a higher price it would lose all its sales and there is no point charging a lower price as it can sell all its output at the given price. The demand curve is thus also the marginal revenue curve; every new unit sold at price P_1 increases total revenue by an amount P_1.

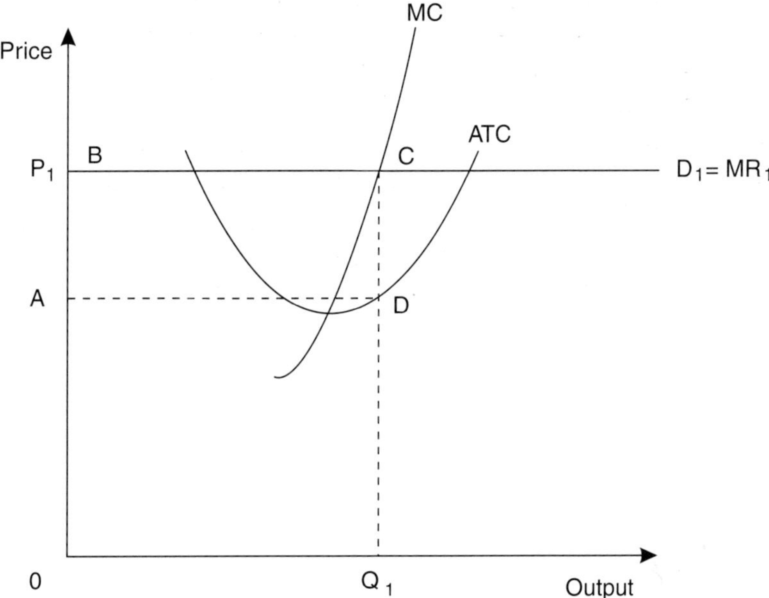

Figure 1 Supernormal profits in the short run

Figure 1 also shows the average total cost curve (ATC) and the marginal cost curve (MC), with the MC cutting the ATC at the lowest point of the ATC. Given these cost curves and the demand curve D_1, the firm will produce the output Q_1, where the MC curves cuts the MR horizontal curve at the point C. This is the **profit maximising level of output** (see Chapter 5 Section 3).

At the output Q_1 the firm is making **supernormal profits** indicated by the rectangle ABCD. This will attract new firms into the industry and the price will be bid down, possibly to price P_2 as shown in Figure 2. Here the firm makes a loss shown by the rectangle WXYZ. Once again the firm produces where MC = MR giving an output of Q_2. A firm could choose to do this for a short period so long as revenues covered its **variable** costs, since any excess of revenue **over** variable cost will help to pay the fixed costs. In the long term, however, revenues must cover both fixed and variable costs in full.

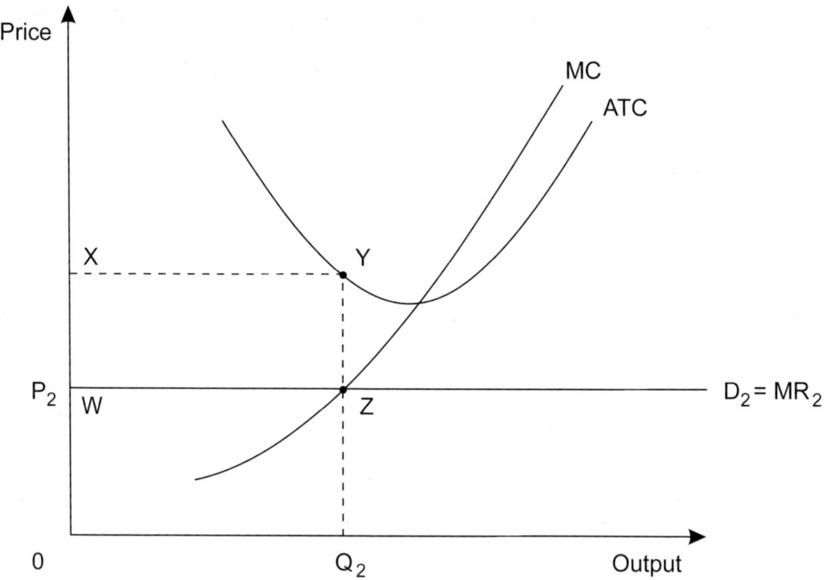

Figure 2 Losses in the short run

In the long run, whenever profits are being made new firms will enter the industry and the price will fall. Similarly, when losses are made firms will leave the industry and the price will rise.

Question — Perfect competition

In conditions of perfect competition, the demand curve for a firm's product is:

(a) Identical to the firm's marginal revenue curve. True or false?
(b) Perfectly inelastic. True or false?

Answer

(a) True. The firm can sell whatever output it produces at the market price.
(b) False. (a) above implies that the demand curve is perfectly elastic.

1.4 Equilibrium in the long run

In a perfectly competitive market in the **long run**, the firm **cannot influence** the market price and its average revenue curve is horizontal. The firm's average cost curve is U shaped. The firm is in equilibrium and earns normal profits only (and so no supernormal profits) when the AC curve is at a tangent to the AR curve as shown in Figure 3(b). In other words, long-term equilibrium will exist when supernormal profits and losses are eliminated. There is no incentive for firms to enter or leave the industry and the price will remain at P with the firm making normal profits only.

Note the following points about Figure 3.

(a) The market price P is the price which all individual firms in the market must take.

(b) If the firm must accept a given MR (as it must in conditions of perfect competition) and it sets MR = MC, then **the MC curve is in effect the individual firm's supply curve** (Figure 3(b)). The **market supply curve** in Figure 3(a) is derived by aggregating the individual supply curves of every firm in the industry.

(c) Consumer surplus is represented by the area to the left of the demand curve above P.

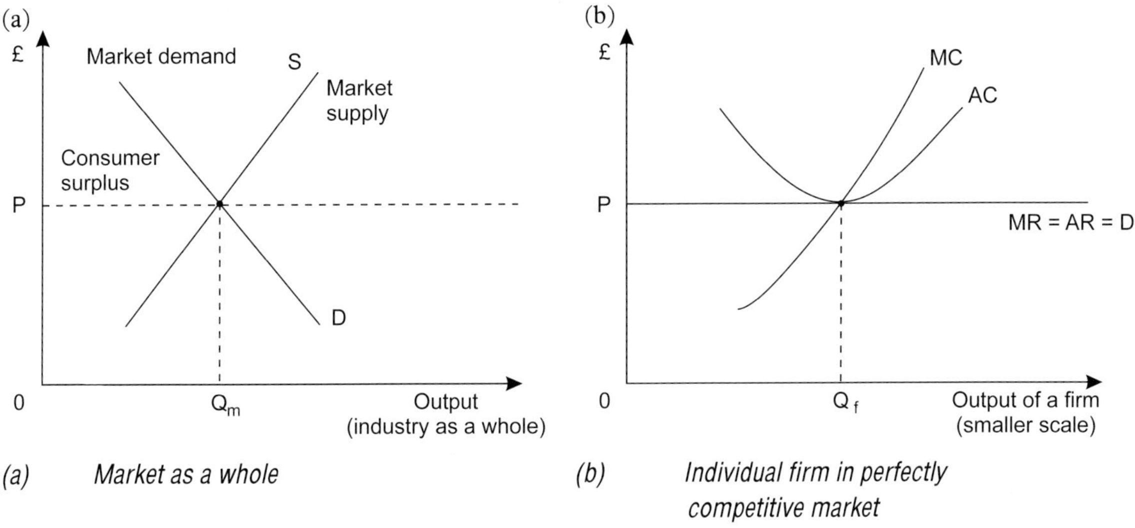

(a) Market as a whole

(b) Individual firm in perfectly competitive market

Figure 3

Long-run equilibrium will, then, occur in the industry when there are no more firms entering or leaving the industry because no new firm thinks it could earn higher profits by entering and no existing firm thinks it could do better by leaving. In the **long run**, then, all firms in the industry will have MR = MC = AC = AR = price, as in Figure 3(b).

ssessment cus point

This explanation of long run equilibrium under perfect competition and the accompanying diagrams are fundamental knowledge.

Question

Equilibrium perfect competition

A perfectly competitive firm will be in equilibrium where price is equal to marginal cost. True or false?

Answer

True. Price is at average revenue (AR) which is equal to MC.

Question

Small firm

A small perfectly competitive firm manufactures 200 wooden garden benches each month which it sells for £40 each. The table below shows the firm's costs.

Total variable cost	£7,200
Marginal cost	£40
Total fixed cost	£1,800

What should the firm do in the short term?

A Increase output
B Cease production
C Lower its price
D Maintain output at its present level

Answer

D The firm is producing and selling at a level of output where marginal cost is equal to marginal revenue. It is therefore already maximising its profit or minimising its loss. In fact, its monthly total revenue is £40 × 200 units = £8,000. This covers the variable costs and makes a contribution of £800 towards its fixed costs. Ceasing production would cause this contribution to be lost. There would be no point to reducing price since under perfect competition it can sell as much as it can produce at the prevailing market price. If the firm increased production, it would find that its marginal cost rose.

2 Equilibrium for a monopoly

FAST FORWARD

Firms will generally try to earn **supernormal profits** if they can. Competition, though, tends to erode supernormal profits, and firms may have to be satisfied, when equilibrium is reached, with just normal profits. The ability to sustain supernormal profits depends on the nature of competition.

2.1 The monopoly market

Key term

In a **monopoly**, there is only one firm, the sole producer of a good which has no closely competing substitutes.

A firm's monopolistic position may result from some natural factor which makes it too costly for another firm to enter the industry. For example, in the domestic water supply industry it will normally be too costly for a second firm to lay a second water supply system to compete for part of the business of an existing sole supplier: the sole supplier enjoys a **natural monopoly**. In other cases, a monopoly may be formed by mergers of a number of firms in an industry. However formed, **monopoly can only exist if potential competitors are kept out of the market by barriers to entry** (see below). For a monopoly, the total market supply is identical with the single firm's supply and the average revenue curve in monopoly is the same as the total market demand curve.

If price must be reduced to increase unit sales, average revenue is falling and marginal revenue will always be lower than average revenue; if the monopolist increases output by one unit the price per unit received will fall, so the **extra revenue** generated by the sale of the extra unit of the good is **less** than the **price** of that unit. The monopolist therefore faces a downward sloping AR curve with an MR curve below the AR curve (Figure 4).

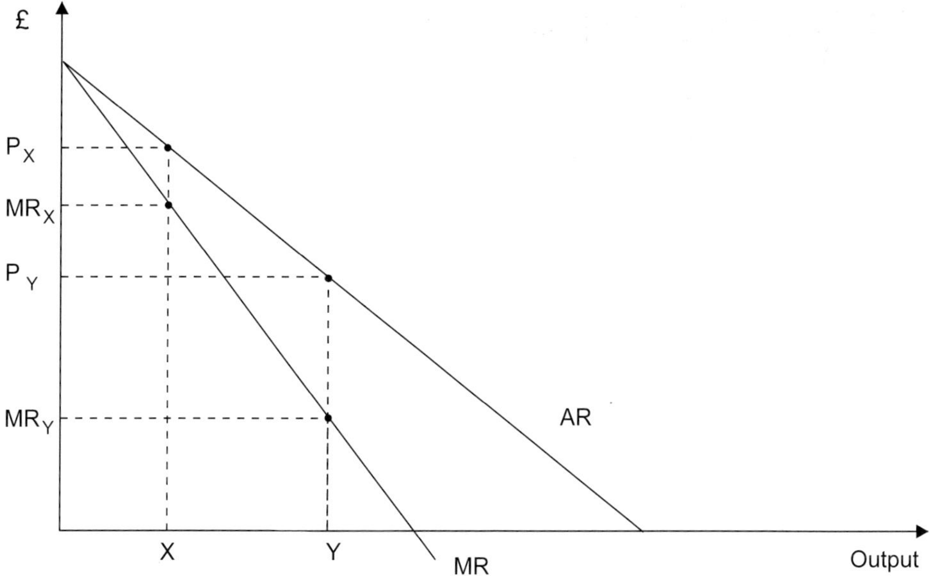

Figure 4 A monopolist's average revenue (AR) and marginal revenue (MR) curves

Marginal revenue can be negative. This occurs when demand is price inelastic and, although lowering the price increases sales demand, the volume increase is small and so total revenue falls.

Question

Price and output level

Study the diagram above. At what price and output level would the firm maximise its sales revenue?

Answer

At the point where MR = 0. Further sales will lead to negative MR, and hence a reduction in total revenue.

It is obviously important that you should understand what the MR and AR (demand) curves are showing us in Figure 4.

(a) At output quantity X, the marginal revenue earned from the last unit produced and sold is MR_X, but the price at which all the X units would be sold is P_X. This is found by looking at the price level on the AR curve associated with output X.

(b) Similarly, at output quantity Y, the marginal revenue from the last unit produced and sold is MR_Y, but the price at which all Y units would be sold on the market is, from the AR curve for Y output, P_Y.

2.2 Profit-maximising equilibrium of a monopoly

The condition for profit maximisation is, as we have seen, that marginal revenue should equal marginal cost. This is true for any firm. As long as marginal revenue exceeds marginal cost, an increase in output will add more to revenues than to costs, and therefore increase profits.

2.3 Monopolist earning normal profits

Figure 5 shows a monopoly equilibrium where the AC curve touches the AR curve at a tangent, at exactly the same output level where MC = MR. Since AC = AR and AC includes normal profits, the monopolist will be earning normal profits but no supernormal profits.

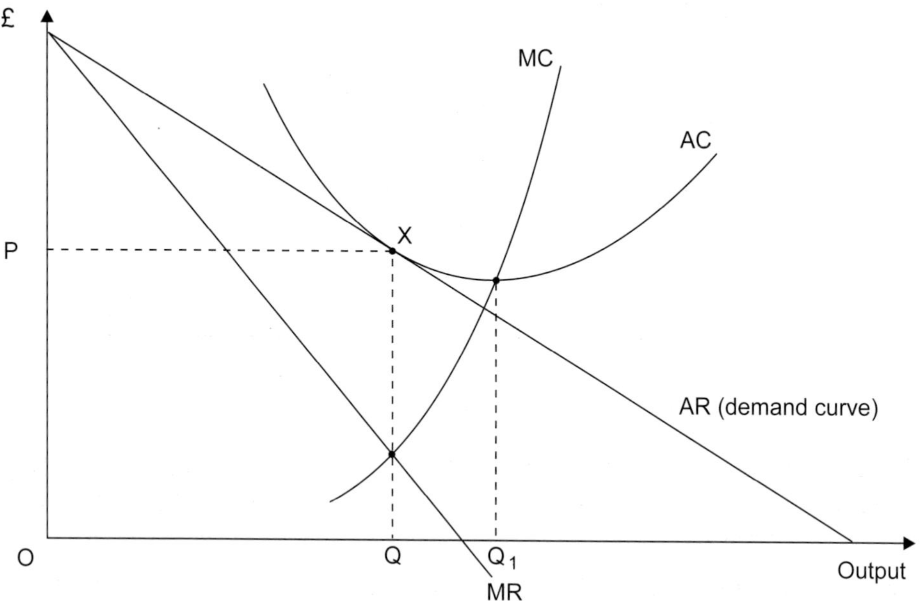

Figure 5 Equilibrium of a monopoly firm earning normal profits

In this situation, the monopoly will make a loss by producing at output higher than Q, and so it will have to produce at an output level which is well below the capacity at which its average costs are minimised (output Q_1).

Monopolies are usually able to earn 'monopoly' or supernormal profits in the **long run** as well as the short run, and the situation illustrated in Figure 5 will be **rare** for a monopoly, although (as we shall see later) it is a long-run equilibrium situation for firms in the type of market structure known as monopolistic competition.

In perfect competition, a firm should not be able to earn supernormal profits in the long run because they would be 'competed away' by new entrants to the industry. A monopoly firm can however earn **supernormal profits** in the long run as well as in the short run, because there are **barriers to entry** which prevent rivals entering the market.

2.4 Monopolist earning supernormal profits

Figure 6 shows the position of the monopolist earning supernormal profits in the short run. SMC is the short-run marginal cost curve and SAC represents short-run average costs.

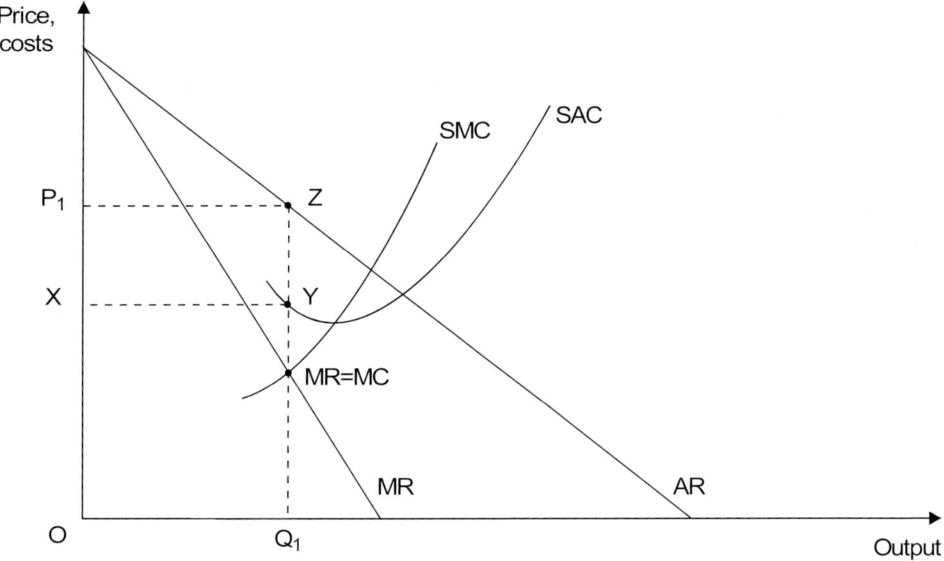

Figure 6 Monopolist's short-run equilibrium

In Figure 6, the monopolist's profit is maximised at output Q_1, where marginal cost (MC) equals marginal revenue (MR), and the price charged is the average revenue P_1. The monopolist is earning supernormal profits represented by the rectangular area P_1 ZYX.

The monopolist will charge a higher price than a perfectly competitive firm, and produce less output. The output of the monopolist will be at a level where AC is not at a minimum.

2.5 Consumer surplus and deadweight loss

If we superimpose the perfect competition demand curve on Figure 6 we can see a further potential effect of monopoly on economic welfare.

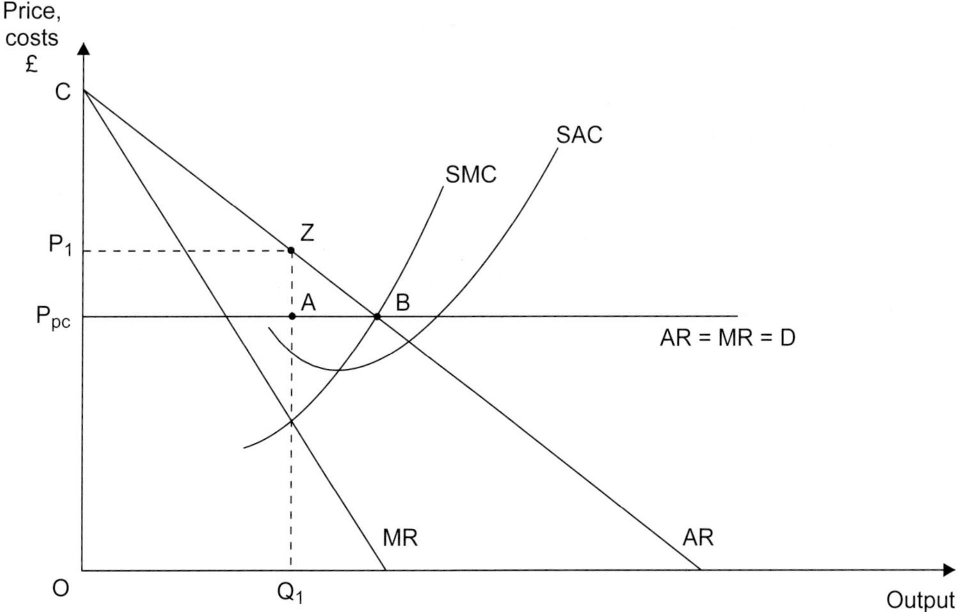

Figure 7 Consumer surplus and dead weight loss

Under perfect competition, the area CBP_{pc} would constitute consumer surplus. Under monopoly, with price P_1 being charged, this is reduced to CZP_1. Part of the consumer surplus has been transformed into super normal profit.

The small triangular area ZBA is called the **dead weight loss** due to monopoly, since it is a benefit totally lost.

3 More about monopoly

3.1 Price discrimination

Price discrimination occurs when a firm sells the same product at different prices in different markets.

Question

Price discrimination

You are likely to have encountered examples of price discrimination in practice. Can you recall any?

Answer

You might have thought of:

- Telephone calls (different prices for peak and off-peak calls)
- Rail travel (there are many different tickets you can buy for an identical journey)
- Package holidays (more expensive during school holidays)

Three basic conditions are necessary for price discrimination to be effective and profitable

(a) The seller must be able to **control the supply of the product**. Clearly, this will apply under monopoly conditions. The monopoly seller has control over the quantity of the product offered to a particular buyer.

(b) The seller must be able to **prevent the resale of the good** by one buyer to another. The markets must, therefore, be clearly separated so that those paying lower prices cannot resell to those paying higher prices. The ability to prevent resale tends to be associated with the character of the product, or the ability to classify buyers into readily identifiable groups. Services are less easily resold than goods while transportation costs, tariff barriers or import quotas may separate classes of buyers geographically and thus make price discrimination possible.

(c) There must be significant differences in the willingness to pay among the different classes of buyers. In effect this means that the **elasticity of demand must be different in at least two of the separate markets** so that total profits may be increased by charging different prices.

3.2 Diagrammatic explanation

We can see how the monopolist seller practising price discrimination can maximise revenue using a diagram.

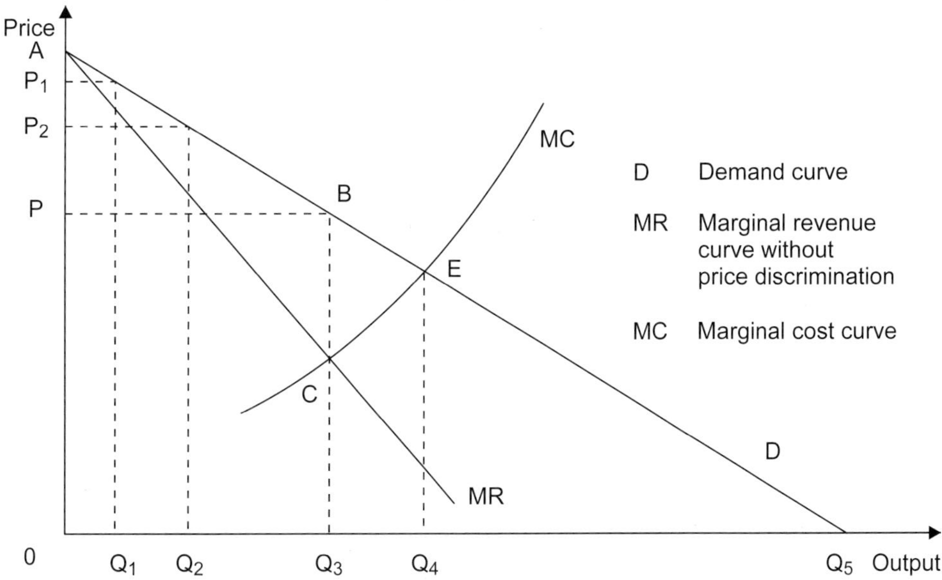

Figure 9 Price discrimination

Figure 9 demonstrates firstly the equilibrium position of a monopolist who does not discriminate. He produces at the point C where marginal cost equals marginal revenue, producing output Q_3 and selling at price P. His total revenue is given by the rectangle $OPBQ_3$.

Figure 9 also illustrates how the monopolist can improve on this position, both from the point of increased revenue and increased profits. **The discriminating monopolist does not charge the same price for all units sold.** If we assume that the monopolist can discriminate **perfectly**, then he can sell each unit for a different price as indicated on the demand curve. Thus he can sell the first unit Q_1 at the price P_1, and the second unit Q_2 at the price P_2. This follows for all units sold so that the demand curve now becomes the marginal revenue curve; each extra unit sold is sold for the price indicated on the demand curve, each previous unit being sold for the higher price relevant to that unit.

The perfectly discriminating monopolist will still maximise profits by producing at the level of output where MC = MR, but the marginal revenue curve is now the curve D, the demand curve. He thus produces at the point E where marginal cost equals the new marginal revenue, producing Q_4 units.

Recall that the total revenue for the non-discriminating monopolist by producing at the level of output was equivalent to area $OPBQ_3$. The **additional** revenue of the discriminating monopolist is represented by the areas APB plus Q_3BEQ_4. The discriminating monopolist has thus maximised his revenue (consistent of course with maximising his profit). If the monopolist did not wish to maximise profit but wished simply to maximise revenue he would expand production to the point Q_5 when his total revenue would be the area OAQ_5.

Take care not to confuse maximising revenue with maximising profit. Increasing output beyond Q_4 in the example will not increase profit as marginal costs exceed marginal revenue for each additional unit sold.

3.3 Examples of price discrimination

Various examples show that these conditions can be met and that it is possible for a monopolist to engage in price discrimination. Markets may be separated by a **time barrier**, for example where the cost of telephone calls varies according to the time of day at which they are made. Rail operating companies charge cheaper rates for off peak travel.

Holiday companies charging a higher price for a given holiday at certain times of the year is another example. These are examples of services which cannot be transferred from the cheaper to the more expensive market.

Price discrimination also occurs where it is possible to separate buyers into clearly defined **groups**. Industrial users of gas and electricity are able to purchase these fuels more cheaply than are domestic users. Similarly milk is sold more cheaply to industrial users, for example for making into cheese or ice cream, than to private households.

Question **Price discrimination**

Explain why it is possible for a railway or airline to charge different fares for passengers using the same service.

Answer

(a) **Consumers' ignorance**. Not all consumers may be aware of the availability of low-rate tickets such as lower prices for booking in advance, special offers and so on. This means that two customers on the same journey and in similar seats might pay different prices because one of the customers is unaware that a cheaper price could have been obtained.

(b) **The nature of the good**

(i) Prices can be varied according to the time of day or day of the week. Many customers will be forced to travel at peak times and pay top prices and some will switch to travelling at a cheaper time when the railway or airline has spare capacity to be filled up. Demand for journeys at peak times will be relatively inelastic, since demand will be from commuters who must travel in these periods in order to reach their workplace on time.

(ii) A cheaper rate might be offered to children. Since a child cannot transfer his ticket to an adult there is no danger that adults can buy cheaper tickets by using children to obtain tickets on their behalf.

(c) **Geographical separation of market segments**: a railway can sell cheap travel to customers travelling from say, Manchester to London, but still charge full rates to customers travelling from London to Manchester.

3.4 Are monopolies beneficial or harmful?

FAST FORWARD

Monopoly may be **beneficial** (because of economies of scale) or **harmful**. Government policies have been directed at the harmful aspects of monopoly. Rather than keeping nationalised monopolies in public ownership, the UK government has privatised them, setting up **consumer watchdog bodies** to regulate the newly privatised industries.

We have now seen two things.

(a) A monopolist is likely to produce less output but charge a higher price for it than a comparable firm operating in conditions of perfect competition, unless the monopolist can achieve economies of scale that a smaller firm could not. This leads to the monopolist earning extra profits and also a social cost or **deadweight burden** of monopoly.

(b) Monopolists can practise price discrimination.

These two points might suggest that monopolies are a bad thing. But there are economic arguments both for and against monopolies.

3.5 Arguments in favour of monopolies

A firm might need a monopoly share of the market if it is to achieve maximum economies of scale. Economies of scale mean lower unit costs, and lower marginal costs of production. The consumer is likely to benefit from these cost efficiencies through lower prices from the monopoly supplier. Economies of scale shift the firm's cost curves to the right, which means that it will maximise profits at a higher output level, and quite possibly at a **lower selling price** per unit too.

So-called **natural monopolies** exist because of a very high ratio of fixed costs to variable costs. Such a cost structure makes it very likely that significant economies of scale will exist.

Monopolies can afford to spend more on research and development, and are able to exploit innovation and technological progress much better than small firms.

Monopolies may find it easier than small firms to raise new capital on the capital markets, and so they can finance new technology and new products. This may help a country's economy to grow.

Monopolies will make large profits in the short term, but in many cases their profits will eventually encourage rival firms to break into their market, by developing rival products which might have a better design, better quality or lower price. It can therefore be argued that **temporary monopolies can stimulate competition**, and are in the longer term interests of consumers.

There is also an argument that firms which show entrepreneurial flair and innovation deserve rewarding for the risks they have taken and the new products they have made. They should therefore be rewarded by legal protection of the monopoly through the award of **patent rights**. Monopolies can spend more on research and development and will therefore tend to be innovative.

3.6 Arguments against monopolies

AST FORWARD

It may be that monopolies encourage **complacency about costs** (X-inefficiency) and may produce allocative inefficiency. Goals other than profit maximisation pursued in large companies could also result in **inefficiencies**.

Arguments against monopolies include the following.

(a) The profit-maximising output of a monopolist is likely to be at a price and output level which give it **supernormal profits**. This is a benefit for the monopoly producer at the expense of the consumer.

(b) The profit-maximising output of a monopoly is at a point where **total market output is lower and prices are higher** than they would be if there were a competitive market instead of a monopoly.

(c) **Monopolies do not use resources in the most efficient way possible**. Efficient use of resources can be defined as combining factors of production so as to minimise average unit costs. The profit-maximising output of a monopoly is not where average costs (AC) are minimised (at the lowest point of the firm's AC curve), and so monopolies are not efficient producers.

(d) Monopolists can carry out restrictive practices, such as price discrimination, to increase their supernormal profits.

(e) The higher prices and supernormal profits encourage firms in competitive markets to want to become monopolies, and they can do this by trying to create **product differentiation**, by introducing differences between their own products and the products of rival competitors. These differences might be real product design or quality differences, or imaginary differences created by a brand name and a brand image. This can be beneficial for producers, but at the expense of consumers.

(f) Because they are not threatened by competition and can earn supernormal profits, **monopolies might become slack about cost control**, so that they fail to achieve the lowest unit costs they ought to be capable of. They may also adopt a complacent attitude to innovation, instead of investing in it.

(g) Monopolies might stifle competition, by taking over smaller competitors who try to enter the market or by exploiting barriers to entry against other firms trying to enter the market.

(h) If a monopoly controls a vital resource, it might make decisions which are damaging to the public interest. This is why the government often chooses to put vital industries under state control (for example, health care, the fire service and the nuclear power industry at the time of writing).

(i) There might be diseconomies of scale in a large monopoly firm.

3.7 Barriers to entry

Key term

Barriers to entry: factors which make it difficult for suppliers to enter a market.

Barriers to entry can be classified into several groups.

(a) **Product differentiation barriers**. An existing monopolist or oligopolist would be able to exploit his position as supplier of an established product that the consumer/ customer can be persuaded to believe is better. A new entrant to the market would have to design a better product, or convince customers of the product's qualities, and this might involve spending substantial sums of money on research and development, advertising and sales promotion.

(b) **Absolute cost barriers**. These exist where an existing monopolist or oligopolist has access to cheaper raw material sources or to know-how that the new entrant would not have. This gives the existing monopolist an advantage because his input costs would be cheaper in absolute terms than those of a new entrant.

(c) **Economy of scale barriers**. These exist where the long run average cost curve for firms in the market is downward sloping, and where the minimum level of production needed to achieve the greatest economies of scale is at a high level. New entrants to the market would have to be able to achieve a substantial market share before they could gain full advantage of potential scale economies, and so the existing monopolist would be able to produce its output more cheaply.

(d) The amount of **fixed costs** that a firm would have to sustain, regardless of its market share, could be a significant entry barrier.

(e) **Legal barriers**. These are barriers where a monopoly is fully or partially protected by law. For example, there are some legal monopolies (nationalised industries perhaps) and a company's products might be protected by patent (for example computer hardware or software).

3.8 Allocative inefficiency and X-inefficiency

One of the arguments against monopolies is that they are inefficient compared with firms in conditions of perfect competition because, unlike perfectly competitive firms, they do not produce at an output level that minimises average costs. Instead, they restrict production and raise price to the level that **maximises profit**. As a result, less is produced and consumed than would be the case under perfect competition. The resources that would have been used are diverted elsewhere, to produce things that households actually want less than the monopolist's product. This implies **that monopolies are inefficient in allocating resources**. This is called **allocative inefficiency**.

A second and different criticism of monopolies is that they are wasteful of costs, and spend more than they need to. The lack of competition, perhaps, makes monopolies **complacent**, and **resources are not used with maximum efficiency**. This type of over-spending inefficiency is called **X– inefficiency**.

The difference between allocative inefficiency and X-inefficiency is illustrated in Figure 10.

(a) **Figure 10(a).** If a monopolist maximises profit at output level Q_2, there is allocative inefficiency because the firm would produce more at lower cost at output Q_1. (This diagram also illustrates **technical** (or productive) inefficiency, which exists when a firm does not achieve the lowest possible cost per unit of output.)

(b) **Figure 10(b).** If a monopolist has an average cost curve AC_1, when it ought to use resources more efficiently and have an average cost curve AC_2, there is X-inefficiency.

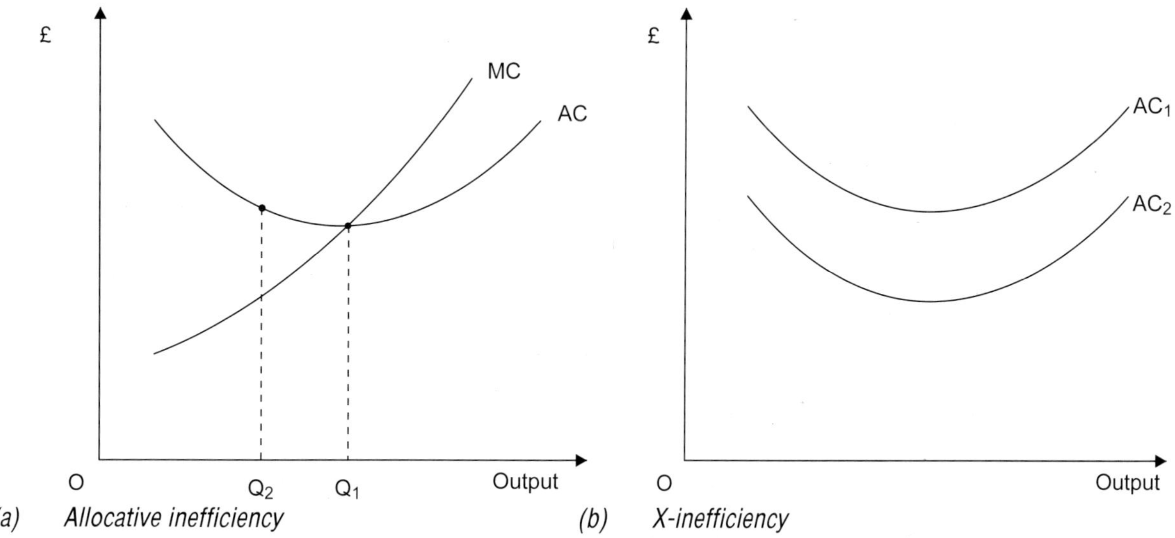

(a) Allocative inefficiency *(b) X-inefficiency*

Figure 10

All monopolies might be accused of some X-inefficiency, but there has been a view that **state owned monopolies** have a tendency to be more X-inefficient than monopolies which are private companies. This may be because they have different objectives from those of private sector organisations.

Chapter roundup

- In **perfectly competitive markets**, firms are **price takers**, and so their decisions are concerned with what output level will maximise profits. In imperfect competition, firms can influence the market price, and so their decisions are about what price to set as well as what volumes of output to produce. **Pure monopoly** is an extreme form of **imperfect competition**.
- Firms will generally try to earn **supernormal profits** if they can. Competition, though, tends to erode supernormal profits, and firms may have to be satisfied, when equilibrium is reached, with just normal profits. The ability to sustain supernormal profits depends on the nature of competition.
- **Monopoly** may be **beneficial** (because of economies of scale) or **harmful**. Government policies have been directed at the harmful aspects of monopoly. Rather than keeping nationalised monopolies in public ownership, the UK government has privatised them, setting up **consumer watchdog bodies** to regulate the newly privatised industries.
- It may be that monopolies encourage **complacency about costs** (X-inefficiency) and may produce allocative inefficiency. Goals other than profit maximisation pursued in large companies could also result in **inefficiencies**.

Quick quiz

1 In what way does monopoly differ from perfect competition?

In a monopoly:

A Products are differentiated
B Supernormal profit is possible
C There are barriers to entry
D There are economies of scale

2 How can a firm in perfect competition make supernormal profits?

3 What is price discrimination?

4 Distinguish allocative inefficiency from X-inefficiency.

5 Which of the following defines the long-run equilibrium position of a firm operating under conditions of perfect competition?

A MC = MR, AC < AR, MR < AR
B MC = MR, AC = AR, MR < AR
C MC > MR, AC = AR, MR = AR
D MC = MR, AC = AR, MR = AR

6 Selling the same good at different prices to different customers is termed:

A Monopolistic exploitation
B Protectionism
C Price discrimination
D Non-price competition

7 In the diagram the firm is currently producing at output level E. The firm will seek to:

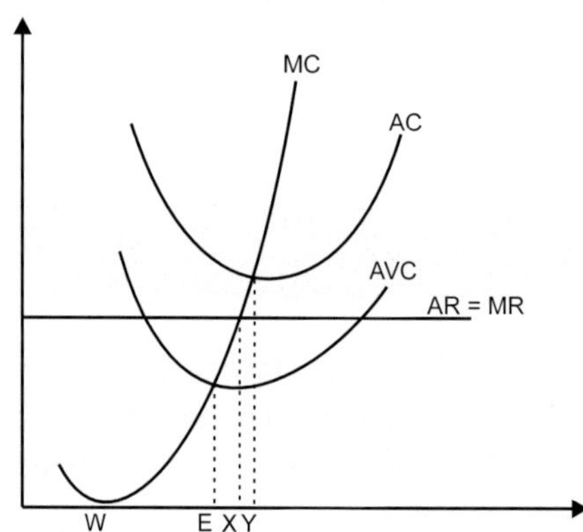

The firm will seek to:

A Leave the industry because AC > MR at all outputs and so losses are inevitable
B Increase output to point Y in order to maximise profits
C Reduce output to point W in order to maximise profits
D Increase output to point X in order to maximise profits

8 The diagram shows the cost curves and revenue curves for Hans Tordam Ltd, a firm of tulip growers. Which of the following statements is true? 1. Price P and output Q are the profit-maximising price and output levels for the firm. 2. Price P and output Q are price and output levels at which the firm makes normal profits. 3. Price P and output Q are the revenue-maximising price and output levels.

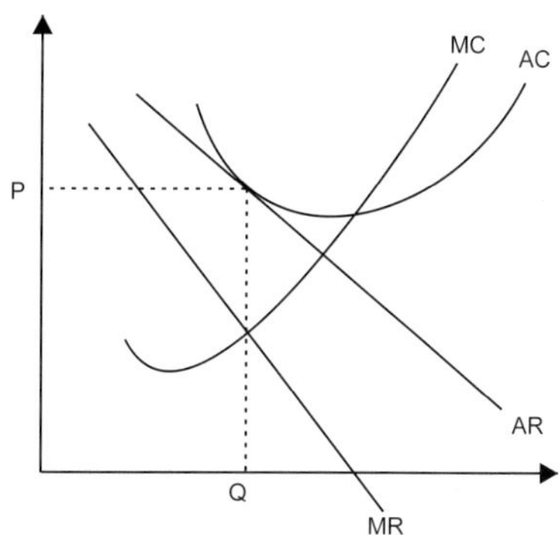

A Statement 1 only is correct
B Statements 1 and 2 only are correct
C Statements 2 and 3 only are correct
D Statements 1, 2 and 3 are correct

9 The diagram shows the revenue and cost curves for a profit-maximising monopoly firm, Lord and Masters Ltd. Which of the following statements are correct? 1. If the firm has zero marginal costs and 100% fixed costs, its profit-maximising output would be OZ; 2. At profit-maximising output OY, supernormal profits for Lord and Masters Ltd are STWX; 3. If the firm's fixed costs increased, so that the AC curve rose to a level where it is at a tangent to the AR curve at point W, it would cease to make supernormal profit.

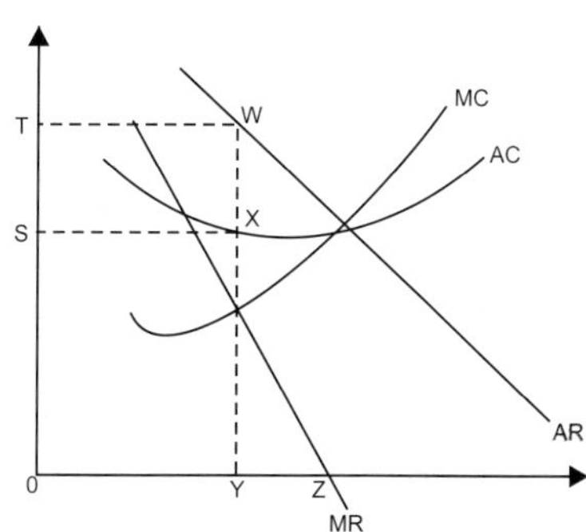

A Statements 1 and 2 are correct
B Statements 2 and 3 are correct
C Statements 1 and 3 are correct
D Statements 1, 2 and 3 are all correct

10 These diagrams show long term equilibrium under perfect competition for both the firm and the industry.

Label these diagrams.

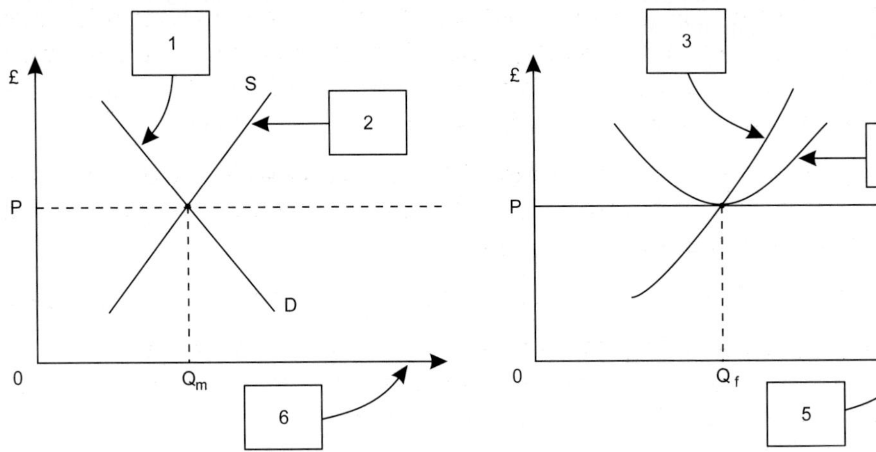

A Firm's average cost
B Output of the firm
C Market supply
D Firm's marginal cost
E Market demand
F Total industry output

Answers to quick quiz

1 C All firms produce homogenous goods under perfect competition. Under a monopoly there is only one producer so the concept of product differentiation is not applicable. Both market forms permit supernormal profit (however, only the monopoly can make supernormal profit indefinitely). Economies of scale may be possible under any market form, though they are, perhaps, less likely under perfect competition.

2 In the short run, the number of firms in the market is fixed. If the prevailing market price is above the lowest point on a firm's average total cost curve, it will make supernormal profits. This will continue until new entrants are attracted into the market and drive the market price down by increasing supply.

3 Price discrimination exists when the same product is sold at different prices in different markets or market segments.

4 A monopolist will produce at a lower level of output and therefore higher cost than a perfectly competitive firm. There is thus inefficient allocation of resources in a monopoly. X-inefficiency arises because monopolists need not control their costs in order to survive. They tend to be inefficient in their use of resources.

5 D For long run equilibrium, MC = MR = AC = AR.

6 C

7 D The firm will produce where MR = MC.

8 B 1. Profit is maximised at price P and output Q, because this is where MC = MR; 2. At this price/output level, average cost equals average revenue. Normal profit is included in cost, and so the firm is making normal profits only, but no supernormal profits; 3. Total revenue is not being maximised because this price/output level is not where MR = 0.

9 D Statement 1 is correct, because if MC = 0, profits would be maximised where MC = MR, which would be at output 0Z, where MR = 0. Statement 2 is correct. Supernormal profits per unit are the difference between AR and AC (price and average cost). This is (W – X) or (T – S). Total supernormal profits for output 0Y are therefore illustrated by area STWX. Statement 3 is probably more difficult to understand. If fixed costs increase, but variable costs remain the same, the MC curve will be unchanged, and so the profit-maximising price will still be 0T and the profit-maximising output 0Y. But if higher fixed costs have raised average costs (AC) to point W, at this price and output level AR = AC, and so there will be no supernormal profits.

10 1 E

2 C

3 D The profit maximising level of output is where marginal costs equals marginal revenue.

4 A Long-term equilibrium is at an output where average cost equals marginal cost and marginal revenue.

5 B

6 F

Now try the questions below from the Exam Question Bank

Question numbers	Page
19–21	368

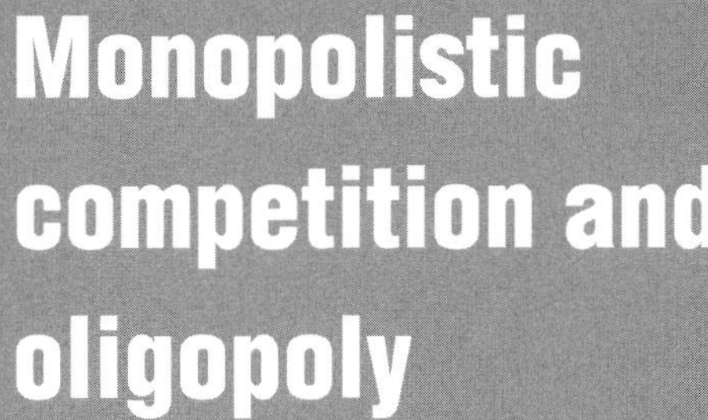

Monopolistic competition and oligopoly

7

Introduction

Economic theorists have noted that actual market structures often do not correspond with the extreme cases of perfect competition and monopoly, which we examined in Chapter 6.

This leads to the analysis of other forms of imperfect market structure, including monopolistic competition and oligopoly, which we now consider.

Topic list	Learning outcomes	Syllabus references	Ability required
1 Monopolistic competition and non-price competition	B (v)	B (6)	Comprehension
2 Oligopoly	B (v)	B (6)	Comprehension
3 Contestable markets	B (v)	B (6)	Comprehension
4 Market concentration	B (iii)	B (5)	Knowledge

1 Monopolistic competition and non-price competition

FAST FORWARD

When **price competition** is restricted, firms usually go in for other forms of competition, such as **sales promotion** and **product differentiation**.

1.1 Monopolistic competition

Key term

Monopolistic competition is a market structure in which firms' products are comparable rather than homogeneous. **Product differentiation** gives the products some market power by acting as a barrier to entry.

A firm operating in conditions of **monopolistic competition** has a downward sloping demand curve like a monopoly (the quantity of output demanded responds to the price at which the firm is prepared to sell). The downward sloping demand curve is possible because of product differentiation created by the firm. Also, unlike a monopoly firm, it is unable to utilise barriers to entry against other firms. (Indeed, the firm already competes with rivals, which can take retaliatory competitive action if the firm makes big profits.)

Firms in monopolistic competition (as well as oligopoly, which we discuss later in this chapter) will **try to avoid competition on price** in order to preserve their position as price maker. They will often resort to **non-price competition** instead, perhaps through advertising and sales promotion, or through **product differentiation**. With product differentiation, suppliers try to create differences between their products and other similar products. These differences might be real (for example, design differences) or largely imaginary and created mainly by advertising and brand image (for example, 'designer label' clothing and washing powders).

Question **Product differentiation**

See if you can think of other examples of product differentiation.

Answer

One example would be in the sale of petrol, where from time to time petrol suppliers advertise the cleanliness of their product, or give information about detergent additives.

1.2 Profit-maximising equilibrium

A firm which operates in conditions of monopolistic competition will have a **short-run** equilibrium, in which it can make **supernormal profits** and a **long-run** equilibrium in which it cannot. In the **long run**, the monopolistic competitor **cannot** earn supernormal profits since there are no **entry barriers**. Its short-run supernormal profits will be **competed away** by new entrants. As a result of competition, the demand curve will move to the left and the firm will eventually be able to achieve normal profits only.

The **short-run equilibrium** for a firm in monopolistic competition is illustrated in Figure 1 below. This is the same as the equilibrium of a monopoly firm earning supernormal profits. The firm makes supernormal profits of (P – A) × Q units, shown by the area of the rectangle PQBA.

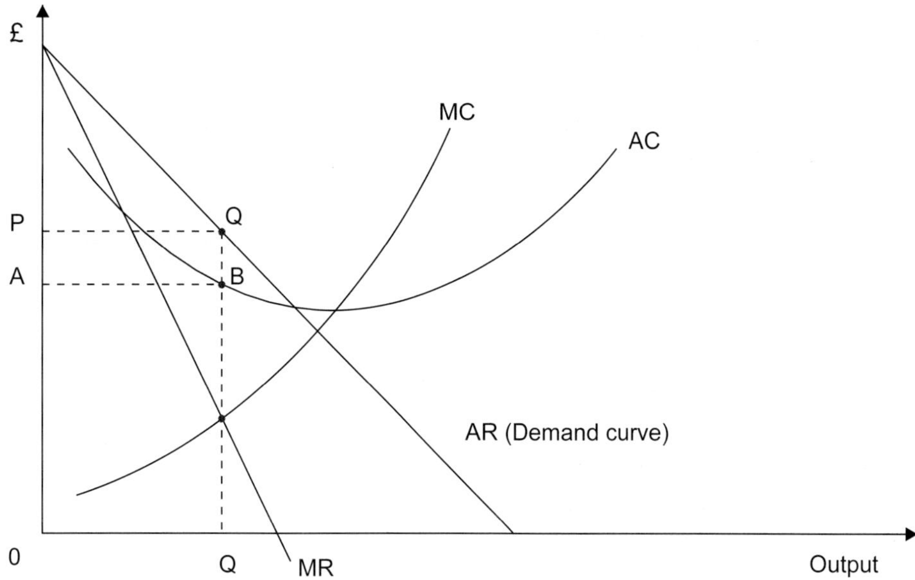

Figure 1 The short-run equilibrium of a firm in monopolistic competition

The **long-run equilibrium** for a firm in monopolistic competition is illustrated by Figure 2. This is the same as the equilibrium of a monopoly firm which earns no supernormal profits, and so normal profits only.

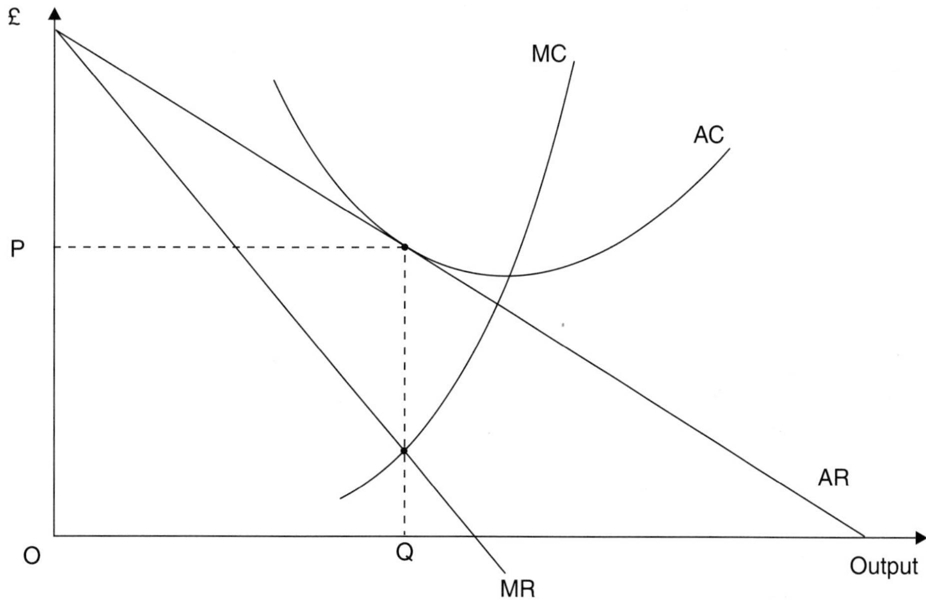

Figure 2 The long-run equilibrium of a firm in monopolistic competition

Price is higher and output lower than in perfect competition for the same reasons described earlier when comparing monopoly with perfect competition.

1.3 Implications of monopolistic competition

Because profit-maximising output is lower compared to perfect competition and is at a point where average costs are not minimised, monopolistic competition, like monopoly, is arguably more **wasteful of resources** than perfect competition.

Since firms in monopolistic competition cannot expand their output to the level of minimum average cost output without making a loss, the **excess capacity theorem** predicts that industries marked by monopolistic competition will always tend to have excess capacity. (Check this in Figure 2, where profit is maximised at output Q, and output Q is lower than the output level where AC would be minimised.)

It can be argued that it is wasteful to produce a wide variety of differentiated versions of the same product. If a single version of the same product were made, firms might be able to achieve economies of scale with large-volume production (and so shift their cost curves to the right).

Some methods that are used to create product differentiation are a waste of resources. Advertising costs are arguably an example of this, although some would argue that promotional activity actually adds utility to a product.

There is reason to argue that monopolistic competition is **not** so wasteful of resources.

(a) Some product differentiation is 'real', where there are technical differences between similar goods from rival firms. Consumers therefore have more to choose from when there is product differentiation. Their requirements are likely to be satisfied better than if there were just a single, basic, low-price good, without any choice.

(b) If product differentiation is entirely imaginary, created by brand image and advertising when the goods of rival firms are exactly the same, rational buyers should opt for the least-cost good anyway.

Question **Monopolistic competition**

Now draw a diagram yourself showing the long-run profit-maximising equilibrium of a firm in monopolistic competition.

Compare your diagram with Figure 2 in this chapter.

2 Oligopoly

FAST FORWARD

Oligopolies might collude and make a formal or informal **cartel** agreement on the price for the industry and output levels for each firm. The **kinked oligopoly demand curve** may explain why there is price stability (and non-price competition) in many oligopoly markets.

2.1 The nature of oligopoly

Key term

Oligopoly: a market structure where a few large suppliers dominate.

Oligopoly differs from **monopoly** in that there is more than one firm in the market and from **monopolistic competition** because in oligopoly the number of rival firms is small. An oligopoly consisting of only two firms is a **duopoly**.

Oligopolists may produce a homogeneous product (oil, for example) or there may be **product differentiation** (cigarettes and cars, for example).

The essence of oligopoly is that **firms' production decisions are interdependent**. One firm cannot set price and output without considering how its rivals' response will affect its own profits. How an oligopolist will actually set his output and price depends on what assumption firms make about their competitors' behaviour.

Assessment focus point

The examiner regards this **interdependence of decision making** as fundamentally important to any discussion of oligopoly.

2.2 Price cartels by oligopolist producers

A **price cartel** or **price ring** is created when a group of oligopoly firms combine to **agree** on a price at which they will sell their product to the market. The market might be willing to demand more of the product at a lower price, while the cartel agreement attempts to impose a higher price (for higher unit profits) by restricting supply to the market to a level which is consistent with the volume of demand at the price they wish to charge.

Each oligopoly firm could increase its profits if all the big firms in the market charge the same price as a monopolist would, and split the output between them. This is known as **collusion**, which can either be tacit or openly admitted.

Cartels are illegal but difficult to prevent. There might still be price leadership. This occurs when all firms realise that one of them is initiating a price change that will be of benefit to them all, and so follow the leader and change their own price in the same way.

Figure 3 shows that in a competitive market, with a market supply curve S_1 and demand curve D, the price would be P_1 and output Q_1. A cartel of producers might agree to fix the market price at P_2, higher than P_1. But to do so, the cartel must also agree to cut market supply from Q_1 to Q_2, and so fix the market supply curve at S_2.

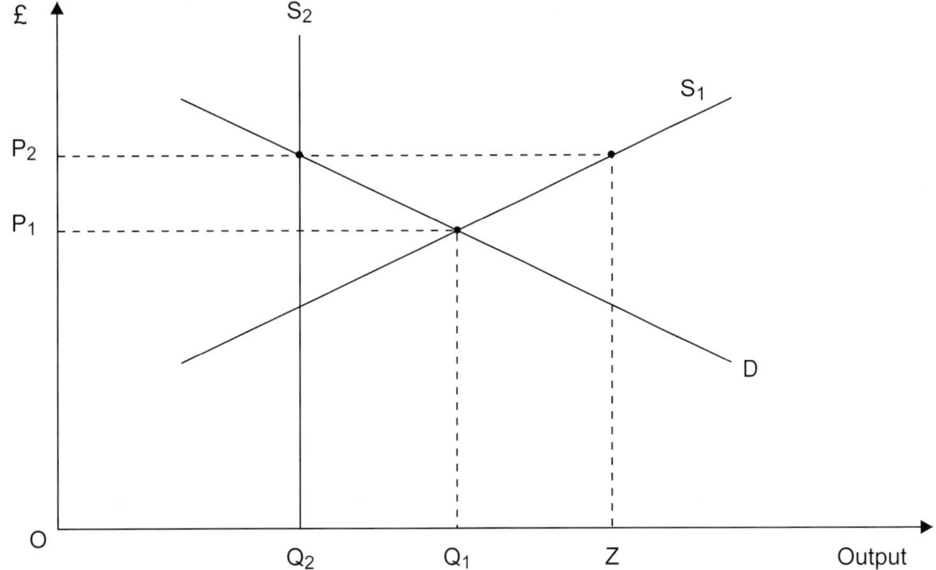

Figure 3 Price cartel

2.3 Establishing a cartel

Establishing a cartel depends on two things.

- The firms in the cartel must be able to control supply to the market.
- The firms must agree on a price and on the output each should produce.

In Figure 3, if the market price is fixed at P_2, firms would want to supply output Z in a free market. This cannot be allowed to happen; otherwise market price P_2 could not be sustained.

The main **weakness** with cartels is that each firm is still seeking the best results for itself, and so there is an incentive for an individual firm to break the cartel agreement by secretly increasing its output and selling it at the fixed cartel price. However, if all firms increased their output in this way, the cartel would collapse because the high price could not be sustained without a restricted output, and excess supply on the market would force down the price.

This has been the common experience of the oil-producing countries of the Organisation of Petroleum Exporting Countries. Attempts to agree on a restricted output quota for each country in order to push up oil prices have often broken down because some member countries exceeded their quota, or sold below the cartel's agreed price.

The **success** of a price cartel will depend on several factors.

(a) Whether it consists of most or all of the **producers** of the product.

(b) Whether or not there are **close substitutes** for the product. For example, a price cartel by taxi drivers might lead to a shift in demand for transport services to buses, cars and trains.

(c) The ease with which supply can be **regulated**. In the case of primary commodities, such as wheat, rice, tea and coffee, total supply is dependent on weather conditions and even political events in the producing country.

(d) The **price elasticity** of demand for the product. An attempt to raise prices by cutting output might result in such a large a fall in demand and such a small rise in price that the total income of producers also falls (price elasticity is greater than 1).

(e) Whether producers can agree on their **individual shares** of the total restricted supply to the market. This is often the greatest difficulty of all.

2.4 The kinked oligopoly demand curve

Price cartels do not always exist in an oligopoly market. So how does an oligopoly firm which is **competing** with rival oligopoly firms decide on its price and output level? A feature of oligopoly markets, remember, is that each firm's pricing and output decisions are influenced by what its rivals might do.

When demand conditions are stable, the major problem confronting an oligopolist in fixing his price and output is judging the response of his competitor(s) to the prices he has set. An oligopolist is faced with a downward sloping demand curve, but the nature of the demand curve is dependent on the reactions of his rivals. Any change in price will invite a competitive response. This situation is described by the **kinked oligopoly demand curve** in Figure 4, in which the oligopolist is currently charging price P, for output OQ, which is at the kink on the demand curve DD.

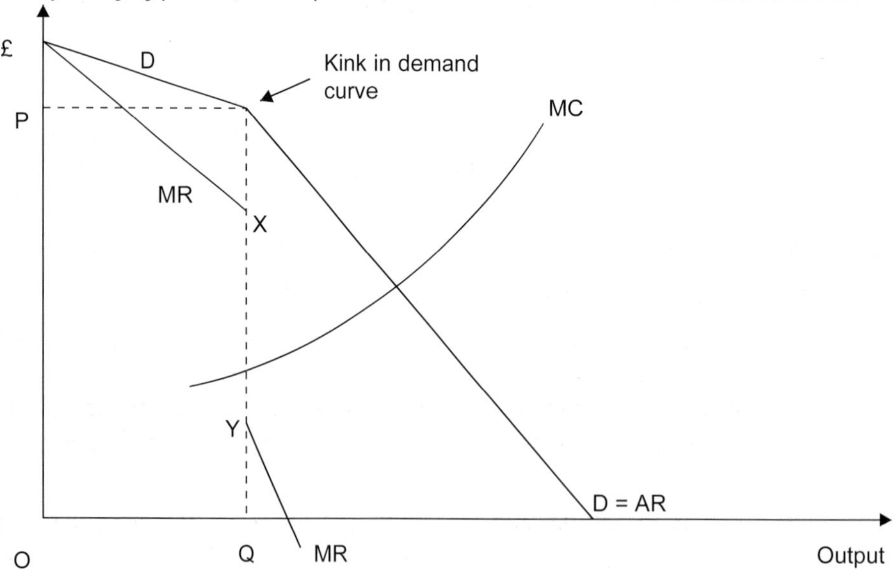

Figure 4 Kinked oligopoly demand curve

The kinked demand curve is used to explain how an oligopolist might have to **accept** price stability in the market.

(a) If the oligopolist were to **raise** his prices above P, his competitors would keep their price **lower** and so many consumers would buy from them instead. An example is the difficulty which individual petrol companies have in raising the price of petrol at garages. If competitors do not raise their prices too, the firm usually soon has to restore its prices to their previous level. The demand curve would therefore be quite **elastic** at these higher prices.

(b) If, on the other hand, the oligopolist were to **reduce** his prices below P, competitors would probably **do the same**. Total market demand might rise, but the increase in demand for the oligopolist's products would probably be quite low. Demand is thus likely to be **inelastic** at prices below P hence the kink in the demand curve.

The marginal revenue (MR) curve is **discontinuous** at the output level where there is the kink in the demand curve. The kink in the demand curve explains the nature of the marginal revenue curve MR. At price P, output OQ, the MR curve falls vertically because at higher prices the MR curve corresponds to the more elastic demand curve, and at prices below P the MR curve corresponds to the less elastic demand.

2.5 Profit maximisation

A firm maximises its profit at the point where MR = MC. The more inelastic the demand curve is below price P, the longer the discontinuous portion (XY) of the MR curve will be. There is thus a wide range of possible positions for the MC curve that produce the same profit maximising level of output.

The oligopolist's cost structure can change, with worsening or improved efficiencies, but as long as the MC curve cuts the MR curve through its vertical portion XY, the oligopolist's price and output decision should not alter. Hence, there will be price and output stability, with cost changes for the oligopoly firm, which change its MC curve, not affecting output and price.

Only if marginal costs rise far enough for the MC curve to pass through the MR curve above point X in Figure 4 is there a case for raising price, and only if MC falls far enough to pass through the MR curve below point Y is there a case for lowering price.

In general, oligopoly prices will rise only if all the firms follow the lead of a rival in raising its price, so that the AR curve shifts outwards. The kink rises to the new common price level, which is again stable. The converse holds for price falls, perhaps occurring because of technological advance.

2.6 Price leadership and price wars

In oligopoly markets there is a tendency for one firm to set the general industry price, with the other firms following suit. This is called **price leadership**. It is one source of stability in a market where there may be cartels which tend to be undercut, and price wars.

When demand conditions change, the situation becomes somewhat different and price stability might no longer exist.

(a) If total market demand falls, oligopolists might try to increase their share of the market by cutting prices.

(b) Similarly, if one oligopolist begins to lose his share of the market, he might try to restore it by cutting prices. The consequence would be a price war. In the UK in recent years there have been price wars by supermarkets and oil companies in selling petrol, for example. The effect of price wars is usually beneficial to consumers, but they are of limited duration because it is not in the interests of oligopolists to sustain them for long.

Economists sometimes model the strategies of oligopolists and market participants in other types of market structure using **game theory**, which involves examining participants' strategies according to what they stand to gain or lose from each strategy.

Question **Cartels and oligopoly**

(a) Draw a diagram to show the effect of a cartel on price and output to the market.
(b) Draw a diagram to show a kinked oligopoly demand curve.

Compare your diagrams with Figures 3 and 4 respectively in this chapter.

3 Contestable markets

FAST FORWARD

A firm in a **contestable market** in which there are close substitutes will earn normal profit only and no supernormal profit.

3.1 The theory of contestable markets

The theory of contestable markets postulates that although there might be just a **few firms** in the market, the market might operate more efficiently than an oligopoly (or monopolistic competition). In equilibrium, a firm in a **contestable market** in which there are close substitutes will earn normal profits only and no supernormal profits and produce at an output level where AC is minimised. Thus the firm will be at equilibrium MR = MC = AC = AR, just as in perfect competition. Here is an exercise to help you to refresh your memory.

Question **Long-run equilibrium**

Draw a diagram to show the long-run equilibrium position for a firm in a perfectly competitive market. Include on your diagram marginal cost (MC), average cost (AC), marginal revenue (MR) and average revenue (AR).

Compare your diagram with Figure 3(b) in Chapter 6.

Firms in contestable markets are forced into this situation because there are neither entry nor exit barriers.

If they were to be inefficient and produce at a level where AC is *not* minimised, or if they were to raise prices to earn supernormal profits, other firms would quickly enter the market knowing they could just as easily leave if supernormal profits were to be eroded by the extra competition.

Thus, the theory of contestable markets shows that **it is not necessary to have many firms supplying to a market for conditions similar to perfect competition to apply**. It is enough for the few firms in the market to know that many more firms **could** enter the market for the few firms to act in a **similar way** to firms in the **perfect competition** model.

Assessment focus point

For assessments, knowing the relevant diagrams is important. Check that you understand how the diagram is built up, and why curves slope in a particular direction.

4 Market concentration

FAST FORWARD

Market concentration is the extent to which a market is controlled by a few large firms. It can be measured by a **concentration ratio**, which only considers a few firms, or by the **Herfindahl index** and the **Gini coefficient**, both of which consider them all. The Gini coefficient is supplementary to the Lorenz curve graphical depiction of concentration.

We have shown that very large suppliers are able to exert influence over market price. The extreme case is the monopoly, but it is not necessary to achieve monopoly in order to exert market power. **Oligopolists**, whether collusive or not, are also capable of influencing market price and even when there are a large number of suppliers in a market, it is possible for the larger ones to wield **market power**.

Key terms

Market concentration is the extent to which supply to a market is provided by a small number of firms. **Industry concentration** is a similar concept, dealing with a complete industry (or group of related markets) rather than a single market.

The **degree of concentration in an industry**, and thus the potential for uncompetitive price-fixing, is of interest to both customers and suppliers and to government regulatory bodies.

4.1 Measuring market concentration

4.1.1 The market concentration ratio

A simple measure of concentration is the proportion of output (or employment, if that is easier to measure) accounted for by the largest producers: this is called the **concentration ratio**. Concentration ratios for single markets might be calculated for the top three, four or five producers.

In the UK manufacturing sector as a whole, a one hundred firm concentration ratio was measured on a constant basis from 1909 to 1992. This ratio rose from 16% in 1909 to 42% in 1975, indicating the increasing concentration of market power in the manufacturing sector. Between 1975 and 1992, the ratio fell to 33%, indicating an increase in the number of smaller manufacturing firms.

Here for example, are some UK five firm concentration ratios for 1992.

Industry	Output	Employment
Tobacco	99	98
Aerospace	73	68
Footwear	48	44
Leather goods	15	12

4.1.2 The Herfindahl index

The **Herfindahl index** reflects the degree of concentration in an entire industry by including data **on all the firms in it**, rather than just that relating to a small number of large firms. It was introduced in the USA in 1982 as a means of alerting the US Justice Department to the possible oligopolistic consequences of **proposed mergers**. The construction of the index is based on **squaring the market share percentages** of all the firms in the market; the process of squaring tends to emphasise the position of the larger firms in the market. The squares are summed to find the index. The higher the index, the less competitive and more concentrated the market is.

4.1.3 Example: Herfindahl index

Consider two industries: both have forty small firms, each with one percent of the total turnover in its market. Market A also has four slightly larger firms that each have two percent of the market and a single very large firm that controls the remaining fifty two percent of turnover. Market B is completed by five large firms, each controlling twelve percent of the market. It is reasonably clear that Market A is likely to be much less competitive than Market B. Nevertheless, the two markets' five firm concentration ratios are identical, since in both markets the top five firms have sixty percent of the total turnover.

The Herfindahl indices for the two markets are calculated as below.

Index A = $52^2 + 4(2^2) + 40(1^2) = 2704 + 16 + 40 = 2760$

Index B = $6(12^2) + 40(1^2) = 864 + 40 = 904$

The difference in size of the two indices reflects the degree of concentration in the two markets much more effectively than does the market concentration ratio.

4.1.4 Regulation and the Herfindahl index

A Herfindahl index of zero indicates perfect competition; an index of 10,000 indicates pure monopoly. When used in the USA as an **aid to the regulation of mergers and acquisitions**, potential indices below 1000 are unlikely to attract attention, while those above 1800 are unlikely to be approved if they represent an increase of more than 100 in the index. Mergers and acquisitions producing potential indices between 1000 and 1800 will only be allowed if it can be shown that there is no collusion between members and that there is easy entry to the market and freely available substitutes.

4.1.5 The Lorenz curve and Gini coefficient

The **Lorenz curve** and **Gini coefficient** are most commonly used to show the distribution of income within a population, but they may also be used to show market concentration.

4.1.6 The Lorenz curve

A Lorenz curve of market concentration would be drawn on a horizontal axis representing the cumulative percentage of the total number of firms in the industry or market, starting with the smallest, and a vertical axis showing the cumulative percentage of industry or market turnover attributable to the firms.

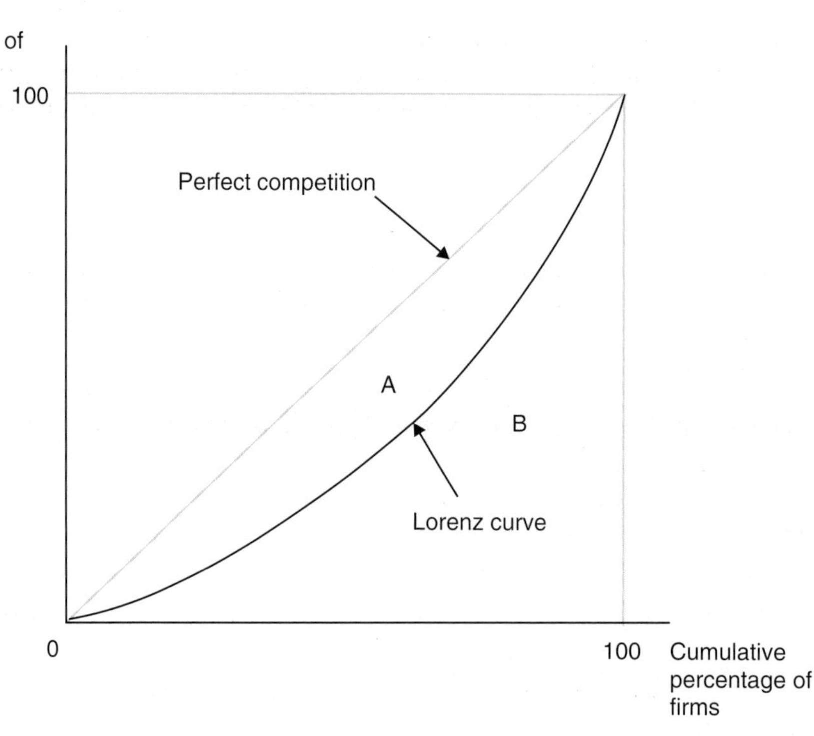

Figure 5 Lorenz curve

A straight line at forty five degrees from the origin would show perfect competition: cumulative market share increases at exactly the same rate as the cumulative number of firms, since all have the same turnover.

This, however, is unrealistic: Lorenz curves (whether showing income distribution or market concentration) typically display **increasing gradients** as the horizontal coefficient increases towards one hundred percent. This is because the smaller firms by definition, have less than an average share of the market. As the cumulative percentage increases, the larger firms come into consideration and when the firm with the exact average market share is reached, the gradient of the curve reaches forty five degrees. Larger firms are then included and since they have above average market shares, the gradient increases until the largest is reached.

4.1.7 The Gini coefficient

The construction of the Lorenz curve is such that the greater the area between the curve and the forty five degree line, the greater is the concentration in the market. The **Gini coefficient** measures the deviation of the Lorenz curve from the forty five degree line. It is the ratio of the area between the curve and the forty five degree line to the whole area below the forty five degree line. In Figure 5, this is the ratio of area A to (area A + area B). The Gini coefficient of **perfect competition** would thus be **zero**: that is to say, the Lorenz curve would not deviate from the forty five degree line, as explained above. The Gini coefficient of pure **monopoly** would be **unity**: area B would disappear completely, since the Lorenz curve would run along the horizontal axis until the one hundred percent market share point was reached and then would rise vertically. Thus, any Gini coefficient will be between zero and one: **the higher it is, the greater the degree of market concentration**.

4.2 Problems with measures of market concentration

4.2.1 Defining the market

An important problem for all measures of market concentration is the way in which the market or industry is defined, since firms tend to **specialise**; a broad definition of a market might show limited concentration, but this might conceal a high degree of market power within specialised aspects of the market. Take, for example, the market for screwdrivers: this might show up as highly competitive, with several medium sized firms trading in it. However, closer inspection might reveal that one of these firms has specialised in very long screwdrivers and has achieved a near monopoly in supplying them.

4.2.2 New entrants

The entry of a new firm into a market should reduce concentration. However, it will not affect the concentration ratio unless it immediately seizes a significant market share and it may not affect either the Lorenz curve or the Gini coefficient.

Chapter roundup

- When **price competition** is restricted, firms usually go in for other forms of competition, such as **sales promotion** and **product differentiation**.
- **Oligopolies** might collude and make a formal or informal **cartel** agreement on the price for the industry and output levels for each firm. We have seen that the **kinked oligopoly demand curve** may explain why there is price stability (and non-price competition) in many oligopoly markets.
- A firm in a **contestable market** in which there are close substitutes will earn normal profit only and no supernormal profit.
- Market concentration is the extent to which a market is controlled by a few large firms. It can be measured by a **concentration ratio**, which only considers a few firms, or by the **Herfindahl index** and the **Gini coefficient**, both of which consider them all. The Gini coefficient is supplementary to the Lorenz curve graphical depiction of concentration.

Quick quiz

1 What is meant by non-price competition?

2 What forms does product differentiation take?

3 What are the implications of the kinked oligopoly demand curve for price and output by an oligopoly firm?

4 What is meant by the term 'contestable market'?

5 Which of the following statements best describes long run equilibrium in a market where there is monopolistic competition?

A Marginal revenue equals average cost
B There is excess capacity in the industry since firms reduce average costs by expanding output
C Firms will earn supernormal profits because price exceeds marginal cost
D Price equals marginal cost, but does not equal average cost

6 Which one of the following statements about price discrimination is incorrect?

A Dumping is a form of price discrimination.
B For price discrimination to be possible, the seller must be able to control the supply of the product.
C Price discrimination is only profitable where the elasticity of demand is different in at least two of the markets.
D An example of price discrimination is the sale of first class and second class tickets on an aeroplane journey.

7 The oligopolist is *least* likely to compete through:

A Advertising
B Improving product quality
C Cutting price
D Providing incidental services as an 'add-on' to the basic good

8 This question consists of two statements. Which, if either, is correct? First statement: In conditions of *monopolistic competition,* firms will eventually reach an equilibrium output which is less than the output level at which average total cost is at a minimum. Second statement: In *perfect competition,* at the output level where marginal revenue equals marginal cost, a firm's average variable costs are minimised.

A Both statements are correct
B The first statement is correct but the second statement is false
C The first statement is false but the second statement is correct
D Both statements are false

9 Which of the following factors would weaken the long-term survival of a cartel?

A Greater price elasticity of demand for the product in the long run
B A high concentration of production in the hands of a few firms
C Substantial costs associated with entry into the industry
D Broadly similar cost structures between industry members

10 Are the following statements correct?

1 Firms operating under conditions of monopolistic competition will often engage in advertising

2 The profits of a firm operating under conditions of monopolistic competition can be increased by a shift of its average revenue curve or a fall in the elasticity of demand for the firm's product

A Both statements are correct
B The first statement is correct but the second statement is false
C The first statement is false but the second statement is correct
D Both statements are false

Answers to quick quiz

1 Non-price competition occurs when firms attempt to increase their sales by product differentiation or various forms of promotion.

2 Product differentiation can be achieved by actual differences in design or level of service. It can also be achieved by advertising and promotion, when there may be no actual material differences at all.

3 The kinked demand is a descriptive device which illustrates the tendency to stability of prices in oligopoly markets. Oligopolists avoid price competition since a price cut will be matched by competitors and produce little lasting benefit.

4 A contestable market is one in which just a few firms operate but there are no barriers to entry or exit. Firms therefore tend to operate as under perfect competition since they know that any abnormal profits will attract new entrants very rapidly.

5 B For long run equilibrium in monopolistic competition, MR = MC and AR = AC, but it is *wrong* to say that MR = AC or that AR = MC Since AR = AC, the firm does *not* earn any supernormal profits. There is excess capacity because at the profit-maximising output, average cost is not at a minimum. AC is minimised at a higher output. Since firms could produce more output at a lower AC, we would say that there is excess capacity in the industry.

6 D First and second class tickets are not an example of price discrimination, because even though they are tickets for the same aeroplane journey, they are different products - e.g. in terms of service and travel comfort - rather than the same product being sold at two or more different prices. All the other statements are true.

7 C Oligopoly is usually characterised by price stability, as illustrated by the so-called kinked oligopoly demand curve. Oligopolists are unlikely to cut prices, and are more likely to resort to *non-price competition* such as advertising and sales promotion, innovation and technical differences and incidental services.

8 B In monopolistic competition, a firm's equilibrium is where MR = MC, and this is at an output level below minimum AC. Statement 2 is false because although average *total* cost is minimised, average *variable* costs are not at a minimum and diminishing returns already apply.

9 A Few suppliers; barriers to entry and similar cost structures are prerequisites for an effective collusive oligopoly. Greater elasticity of demand for a product in the long run would affect the cartel's ability to charge a higher price whilst maintaining the same volume of sales. This would lead to firms leaving the cartel and cutting prices in order to sell more of their own production.

10 A The second statement in fact *explains* why the first statement is correct. Firms in monopolistic competition will often use advertising to try to shift their demand curve to the right, or to make demand for their product more price-inelastic (enabling them to earn bigger profits by raising prices).

Now try the questions below from the Exam Question Bank

Question numbers	Page
22 – 24	369

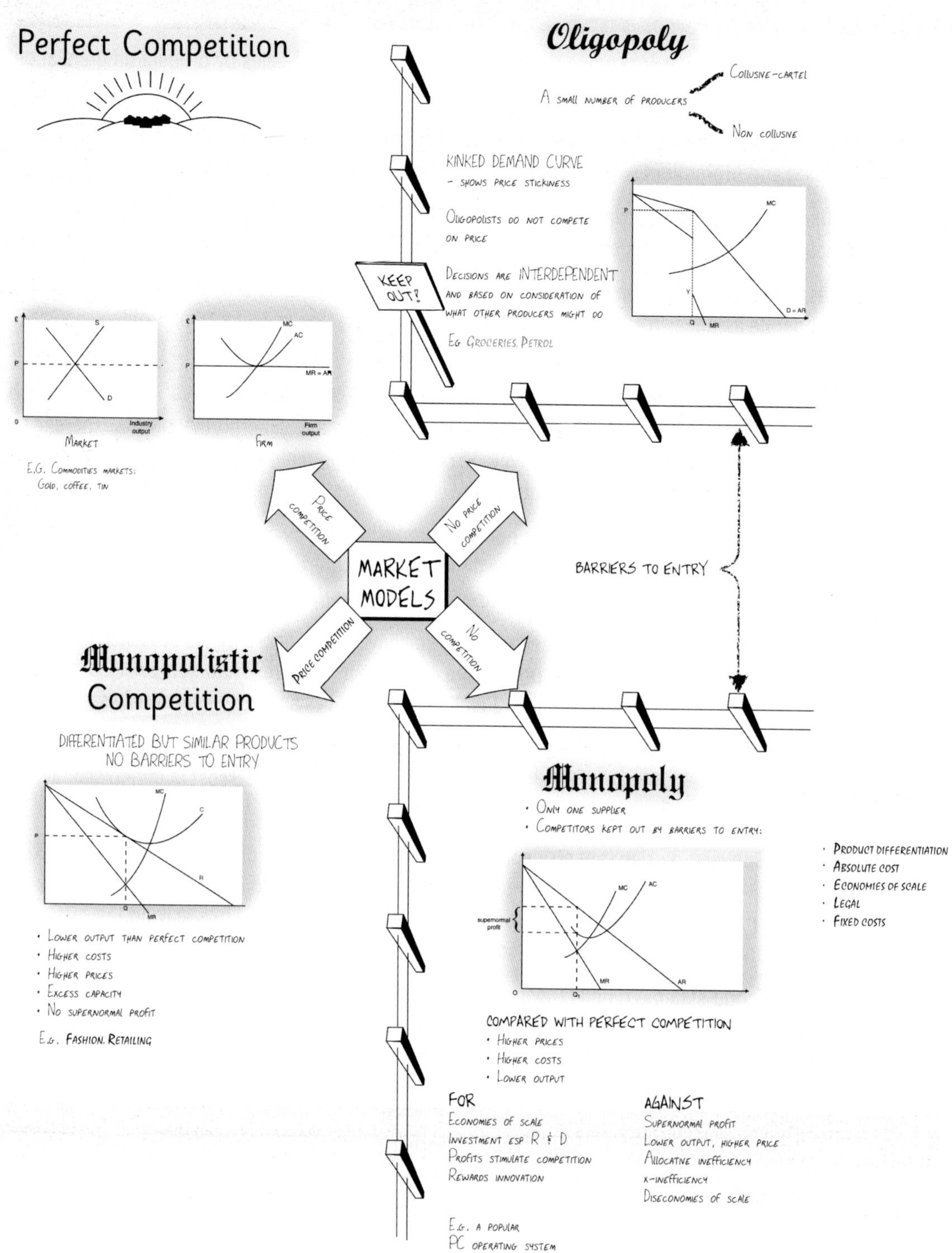

Chapter 7 Mindmap

Public policy and competition

Introduction

There is a potential role for government in the regulation of private markets where these fail to bring about an efficient use of resources.

We now examine this role of government in relation to monopolies and other aspects of competition.

Since monopolies have both economic disadvantages and economic advantages, there are reasons why a government might wish either to restrict or to encourage the development of private enterprise monopolies within its country.

Topic list	Learning outcomes	Syllabus references	Ability required
1 Government regulation and privatisation	–	B (11)	–
2 Public policy towards monopolies	–	B (6)	–

1 Government regulation and privatisation

1.1 Market failure and regulation

FAST FORWARD

Market failure is said to occur when the market mechanism fails to result in economic efficiency, and therefore the outcome is sub-optimal.

In response to the existence of market failure, and as an alternative to taxation and public provision of production, the state often resorts to **regulation of economic activity** in a variety of ways. Of the various forms of market failure, the following are the cases where regulation of markets can often be the most appropriate policy response.

Market failure	Regulation
Imperfect competition	Where monopoly power is leading to inefficiency, the state will intervene through controls on, say, prices or profits in order to try to reduce the effects of the monopoly.
Externalities	A possible means of dealing with the problem of external costs and benefits is via some form of regulation. Regulations might include, for example, controls on emissions of pollutants, restrictions on car use in urban areas, the banning of smoking in public buildings, compulsory car insurance and compulsory education.
Imperfect information	Regulation is often the best form of government action whenever informational inadequacies are undermining the efficient operation of private markets. This is particularly so when consumer choice is being distorted. Examples here would include legally enforced product quality/safety standards, consumer protection legislation, the provision of job centres and other means of improving information flows in the labour market and so on.
Equity	The government may also resort to regulation for social reasons. For example, legislation to prevent racial and/or sexual discrimination in the labour market; regulation to ensure equal access to goods such as health care, education and housing; minimum wage regulations and equal pay legislation.

1.2 Types of regulation

Regulation can be defined as any form of state interference with the operation of the free market. This could involve regulating demand, supply, price, profit, quantity, quality, entry, exit, information, technology, or any other aspect of production and consumption in the market.

1.3 Self-regulation

Bear in mind that in many markets the participants (especially the firms) may decide to maintain a system of voluntary self-regulation, possibly in order to try to avert the imposition of government controls. Self-regulation often exists in the professions (eg the Law Society, the Chartered Institute of Management Accountants, the British Medical Association and other professional bodies).

1.4 Costs of regulation

Potential costs of regulation

(a) **Enforcement costs**. Direct costs of enforcement include the setting up and running of the regulatory agencies. Indirect costs are those incurred by those regulated in conforming to the restrictions. These requirements will add to the firms' costs of production and ultimately to their prices.

(b) **Regulatory capture** refers to the process by which the regulator becomes dominated and controlled by the regulated firms, such that it acts increasingly in the latter's interests, rather than those of consumers. This is a phenomenon which has been observed in the USA.

(c) **Unintended consequences of regulation.** Firms will not react passively to regulatory constraints on their behaviour; they will instead try to limit their effectiveness. In general, theory and observation suggest that firms will substitute away from the regulated activity towards those which are less constrained or completely unregulated.

1.5 Deregulation

Deregulation can be defined as the removal or weakening of any form of statutory (or voluntary) regulation of free market activity. Deregulation allows free market forces more scope to determine the outcome.

There was a shift in policy in the 1980s in the UK and in the USA towards greater deregulation of markets, in the belief that this would improve efficiency. Indeed, many politicians and commentators believed that it was over-regulation of British industry that was largely responsible for Britain's comparatively uncompetitive and inefficient performance.

A rational assessment of deregulation should weigh the potential **social** benefits against the **social** costs. If there will be a net gain to society, we can say that the deregulation should proceed. It would be simplistic to contend that **all** regulation is detrimental to the economy. As we have seen, where there is a clear case of market failure, then state regulation may be required.

1.6 Advantages and disadvantages of deregulation

Deregulation measures, whose main aim is to introduce more competition into an industry by removing statutory or other entry barriers, are also known as **liberalisation**. The benefits of liberalising an industry include the following.

(a) **Improved incentives for internal/cost efficiency**. Greater competition compels managers to try harder to keep down costs.

(b) **Improved allocative efficiency**. Competition keeps down prices closer to marginal cost, and firms therefore produce closer to the socially optimal output level.

In some industries, liberalisation could have certain disadvantages.

(a) **Loss of economies of scale**. If increased competition means that each firm produces less output on a smaller scale, unit costs will be higher.

(b) **Lower quality or quantity of service**. The need to reduce costs may lead firms to reduce quality or eliminate unprofitable but socially valuable services.

(c) **Need to protect competition**. It may be necessary to **implement** a regulatory regime to protect competition where inherent forces have a tendency to eliminate it, for example if there is a dominant firm already in the industry, such as BT in telecommunications. In this type of situation, effective regulation for competition will be required, ie regulatory measures aimed at maintaining competitive pressures, whether existing or potential.

1.7 Deregulation and liberalisation in the UK

In the UK, deregulation and liberalisation have taken place in the areas of financial markets, broadcasting, transport and the professions.

(a) **The 1986 'Big Bang' in the Stock Exchange** abolished the old system of separate jobbers and brokers, and fixed brokerage commissions. Barriers to the entry of new firms were also lifted. One result of this was the merging of many broking and jobbing firms in the City into larger groupings, owned in most cases by 'outside' financial institutions.

(b) The Cable and Broadcasting Act (1984) laid the groundwork for both **cable and direct satellite broadcasting** to develop, in competition with the existing over-the-air BBC and ITV transmissions.

(c) Liberalisation of **road passenger transport** – both buses (stage services) and coaches (express services) – was brought about by the Transport Acts of 1980 and 1985. There is now effective free entry into both markets (except in London).

(d) The monopoly position enjoyed by some **professions** has been removed; for example, in opticians' supply of spectacles and solicitors' monopoly over house conveyancing. In addition, the controls on advertising by professionals have been loosened.

A further instance of liberalisation was the introduction of **compulsory competitive tendering** into public sector organisations. Both local authorities (eg refuse collection, office cleaning and management of leisure facilities) and health authorities (eg hospital cleaning, laundry and catering) have had to contract out the supply of these services, where private sector firms have offered to provide the services at a lower price than their own internal producers.

1.8 Privatisation and denationalisation

Key term

Privatisation the transfer by government of state owned activities to the private sector.

Privatisation as originally envisaged takes three broad forms.

(a) The **deregulation of industries**, to allow private firms to compete against state owned businesses where they were not allowed to compete before (for example, deregulation of bus and coach services; deregulation of postal services).

(b) **Contracting out** work to private firms, where the work was previously done by government employees – for example, refuse collection or hospital laundry work.

(c) **Transferring the ownership of assets** from the state to private shareholders, for example the denationalisation of British Gas, BT and many other enterprises.

The UK government, like many other governments of developed countries, has carried out a policy of denationalisation. British Gas, BT, the regional water authorities and much of the electricity industry have been among the enterprises which have been privatised. Many of the utility industries which have been privatised are still subject to regulations, for example limiting price increases to the rate of retail price inflation (RPI) minus a specified percentage.

The Private Finance Initiative

A fourth type of privatisation has been established in the UK in recent years. The **Private Finance Initiative** (PFI) enlists private sector **capital** and **management expertise** to provide public services at reduced cost to the public sector budget. The capital aspect of the scheme has been particularly welcome to government as it allows for expansion of public services without an increase in the Public Sector Net Cash Requirement.

A typical PFI contract would involve a consortium of private companies that undertakes to design, build, manage and finance a facility such as a school or hospital over a thirty year period. The consortium accepts the **risk** of the project and takes its **returns** in the form of **periodic fees**. Because they usually involve the provision of services, PFI contracts tend to be very complex in order to ensure that performance standards are rigorously defined.

Claimed advantages of PFI

(a) Government is able to finance improved provision of goods and services for the public without increasing its borrowing.

(b) Risks are transferred to the private sector.

Criticisms of PFI

(a) Public projects will be more expensive because a private company cannot borrow as cheaply as the government.

(b) There is no real transfer of risk, as the government will be forced to support projects that suffer financial failure.

1.9 For and against privatisation generally

The following are **possible advantages of privatisation**.

(a) Privatised companies may be **more efficient**.

(b) Denationalisation provides an immediate **source of money** for the government.

(c) Privatisation **reduces bureaucratic and political meddling** in the industries concerned.

(d) Privatised companies may have a **more flexible** and **profit-oriented management culture**.

(e) There is a view that **wider share ownership** should be encouraged. Denationalisation is one method of creating wider share ownership, as the sale of BT, British Gas and some other nationalised industries have shown in the UK.

There are arguments against privatisation too.

(a) State owned industries are more likely to respond to the **public interest**, ahead of the profit motive. For example, state owned industries are more likely to cross-subsidise unprofitable operations from profitable ones; for example the Post Office will continue to deliver letters to the isles of Scotland even though the service might be very unprofitable.

(b) Encouraging private competition to state-run industries might be inadvisable where **significant economies of scale** can be achieved by monopoly operations.

(c) Government can **provide capital more cheaply** than the market to industries whose earning potential is low, but which are deemed to be of strategic importance, such as aircraft manufacture. Opponents of this idea suggest that the very idea of a strategic industry is spurious.

(d) State-owned industries can be run in a way that **protects employment**, as was the case in the UK coal industry, for instance. The problem with this is that the taxpayer is effectively **subsidising technical inefficiency**.

(e) Surpluses from state-run industries can be used for **public welfare** rather than private wealth. The problem here is that points (a) and (d) above tend to preclude the creation of surpluses.

1.10 Privatisation, efficiency and competition

The inefficiency associated with state monopolies was discussed earlier and could be said to be of three types.

(a) **Technical inefficiency**. A firm is technically efficient when it uses the **least-cost combination of productive resources** for a given level of output. Failure to do this leads to its not operating at the lowest possible cost per unit of output. This is also known as **productive** inefficiency.

(b) **Allocative inefficiency**. Secondly, there is allocative inefficiency where price is higher than marginal cost such that the good or service is under-produced and under-consumed.

(c) **X-inefficiency**. The monopolist's privileged position relieves it of the need to exert constant effort to keep costs down. The resulting rise in costs is called x-inefficiency.

The contention that privatisation will lead to efficiency improvements is based on a number of assumptions. The most important assumption is that privatisation will place the industry in a market subject to **competitive pressures** approaching the perfectly competitive ideal. In practice, however, there are few examples of perfectly competitive markets and the likelihood is of restricted competition between a small number of large firms, with a degree of inefficiency persisting. If there are no legal restrictions, it is also possible that state monopolies will merely become private monopolies with even less regard than before for the consumer.

Another assumption of the analysis is that there are no economies of scale. Where there are significant economies of scale there *may* be a **natural monopoly**, with room in the market for one firm only, and monopoly may be productively more efficient than a market with competing firms.

It is believed that **management and working practices** will be changed under private sector control. Management will become largely free of interference from the government, working practices should become more efficient and trade union power may be reduced.

It is claimed that with the central objective of profit maximisation, privatised firms will be **responsive to the wants of consumers** as revealed by market research and signalled by the operation of the price mechanism. The profit objective induces firms to innovate and to seek out new markets, a process which promotes the efficient allocation of resources.

Where privatisation increases competition, the **greater competition** is likely to make firms produce output more cheaply and to sell it at a lower price. Nationalised organisations have often acted as monopolists, with the consequences of higher prices and lower output characteristic of non-competitive markets.

1.11 Privatisation in practice

In the UK, there has been only a **limited** increase in competition following some privatisations. Indeed, some organisations have been sold as monopolies to increase their attractiveness to shareholders. The example of BT can be used to illustrate the attempt to encourage **competition** along with privatisation. Firstly, BT's pricing is regulated by a 'Retail Prices Index minus *x* percent' formula. Secondly, a relatively small competitor, Mercury, a subsidiary of Cable and Wireless, was licensed to compete for part of BT's activities. However, these were relatively **minor restrictions** on a company with great market power (although since the mid-1990s, new operators have been entering as competitors in the market). The alternative strategy adopted in the USA for the telecommunications giant AT&T was to break down its operations into smaller units which could compete with one another.

Privatisation alone is often not sufficient to **improve** the **performance** of a monopoly and other steps may need to be taken to increase competition. On the other hand, improvements to the competitive environment might equally be achieved without privatisation.

Public provision of education

What economic arguments could be used to justify the public provision of education?

Answer

Education is widely considered to be a merit good, that is, a good judged to be desirable for people to consume or to receive, regardless of their income. There are various moral and political grounds on which education could be judged as desirable. However, here we are concerned with economic arguments. Arguments for the public provision of education may focus on the desirability of education, or alternatively on its provision by the public sector rather than by the private sector. Below, we look first at economic arguments in favour of education in general before considering arguments specifically in favour of its public provision as compared with private provision.

Economic benefits of education

Basic literacy and numeracy are requirements for a wide range of productive tasks, while at higher levels of skill vocational education helps individuals acquire the competence necessary for specific job roles. The existence of widespread illiteracy and innumeracy in the population necessarily diminishes the prospect of economic growth. Third world countries, in particular, are aware of the difficulties of poor education: it may be impossible to train enough people to cope with new technology, because of their inability to read or manipulate simple numbers.

How should education be provided?

It might be argued that since education equips labour with appropriate skills, then it should be provided by employers. However, although many employers do provide 'on-the-job' training and education to employees, it is not practicable for them to make full educational provision for individuals. This is because most education needs to take place before adulthood when people enter employment and in the case of employees the benefit to employers of providing education is limited by the problem that individuals may leave the employer soon after the education is provided, a problem which often inhibits the provision of any training by employers.

Where employers provide education to employees, there is an externality effect since the education provided may benefit the wider economy. Such benefits will be evident when the employees move to other employment and use their skills more widely. (It is also arguable that more education raises productivity (output per worker) not just for the individual involved but for other workers with whom this individual co-operates.)

Given such externality effects, and given the wider moral or political arguments in favour of education, society should encourage the provision of education if individuals are likely to demand too little of it. They may demand too little because they do not take full account of the social benefits (externality effects) of their receiving education or because they do not take full account of the private benefits to themselves. One way to achieve this is the public provision of free schooling to ensure a minimum level of education and socialisation.

Types of public provision

It is important however to note that a government can ensure the provision of minimum levels of education in different ways. In particular, it is not necessary for the education to be provided by government-run organisations. As with many other activities within government's responsibility, such as refuse collection and road building, it could be 'contracted out' to private sector organisations. 'Vouchers' could be issued for all individuals of school age, which parents could use at the recognised school of their choice, whether in the private or public sector. The school would then redeem the voucher with the government, which would pay the individual's fees. As at present, some regulation would be necessary to ensure that all children are schooled – in other words, to ensure that parents 'spend' their vouchers. Alternatively, government could fund individual places at private sector schools.

2 Public policy towards monopolies

FAST FORWARD

You should understand the various arguments in favour of **public (or 'nationalised') ownership of production** concerning public goods, merit goods and natural monopoly. You should also be aware of the **efficiency arguments** against public ownership.

2.1 Public policy towards monopolies

Monopolies might be harmful or beneficial to the public interest.

(a) A beneficial monopoly is one that succeeds in achieving economies of scale in an industry where the minimum efficiency scale is at a level of production that would mean having to achieve a large share of the total market supply.

(b) A monopoly would be detrimental to the public interest if cost efficiencies are not achieved. *Oliver Williamson* suggested that monopolies might be inefficient if 'market power provides the firm with the opportunity to pursue a variety of other-than-profit objectives'. For example, managers might instead try to maximise sales, or try to maximise their own prestige.

2.2 Methods of government control

There are several different ways in which a government can attempt to control monopolies.

(a) It can stop them from developing, or it can break them up once they have been created. Preventing monopolies from being created is the reason why a government might have a public policy on mergers.

(b) It can take them over. Nationalised industries are often government-run monopolies, and central and/or local government also have virtual monopolies in the supply of other services, such as health, the police, education and social services. Government-run monopolies are **potentially advantageous.**

    (i) They need not have a profit-maximising objective so that the government can decide whether or not to supply a good or service to a household on grounds other than cost or profit.

    (ii) The government can regulate the quality of the good or service provided more easily than if the industry were operated by private firms.

    (iii) Key industries can be protected (for example health, education).

(c) It can allow monopolies or oligopolies (firms with few competitors) to operate, but try to control their activities in order to protect the consumer. For example, it can try to prohibit the worst forms of restrictive practice, such as price cartels. Or it may set up regulatory 'consumer watchdog' bodies to protect consumers' interests where conditions of natural monopoly apply, as in the recently privatised utility industries of the UK.

Control over markets can arise by firms eliminating the opposition, either by merging with or taking over rivals or stopping other firms from entering the market. When a single firm controls a big enough share of the market it can begin to behave as a monopolist even though its market share is below 100%.

Several firms could behave as monopolists by agreeing with each other not to compete. This could be done in a variety of ways – for example by exchanging information, by setting common prices or by splitting up the market into geographical areas and operating only within allocated boundaries.

In a perfect monopoly, there is only one firm that is the sole producer of a good that has no closely competing substitutes, so that the firm controls the supply of the good to the market. The definition of a monopoly in practice is wider than this, because governments seeking to control the growth of monopoly firms will probably choose to regard any firm that acquires a certain share of the market as a potential monopolist.

2.3 The Competition Commission in the UK

sessment cus point

Although the Competition Commission is specific to the UK, questions could be set on it in relation to public control of monopolies and mergers.

The Director General of Fair Trading may ask the Competition Commission (CC) to investigate if any firm or group of firms controls 25% or more of the market, or the Secretary of State may do the same if any proposed takeover or merger would create a firm that controlled 25% or more of the market. The CC may also investigate proposed mergers where the assets involved exceed £70 million in value. The Commission will then investigate the proposed merger or takeover and recommend whether or not it should be allowed to proceed.

The **public interest** includes the promotion of competition and the extension of consumer sovereignty, efficiency and enterprise.

The **interpretation** of the public interest leads to conflicts in many cases. For example, actions which enhance competition and consumer sovereignty may conflict with the objective of allowing firms to be large enough to take advantage of competitive conditions in the international economy.

(a) The CC may agree to a merger, but set conditions which are designed to protect consumers, or it may require that some assets be sold by the merged enterprise in order to prevent a dominant market position being established in a particular area of its operations.

(b) The CC will consider whether any **excessive profits** have been made. In the *Roche Products* case for example, a return on capital of 70% was deemed to be evidence of **excessive pricing.** In another case, *Pedigree Petfoods*, 44% was held to be **not excessive**.

(c) The CC will also see whether there is on the face of it a **high degree of interdependence** between a small number of firms. This evidence could be in the form of parallel pricing, predatory pricing or price discriminating policies, sometime prevalent in oligopolies in which there are say only four or five firms.

(d) A firm carrying out 'anti-competitive' practices will not be favoured. An example of this could be 'socially unproductive advertising', where firms in a dominant position have huge advertising spends with the objective of building a barrier over which firms unable to spend a lot on advertising cannot climb. If the merger involves any anti-competitive **distribution policies** such as single supplier agreements, it could be opposed.

(e) The CC will wish to avoid splitting up large companies, thus depriving them of economies of sale. The CC may also throw out applications if they could aggravate unemployment in an area in which unemployment is already significantly high.

(f) The CC will be mindful to protect the needs of merging firms to secure adequate returns for enterprise, risk taking, innovation, improved efficiency research and development, and the need to compete with multinational firms on a global scale. Supernormal profits will not in themselves be a reason to refer merger proposals.

The conflicts between objectives present one problem for the CC, while another problem is that governments may be motivated by other political and economic considerations in deciding whether to adopt CC recommendations.

2.4 Enterprise Act 2002

The Enterprise Act 2002 includes provisions to reform UK competition law.

Under this Act, criminal sanctions for operating a cartel are introduced with a maximum penalty of five years in prison for those found guilty of dishonestly operating deliberate agreements to fix prices, share markets, limit production and rig bids.

Chapter roundup

- **Market failure** is said to occur when the market mechanism fails to result in economic efficiency, and therefore the outcome is sub-optimal.
- You should understand the various arguments in favour of **public (or 'nationalised') ownership of production** concerning public goods, merit goods and natural monopoly. You should also be aware of the **efficiency arguments** against public ownership.

Quick quiz

1 In what circumstances might government regulation of markets have an economic justification?

2 What different forms can privatisation take?

3 Why might a government wish to control monopolies?

4 How might a government be able to control monopolies?

5 What cases may the Competition Commission investigate?

6 Which one of the following statements is incorrect?

A If the effect of privatisation is to increase competition, the effect might be to reduce or eliminate allocative inefficiency

B Privatisation means selling off nationalised industries by the government to the private sector

C The effect of denationalisation could be to make firms more cost-conscious, because they will be under the scrutiny of stock market investors

D The government might appoint consumer watchdogs to regulate privatised industries

Answers to quick quiz

1 The undesirable effects of various forms of market failure can be reduced by government action. Monopoly power can be attacked by regulation of price or profit or even the break-up of the monopoly firm. Externalities can be reduced by bans on some forms of behaviour, such as dangerous pollution, and by levying taxes on others such as the consumption of alcohol. Where imperfect information distorts consumer choice, legally enforceable product standards and disclosure requirements can improve the operation of the market. Finally, governments may intervene for social and political reasons, banning racial discrimination and enforcing a minimum wage, for example.

2 Privatisation can take three forms.

- Deregulation allows private firms to compete against state owned organisations.
- Work done by government employees may be contracted out.
- State owned businesses may be sold to private shareholders.

3 There are arguments both for and against monopolies. Monopolies are detrimental to the public interest when they are inefficient in their allocation of resources and their operations generally. They may also be objected too on the grounds that they obtain higher prices, and hence profits, than would be possible under competition; and they restrict choice.

4 Governments can regulate monopolies, particularly their prices and the quality of their goods and services; prevent them from developing; break them up; or take them into public ownership.

5 The Director General of Fair Trading may ask the Competition Commission (CC) to investigate if any firm or group of firms controls 25% or more of the market, or the Secretary of State may do the same if any proposed takeover or merger would create a firm that controlled 25% or more of the market. The CC may also investigate proposed mergers where the assets involved exceed £70 million in value. The Commission will then investigate the proposed merger or takeover and recommend whether or not it should be allowed to proceed.

6 B Privatisation *could* mean selling off nationalised industries, but it can also refer to deregulation of industries to allow private firms to compete with state-run business (eg private bus companies) and contracting out work previously done by government employees to private firms (eg refuse collection).

Now try the questions below from the Exam Question Bank

Question numbers	Page
25, 26	370

Part C
The financial system

Finance

Introduction

A national economy depends on a vast network of economic relationships. Among the most important are those that facilitate the flow of value between households, firms and governments. In this chapter we look at the institutions that perform this function and how they do it.

Topic list	Learning outcomes	Syllabus references	Ability required
1 The flow of funds and financial intermediation	C (i)	C (1), (2), (3)	Comprehension
2 Households	C (i)	C (1), (2), (3)	Comprehension
3 Firms	C (i)	C (1), (2), (3)	Comprehension
4 Government	C (i)	C (1), (2), (3)	Comprehension
5 The flow of funds	C (ii)	C (1), (2), (3)	Comprehension
6 Financial markets	C (ii)	C (4)	Comprehension
7 The main financial intermediaries	C (ii)	C (5)	Comprehension
8 The insurance markets	C (iii)	C (9)	Comprehension

1 The flow of funds and financial intermediation

FAST FORWARD

Within an economy, some people, firms and organisations will have money which is surplus to their needs, and others will have less money than they need for their spending requirements. **Credit** involves lending money, and the transfer (usually in return for interest payments) of money from surplus units to deficit units. **Financial intermediaries**, such as banks and building societies, make the provision of credit much easier, by taking deposits from savers and re-lending to borrowers.

1.1 The flow of funds

The flow of funds is the movement of money between people or institutions in the economic system.

If we begin by ignoring imports and exports and foreign investments, we can start to build up a picture of the flow of funds by identifying three main sectors in the economy that make payments and receipts.

(a) Households and individuals or the **personal sector**

(b) Firms or the **business sector** – ie companies and other businesses

(c) Governmental organisations or the **government sector** – ie central government, local government and public corporations

Within each of these three sectors, there is a continual movement of funds, payments and receipts on a short-term, medium and long-term basis.

Key terms

The role of **financial intermediaries** such as banks and building societies in an economy is to provide means by which funds can be transferred from **surplus units** in the economy to **deficit units**. Financial intermediaries develop the facilities and **financial instruments** which make lending and borrowing possible.

2 Households

FAST FORWARD

Credit for households comes from a variety of sources including credit agreements, bank loans and mortgages.

Households and individuals receive income from employment usually on a weekly or monthly basis. This month to month cash inflow needs to finance the short term needs for food, shelter and clothing and the longer term needs of households and individuals to acquire property and provide for retirement.

Most households will attempt to spend less than their monthly earnings in order to be able to provide for medium and long term aims to acquire property and provide for retirement. However, savings alone may not be able to finance the purchase of a house as the price may account to several times a households' annual income.

In order to achieve their long term aims, eg access the property market, households will need to obtain funds from those with funds surplus to their current requirements. In order to provide for retirement households may not only save but also seek to acquire assets whose value they expect will rise faster than cash savings.

2.1 Credit

Credit for the purpose of this chapter and the next concerns **lending and borrowing money**, rather than with buying goods on **trade** credit.

The functions of credit can be seen from the point of view either of the borrower or the lender.

(a) For the borrower, the reason for borrowing money is to be able to purchase goods or services now that he might not otherwise be able to afford. The borrower wants to buy now and pay later.

(b) For the lender, the reason for lending money is that there is nothing that he now particularly wants to spend his money on, and by lending it, he can earn some interest.

2.2 Sources of credit for households

Credit for households comes from a variety of sources, including the following.

(a) **Credit agreements** allow people to borrow money for the immediate purchase of goods or services and to pay for them over an extended period of time. These agreements take a variety of forms including bank loans, overdraft facilities, credit card, trade credit, hire purchase and lease finance.

(b) **Bank loans** allow people to borrow money for the immediate purchase of goods or services and to pay for them over an extended period of time. These agreements take a variety of forms including bank loans, overdraft facilities, credit card, trade credit, hire purchase and lease finance.

(c) **Mortgages** are loans used to acquire an asset, typically property such as a house or factory. The asset is conveyed to the lender as security for the loan and ownership does not pass to the buyer until the mortgage is repaid in full.

3 Firms

A business will have receipts from several sources, which might include sales, investment income and proceeds from the disposal of fixed assets. A firm's outlays include the need to finance working capital, pay wages and salaries, rent and utility bills. For its medium long term needs the company will need to purchase long term assets such as premises, machinery and equipment.

In order to achieve profit and function as a going concern, most companies will need funding over and above the contribution by shareholders.

The need for finance for firms arises for two reasons. First, production takes place before products are sold. A firm has to finance production (labour, raw material, inventory) before any receipts accrue and therefore needs funds in the form of working capital in order to operate. This type of finance is a bridging type and is short term. A second reason for a firm to need funds is for investment purposes. Like individuals, companies that need to expand or replace their plant and equipment may need funds far in excess of the income that the company earns from its activities. These types of funds are typically long-term.

3.1 Sources of capital for companies

FAST FORWARD

A company must have **capital** to carry out its operations. Many companies start in a small way, often as family businesses, then grow to become **public companies**, which can invite the public to subscribe for shares.

New capital enables the firm to expand its activities and achieve the advantages of large-scale production.

Credit may be short-term, medium-term or long-term. The length of credit ought to match the life of the assets they finance, and should not exceed the asset's life.

(a) The amount of short-term credit taken by a firm should be limited by considerations of liquidity. The firm must have the cash to pay creditors on time, and so short-term credit should not become excessive in relation to current assets, which are short-term sources of cash.

(b) The amount of long-term credit is effectively measured by the gearing ratio, which should remain at an acceptable level.

Principal sources of short-term capital

(a) **Credit agreements** allow people to borrow money for the immediate purchase of goods or services and to pay for them over an extended period of time. These agreements take a variety of forms including bank loans, overdraft facilities, credit card, trade credit, hire purchase and lease finance.

(b) **Bank overdrafts** are loans used to acquire an asset, typically property such as a house or factory. The asset is conveyed to the lender as security for the loan and ownership does not pass to the buyer until the mortgage is repaid in full.

(c) **Bills of exchange** are a means of one business providing credit to another business for a short period, usually for 3 months. The lender makes up the bill for a specified sum payable at a future date and the borrower accepts the bill by signing it. Once the loan has been made there may be secondary trading in the bill, that is the loan will be sold on to a third party. The bill will be bought from the drawer at a discount form the face value of the loan, this discount representing an interest charge on the amount owed.

(d) **Commercial Paper:** Banks and companies with good credit ratings raise funds by issuing unsecured promissory bearer notes that can be interest-bearing or discounted. These notes usually have short lives of up to 270 days.

Principal sources of long-term capital

(a) **Issued share capital**. Share capital might be in the form of ordinary shares (equity) or preference shares. Bear in mind that only the ordinary shareholders are owners of the company, and preference shares are comparatively rare.

(b) **Retained profits and other reserves**. Retained profits are profits that have been kept within the company, rather than paid out to shareholders as dividends.

(c) **Borrowing**. Companies borrow from banks and from private or institutional investors. Investors might purchase debt securities issued by the company. The company promises to repay the debt at a date in the future, and until then, pays the investors interest on the debt. Debt capital includes debentures and, for larger companies, eurobonds and commercial paper.

(d) **Venture capital**. Venture capitalists are prepared to finance risky ventures such as start ups. Because they accept a high degree of risk (with many of their ventures producing little or no return) they require a very high return from the ones that do succeed. They also require a clear exit route that allows them to realise their capital, such as a public flotation issue of shares.

(e) **Debentures and other loan stock** are long-term loans, the terms of which are set out in a debenture trust deed. Debentures issued by large companies are traded on the stock market.

(f) **Bonds** are financial securities issued by government or businesses to provide them with long-term borrowing. The bonds bear a fixed nominal (or coupon) rate of interest. The market in secondary dealings for bonds involves selling the bonds at various prices in order to keep the effective interest rate in line with current interest rates. **Eurobonds** are bonds sold outside the jurisdiction of the country in whose currency the bond is denominated.

3.2 Raising capital

If a company wants to raise new capital from sources other than retained profits, it should establish whether it needs long-term (usually meaning three years or longer) or short-term capital. Short-term capital can be obtained either by taking longer credit from suppliers, or by asking the company's bank for a short-term loan or bigger overdraft facility. Ideally, a company should use long-term finance to finance commitments with a long payback period, such as fixed assets or research and development.

Raising more long-term capital would require the issue of more share capital or more debt. The ability to raise capital by issuing new shares will depend on the status of the company. A company listed on the Stock Exchange or AIM could go to the market to raise funds. A private company would have to try to raise new share capital privately, without being able to use the institutions of an organised market place; the task for private companies is therefore much more difficult.

A large public limited company is usually in a better position to raise capital than smaller companies, private companies and non-incorporated businesses.

(a) The high standing of such companies makes investors and other creditors more willing to offer finance.

(b) There is a well established machinery for raising capital through the Stock Exchange. A share issue will be organised for a firm by an investment bank (known as an issuing house) or similar organisation.

(c) The limited liability of company shareholders usually makes large companies more willing to borrow, in contrast to small company owner-directors, sole traders and partners, who accept greater personal financial risks when they borrow large amounts of capital.

The main source of external lending to companies, both long and short-term, is the banks. New debenture (loan) stock is not often issued by companies to raise new funds because this stock must compete with government loan stock (gilts) to attract investors, and because they are higher risk, company debentures must generally offer a higher rate of interest than the interest rate on gilts, which has been very high itself in recent years.

3.3 Retained earnings

Advantages of funds generated from retained earnings

- Absence of brokerage costs
- Simplicity and flexibility
- All gains from investment will accrue to existing shareholders

Disadvantages

(a) Shareholders' expectation of dividends may present a problem, particularly for a public company quoted on the Stock Exchange.

(b) Insufficient earnings may be available.

3.4 Difficulties in raising finance

Despite the existence of various capital markets and money markets, it is not necessarily easy for firms to raise new capital, except by retaining profits. Small firms in particular find it difficult to attract investors without surrendering a measure of **control**, with the banks remaining as the major source of funds for such companies. The capital markets are dominated by institutional investors who have tended to channel their funds into safe investments such as 'blue chip' stocks and shares which are traded on the Stock Exchange main market or on the Alternative Investment Market (AIM), as well as government securities. The venture capital providers take a more adventurous approach, although it should be noted that some of the venture capital organisations have been set up by the large institutional investors.

Banks in the UK have also traditionally been thought of as conservative in their approach to finance, avoiding risky investments. However, the high number of company receiverships experienced in the economic recession of the early 1990s suggests that bankers' traditional reputation for excessive caution may have been undeserved during the late 1980s.

4 Governments

4.1 Government payments and receipts

FAST FORWARD

During any given period of time governments need to spend money on outlays of a **short**, **medium** and **long-term** nature. To pay for these outlays governments collect taxes.

4.1.1 Government payments

Governments need to spend money on a number of outlays of a current on long term nature. These can be analysed into the following categories:

(a) **Government purchases of goods and services**

This is the largest outlay and consists of expenditure on current goods and services such as

- salaries of public servants
- repairs, maintenance of public buildings

as well as long term investment on infrastructure such as building roads and hospitals.

(b) **Transfer payments**

These are payments made for which the government received no goods or services in return. Examples include

- unemployment and welfare payments
- other social security payments
- state pension

4.1.2 Government receipts

To pay for expenditure governments collect revenues, mainly taxes. There are four main types of government revenues.

(a) **Taxes on income and capital gains**

- Taxes paid by individuals
- Taxes paid by companies

(b) **Taxes on expenditure** or sales taxes whereby consumers pay a tax on their consumption of goods and services. The main sales taxes are **excise duties** on tobacco, alcohol and petrol and **value added tax**.

(c) **Social security contributions**

In the UK these are a fixed percentage of a worker's salary up to a certain ceiling and they are matched by contributions from the employer.

(d) **Other revenues**

One of the main element of this category is income from government corporations such as the Post Office. Prior to the privatisation of the late eighties and early nineties this was a higher proportion of total revenues.

4.2 Government deficits/surpluses

FAST FORWARD

The government budget deficit is the **difference** between government **expenditures** and **revenues** in any one period, normally a year referred to as a fiscal year.

Key terms

A **fiscal year** is the period over which the government revises its revenue and expenditure plans.

Government expenditure does not need to be equal to government revenues in each fiscal year.

When revenues exceed outlays there is a budget surplus. When outlays exceed revenues there is a budget deficit.

The deficit can therefore be represented as

Budget deficit = government outlays – government revenues
= government purchases (P) + transfers (TR) + net interest (INT) – government revenues (T)
= P + TR + INT – T

Financing the budget deficit

When governments spend more than they raise in taxes and therefore incur a budget deficit, they have to borrow. Governments borrow by issuing debt and in the UK, government debt is referred to as gilt edged securities. These will be discussed later.

4.3 Government deficit and government debt

FAST FORWARD

The government deficit in any one fiscal year represents the **new borrowing** that the government needs to undertake.

It is important to understand the distinction between government deficit and government debt.

The government deficit represents the excess of government spending over government revenues in any one period. As such, the government deficit is a flow concept, just like the profit and loss is a flow concept in the financial statements of a company.

In any one year, the budget deficit represents the amount of new borrowing that the government must undertake.

Therefore,

New borrowing	=	Government budget deficit
Or change in borrowing	=	Government budget deficit
Expressed as Δ ß	=	Government budget deficit

Government debt is the accumulation of government deficits over time and represents all the debt issued to fund the deficits. Since deficits in the UK are funded by issuing government bonds (known as gilts), government debt is the total outstanding amount of gilts issued.

5 The flow of funds

Having discussed the main units of the economy and the reasons why there is a demand and supply of funds to the economy, we discuss now how **surplus units** are able to transfer surplus funds to **deficit units**, and how the deficit units can raise the requisite funds,

There are two ways in which the transfer of funds takes place. First, there is the direct way, in which economic units transact directly in organised market. There are many markets that cater for all the needs of the economic units in terms of maturity or currency. A schematic approach of the flow of funds is shown as

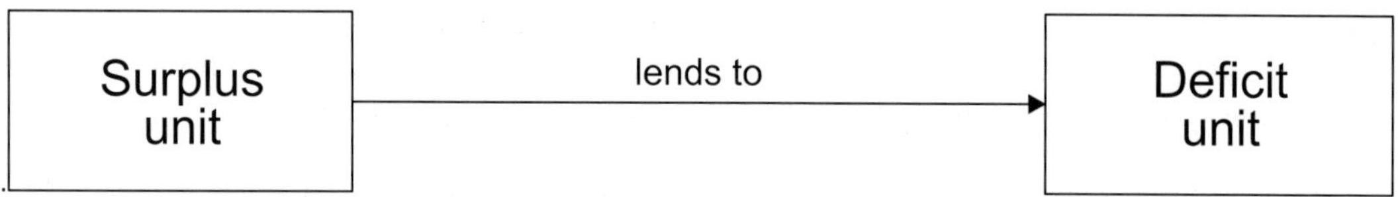

The second way of bringing together surplus and deficit units is through a **financial intermediary**. The intermediary provides a service to both the surplus unit and the deficit unit, by accepting surplus funds and making these funds available to a deficit unit.

The main advantage of financial intermediation is that it provides a way of channelling funds for large and small economic units. For example, a person might deposit savings with a bank, and the bank might use it collective deposits of savings to provide a loan to a company.

The two methods of channelling funds is shown schematically bellow

Flow of funds in the economy

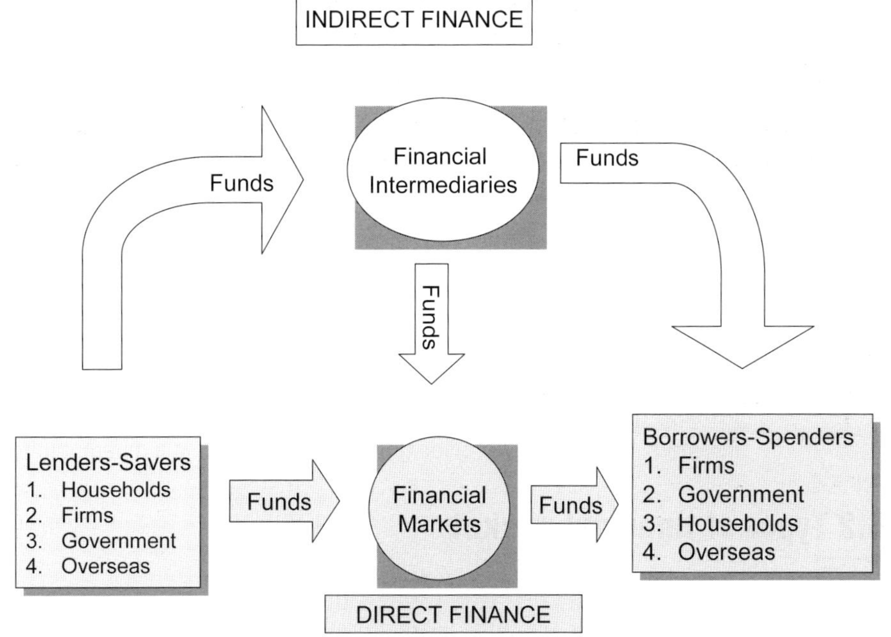

Flow of funds in an open economy, showing the role of financial intermediation

In the next sections we shall discuss the main financial intermediaries and financial markets in the financial system.

5.1 Financial intermediaries

ST FORWARD

An intermediary is a go-between, and a financial intermediary is an institution which **channels funds from savers to borrowers**, by obtaining deposits from lenders and then re-lending them to borrowers. intermediaries can, for example, provide a link between savers and investors.

UK financial intermediaries

(a) Banks
(b) Building societies
(c) Insurance companies, pension funds, unit trust companies and investment trust companies

In spite of competition from building societies, insurance companies and other financial institutions, banks arguably remain the major financial intermediaries in the UK.

(a) The clearing banks are the biggest operators in the retail banking market, although competition from the building societies has been growing in the UK.

(b) There is greater competition between different banks (overseas banks and the clearing banks especially) for business in the wholesale lending market.

Benefits of financial intermediation

(a) Financial intermediaries provide obvious and convenient ways in which a lender can **save money**. Instead of having to find a suitable borrower for his money, the lender can deposit his money with a financial intermediary that offers a financial instrument to suit his requirements.

(b) They can package up the amounts lent by savers and lend on to borrowers in bigger amounts (a process called **aggregation**).

(c) Provided that the financial intermediary is itself financially sound, **the lender's capital is secure**. Bad debts would be borne by the financial intermediary in its re-lending operations.

(d) They provide a **ready source of funds for borrowers**. Even when money is in short supply, a borrower will usually find a financial intermediary prepared to lend some.

(e) Financial intermediaries, most importantly, provide **maturity transformation**; ie they bridge the gap between the wish of most lenders for liquidity and the desire of most borrowers for loans over longer periods. They do this by providing investors with financial instruments which are liquid enough for the investors' needs and by providing funds to borrowers in a different longer term form.

5.2 Types of financial market

Types of financial market in terms of maturity

These are types of market for dealing in capital.

(a) **Capital markets** are financial markets for **raising** and **investing** largely long-term capital.
(b) **Money markets** are financial markets for lending and borrowing largely short-term capital.

What do we mean by **long-term** and **short-term** capital? We have already indicated that these terms are not very precise.

(a) By **short-term capital**, we mean usually capital that is lent or borrowed for a period which might range from as short as overnight up to about one year, and sometimes more.

(b) By **long-term capital**, we mean capital invested or lent and borrowed for a period of about five years or more, but sometimes less.

(c) There is a **grey area** between long-term and short-term capital, which is lending and borrowing for a period from about 1-2 years up to about 5 years (**medium-term** capital).

Primary and secondary markets

A **primary market** if a market for new securities issues where the security is purchased direct from the issuer.

A **secondary market** is a market where the instruments are traded between investors after they have been issued.

Question **Sources of finance**

Try to think of some of the markets that firms can use to obtain finance. A number of them will be listed in the next few paragraphs.

Exchanges

Most financial markets are organised as exchanges in which trading takes place either face to face or most commonly electronically. Examples of exchanges include the London Stock Exchange and the New York Stock Exchange.

Over-the-Counter Markets

Shares and other financial instruments are also bought and sold outside the supervised and regulated official exchanges in the over-the-counter (OTC) markets. OTC market prices are negotiated rather than set by auction, as is the case in most stock exchanges. In the USA, OTC market prices are reported via the National Association of Securities Dealers Automatic Quotation System (NASDAQ). Most OTC trading deals with shares that are not quoted on any public stock exchange.

6 Financial markets

FAST FORWARD

Firms may obtain long-term or medium-term capital as **share capital** or as **loan capital**. Debentures, loan stock, bonds and commercial paper are all types of loan capital.

In section we discuss short-term instruments which trade in the money markets and long-term instruments such as bonds and shares.

6.1 Money market instruments

The UK money markets are operated by the banks and other financial institutions. Although the money markets largely involve wholesale borrowing and lending by banks, some large companies and the government are also involved in money market operations. **The money markets are essentially shorter term debt markets**, with loans being made for a specified period at a specified rate of interest.

The money markets operate both as a **primary market**, in which new financial claims are issued and as a **secondary market**, where previously issued financial claims are traded.

Amounts dealt in are relatively large, generally being above £50,000 and often in millions of pounds. Loans are transacted on extremely 'fine' terms – ie with small margins between lending and borrowing rates – reflecting the **economies of scale** involved. The emphasis is on liquidity: the efficiency of the money markets can make the financial claims dealt in virtually the equivalent of cash.

There are various markets, including the following.

(a) **The primary market** is the market where, as already described, the Bank of England carries out 'open market operations' in short-term financial instruments in order to ensure the liquidity of the banking system and to exert influence over interest rates.

(b) **The interbank market** is the market in which banks lend short-term funds to one another. The principal interest rate in this market is the London Inter-Bank Offer Rate or LIBOR, which is used by individual banks to establish their own base interest rates and interest rates for wholesale lending to large borrowers.

(c) **The Certificate of Deposit market** is a market for trading in **certificates of deposit**, a form of deposit which can be sold by the investor before maturity. A certificate of deposit (CD) is a certificate issued by a bank that shows a specific amount of money has been deposited at the issuing institution. CDs are issued by banks to access funds for their finance and lending activities. The CD bears a specific maturity date, interest rate, and denomination.

CDs issued in amounts up to $100,000 are insured by the Federal Deposit Insurance Corporation (FDIC). A CD may be issued in either a negotiable or nonnegotiable form. Negotiable CDs provide the investor with the opportunity to sell the CD in the open market prior to the maturity date. CD yields are quoted on an interest-bearing basis, versus the discounted basis used for Treasury bills, commercial paper, and bankers' acceptances. A CD with a maturity of one year or less posts interest income at maturity. In contrast, term CDs pay interest on a semiannual basis. The yield on CDs is higher than that on Treasury securities of the same maturity due to the credit rating of the issuing bank, the liquidity of the CD market, and the supply and demand for CDs.

(d) **The local authority market** is a market in which local authorities borrow short-term funds from banks and other investors, by issuing and selling short-term 'debt instruments'.

(e) **The finance house market** covers the short-term loans raised from the money markets by finance houses (eg hire purchase finance companies).

(f) **The inter-company market** refers to direct short-term lending between companies, without any financial intermediary. This market is very small, and restricted to the treasury departments of large companies, and has largely been superseded by the sterling commercial paper market.

(g) **The sterling commercial paper market** is a market in which companies issue debt securities carrying interest, known as commercial paper (CP) with a maturity of up to one year, or medium term notes (MTNs) with a period of between one and five years.

A distinction is sometimes made between the primary market and all the other money markets which are referred to collectively as the parallel markets or 'unofficial' markets.

6.2 Bond markets and instruments

Bonds are long-term debt instruments. Depending on the country of issue, the bond will usually pay interest (coupons) either annually or semi-annually. US and UK bonds pay semi-annual interest, while Eurobonds pay interest annually.

Government bonds

Government bond are issued by governments to finance public expenditure. In the UK, government bonds are known as gilt-edged securities or gilts and are classified according to the number of years remaining to redemption as:

- Short-dated: seven years or less to maturity
- Medium dated: over seven but less than 15 years to maturity
- Long-dated: 15 years or more to maturity

Gilts may be issued either by selling them direct to dealers, or by selling them to the Bank of England first, and then releasing them gradually ('on tap') to the market at a suitable time.

The primary gilts market is the market for the sale of new gilt issues. There is an active market in second-hand gilts with existing holders selling their holdings of gilts to other investors in the gilts market.

Corporate bonds

Corporate bonds are issued by corporations in order to raise funds. Corporate bonds and investor demand therefore a higher yield. Corporate bonds in the UK take the form of debenture stocks which are traded on the London Stock Exchange or OTC. Debentures usually pay semi-annual fixed coupons as a percentage of the face value and holders receive a certificate of ownership. Debentures are loans secured by fixed and/or floating charges usually based on the corporation's property or financial assets.

- Fixed charge debentures specify which assets the corporation is unable to dispose of. If the corporation goes into liquidation, then these assets are sold to repay the debentures.
- Floating charge debentures cover all the assets of the corporation. If the corporation goes into liquidation, then all the assets are sold to repay the debenture.

Fixed rate bonds

Fixed rate bonds pay a constant rate of interest throughout their lives.

Floating rate notes

A floating rate note is a medium, to long-term debt instrument, that pays a variable interest rate linked to a financial index and adjusted periodically, typically every three or six months.

New issues of bonds normally set a coupon rate close to the current interest rates. When there is uncertainty about interest rates, the issuer would line to issue bonds where the coupon can go down when interest rates falls. Floating Rate Notes (FRNs) are instruments which have this feature. The coupon on a FRN is expressed as LIBOR plus or minus a number of points (bp), for example, LIBOR + 406bp.

The fixing of the coupon in this way means that issuers pay and investors receive a rate which is close to the market rate.

Zero coupon bonds

A zero-coupon bond pays no coupon during its life. The bond is issued at a deep discount to the face value and it is redeemed at par. The return for the investor is determined by the difference between the price paid and the principal received at maturity. Zero coupon bonds are issued by issuers who want to delay repayment. Given the increased credit risk due to the delayed payment, they are normally issued only by institutions governments or corporations with the highest credit rating. Zero coupon bonds can be created from coupon bearing bonds by 'stripping' the coupons.

Undated (perpetual) bonds

An undated bond is a bond that pays a fixed coupon in perpetuity, ie it has no maturity date. Typically these bonds pay low coupons and are issued only when interest rates are very low. An example of such a bond is the 3.5% War Loan, a gilt issued by the UK government. Some undated bonds have a call provision that allows for early redemption when interest rates fall below the coupon rate.

Index linked bonds

These are bonds issued by the UK government with coupons and redemption values linked to the Retail Price Index.

Callable bonds

A callable bond gives the issuer the right, but not the obligation, to redeem a bond of an agreed specific price before the scheduled redemption date.

The call feature makes it attractive to the issuer because it will allow early redemption when interest rates decline, allowing refinancing at a lower cost. Because of the call option embedded in the bond, investors will require a higher coupon to compensate for the possibility of early redemption.

Convertible bonds

If a corporation issues equity as well as debt, then it is able to issue secured or unsecured debt instruments that can convert part or all of the debt to equity. The terms of the bond set out the number of shares for conversion and usually the time period over which the conversion can take place.

6.3 Equity market instruments

Ordinary Shares

Ordinary shares represent a claim on the future income of the corporation.

Preference Shares

Preference shares are **hybrid securities** with characteristics of both **debt** and **ordinary shares.** Preference share dividends are similar to interest payments in that they are generally fixed in amount and must be paid before common stockholders can receive any dividends. However, **interest on debt** (both short and long term) must be paid before preference share holders can receive anything; therefore, creditors look at **preference shares** as **equity**. Further, if the profits are not sufficient to pay dividends to preference shareholders the firm may omit it without leading the firm into bankruptcy. In contrast, not paying **interest** on borrowed money is an act of **default**. If the company goes bankrupt, preference shares have priority over ordinary shares in terms of claim on assets in liquidation. Once creditors have been paid in full, any money left over from the sale of assets can be used to settle the claims preference shareholders.

When a preference share is issued the dividend rate is specified as percentage of the share's par value or its offering price.

There a variety of preference shares but in terms of their distinguishing features they can be grouped into 5 categories as follows.

- **Cumulative preference shares .** Virtually all preference shares have a cumulative feature. If the firm does not distribute dividends in any year, these unpaid dividends are carried forward from year to year.
- **Non-Cumulative preference shares.** In this case any dividend arrears are not carried forward. Dividends are only paid out of current profits.
- **Redeemable preference shares.** Although preferred stock has no fixed maturity date, firms generally make provisions for its retirement. As with most bond issues, almost all preferred stock issues have a call provision giving the company the right to buy back the issue at a price specified when it first came to market. This option is valuable in a declining interest rate environment because it allows the issuing company to replace an existing issue with a less expensive one.
- **Participating preference shares.** This is not a common type of preference share. In effect it offers the possibility of higher dividends than the specified rate. Should the level of profits exceed a certain level specified in the conditions for the preference share, then the shareholder receives a greater dividend.
- **Convertible preference shares.** This hybrid instrument is becoming increasingly more popular as it carries the right to switch to ordinary shares at specified dates and specified terms. They are profitable if the ordinary shares do well.

Some preference shares issues also have a sinking fund requiring the company to set aside money to retire a certain number of shares annually.

Finally, we should note that unlike interest payments on debt, dividends on preference shares are not deductible as expenses for tax purposes.

Most preference shares are non-participating, cumulative and irredeemable. As such these shares have similarities with both bonds, which are debt instruments, and shares, which are equity instruments.

Preference shares are similar to bonds in that

(a) They pay a fixed annual dividend expressed as a percentage of the share's par value which does not vary with the profits made by the organisation.

(b) Holders receive their dividend before ordinary shareholders which means the income from preference shares is more reliable than for ordinary shares.

Preference shares are similar to ordinary shares in that

(a) Failure to pay the dividend does not mean the organisation will face bankruptcy since most preference shares are cumulative.

(b) If the organisation does go into liquidation, then preference shareholders are usually entitled to be repaid only the par value of their holding, if anything.

Normally, holders of preference shares do not enjoy voting rights unless the firm violates the provisions of the agreement with them.

6.4 Main Exchanges

The **London Stock Exchange** is an organised capital market based in London which plays an important role in the functioning of the UK economy. It is the main capital market in the UK.

(a) It makes it easier for large firms and the government to raise long-term capital, by providing a market place for borrowers and investors to come together.

(b) The Stock Exchange publicises the prices of quoted (or 'listed') securities, which are then reported in daily national newspapers such as the Financial Times. Investors can therefore keep an eye on the value of their stocks and shares, and make buying and selling decisions accordingly.

(c) The Stock Exchange tries to enforce certain rules of conduct for its listed firms and for operators in the market, so that investors have the assurance that companies whose shares are traded on the Exchange and traders who operate there are reputable. Confidence in the Stock Exchange will make investors more willing to put their money into stocks and shares.

The **Alternative Investment Market** (AIM), which opened in 1995, is a market where smaller companies which cannot meet the more stringent requirements needed to obtain a full listing on the Stock Exchange can raise new capital by issuing shares. Like the Stock Exchange main market, the AIM is also a market in which investors can trade in shares already issued. It is regulated by the Stock Exchange.

The price of shares on a stock market fluctuate up and down.

(a) The price of shares in a particular company might remain unchanged for quite a long time; alternatively, a company's share price might fluctuate continually throughout each day.

(b) The **general level** of share prices, as measured by share price indices such as the All-Share Index and the FTSE 100 Index, may go up or down each minute of the day.

The indices of share prices on the Stock Exchange act as indicators of the state of **investor confidence** in the country's economy. For example, if investors believe that interest rates are too low to curb inflation, they may sell shares and move their funds to other countries, causing a decline in share prices.

Question — **Share prices**

From your reading of business pages (which should be a central feature in anyone's study of economics) what factors have you noticed as having an influence on share prices?

Answer

Share prices respond to:

(a) Factors related to the circumstances of individual companies – eg news of a company's annual profits, or a proposed takeover bid

(b) Factors related to the circumstances of a particular industry – eg new government legislation or regulations for an industry, such as new laws on pollution controls or customer protection measures

(c) Factors related to the circumstances of the national economy – eg changes in interest rates, the latest official figures for the balance of trade, or price inflation

Assessment focus point

You should be aware of the types of factors set out in the Question above, but detailed knowledge of theories of share price behaviour is not expected.

6.5 Changes in the capital markets

Recent years have seen very big changes in the capital markets of the world.

(a) **Globalisation of capital markets**

The capital markets of each country have become internationally integrated. Securities issued in one country can now be traded in capital markets around the world. For example, shares in many UK companies are traded in the USA. The shares are bought by US banks, which then issue ADRs (American depository receipts) which are a form in which foreign shares can be traded in US markets without a local listing.

(b) **Securitisation of debt**

Securitisation of debt means creating tradable securities which are backed by less liquid assets such as mortgages and other long term loans.

(c) **Risk management (and risk assessment)**

Various techniques have been developed for companies to manage their financial risk such as swaps and options. These 'derivative' financial instruments may allow transactions to take place off-balance sheet and the existence of such transactions may make it more difficult for banks and other would-be lenders to assess the financial risk of a company that is asking to borrow money.

(d) **Increased competition**

There is much fiercer competition than there used to be between financial institutions for business. For example, building societies have emerged as competitors to the banks, and foreign banks have competed successfully in the UK with the big clearing banks. Banks have changed too, with some shift towards more fee-based activities (such as selling advice and selling insurance products for commission) and away from the traditional transaction-based activities (holding deposits, making loans).

6.6 Securitisation of debt

The securitisation of debt involves disintermediation. **Financial disintermediation** is a process whereby ultimate borrowers and lenders by-pass the normal methods of financial intermediation (such as depositing money with and borrowing money from banks) and find other ways of lending or borrowing funds; or lend and borrow directly with each other, avoiding financial intermediation altogether.

Securitisation of debt provides firms with a method of borrowing directly from non-banks. Although banks might act as managers of the debt issue, finding lenders who will buy the securitised debt, banks are not doing the lending themselves.

7 The main financial intermediaries

ST FORWARD

Financial intermediaries include **banks** and **institutional** investors such as pension funds, investment trusts and unit trusts.

Having discussed the main financial markets and the instruments traded in those markets we can now turn in this section to the financial intermediaries.

7.1 Banks

Banks are major providers of credit. Banks create money when they give credit (see Chapter 10), and so bank lending has two aspects which are important for the economy.

- The growth of credit and hence expenditure in the economy
- Increases in the money supply

Banks lend money that has been deposited with them by customers. A bank is really only a go-between or intermediary between the initial lender and the ultimate borrower. When explaining the role of financial intermediaries such as banks, we looked earlier at the flow of funds within an economy.

7.2 Other intermediaries

The providers of capital include private individuals, such as those who buy stocks and shares on the Stock Exchange, and those who deposit money with banks, building societies and National Savings & Investments (NS&I). (NS&I is a government institution set up to borrow on behalf of the government, mainly from the non-bank private sector of the economy. NS&I operates through Post Offices throughout the UK, so that individuals can deposit and withdraw savings with relative ease.)

There are also important groups of **institutional investors** which specialise in providing capital and act as financial intermediaries between suppliers and demanders of funds. Many financial services organisations now have diversified operations covering a range of the following activities.

(a) **Pension funds**. Pension funds invest the pension contributions of individuals who subscribe to a pension fund, and of organisations with a company pension fund.

(b) **Investment trusts**. The business of investment trust companies is investing in the stocks and shares of other companies and the government. In other words, they trade in investments.

(c) **Unit trusts**. Unit trusts are similar to investment trusts, in the sense that they invest in stocks and shares of other companies. A unit trust comprises a 'portfolio' – ie a holding of stocks or shares in a range of companies or gilts, perhaps with all the shares or stocks having a special characteristic, such as all shares in property companies or all shares in mining companies. The trust will then create a large number of small units of low nominal value, with each unit representing a stake in the total portfolio. These units are then sold to individual investors and investors will benefit from the income and capital gain on their units – ie their proportion of the portfolio.

(e) **Venture capital.** Venture capital providers are organisations that specialise in raising funds for new business ventures, such as 'management buy-outs' (ie purchases of firms by their management staff). These organisations are therefore providing capital for fairly risky ventures. A venture capital organisation that has operated for many years in the UK is Investors in Industry plc, usually known as '3i'. In recent years, many more venture capital organisations have been set up, for example by large financial institutions such as pension funds.

The role of financial intermediaries in capital markets is illustrated in the diagram below.

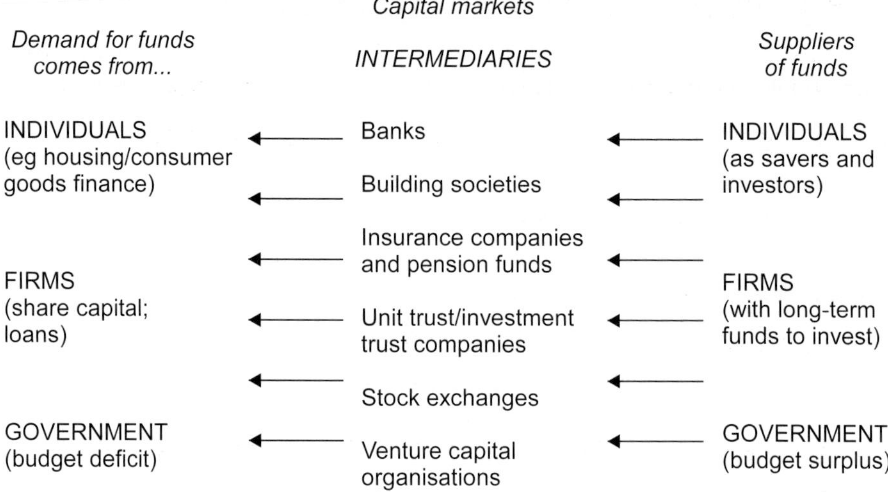

8 The insurance market

8.1 Insurance companies' intermediation role

We discussed above that the role of banks as financial intermediaries is to provide liquidity and bring together units with excess funds and units with a shortage of funds.

FAST FORWARD

Insurance companies act as **intermediaries** by bringing together units which want to **shed risk** and **uncertainty** together with units which are prepared to **take the risk** at a **price.**

Insurance companies, like banks, perform an intermediation role, but they **transfer risk** rather than funds.

The insurance market brings together units that want to shed risk and uncertainty about future outcomes and units which are prepared to take the risk at a price.

There are different types of risk that economic units face and like financial intermediaries insurance companies provide a range of risk transfer instruments to cater for these different types of risk.

Key terms

An **insurance contract** or policy is an instrument through which risk is transferred from one unit to another at a price which is determined to a large extent by demand and supply.

8.2 Risk and uncertainty

FAST FORWARD

Risks associated with everyday life can be mitigated or eliminated through insurance.

Individuals, firms and governments face uncertainty in all spheres of their activity.

8.3 The risk facing individuals

- Their longevity
- Their future earnings
- Their personal safety
- The state of their health
- The safety of their possessions

and many other aspects of their lives.

All the uncertainties relating to the above, (for example death, relating to longevity above), unemployment relating to uncertainty of earnings, can have serious repercussions on an individual's life.

The repercussions can be mitigated or completely eliminated by taking insurance.

Question — **Uncertainty**

The use of a car involves uncertainty. Think of ways in which this uncertainty can be mitigated or eliminated.

Answer

By buying insurance we can mitigate or completely eliminate the uncertainty relating to our own use of the car.

If the car is stolen it will be replaced or, if it is damaged, insurance can cover the cost.

Whether we mitigate or completely eliminate the risk will depend on the premiums we will be prepared to pay.

Breakdown services such as the AA or RAC mitigate risks of high recovery and roadside repair costs.

8.4 The nature of insurance contracts

FAST FORWARD

Insurance claims are **contingent claims**. The insured party benefits only if something adverse happens.

Insurance contracts will only benefit the insured party if something adverse happens for which he has taken cover. Because the insured party will benefit only if a particular contingency occurs, claims are referred to as contingency claims. This is why the level of insurance varies among individuals. The level of insurance that different individuals take depends on their degree of aversion to risk and the price of the insurance product.

8.5 Organisation of the insurance industry

FAST FORWARD

The insurance industry is organised in **two** main types of company:

(a) General insurance companies
(b) Life companies.

(a) General insurance companies cover all risks other than the risk of death. Examples include:

- Motor insurance
- Household insurance
- Property
- Accident
- Liability
  - Public liability
  - Employer's liability
  - Professional liability
- Marine
- Aviation

The above are only examples and do not provide an exhaustive list.

(b) Life Companies insure against the possibility of death. Life insurance is sometimes referred to as 'life assurance'.

Many large corporations which face a multitude of risks for which there is a regulatory obligation to insure have set up their own insurance companies.

An example is BP which has set up its own insurance company to cover a large part of its everyday risk. These companies are called **captive insurance companies**.

8.6 Insurance underwriters and insurance brokers

Key terms

An **insurance broker** acts as an intermediary between those seeking insurance and the insurers.

An **insurance underwriter** is the person who accepts the risk in exchange for a premium based on a calculation of the level of risk from the insured.

8.7 Re-insurance

FAST FORWARD

Sometimes the underwriter wants to share some of the risk and he will do this by a process of re-insurance whereby he passes a risk to another insurer in exchange for part of the premium.

The nature of risk is such that the ultimate liability may be too big for an individual insurance company.

The costs involved in a large natural catastrophe for instance could completely wipe out the assets of a single insurance company. For this reason insurance companies themselves take insurance against their own exposure to the risk they undertake through what is referred to as re-insurance.

8.8 Lloyds of London

The largest insurance market in the world is Lloyds of London where individual insurance companies or underwriters trade their risks.

8.9 The main life insurance (or assurance) contracts

(a) **Whole life contract**

A whole life contract pays a certain amount on death of the insured party. The premium is fixed when the policy is issued.

(b) **Universal life contract**

This contract is similar to a whole life contract but it allows the premiums paid to vary.

(c) **Term life**

This is a contract that insures against the risk of death for a specific period of time. This insurance product would benefit the insured party's beneficiaries if death happened during that specified period.

Diversification of life insurance contracts

Over recent years the life assurance industry has launched a number of products to make this type of insurance more attractive.

Many life insurance products, although they retain an element of life cover, are essentially savings policies rather than protection policies. **Endowment assurance** pays out a sum on death or on maturity of the policy, and has often been used as a way of saving to pay off a mortgage. Such policies may be '**with profits**' – sharing in the long-term performance of the life company's funds – or the returns on the investment element of the policy may be linked to the performance of specific '**unit-linked**' funds.

With **single premium bonds**, a single lump sum is allocated to one or more funds.

Chapter roundup

- Within an economy, some people, firms and organisations will have money which is surplus to their needs, and others will have less money than they need for their spending requirements. **Credit** involves lending money, and the transfer (usually in return for interest payments) of money from surplus units to deficit units. **Financial intermediaries**, such as banks and building societies, make the provision of credit much easier, by taking deposits from savers and re-lending to borrowers.
- Credit for households comes from a variety of sources including credit agreements, bank loans and mortgages.
- A company must have **capital** to carry out its operations. Many companies start in a small way, often as family businesses, then grow to become **public companies**, which can invite the public to subscribe for shares.
- During any given period of time governments need to spend money on outlays of a **short**, **medium** and **long-term** nature. To pay for these outlays governments collect taxes.
- The government budget deficit is the **difference** between government **expenditures** and **revenues** in any one period, normally a year referred to as a fiscal year.
- The government deficit in any one fiscal year represents the **new borrowing** that the government needs to undertake.
- An intermediary is a go-between, and a financial intermediary is an institution which **channels funds from savers to borrowers**, by obtaining deposits from lenders and then re-lending them to borrowers. They can, for example, provide a link between savers and investors.
- **Firms** may obtain long-term or medium-term capital as **share capital** or as **loan capital**. Debentures, loan stock, bonds and commercial paper are all types of loan capital.
- **Financial intermediaries** include **banks** and **institutional** investors such as pension funds, investment trusts and unit trusts.
- Insurance companies act as **intermediaries** by bringing together units which want to **shed risk** and uncertainty together with units which are prepared to **take the risk** at a price.
- Risks associated with everyday life can be mitigated or eliminated through insurance.
- Insurance claims are **contingent claims**. The insured party benefits only if something adverse happens.
- The insurance industry is organised in **two** main types of companies

  (a) General insurance companies
  (b) Life companies.
- Sometimes the underwriter wants to share some off the risk and he will do this by a process of **re-insurance** whereby he passes a risk to another insurer in exchange for part of the premium.

Quick quiz

1 List the main sources of credit available to businesses.

2 What is meant by 'maturity transformation'?

3 The functions of commercial financial intermediaries include all the following except:

A Maturity transformation
B Reduction of transactions costs
C Aggregation
D Gilt issuing

4 A 'money market' is best defined as:

A A market where organisations raise any form of finance
B A market where organisations raise long-term finance
C A market where organisations raise short-term finance
D A market where Treasury Bills are traded

5 Advantages of obtaining a stock market listing include all the following except:

A Better access to capital markets
B Ability to make share for share deals
C Ability to liquidate holdings
D Greater public scrutiny

6 A money market financial intermediary is best defined as:

A An institution which matches surplus funds holders to deficit funds units.

B An institution which operates on the Stock Exchange, matching buyers and sellers of stocks and shares.

C An institution which allows firms to obtain equipment from suppliers by providing leasing or hire purchase finance.

D An institution which acts as a buffer between the Bank of England and the rest of the UK banking system.

Answers to quick quiz

1 Short term credit may be had in the form of overdraft, trade credit and the issue of bills of exchange. Medium term credit often takes the form of term loans from banks, hire purchase and finance leases. Longer term credit may be obtained by issuing debentures and mortgages.

2 Financial intermediaries accept sight deposits but make term loans. They thus convert the immediate maturity of their own short term borrowings into loan assets which will mature at some more distant future time.

3 D This is a function of the Bank of England.

4 C

5 D Greater public scrutiny may attract takeover bidders and will require the firm to pay more attention to public relations.

6 A An institution on the Stock Exchange is a capital market player. C is a financial intermediary but is not the best definition. D is a financial intermediary but is not the best definition.

Now try the questions below from the Exam Question Bank

Question numbers	Page
27 – 29	370

Credit and banking

Introduction

In this chapter, we look closer at three issues. First, we discuss the **role of the banks** in the **financial system** and in particular how they create **credit** and provide **liquidity**. Secondly we discuss the role of the central bank, and how it influences the functioning of the financial system. Finally we discuss the structure of yields of the various instruments that trade in the financial markets.

The three areas are intertwined because the monetary policy of a government operated through its central bank influences the behaviour of banks, by influencing their credit creation activities, and affects the level and structure of financial yields by setting short run interest rates. As both banks and financial markets are the major sources through which firms and individuals raise capital, the **central bank** can have a potent **impact on the financial markets** and the **real economy**.

Topic list	Learning outcomes	Syllabus references	Ability required
1 Credit creation and the banking system	C (ii)	C (6)	Comprehension
2 The role of the central bank	C (ii), C (v)	C (8)	Comprehension
3 Yield on financial instruments	C (ii)	C (7)	Comprehension

1 Credit creation and the banking system

FAST FORWARD

Banks (and building societies) create **credit** when they lend or grant overdrafts, and their activities thus contribute significantly to the increase in the money supply. In practice, the size of the **credit multiplier** is restricted by 'leakages' and by central bank controls over the liquidity and capital structure of banks.

1.1 The banks and the banking system

As has already been discussed, banks are major financial intermediaries in a financial system. The term 'bank' is generic and there are different types of banks that operate within a banking system. You will probably have come across a number of terms which describe the types.

(a) **Clearing banks** operate the clearing system for settling payments (eg payments by cheque by bank customers).

(b) The term **retail banks** is used to describe the traditional High Street banks. The term **wholesale banks** refers to banks which specialise in lending in large quantities to major customers. The clearing banks are involved in both retail and wholesale banking but are commonly regarded as the main retail banks.

(c) **Investment banks** (which used to be referred to as **merchant banks**) offer services, often of a specialised nature, to corporate customers.

(d) **Commercial banks** make commercial banking transactions with customers. They are distinct from the country's central bank.

Question — Bank balance sheet

In the balance sheet of a retail bank, which one of the following items do you think would constitute the largest asset?

(a) Customers' overdrafts and bank loans
(b) Customers' deposits
(c) Land and buildings

Answer

The answer is (a). Item (b) is not an asset of the bank – it is a liability (a sum of money owed by the bank to its customers). It might be tempting to choose item (c), if you think about the large number of High Street sites owned by the retail banks, but in fact the value of this asset is dwarfed by the banks' lending.

1.2 The functions of the commercial banks

(a) **Providing a payments mechanism**. The clearing system is the major payments mechanism in the UK, and it enables individuals and firms to make payments by cheque. The banks are also a source from which individuals and firms can obtain notes and coin.

(b) **Providing a place for individuals, firms and government to store their wealth**. Banks compete with other financial institutions to attract the funds of individuals and firms.

(c) **Lending money** in the form of loans or overdrafts.

(d) **Acting as financial intermediaries** by accepting deposits and lending, and in doing so transforming the risk characteristics and maturity characteristics of the lending.

(e) **Providing customers with a means of obtaining foreign currency, or selling foreign currency**, whenever they require it. Banks play a central role in the foreign exchange markets.

The banks also provide a wide range of other **commercial services** to customers.

(a) Advising and assisting companies, for example advising firms in a takeover bid and assisting companies to issue shares on the stock market.

(b) Providing assistance to exporters and importers, for example helping exporters to obtain payment from buyers abroad, and helping importers to pay for goods they buy from foreign suppliers

(c) Leasing

(d) Debt factoring services

(e) Executorship and trustee services

(f) Acting as insurance brokers for insurance companies by selling some insurance policies

(g) Selling insurance policies of their own, notably life assurance policies

(h) Selling pensions

(i) Share registration and share dealing services

(j) Unit trust business

(k) Giving investment advice

1.3 Credit creation

Key terms

The **bank multiplier** or **credit multiplier** is the name given to banks' ability to create credit, and hence money, by maintaining their cash reserves at less than 100% of the value of their deposits.

When someone deposits money in a bank, the banks are able as a result to 'create' credit of a much greater magnitude than the amount of money originally deposited.

Suppose, for example, that in a country with a single bank, customer deposits total £100,000. The bank, we will assume, re-lends all these deposits to other customers. The customers will use the money they have borrowed to buy goods and services and they will pay various firms and individuals for these purchases. If the firms and individuals receiving payment then put the money into their own accounts with the bank, the bank's deposits will have doubled.

It is this fact that most additions to bank lending end up as money in someone's bank account, adding to total customer deposits with the banks, that give banks this special **ability to create credit**. This is an ability that is also shared in the UK by building societies, since building society deposits are included in definitions of the money supply (M2 and M4).

1.4 Illustration of credit creation

Illustrating the process with some figures may be helpful. We shall assume for simplicity that there is only one bank in the banking system, and that all money lent by the bank is re-deposited by various customers.

A customer depositing £1,000 in cash with the bank **creates an asset**, in the sense that the bank, in return for the deposit, gives the customer a promise to pay on demand, or subject to notice, the £1,000 deposited. The promise is, of course, an account opened under the name of the client.

To the bank, the deposit is a **liability**. However, the deposit provides funds for the bank to acquire **assets**. We shall begin by assuming that the bank holds these assets entirely in the form of cash.

If the bank keeps the full £1,000 and does nothing with it, then it would simply operate as a 'cloakroom' in which the client's money is deposited. However, if the bank believes that the client is unlikely to claim the full £1,000 for some time, there will be some incentive to use the money rather than to keep it idle. One possibility would be to lend it; the bank would be taking a risk that it will not have the cash when its customer wants to have it back, but at the same time it would expect to make a profit by charging interest on the sum of money so lent.

On one hand the deposit of the £1,000 creates the opportunity for the bank to make a profit in the form of the interest that it can charge on the money it lends (the incentive being all the stronger if the bank is paying interest on the deposits it accepts), but on the other hand there is a risk that when the money is out on loan the client may claim it back. The bank will then be unable to meet its obligation to repay the cash to the client unless it can recall the loan instantly, which is unlikely.

As long as the bank feels that the likelihood is small that its depositors will demand a substantial proportion of their deposits in cash, then it faces an acceptable risk in lending some of the money. In other words, the bank strikes a balance between the desire to play safe by holding the cash and the desire to make profits by lending.

In the example in the table below, it is assumed that the bank has decided on the basis of past experience and observation to keep 50 pence in cash for every £1 deposited, and then lend out the other 50 pence. In other words, the bank in this example is operating a **50% cash ratio**. At step (1) below, the bank has £1,000 in cash. This is enough to support total liabilities of £2,000 and maintain a 50% cash ratio. If the bank now lends £1,000, and if all of that £1,000 is then spent by the borrowers but ends up back with the bank as deposits of other customers, the new situation for the bank will be as in (2) below.

	Bank's liabilities (= customer deposits)	*Bank's assets (= cash or loans to customers)*
(1)	£1,000 deposits	£1,000 cash
(2)	£2,000 deposits	£1,000 cash £1,000 loans

There is a doubling effect in relation to the money supply.

1.5 The credit multiplier

If the bank decided that the **50% cash ratio** was too conservative and reduced it to 25%, then for £1,000 cash deposited with the bank, deposits could be expanded fourfold. It is important to understand that banks in the process of lending are also potentially creating money because clients either borrowing or receiving the proceeds of borrowers' expenditure can use their deposits to make money transactions. In a modern economy most money transactions are by cheque or other bank transfer such as direct debits or standing order, thus transferring bank deposits from person to person or from firm to firm. Consumers and producers thus use the liabilities of a private institution as money.

The fact that banks do not need to keep a 100% cash reserve ratio automatically implies that they have the capacity to create money out of nothing. The size of this credit expansion depends primarily on the size of their cash reserve ratio.

We can summarise the quantitative side of credit creation in banks as follows:

$$\text{Deposits} = \frac{\text{Cash}}{\text{Cash ratio}} \quad \text{or } D = \frac{c}{r}$$

The smaller the cash ratio or **credit multiplier**, the bigger the size of the deposits that a given amount of cash will be able to support and hence the larger the money supply.

This theoretical description of the credit multiplier applies only to some extent in practice. If a bank decides to keep a cash reserve ratio of 10%, and it receives additional deposits of £1,000, the total increase in bank deposits will not be £1,000 ÷ 10% = £10,000, but considerably less than this.

Question — Cash reserve ratio

Suppose that all the commercial banks in an economy operated on a cash reserve ratio of 20%. How much cash would have to flow into the banks for the money supply to increase by £80 million?

Answer

Call the extra cash £C. Then:

$$\frac{C}{20\%} = 80 + C$$

$$C = 20\% \times (80 + C)$$

$$0.8C = 16$$

$$C = £20 \text{ million}$$

If an extra £20 million is deposited, the total money supply will rise to £20 million ÷ 20% = £100 million. This includes the initial £20 million, so the increase is £80 million.

There are constraints on the growth of a bank's deposits (and on the growth of the deposits of all banks in total).

- Cash leaks out of the banking system into less formal accumulations.
- Customers might not want to borrow at the interest rates the bank would charge.
- Banks should not lend to high-risk customers without good security.

A **cash ratio** or similar **fractional reserve system** might be imposed on banks by the government. Until 1971, a mandatory cash ratio of 8% was applied to the London clearing banks. Between 1971 and 1981 banks were required to maintain 12½% reserve asset ratio requirement. Although not intended as a direct monetary control (on credit growth), in effect it applied a credit multiplier limit of 8 – ie every initial £1 increase in bank deposits would result in up to £8 more in deposits.

1.6 Liquidity, profitability and security: aims of the banks

A commercial bank has three different and potentially conflicting aims which it must try to keep in balance. These are as follows.

(a) **Profitability.** A bank must make a profit for its shareholders. The biggest profits come from lending at higher interest rates. These are obtained with long-term lending and lending to higher risk customers.

(b) **Liquidity**. A bank must have some liquid assets. It needs notes and coin (till money) to meet demands from depositors for cash withdrawals. It also needs to be able to settle debts with other banks. For example, if on a particular day, customers of the Barclays Bank make payments by cheque to customers of Lloyds Bank totalling £200 millions, and customers of Lloyds Bank make payments by cheque to customers of Barclays totalling £170 millions, Barclays will be expected to pay Lloyds £30 million to settle the net value of transactions. This is done by transferring funds between the bank accounts of Barclays and Lloyds, which they keep with the Bank of England (as 'operational deposits'). A bank might also need to have some 'near liquid' assets which it can turn into liquid assets quickly, should it find itself with a need for more liquidity. Near-liquid assets earn relatively little interest. A bank will try to keep the quantity of such assets it holds to a safe minimum.

(c) **Security**. People deposit their money with banks because they are regarded as stable and secure institutions. A bank might lend to some high-risk customers, and suffer some bad debts, but on the whole, a bank will be expected to lend wisely and securely, with a strong likelihood that the loans will be repaid in full and with interest. If it did not, people might put their money somewhere else instead, not with the bank. This is why banks usually give careful consideration to the reliability of the borrower. Often, in doubtful cases, they will ask for security for a loan or overdraft. Security means that in the event of a default on loan repayments by the borrower, the bank can realise the security by selling the secured asset or assets and using the sale proceeds to pay off the debt.

1.7 Assets and liabilities of commercial banks

The distribution of assets for all UK commercial banks aggregated together is summarised in the table below.

UK commercial banks' assets, May 1993

	%
Cash	0.5
Balance with Bank of England	0.2
Market loans	24.0
Bills of exchange	1.8
Investments	6.7
Advances	62.0
Miscellaneous	4.8
	100.0

The triple aspects of bank lending – profitability, liquidity, and security – are evident in a commercial bank's **asset structure**.

(a) About 0.5% to 2% or so of a retail bank's assets might be till money (notes and coin) and deposits with the Bank of England. Most of these assets are held to meet the need for immediate liquidity, and earn no interest.

(b) Some assets are 'near-liquid' which means that they can quickly be converted into liquid deposits.

(i) The most important near-liquid assets are loans to the money markets and other money market securities.

(ii) Other near-liquid assets are bills, mainly eligible bank bills. Bills are short-term debt instruments. Eligible bills are bills of exchange that the Bank of England would be prepared to buy when the banking system is short of money. Most eligible bills are issued by top-class banks who are granted eligible status by the Bank of England.

(iii) Banks also hold some gilt-edged securities, mainly British government stocks. These can be sold on the stock market should a bank wish to obtain immediate liquid funds, but often, banks will buy gilts on the stock market with a fairly short term to maturity, and then hold them until they mature and the government redeems the debt.

Near-liquid assets – market loans, bills of exchange and gilt-edged security investments – might represent around 25% to 30% of a retail bank's assets.

(c) The biggest returns are earned by banks on their longer term **illiquid assets** – ie their overdrafts and bank loans to customers. Advances to customers are the biggest proportion of a retail bank's assets (over 70%) and the rate of interest on the loans varies according to the perceived risk of the customer as well as current interest rates.

(d) Banks' assets include the normal type of fixed assets found in any large organisation – eg property and equipment. However, the value of these operational assets is small in relation to the size of loans, even for the big clearing banks.

Sterling sight and time deposits of the retail banks account for most of their **liabilities**. Most sterling deposits are provided by the UK private sector (individuals and firms). **Other currency deposits** are the other main type of liability, consisting of deposits held by customers of UK banks in US dollars, euros and so on. In the UK there are no exchange control regulations currently in operation, and so private individuals as well as commercial firms and financial institutions are allowed to maintain foreign currency accounts. The bulk of other currency deposits, however, are held by overseas customers of UK banks.

1.8 Definition of money

Although we have talked about money in the context of the flow of funds we have not used a precise definition of money so far. The Bank of England uses two definitions of money, narrow money (known as MO) and broad money (known as M4). The precise definition of the two measures is as follows:

Key terms

MO: Notes and coins in circulation

M4: MO Plus sterling deposit accounts with barks and building societies.

Other less important definitions used include M1, M2 and M3 which all contain MO but are differentiated by the type of deposits they include.

1.9 Building societies

The building societies of the UK are **mutual** organisations whose main assets are mortgages of their members, and whose main liabilities are to the investor members who hold savings accounts with the society.

The distinction between building societies and banks has become increasingly blurred, as the societies have taken to providing a range of services formerly the province mainly of banks, and banks have themselves made inroads into the housing mortgage market. Some building societies now offer cheque book accounts, cash cards and many other facilities that compete directly with the banks.

The growing similarity between retail banks and building societies is recognised by the inclusion of building society deposits in the broader monetary aggregate M4 (see 1.8 above). The building society sector has shrunk in size as a number of the major societies have either converted to public limited companies and therefore become banks or have been taken over by banks or other financial institutions.

2 The role of the central bank

FAST FORWARD

The **central bank** has various functions. These include acting as a **banker to the central government** and to the **commercial banks**. The Bank of England has responsibility for controlling sterling inflation by setting interest rates.

Assessment focus point

The examiner has stated that, where possible, references to institutions will be to generic types (eg central banks) rather than to particular national institutions. You might be able to make use of your knowledge of institutions in any country in answering questions.

A central bank is a bank which acts on behalf of the government. The central bank for the UK is the Bank of England. The Bank of England ('the Bank') is a nationalised corporation run by a Court of Directors, consisting of the Governor, Deputy Governor, and some Executive Directors and part-time Directors.

Functions of the Bank of England

(a) It acts as **banker to the central government** and holds the 'public deposits'. Public deposits include the National Loans Fund, the Consolidated Fund and the account of the Paymaster General, which in turn includes the Exchange Equalisation Account.

(b) It is the **central note-issuing authority** in the UK – it is responsible for issuing bank notes in England.

(c) It is the **manager of the National Debt** – ie it deals with long-term and short-term borrowing by the central government and the repayment of central government debt.

(d) It is the manager of the Exchange Equalisation Account (ie the UK's **foreign currency reserves**).

(e) It acts as advisor to the government on **monetary policy**.

(f) It acts as agent for the government in carrying out its monetary policies. Since May 1997, it has had operational responsibility for **setting interest rates** at the level it considers appropriate in order to meet the government's inflation target.

(g) It acts as a **banker to the commercial banks**. The commercial banks keep a bank account with the Bank of England.

(h) It acts as a **lender to the banking system**. When the banking system is short of money, the Bank of England will provide the money the banks need – at a suitable rate of interest.

Supervision of the banking system is the responsibility of the Financial Services Authority.

2.1 The central bank as lender of last resort

In the UK, the short-term money market provides a link between the banking system and the government (Bank of England) whereby the Bank of England lends money to the banking system, when banks which need cash cannot get it from anywhere else.

(a) The Bank will supply cash to the banking system on days when the banks have a cash shortage. It does this by buying eligible bills and other short-term financial investments from approved financial institutions in exchange for cash.

(b) The Bank will remove excess cash from the banking system on days when the banks have a cash surplus. It does this by selling bills to institutions, so that the short-term money markets obtain interest-bearing bills in place of the cash that they do not want.

The process whereby this is done currently is known as **open market operations** by the Bank. This simply describes the buying and selling of eligible bills and other short-term assets between the Bank and the short-term money market.

2.2 Open market operations and short-term interest rates

Key term

Open market operations: the Bank of England's dealings in the capital market. The bank uses open market operations to control interest rates.

Open market operations provide the Bank of England with a method of control over short-term interest rates. They are thus an important feature of the government's monetary policy, which the Bank implements on its behalf.

When bills are bought and sold, they are traded at a discount to their face value, and there is an implied interest rate in the rate of discount obtained. Discounts on bills traded in open market operations have an immediate influence on other money market interest rates, such as the London Inter-Bank Offered Rate (LIBOR), and these in turn influence the 'benchmark' base rates of the major banks.

Because the eligible bills and other assets which the Bank of England acquires in its money market operations are short-term assets, a proportion mature each day. The market is then obliged to redeem these claims and must seek further refinancing from the bank. This continual turnover of assets gives the Bank of England the opportunity to determine the level of interest rates day by day.

2.3 The independence of the Bank of England

The Bank is an adviser to the government, but not an agent of the government. How much independence of action does the Bank have?

Proponents of **independence for central banks** argue that independence can prevent the worst government monetary excesses, which in some cases result in **hyperinflation**. High levels of existing public expenditure commitments combined with electoral pressures (along with other factors) build in strong underlying inflationary pressures. An independent central bank is seen as an essential counterweight to the potentially reckless decisions of politicians. As well as avoiding the worst excesses, a strong central bank is regarded as vital for the shorter term stability of domestic prices and of the currency, and so is important to overseas trade. Any government wishing to reduce an already high rate of inflation will, however, have to listen carefully to the advice of its central bank if it is to have any real success.

Those arguing against independence point out that the central bank is an unelected body and therefore does not have the open responsibility of politicians. Danger in this respect is minimised by the formal publication of decisions and recommendations of the central bank.

Further, it is claimed that central bank views on monetary policy could be in conflict with other economic objectives of the government. For example, excessively strict pursuit of monetary policy in order to pursue an inflation target might result in prolonged recession and heavy under-utilisation of resources.

In May 1997, the new Labour government of the UK announced important changes to the role of the UK central bank, the Bank of England. As already mentioned, the Chancellor of the Exchequer handed over to the Bank the power to set interest rates. Rates are set by a **Monetary Policy Committee** including the Governor of the Bank, his two deputies and four outsiders, but no politicians. The Committee sets interest rates with the aim of meeting the inflation target set by government.

The 1997 changes did not make the Bank of England fully independent, as the UK government can still override the Bank in an emergency. The role of the Bank of England also falls short of that of many other central banks in that responsibility for setting inflation or monetary targets rests with government.

One of the more independent central banks is the European Central Bank which is designed to be totally free of political interference. It came into existence at the end of 1998, ready for the European single currency.

3 Yield on financial instruments

FAST FORWARD

In practice, there is a variety of **interest rates**. To make a profit, institutions that borrow money to re-lend, or that accept deposits which they re-lend (eg banks) must pay lower interest on deposits than they charge to customers who borrow.

3.1 Interest rates and yields

Credit is a scarce commodity, priced through **interest rates**. Although there are many different interest rates in an economy, including building society mortgage rates, banks' base rates and yields on gilt-edged securities, they tend to move up or down together.

(a) If some interest rates go up, for example the banks' base rates, it is quite likely that other interest rates will move up too, if they have not gone up already.

(b) Similarly, if some interest rates go down, other interest rates will move down too.

A central bank affects the general level of interest rates through its influence on short term interest rates.

A **yield** is a general term to describe the return from an investment. Yields and interest rates are linked and changes in interest rates lead to changes in yields.

3.2 Nominal and real rates of interest

FAST FORWARD

The real value of income from investments is eroded by **inflation**. The real rate of interest can be calculated by using the formula below.

$$\frac{1+\text{money rate}}{1+\text{inflation rate}} = 1 + \text{real rate}$$

Nominal rates of interest are rates expressed in money terms. For example, if interest paid per annum on a loan of £1,000 is £150, the rate of interest would be 15%. The nominal rate of interest might also be referred to as the **money rate of interest**, or the **actual money yield** on an investment.

Real rates of interest are the rates of return that investors get from their investment, adjusted for the rate of inflation. The real rate of interest is therefore a measure of the increase in the real wealth, expressed in terms of buying power, of the investor or lender. Real rates of interest are lower than nominal rates when there is price inflation. For example, if the nominal rate of interest is 12% per annum and the annual rate of inflation is 8% per annum, the real rate of interest is the interest earned after allowing for the return needed just to keep pace with inflation.

The relationship between the inflation rate, the real rate of interest and the money rate of interest is:

(1+ real rate of interest) × (1+ inflation rate) = 1+ money rate of interest

We may rearrange this to find the real rate of interest in the example above.

$$\frac{1+\text{money rate}}{1+\text{inflation rate}} = 1 + \text{real rate}$$

$$\frac{1.12}{1.08} = 1.037$$

The real rate of interest is thus 3.7%.

The real rate of interest is commonly measured approximately, however, as the difference between the nominal rate of interest and the rate of inflation. In our example, this would be 12% – 8% = 4%.

ST FORWARD

Provision of finance brings **risk**, which will be reflected in the interest charged.

3.3 Interest rates on loans

The influences affecting interest rates in general will play a background part in determining the rate of interest for a particular loan. The main emphasis will be on specific factors concerning the nature of the borrowing and the status of the borrower.

The fundamental consideration in any lending decision is **risk**. The more **speculative** any borrowing proposal is believed to be, the higher will be the rate of interest. The lender is concerned not only with recovering the capital sum on the due maturity date, but also with earning a return on the money lent over the period of the loan. The time period of lending influences risk: the longer the time period, the greater is uncertainty about the ability of the borrower to repay the loan or as to the erosion in the value of money by inflation.

Borrowers and lenders will both take into account **real interest rates**. Consideration as to **future inflation levels** will therefore help determine the nominal rate of interest.

The **status of the borrower** will influence **perceived risk**. Those with a higher credit rating and moderate financial gearing will be granted more favourable borrowing terms and therefore relatively lower interest rates than those with a poor financial record. Whether a borrower can offer security for a loan and the quality of that security will be important: the better the collateral, the lower the rate of interest.

From both parties' points of view, but particularly that of the lender, the **type of any asset purchased by the loan is** important: is the security non-marketable on the one hand, or is it either marketable or redeemable on the other? In the latter case, there is possible escape from the financial commitment and risk, and means of adjustment to changed conditions. The more marketable/redeemable a security, the lower the interest rate.

The **amount** of any proposed loan will also be of some importance. Larger individual amounts will be less costly for a borrower to administer and this may be reflected in a marginally higher rate of interest on offer.

A lender will also be concerned in some instances with the **purpose** of any loan and the **competence of the borrower** in use of the funds. The reputation of a financial institution may be jeopardised by ill-considered lending which subsequently is adversely publicised. The greater the risk in this regard is considered to be, the higher will be the rate of interest.

3.4 Yields on short term money market instruments

Yield on Commercial paper

Commercial paper can be issued at a discount from the face value or it can be issued in interest bearing form. The investor is getting the same rate of return regardless of whether the commercial paper is purchased on a discounted or interest bearing basis.

On a discounted basis, the investor pays less than the face value or principal amount of the commercial paper and receives the full face at maturity. The quoted discount rate of interest is the discount amount expressed as a percentage of the maturing face amount.

On a interest bearing basis, the investor pays for the full face value of the commercial paper and receives the face value plus accrued interest at the time of maturity. The quoted discount or interest rate is converted to a yield to calculate the interest at maturity. This conversion is simply a restatement of the discount rate as a percentage of the initial proceeds rather than the maturing amount.

Yield on Treasury bills

Treasury bills are purchased by investors at less than face value and are redeemed at maturity at face value. The difference between the purchase price and the face value of the bill is the investor's return.

The following formula is used to determine the discount yield for T-bills that have three- or six-month maturities:

$$y = \frac{F - P}{F} \times \frac{360}{M}$$

F = = face value

P = purchase price

M = maturity of bill. For a three-month T-bill (13 weeks) use 91, and for a six-month T-bill (26 weeks) use 182

360 = the number of days used by banks to determine short-term interest rates

3.4.1 Example

What is the discount yield for a 182-day T-bill, auctioned at an average price of $9719.30 per $10,000 face value?

Solution

$$y = \frac{F - P}{F} \times \frac{360}{M} = \frac{10{,}000 - 9{,}719.3}{10{,}000} \times \frac{360}{182} = 0.0555$$

The discount yield is 5.55%

When comparing the return on investment in T-bills to other short-term investment options, the investment yield method can be used. This yield is alternatively called the **bond equivalent yield**, the coupon equivalent rate, the effective yield and the interest yield.

The yield on a Treasury bill varies according to the method of computation. The discount method relates the investor's return to the face value, while the investment method relates the return to the purchase price of the bill. The discount method tends to understate yields relative to those calculated using the investment method.

The following formula is used to calculate the investment yield for T-bills that have three- or six-month maturities:

$$\text{Investment yield} = y = \frac{F-P}{P} \times \frac{365}{M}$$

Note that the investment yield method is based on a calendar year: 365 days, or 366 in leap years.

3.4.2 Example

What is the investment yield of a 182-day T-bill, auctioned at an average price of $9,659.30 per $10,000 face value?

Solution

$$y = \frac{F-P}{P} \times \frac{365}{M} = \frac{10{,}000 - 9{,}719.3}{9{,}719.3} \times \frac{365}{182} = 0.0579$$

Investment yield = 5.79%

3.5 Yields on bonds

Yields on bonds

Yield calculations on bonds aim to show the return on a gilt or bond as a percentage of either its nominal value or its current price. There are three types of yield calculation that are commonly used, the **nominal or flat yield**, the **current or running yield** and the **yield to maturity** or **redemption yield**:

Nominal or flat Yield

This is derived by dividing the annual coupon payment by the par value or nominal value of the bond.

$$\text{Nominal yield} = \frac{C}{F}$$

where C is the coupon and F is nominal or par value .

3.5.1 Example

If the nominal value of a bond is £100 and the bond pays 4% what is the nominal yield on the bond?

Solution

$$\text{Nominal yield} = \frac{4}{100} = 0.04 \text{ or } 4\%$$

Current or Running Yield

This is calculated by dividing the annual coupon income on the bond by its current market price.

$$\text{Running yield} = \frac{C}{P}$$

Where P is the market price.

3.5.2 Example

If the market price of the £100 bond dropped to £96, what is the current yield on the bond?

Solution

Running yield = $\frac{4}{96}$ = 0.0417 or 4.17%

Redemption Yield

The yield to maturity or redemption yield, is the rate of return investors earn if they buy the bond at a specific price (P) and hold it until maturity. Mathematically the yield to maturity (r) is the value that makes the present value of all the coupon payments equal to the purchase price.

Assessment focus point

These computations are most unlikely to be required in your exam.

3.6 Variations in the general level of interest rates over time

FAST FORWARD

Interest rates reflects a number of things, including **inflation**, **risk**, **demand for finance** and **government monetary policy**. A normal yield curve slopes upward.

Interest rates on any one type of financial asset will vary over time. In other words, the general level of interest rates might go up or down. The general level of interest rates is affected by several factors.

(a) **The need for a real return**. It is generally accepted that investors will want to earn a 'real' rate of return on their investment, that is, a return which exceeds the rate of inflation. The suitable real rate of return will depend on factors such as investment risk.

(b) **Uncertainty about future rates of inflation**. When investors are uncertain about what future nominal and real interest rates will be, they are likely to require higher interest yields to persuade them to take the risk of investing, especially in the longer term.

(c) **Changes in the level of government borrowing**. When the demand for credit increases, interest rates will go up. A high level of borrowing by the government, is likely to result in upward pressure on interest rates.

(d) **Higher demand for borrowing from individuals**. If individuals want to borrow more, for example because they feel confident about their level of future earnings, then interest rates will tend to rise.

(e) **Monetary policy**. Governments control the level of investment rates in order to control inflation.

(f) **Interest rates abroad**. An appropriate real rate of interest in one country will be influenced by external factors, such as interest rates in other countries and expectations about the exchange rate.

3.7 The term structure of interest rates

The structure of interest rates refers to the many different interest rates that there are. These various interest rates can be grouped into three broad classes, according to the length of time until the associated debts reach maturity.

- Short-term interest rates
- Medium-term interest rates
- Long-term interest rates

Longer term financial assets should in general offer a higher yield than short-term lending.

(a) The investor must be compensated for tying up his money in the asset for a longer period of time. If the government were to make two issues of 9% Treasury Stock on the same date, one with a term of five years and one with a term of 20 years (and if there were no expectations of changes in interest rates in the future) then the **liquidity preference** of investors would make them prefer the five year stock.

(b) The only way to overcome the liquidity preference of investors is to compensate them for the loss of liquidity; in other words, to offer a higher rate of interest on longer dated stock.

(c) There is a greater **risk** in lending longer term than shorter term for two reasons.

   (i) **Inflation**. The longer the term of the asset, the greater is the possibility that the rate of inflation will increase, so that the fixed rate of interest paid on the asset will be overtaken by interest yields on new lending now that inflation is higher.

   (ii) **Uncertain economic prospects**. The future state of the economy cannot be predicted with certainty. If an organisation wishes to borrow money now for, say, 15 years, there is no certainty about what might happen to that organisation during that time. It might thrive and prosper or it might run into economic difficulties for one reason or another.

   Investors will require a higher return to compensate them for the increased risk.

(d) Note, however, that two other factors also affect the cost of borrowing.

   (i) The risk associated with the perceived ability of the borrower to fulfil the terms of the loan
   (ii) Whether or not the loan is secured by a mortgage on an asset

3.8 Yield curve

A yield curve shows the relationship between interest rates on similar assets with different terms to maturity. A normal yield curve will be upward-sloping, as shown in Figure 1, because of the higher interest rates which are likely to apply to longer terms of lending for the reasons explained in the previous paragraph.

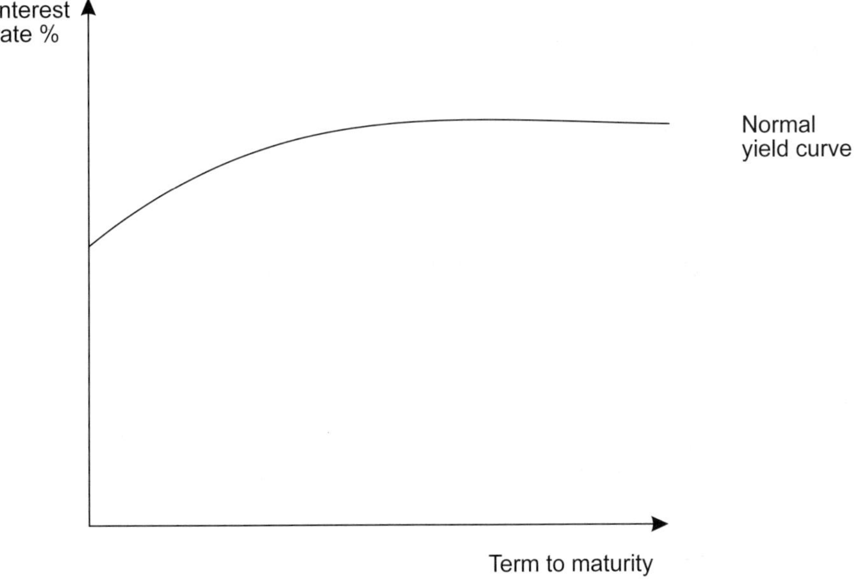

Figure 1 Yield curve

3.9 Returns on equities

As in the case of bonds or capital uncertain assets, the return on equities is made up of two components, the income received and the capital gain or loss for the change in the price of the share.

$$k_E = \frac{D}{P_P} + \frac{P_S - P_P}{P_P}$$

where

D is the dividend paid

P_P is the purchase price

P_S is the selling price

$$\text{Dividend yield} = \frac{D}{P_P}$$

$$\text{Capital gain part} = \frac{P_S - P_P}{P_P}.$$

3.9.1 Example

Consider the following information on a share

Current dividend per share	£0.2
Purchase price	£5
Sale Price	£6

We can calculate the dividend yield, the capital gain and the total return on the stock.

Solution

$$\text{Dividend yield} = \frac{D}{P_P} = \frac{0.2}{5} = 0.04 = 4\%$$

$$\text{Capital gain} = \text{Dividend yield} = \frac{P_S - P_P}{P_P} = \frac{6-5}{5} = 0.2 = 20\%$$

Total Return = Dividend yield + Capital gain = 4% + 20% = 24%

Long term rates of return

As ordinary equities have no maturity and the dividend payments are not constant, it is difficult to calculate a return similar to the yield to maturity. However, approximate measures can be derived if we make assumptions about the dividends. Two such assumptions are normally made. First that the dividend paid is constant for ever at level D. in this case if the price is P, the return on equities is given by the dividend yield since with no growth in dividend payments there will be no growth in the value of the firm.

The second assumption made is that dividends grow at constant rate g. In this case the rate of return is given by

$$k_E = \frac{D}{P}(1+g) + g$$

3.9.2 Example

To illustrate, assume the following values for the expected growth, current dividends and current market price:

g = 0.05
D = £0.06
P = £2

Calculate the rate of return on equity.

Solution

$$k_E = \frac{0.06}{2}(1+0.05)+0.05 = 0.0815 \text{ or } 8.15\%$$

3.10 Risk and return on financial assets

When investors invest in financial assets they receive in return an income as a compensation for giving up funds and therefore potential consumption. The income takes the form of a dividend or coupon or a capital gain. Looking at the various instruments we have examined so far, we can make the following comments regarding the uncertainty surrounding the income and the capital gain element of compensation.

(a) A 91 day **Treasury bill** has no uncertainty regarding its income if it is held to maturity, since the compensation in the form of the discount yield is known at the beginning of the transaction.

(b) A **government bond** has no uncertainty regarding its income, since this is known at the time the bond is issued. It also faces no risk with regard to capital gains if it held to maturity. As our example above shows, it is possible however for the price of the bond to fall and a loss to incur if the bond is sold before maturity.

(c) **Ordinary shares**, on the other hand, have uncertain dividend payments and uncertain selling prices, that makes the holding period return uncertain.

(d) Another aspect of risk that should be taken into account is **credit risk**. A corporate bond for example may pay fixed coupons but it may have a high risk of bankruptcy in which case even the coupon payment is rendered uncertain.

Taking these characteristics into account it is accepted that the ranking of securities in terms of risk is as follows.

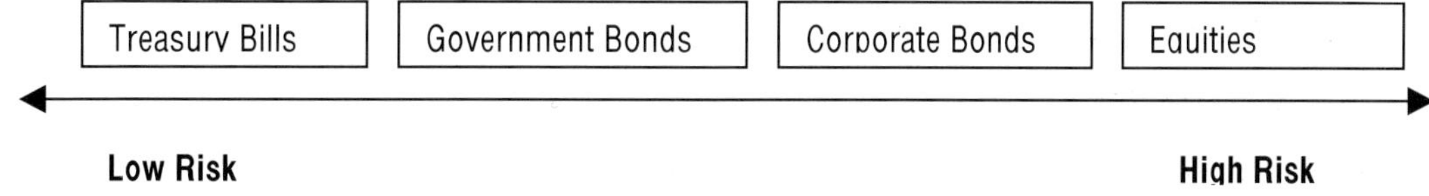

Since individuals are exposed to varying degrees of risk when invest in financial assets, then it follows that investors will demand a higher compensation for the higher risk. The relationship between risk and return is thus positive and the determination of the precise relationship between risk and return is the object of financial theory. The accepted relationship between risk and return is shown in the diagram below.

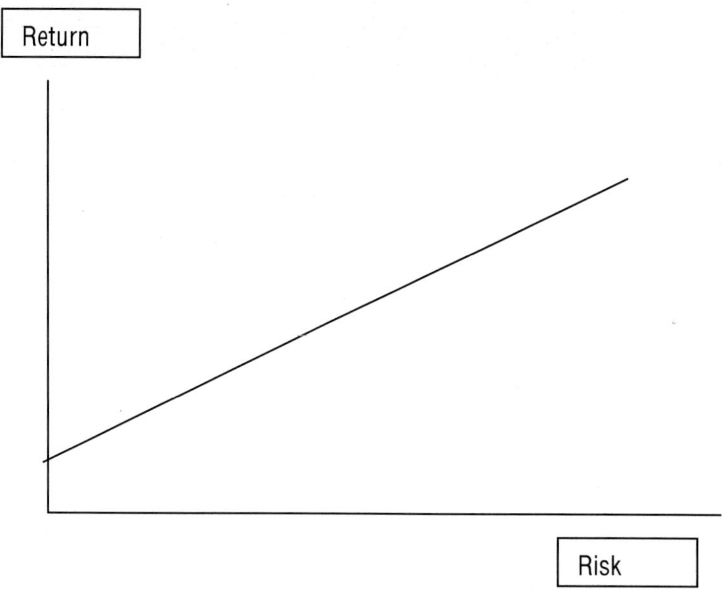

The return on any asset could be seen as made up of two components:

(a) the return from an **asset** which is **free of risk** such as government bond (a **risk free asset**) and

(b) an additional return, referred to as the **risk premium** which represents the compensation for bearing the risk.

3.11 The impact of the central bank on financial market yields

As discussed earlier, central banks may set short term interest rates. At the same time interest rates affect the yields on other financial assets. For example, an investor in equities will require a yield that would be at least equal to the prevailing short-term interest rates plus a risk premium appropriate to the equities held. If interest rates go up following an intervention by the Central Bank the required return by equity holders will go up and share prices will tend to fall.

Central banks can therefore play an important role in affecting yields and prices of financial assets.

Chapter roundup

- Banks (and building societies) create **credit** when they lend or grant overdrafts, and their activities thus contribute significantly to the increase in the money supply. In practice, the size of the **credit multiplier** is restricted by 'leakages' and by central bank controls over the liquidity and capital structure of banks.
- The **central bank** has various functions. These include acting as a **banker to the central government** and to the **commercial banks**. The Bank of England has responsibility for controlling sterling inflation by setting interest rates.
- In practice, there is a variety of **interest rates.** To make a profit, institutions that borrow money to re-lend, or that accept deposits which they re-lend (eg banks) must pay lower interest on deposits than they charge to customers who borrow.
- The real value of income from investments is eroded by **inflation**. The real rate of interest can be calculated by using the formula below.

  $$\frac{1 + \text{money rate}}{1 + \text{inflation rate}} = 1 + \text{real rate}$$
- Provision of finance brings **risk**, which will be reflected in the interest charged.
- Interest rates reflect a number of things, including **inflation**, **risk**, **demand for finance** and **government monetary policy**. A normal yield curve slopes upward.

Quick quiz

1. Define the credit multiplier.
2. What three aims must a commercial bank keep in balance?
3. List the likely functions of a central bank.
4. If the banking system has liquid reserves of £225bn and seeks to maintain a reserve ratio of 13%, what will broad money supply be?

   A £17bn
   B £1,731bn
   C £2,925bn
   D £292,599bn
5. The ability of the banks to create credit is constrained by all the following except:

   A Leakages of cash out of the banking system
   B A reduced reserve ratio
   C Low demand for loans
   D Prudent lending operations

Answers to quick quiz

1. The credit multiplier (or bank multiplier) is the name given to banks' ability to create credit, and hence money, by maintaining their cash reserves at less than 100% of the value of their deposits.

2. Liquidity, profitability and security.

3. Setting interest rates
   Banker to the government
   Central issuer of banknotes
   Manager of the national debt
   Manager of the nation's foreign currency reserves
   Banker to the clearing banks
   Supervision of the banking system

4. B £225bn × credit multiplier = total deposits (broad money) therefore £225bn × (1/0.13) = £1,731bn

5. B A falling reserve ratio will increase the credit multiplier.

Now try the questions below from the Exam Question Bank

Question numbers	Page
30 – 32	370

11

The foreign exchange market

Introduction

In this chapter we look at how exchange rates are determined and how they impact on business. Before we see how the foreign exchange markets operate, in the first section we go through the terminology and basic calculations. The reason for doing this first is that it is absolutely essential knowledge for all levels of your CIMA studies. Examiners even at Strategic level frequently complain that students get basic foreign currency calculations wrong. If you can master the calculations at this stage, this will be a big help later on.

In Section 2 we look at the operation of the foreign exchange markets and look at their impact on a business's competitiveness and ability to trade. An awareness of the factors that cause movements in the foreign exchange rates will help businesses predict what the effects are likely to be, so in Section 3 we consider the main influences on exchange rates. However governments intervene to varying degrees to limit the fluctuations of exchange rate, and therefore in Section 4 we consider various exchange rate systems. Despite these, all businesses trading abroad will face some exchange risk and so in the last section we describe various methods firms use to counter foreign exchange risks, and also credit risks, which can also be significant when trading abroad.

Topic list	Learning outcomes	Syllabus references	Ability required
1 Exchange rates	C (iv)	C (11)	Comprehension
2 Foreign exchange markets	C (iv)	C (10), (11)	Comprehension
3 Influences on exchange rates	C (iv)	C (13)	Comprehension
4 Government policy	C (iv)	C (14)	Comprehension
5 Risks of international trade	C (iv)	C (12)	Comprehension

1 Exchange rates

FAST FORWARD

The **spot rate** is the rate at which currencies are currently quoted on the foreign exchange markets. The **forward rate** is the rate at which currencies will be exchanged on a set future date.

1.1 Types of exchange rates

Key terms

An exchange rate is the market price at which one specific currency exchanges for another specific currency.

An exchange rate is the rate at which one country's currency can be traded in exchange for another country's currency. It is the price of one currency expressed in terms of another currency.

The exchange rate may be set by the interaction of demand and supply of the various foreign currencies (**floating exchange rate**) or by government intervention in order to maintain a constant rate of exchange (**fixed exchange rate**).

1.2 Dealing in foreign exchange

Dealers in foreign exchange make their profit by buying currency at one exchange rate (the **bid price**), and selling it at a more favourable rate for themselves (the **offer price**). This means that there is a **selling rate** and a **buying rate** for a currency.

1.2.1 Example: Buying and selling foreign exchange rates

Dan trades in the UK and wishes to purchase some machinery from a supplier in the United States. The transaction will be in dollars and the cost of the machinery is $500,000. Dan has also just received €100,000 on a contract and wishes to exchange the euros for pounds.

The current exchange rates are:

$/£ 1.8700 – 1.8900
€/£ 1.4600 – 1.4800

Required

Calculate how much Dan will pay in sterling for the machinery and how much he will receive on the contract.

Solution

The key rule to remember is that Dan will always get the worse rate for the transaction and the foreign exchange dealers will always get the better rate.

(a) **The machinery**

Dan needs to **pay in dollars**, so needs to obtain or **buy dollars** with pounds. The rates quoted are how many dollars can be exchanged for each pound. Since Dan gets the worst of it, for each pound he pays to buy dollars, he will only obtain $1.8700, the **lower rate.**

Therefore to obtain $500,000, he needs to pay 500,000/1.8700 = £267,380

(b) **The contract payment**

Here Dan has **received euros** and wishes to **sell the euros** he has received in exchange for £. As Dan again gets the worse bargain, he has to sell more euros to obtain each pound, and so will have to hand over €1.4800 (the **higher rate**) to obtain each £.

He will receive 100,000/1.4800 = £67,568

1.2.2 Mid-market price

Sometimes you will see a single exchange rate quoted, the **mid-market price**. This is, unsurprisingly, the price midway between the bid and offer price. In the situation Dan is facing in the question above, the mid-market $/£ price will be 1.8800.

Question — **Sterling receipts**

Calculate how much sterling the exporter would receive and how much sterling the importer would pay in each of the following situations, if they were to exchange currency and sterling at the spot rate.

(a) A UK exporter receives a payment from a Danish customer of 150,000 kroners.
(b) A UK importer buys goods from a Japanese supplier and pays 1 million yen.

Spot rates are as follows.

	Bank sells		*Bank buys*
Danish Kr/£	9.4340	–	9.5380
Japan ¥/£	203.65	–	205.78

Answer

(a) The exporter is selling Danish kroners. The bank will buy Danish kroners and give

$$\frac{150{,}000}{9.5380} = £15{,}727 \text{ in exchange for the kroners}$$

(b) The importer is buying the yen from the bank. The bank will sell the yen to the importer and will charge

$$\frac{1{,}000{,}000}{203.65} = £4{,}910$$

1.3 Direct and indirect currency quotes

Key terms

A **direct quote** is the amount of domestic currency that is equal to one foreign currency unit.

An **indirect quote** is the amount of foreign currency that is equal to one domestic currency unit.

Currencies may be quoted in either direction. For example, the US dollar and Euro might be quoted as€/$ = 0.8763 or $/€ = 1.1412. In other words €0.8763 = $1 and $1.1412 = €1. One rate is simply the reciprocal of the other.

A further complication to be aware of is that the selling rate in one country becomes the buying rate in the other. For example, Malaysian Ringgit (MR) are quoted in London as:

	Bank sells		*Bank buys*
MR/£	5.5655	–	5.5662

However, in Kuala Lumpur you would see:

	Bank sells		*Bank buys*
MR/£	5.5662	–	5.5655

Key term

If a currency is quoted at $1.50:£, the $ is the **term currency** (the **reference currency**), and the pound sterling is the **base currency**.

1.3.1 Buying low and selling high

When considering the prices banks are using, remember that the bank will **sell the term/reference currency low**, and **buy the term/reference currency high**. For example if a UK bank is buying and selling dollars, the bank's selling price may be $1.41 (the customer obtains fewer dollars for each pound he pays) and the bank's buying price may be $1.43 (the customer needs to give the bank $1.43 for the bank to pay each pound).

Assessment focus point

The assessment will not be confined to the activities of UK companies. Exchange rates given in the examination could be as quoted in foreign countries. Because of these complications you should always double-check which rate you are using. One sure method is to recognise that the bank makes money out of the transaction and will therefore offer you the worse of the two possible rates.

1.4 Spot and forward rates

Key terms

A **spot rate** is the rate set for the immediate delivery of the currency.

A **forward rate** is the rate set for the delivery of the currency at some future date.

A forward price is the **spot price** ruling on the day a forward exchange contract is made plus or minus the **interest differential** for the period of the contract.

The forward rate is **not a forecast** of what the spot rate will be on a given date in the future; it will be a coincidence if the forward rate turns out to be the same as the spot rate on that future date.

1.4.1 Example: Spot and forward rates

Suppose that a spot rate on 1 June is US$1.7430 - 1.7440 to £1, and the three months forward rate (for 1 September) is US$1.7380 - 1.7395 to £1. In this example, three-month interest rates in the UK on 1 June would be higher than interest rates in the USA, which accounts for the forward rates for dollars against sterling being lower than the spot rates on 1 June.

1.4.2 Discounts and premiums

Forward rates are not always quoted in full, but may be quoted at a discount or premium to the spot rates.

FORWARD RATES AS ADJUSTMENTS TO SPOT RATES	
Forward rate cheaper	Quoted at discount
Forward rate more expensive	Quoted at premium

A **discount** is therefore **added** to the spot rate, and a **premium** is therefore **subtracted** from the spot rate. (The mnemonic **ADDIS** may help you to remember that we ADD Discounts and so subtract premiums.) The longer the duration of a forward contract, the larger will be the quoted premium or discount.

1.4.3 Example: Discounts and premiums

The $/£ spot rate is currently quoted at 1.8500 – 1.8700 and the 1 month forward rate at 0.0006 – 0.0010 discount.

Required

Calculate the actual forward rate.

Solution

Because the forward rate is quoted at a discount, that means that more dollars can be obtained for each pound. The rate is therefore 1.8506 – 1.8710.

Question — **Forward rate**

The €/$ spot rate is currently quoted at 0.7800 – 0.8000 and the 3 month forward rate at 0.0012 – 0.0008 premium.

Required

Calculate the actual forward rate.

Answer

Because the forward rate is quoted at a premium, that means that fewer euros can be obtained for each dollar. The rate is therefore 0.7788 – 0.7992.

2 Foreign exchange markets

FAST FORWARD

Activity in foreign exchange markets partly depends on **currency demands** arising from **international trade**, but much dealing is done between banks.

If firms want to develop by doing business abroad, they will have to use foreign currency; however their cash flows may be **threatened** by **adverse exchange rate movements** on the foreign currency markets.

Longer-term adverse exchange rate movements can threaten a firm's **competitiveness** in world markets.

2.1 Operation of foreign exchange markets

Currency markets exist to facilitate the **exchange of one currency** into another. Although demand to buy or sell foreign currencies arises from the demands of individuals (for example tourists going abroad and firms doing business abroad), the main bulk buying and selling of foreign currencies is by banks:

- Banks buy currency from customers and sell currency to customers
- Banks may buy currency from the government or sell currency to governments – this is how governments build up their official reserves
- Banks also buy or sell currencies between themselves

The foreign exchange markets are worldwide with the largest currency dealing centre being London.

2.2 Dealing on foreign exchange markets

As we shall see later on in this chapter, some exchange rates are fixed, but many are allowed to vary. Rates are changing continually, and each bank will offer **new rates** for customer enquiries according to how its dealers judge the market situation. Dealers are kept continually informed of rates at which deals are currently being made by means of computerised information services.

Exchange rates will often change by just small amounts up or down, but factors such as **speculation** may lead to more substantial movements.

2.3 Impact of foreign exchange markets on firms

2.3.1 Need for foreign exchange facilities

As indicated above, banks buy and sell foreign currency to their customers. Firms need to use banks because if they sell their products overseas, they will often not be able to price their products in their own currency, and will have to **price their products in the local currency** of the markets in which they are selling. They may however wish to convert the foreign currency earnings into their own currency, and so will have to use bank facilities to carry out this exchange. Similarly if a firm buys from overseas, it may not be able to settle its account in its own currency, but may **require foreign currency to pay the supplier**.

Thus if they wish to expand into new markets or use cheaper sources of supply, firms have to trade abroad and hence become involved in foreign exchange dealings.

2.3.2 Risks of exchange dealing

Although being able to buy and sell foreign currency they need or earn may significantly enhance the opportunities of firms, it also exposes firms to **currency risk.** This is partly because doing business abroad does not just consist of a series of individual transactions settled instantaneously.

(a) A US company may agree in June to make a payment to a French company in September of €300,000. If the payment was made in June, the exchange rate could be 0.7800€/$ and hence the payment would have cost the company 300,000/0.7800 = $384,615. However by September the dollar may have weakened against the euro with the result that the company will, for each dollar it sells to the bank, obtain fewer of the euros that it needs. Say the rate has moved to 0.7700 by September. The payment will now cost the company 300,000/0.7700 = $389,610

(b) A UK company may budget to receive $15,000,000 from sales in the USA over a year. If it expects the average exchange rate over the year to be 1.8000$/£, it will expect to obtain 15,000,000/1.8000 = £8,333,333 for the dollars it expects to earn and will budget accordingly. Suppose however that the value of the dollar falls, and the average exchange rate for the year turns out to be 1.8500$/£. Then the company will only earn 15,000,000/1.8500 = £8,108,108 and the actual value of sales will be under-budget, even though the quantities sold have been as budgeted.

These examples illustrate how using foreign currencies in business can introduce a significant element of uncertainty into planning. We shall discuss how firms counter exchange risk in Section 5 of this Chapter.

2.3.3 Impact on competitiveness

For individual transactions, a company may be unlucky in being adversely affected by short-term currency movements. However some currency movements may be longer-term. Over time these movements may reduce the **longer-term competitiveness** of a firm. If its own local currency strengthens, then its products will become more expensive overseas and hence demand for them will decrease.

As firms both buy and sell overseas, it is possible that they may suffer adverse exchange rate movements in two ways. Suppose a UK company buys raw materials that are priced in US dollars. It converts these materials into finished products that it exports mainly to Spain. Over a period of several years, the pound depreciates against the dollar but strengthens against the euro. The **sterling value** of the **company's income declines** while the **sterling cost** of its **materials increases**, resulting in a double drop in the value of the company's cash flows.

A company need not even engage in any foreign activities to be subject to **longer-term currency exposure**. For example if a company trades only in the UK but the pound strengthens appreciably against other world currencies, it may find that it loses UK sales to a foreign competitor who can now afford to charge cheaper sterling prices.

Question **Foreign trading**

If a firm makes a lot of sales in one particular overseas countries, why might using suppliers within that country reduce its foreign exchange risk?

Answer

Because the firm is receiving monies and making payments in the same foreign currency, and adverse effect of an exchange rate movement on receipts will be countered by a beneficial effect on payments. This is the technique known as matching which we shall consider further in Section 5.

(There may well be other arguments for using suppliers in the same country that sales are made, and locating manufacturing facilities there as well, for example reduced transport and distribution costs.)

3 Influences on exchange rates

FAST FORWARD

Supply and demand for foreign currency are subject to a number of influences.

- The rate of inflation, compared with the rate of inflation in other countries
- Interest rates, compared with interest rates in other countries
- The balance of payments
- Speculation
- Government policy on intervention to influence the exchange rate

3.1 Factors influencing the exchange rate for a currency

In this section we cover the major factors that influence movements on the foreign exchange markets, other than government intervention, which we cover in Section 4 of this Chapter. Apart from these factors, other factors influence the exchange rate through their relationship with the items identified above.

(a) **Total income and expenditure** (demand) in the domestic economy determines the demand for goods. This includes imported goods and demand for goods produced in the country which would otherwise be exported if demand for them did not exist in the home markets.

(b) **Output capacity and the level of employment** in the domestic economy might influence the balance of payments, because if the domestic economy has full employment already, it will be unable to increase its volume of production for exports.

(c) The **growth in the money supply** influences interest rates and domestic inflation.

3.2 Inflation and the exchange rate

If the rate of inflation is higher in one country than in another country, the value of its currency will tend to weaken against the other country's currency.

3.2.1 Purchasing power parity theory

Purchasing power parity theory attempts to explain changes in the exchange rate exclusively by the rate of inflation in different countries. The theory predicts that the exchange value of a foreign currency depends on the relative purchasing power of each currency in its own country.

As a simple example, suppose that there is only one commodity, which costs £110 in the UK and €165 Euros in France. The purchasing power parity exchange rate would be £1 = €1.5. If, as a result of inflation, the cost of the commodity in the UK rises to £120, purchasing power parity theory would predict that the exchange rate would adjust to:

$$1.5 \times \frac{110}{120} \times £1 = €1.375$$

If the exchange rate remained at £1 = €1.5, it would be cheaper in the UK to import more of the commodity from France for £110 rather than to produce it in the UK, As a result, the UK would have a balance of trade deficit in that commodity. This would only be corrected by an **alteration in the exchange rate**, with the pound weakening against the euro.

Purchasing power parity theory states that an exchange rate varies according to relative price changes, so that:

$$\text{'Old' exchange rate} \times \frac{\text{Price level in country A}}{\text{Price level in country B}} = \text{'New' exchange rate}$$

Assessment formula

The theory is not usually adequate in explaining movements in exchange rates **in the short term**, mainly because it ignores payments between countries (ie demand and supply transactions) and the influence of supply and demand for currency on exchange rates.

The relevant formula is:

$$\text{Future rate US\$/£} = \text{Spot US\$/£} \times \frac{1+\text{US inflation rate}}{1+\text{UK inflation rate}}$$

However you may have to use other currencies in it. Note that 'Future rate' here means the spot exchange rate at a future date. This formula does not relate the forward rate quoted now to the spot rate – a relationship we discussed in paragraph 1.4 of this Chapter, and return to below.

3.2.2 Example: Purchasing power parity theory

Suppose that inflation is running at 8% in the US and 4% in the UK. The exchange rate between the two countries is 1.7600 $/£. What is the predicted rate in one year's time, using purchasing power parity?

Solution

Using purchasing power parity, Future rate US$/£ = 1.7600 $\times$ (1 + 0.08)/(1 + 0.04)

= 1.8277

Question **Purchasing power parity**

Current inflation rates are 6% in the Eurozone and 4% in the UK. The current spot exchange rate is 0.6800 £/€. What is the expected spot exchange rate in one year's time?

Answer

The complications here are that we are using Euros and pounds, and the exchange rate is quoted in terms of £/€. This means that the formula has to be adjusted:

$$\text{Future rate £/€} = \text{Spot £/€} \times \frac{1 + \text{UK inflation rate}}{1 + \text{Euro inflation rate}}$$

= 0.6800 $\times$ (1 + 0.04)/(1 + 0.06)

= 0.6672

3.3 Interest rates and the exchange rate

It would seem logical to assume that if one country raises its interest rates, it will become more profitable to invest in that country, and so an increase in investment from overseas will push up the **spot exchange rate** because of the extra demand for the currency from overseas investors.

This may be true in the short-term, but the market adjusts **forward rates** for this. If this were not so, then investors holding the currency with the lower interest rates would switch to the other currency for (say) three months, ensuring that they would not lose on returning to the original currency by fixing the exchange rate in advance at the forward rate. If enough investors acted in this way (known as **arbitrage**), forces of supply and demand would lead to a change in the forward rate to prevent such risk-free profit making.

3.3.1 Interest rate parity

The **interest rate parity** condition relates the forward and spot rates for two currencies to the interest rates prevailing in those two countries: we introduced this idea at paragraph 1.4 of this Chapter.

$$\text{Forward rate US\$/£} = \text{Spot US\$/£} \times \frac{1 + \text{nominal US interest rate}}{1 + \text{nominal UK interest rate}}$$

3.3.2 Example: Interest rate parity

The current exchange rate between the US and UK is $/£ 1.7500. The current central bank lending rates in both countries are 6% in the US, 5% in the UK. What is the one-year forward exchange rate?

Solution

Here use of the formula is straightforward, as we are given the US and UK figures.

Forward rate US$/£ = 1.7500 × (1 + 0.06)/(1 + 0.05)

= 1.7667

Question

Interest rate parity

The spot rate between Japan and the Eurozone is currently 145.000 ¥/€. The central bank lending rate in Japan is currently 8% and is 4% in the Eurozone. What is the one-year forward exchange rate, using the interest rate parity condition?

Answer

Here we are dealing with two currencies that are not the dollar and the pound. As the exchange rate is quoted in terms of Yen per each Euro, then the Japanese interest rate goes on top of the interest rate parity equation.

Forward rate ¥/€ = 145.000 × (1 + 0.08)/(1 + 0.04)

= 150.577

3.4 The balance of payments and the exchange rate

If exchange rates respond to **demand and supply for current account items**, then the balance of payments on the current account of all countries would tend towards equilibrium. This is not so, and **in practice other factors influence exchange rates more strongly**.

Demand for currency to invest in overseas capital investments and supply of currency from firms disinvesting in an overseas currency have more influence on the exchange rate, in the short term at least, than the demand and supply of goods and services.

If a country has a **persistent deficit in its balance of payments current account**, international confidence in that country's currency will eventually be eroded. In the long term, its exchange rate will fall as capital inflows are no longer sufficient to counterbalance the country's trade deficit.

3.5 Speculation and exchange rate fluctuations

Speculators in foreign exchange are investors who **buy or sell assets in a foreign currency**, in the **expectation of a rise or fall in the exchange rate**, from which they seek to make a profit. Speculation could be destabilising if it creates such a high volume of demand to buy or sell a particular currency that the exchange rate fluctuates to levels where it is overvalued or undervalued in terms of what hard economic facts suggest it should be.

If a currency does become undervalued by heavy speculative selling, investors can make a further profit by purchasing it at the undervalued price and selling it later when its price rises.

Speculation, when it is destabilising, could **damage a country's economy** because the uncertainty about exchange rates disrupts trade in goods and services.

4 Government policy

FAST FORWARD

Government policies on exchange rates might be **fixed exchange rates** or **floating exchange rates** at two extremes.

In practice, 'in-between' schemes have included:

- **Fixed rates**, but with provision for devaluations or revaluations of currencies from time to time ('adjustable pegs') and also some fluctuations ('margins') around the fixed exchange value permitted
- **Managed floating** within a desired range of values

Currency blocs and **exchange rate systems** enhance currency stability, but limit the ability of governments to pursue independent economic policies.

If several currencies adopt a **single currency**, then **transactions** between firms in different countries within the currency zone will become **cheaper** (no commission costs on currency dealings), and **financial markets** across the zone will become **more flexible.**

4.1 Free floating exchange rates

Sometimes governments will not intervene in the foreign exchange markets. Free floating at flexible exchange rates is when **exchange rates are left to the free play of market forces** and there is no official financing at all.

Floating exchange rates are the only option available to governments when other systems break down and fail. Milton Friedman has remarked that 'floating exchange rates have often been adopted by countries experiencing financial crises when all other devices have failed. That is a major reason why they have such a bad reputation.'

4.1.1 Advantages of floating exchange rates

(a) Governments do not have to **spend or even hold foreign currency reserves**

(b) Balance of payments deficits or surpluses are **automatically corrected**. A deficit will result in the exchange rate falling; this will improve competitiveness, raise exports and restore equilibrium.

(c) Governments need **not adopt economic policies** that may be undesirable for other reasons to **maintain exchange rates**.

4.1.2 Disadvantages of floating exchange rates

(a) If exchange rates **appreciate too much** under a floating rate system, then, as we have seen, **firms' international competitiveness** may be reduced, and output and employment may fall across the economy.

(b) If **exchange rates fall too much**, **import prices,** and hence inflation, **will rise.**

(c) **Currency risk** will be **maximised** under a system of floating exchange rates.

4.1.3 Managed floating

In practice, governments prefer generally to operate **managed floating** of their currency and a policy of allowing a currency to float entirely freely is rare.

4.2 Government intervention in foreign exchange markets

A government can intervene in the foreign exchange markets in two ways.

(a) It can **sell its own currency** in exchange for foreign currencies, when it wants to keep down the exchange rate of its domestic currency. The foreign currencies it buys can be added to the official reserves.

(b) It can **buy its own currency** and pay for it with the foreign currencies in its official reserves. It will do this when it wants to keep up the exchange rate when market forces are pushing it down.

The government can also intervene indirectly, by **changing domestic interest rates,** and so either attracting or discouraging investors in financial investments which are denominated in the domestic currency.

By managing the exchange rate for its currency, a government does not stop all fluctuations in the exchange rate, but it tries to keep the fluctuations within certain limits.

(a) **Unofficial limits**: a government might intervene in the foreign exchange markets and sell foreign currency from its official reserves to buy the domestic currency, and so support its exchange rate, even though there is no officially declared exchange rate that it is trying to support.

(b) **Official limits**: the country may be part of a system that allows its currency to fluctuate against the other currencies within the system only within specified limits.

4.2.1 Reasons for a policy of controlling the exchange rate

(a) To **rectify a balance of trade deficit**, by trying to bring about a fall in the exchange rate.

(b) To **prevent a balance of trade surplus** from getting too large, by trying to bring about a limited rise in the exchange rate.

(c) To **emulate economic conditions** in other countries, for example lower inflation.

(d) To **stabilise the exchange rate of its currency**. Exporters and importers will then face less risk of exchange rate movements wiping out their profits. A stable currency increases confidence in the currency and promotes international trade.

4.3 Fixed exchange rates

A policy of rigidly fixed exchange rates means that the government must use its **official reserves** to create an exact match between supply and demand for its currency in the foreign exchange markets, in order to keep the exchange rate unchanged. Using the official reserves will therefore cancel out a surplus or deficit on the current account and non-official capital transactions in their balance of payments. A balance of payments surplus would call for an addition to the official reserves, and a deficit calls for drawings on official reserves.

For simplicity and convenience, the exchange rate is fixed against a standard. The standard might be one of the following.

- **Gold**
- **A major currency**
- **A basket of major trading currencies**

4.3.1 Advantages of fixed exchange rates

(a) A fixed exchange rate system **removes exchange rate uncertainty** and so **encourages international trade**.

(b) A fixed rate system also **imposes economic disciplines** on countries in deficit (or surplus).

4.3.2 Disadvantages of fixed rates

(a) There is inevitably **some loss of flexibility** in economic policy making once a country fixes its exchange rates. A government might be **forced to reduce demand** in the domestic economy (for example by raising taxes and so cutting the demand for imports) in order to maintain a currency's exchange rate and avoid a devaluation.

(b) Countries regard **devaluation** as an indicator of failure of economic policy and often resist devaluation until long after it should have taken place.

4.3.3 A moveable peg system

A moveable or adjustable peg system is a system of fixed exchange rates, but with a provision for the devaluation or revaluation of a currency.

A moveable peg system provides **some flexibility.** Exchange rates, although fixed, are not rigidly fixed, because adjustments are permitted. Even so, it is still fairly inflexible, because governments only have the choice between a revaluation/devaluation or holding the exchange rate steady. A more flexible system would allow some minor variations in exchange rates.

4.4 Currency boards

A currency board is a type of fixed rate system where the local currency is backed by a **major world currency** such as the dollar. The local money supply is matched by **holdings of financial assets** in the **reserve currency.** The country cannot make local currency issues unless they are backed by additional assets in the reserve currency.

4.5 Currency blocs

Currency blocs are where groups of countries **fix their exchange rates** against a major trading currency. The resulting stability is designed to help international trade, since the major currency used will be the currency of a country (countries) with whom members of the bloc carry out a lot of trade.

The currency may be a major world currency or it may be an artificial currency set up as part of a more formal exchange rate system.

4.6 Exchange rate systems

Exchange rate systems are systems where there is **stability** between the currencies of member currencies, even though there are fluctuations with the currencies of countries outside the systems. An example is the European Monetary System established in 1979. Part of this was the Exchange Rate Mechanism under which:

(a) Each country had a **central rate** in the system.

(b) Currencies were only allowed to **fluctuate within certain levels** (bands)

(c) Within the bands, fluctuations of a certain limit should **trigger action** by governments to prevent fluctuations beyond the bands allowed.

4.6.1 Advantages of exchange rate systems

(a) **Reduction of inflation**

Exchange rate stability within an exchange rate system may help dampen inflation by preventing a government from allowing the currency to drift downwards in value to compensate for **price inflation.** This was a major aim of UK Prime Minister John Major, who wanted to establish the UK economy as a permanent low inflation economy.

(b) **Expectations**

There are likely to be effects on people's expectations; in particular the **perceived risk** of **exchange rate movements** between member currencies should be **low.** As well as allowing firms to plan and forecast with greater certainty, exchange rate stability ought to make a currency **less risky to hold**.

4.6.2 Problems with exchange rate systems

The UK's experience within the European Monetary System demonstrates a number of the potential problems of an exchange rate system.

(a) **Wrong initial rates**

In retrospect it is clear that the UK entered the European Monetary System at **too high a rate**, leading to the UK becoming less competitive, resulting in a deep recession and a significant deficit on the balance of payments.

(b) **Interest rate levels**

Interest rate policy must be consistent with keeping the currency stable.The problem the UK faced in the early 1990s was that it had to keep interest rates high for longer than was necessary for the aim of dampening inflation to maintain the pound's value against the deutschmark, as the German interest rate was high. However the two countries were facing different economic situations, with Germany needing to keep interest rates high to counter continuing inflationary pressures caused by the unification of East and West Germany.

(c) **Vulnerability**

Ultimately the currency markets felt that the UK rate within the ERM was not sustainable, and **speculation proved self-fulfilling**. UK attempts to maintain the value of the pound by raising interest rates and spending foreign currency reserves to buy sterling and protect its value proved in vain, and in September 1992 the UK devalued and left the ERM.

4.7 Single currency

A single currency is where a number of countries agree to adopt a single currency. Twelve members of the European Union have adopted a single currency, the euro. The system is administered by the European Central Bank, which issues euros and sets interest rates across the Eurozone. The continuing success depends on **convergence of the economies** of the member economies; as we have seen with EMU, the system could run into serious difficulties if countries have different economic priorities.

4.7.1 Advantages of a single currency

(a) The removal of exchange rate risk makes **cross-border trade and investment easier** and less risky.

(b) The removal of conversion fees paid by business and individuals to banks when converting different currencies makes **transactions** within the currency zone **cheaper.**

(c) **Financial markets** are **opened up** across the region and are more flexible and liquid than when there are many different currencies

(d) **Price parity** or price transparency across borders is thought to **lower prices** across the area.

(e) **Funding** is **easier to obtain**, as there is greater cross-border borrowing.

(f) **Economic stability** within the zone is thought to benefit not just the member countries of the zone but also the **world economy** as a whole.

4.7.2 Disadvantages of a single currency

(a) '**One size fits all**' currency may **not be applicable** to countries with very different industrial structures and at very different levels of economic maturity.

(b) There is a **loss of national self-determination** in monetary matters.

(c) **Agreement and coordination** between the different countries using the currency may be **difficult to achieve**.

Question — **Floating exchange rates**

Which of the following is not a disadvantage of a government allowing a country's exchange rate to float freely?

A Floating may result in currency appreciation and a fall in competitiveness.
B Floating may result in currency depreciation and a rise in inflation.
C Floating will result in firms facing increased foreign exchange risk.
D Floating will mean that government economic policy becomes more restricted.

Answer

D Floating removes the restrictions on economic policy that are necessary to maintain exchange rates at fixed levels.

5 Risks of international trade

5.1 Foreign exchange risk

FAST FORWARD

Basic methods of hedging risk include **matching receipts and payments**, **invoicing in own currency**, and **leading and lagging** the times that cash is received and paid.

A **forward contract** specifies in advance the rate at which a specified quantity of currency will be bought and sold.

Money market hedging involves borrowing in one currency, converting the money borrowed into another currency and putting the money on deposit until the time the transaction is completed, hoping to take advantage of favourable interest rate movements.

More complex methods of hedging include use of derivatives such as **futures**, **options** and **swaps.**

Key terms

Foreign exchange or currency risk is the risk that value will fluctuate due to changes in foreign exchange rates.

The main types of foreign exchange risk are as follows:

5.1.1 Transaction risk

Transaction risk is the risk of adverse exchange rate movements occurring in the course of **normal international trading transactions**. This arises when the prices of imports or exports are fixed in foreign currency terms and there is movement in the exchange rate between the date when the price is agreed and the date when the cash is paid or received in settlement.

5.1.2 Economic risk

This is the risk to the longer-term **international competitiveness** of a company. For example, a UK company might use raw materials that are priced in US dollars, but export its products mainly within the EU. A depreciation of sterling against the dollar or an appreciation of sterling against other EU currencies will both erode the competitiveness of the company.

Economic exposure can be difficult to avoid, although **diversification of the supplier and customer base** across different countries will reduce this kind of exposure to risk.

5.1.3 Translation risk

This is the risk that the organisation will make exchange losses when the **accounting results** of its foreign branches or subsidiaries are translated into the home currency. Translation losses can result, for example, from restating the book value of foreign assets at the exchange rate on the balance sheet date. Such losses will not have an impact on the firm's cash flow unless the assets are sold.

5.2 Dealing with foreign exchange transaction risk

5.2.1 Matching receipts and payments

A company can reduce or eliminate its foreign exchange transaction exposure by matching receipts and payments. Wherever possible, a company that expects to make payments and have receipts in the same foreign currency should plan to **offset** its **payments** against its **receipts** in the currency. Since the company will be setting off foreign currency receipts against foreign currency payments, it does not matter whether the currency strengthens or weakens against the company's 'domestic' currency because there will be **no purchase or sale of the currency.**

Since a company is unlikely to have exactly the same amount of receipts in a currency as it makes payments, it will still be **exposed to the extent of the difference**, and so the company may wish to avoid exposure on this difference by arranging forward exchange cover.

Offsetting (matching payments against receipts) will be cheaper than arranging a forward contract to buy currency and another forward contract to sell the currency, provided that:

- **Receipts occur before payments**, and
- The **time difference** between receipts and payments in the currency is **not too long**

5.2.2 Leads and lags

Companies might try to use:

- **Lead payments**: payments in advance, or
- **Lagged payments**: delaying payments beyond their due date

in order to take advantage of foreign exchange rate movements.

With a lead payment, paying in advance of the due date, there is a finance cost to consider. This is the interest cost on the money used to make the payment.

5.2.3 Currency of invoice

One way of avoiding exchange rate risk is for an exporter to **invoice** his foreign customer in his **domestic currency**, or for an importer to **arrange** with his **foreign supplier** to be **invoiced** in his **domestic currency**.

However, although either the exporter or the importer can avoid any exchange risk in this way, only one of them can deal in his domestic currency. The other must accept the exchange risk, since there will be a period of time elapsing between agreeing a contract and paying for the goods (unless payment is made with the order).

5.3 Forward exchange contracts

Key terms

A **forward exchange contract** is an agreement to exchange different currencies at a specified future date and at a specified rate. The difference between the specified rate and the spot rate ruling on the date the contract is entered into is the discount or premium on the forward contract.

Forward exchange contracts allow a trader who knows that he will have to buy or sell foreign currency at a date in the future to make the purchase or sale at a **predetermined rate of exchange**. The trader will therefore know in advance either how much **local currency** he will **receive** (if he is selling foreign currency to the bank) or how much local currency he must **pay** (if he is buying foreign currency from the bank).

5.3.1 Example: Forward exchange contracts

A UK importer knows on 1 April that he must pay a foreign supplier 26,500 Swiss francs in one month's time, on 1 May. He can arrange a forward exchange contract with his bank on 1 April, where the bank undertakes to sell the importer 26,500 Swiss francs on 1 May, at a fixed rate of say 2.6400 Swiss Francs:£

The UK importer can be certain that whatever the spot rate is between Swiss francs and sterling on 1 May, he will have to pay on that date, at this forward rate:

$$\frac{26{,}500}{2.64000} = £10{,}038$$

(a) If the spot rate is lower than 2.6400, the importer would have **successfully protected himself** against a weakening of sterling, and would have avoided paying more sterling to obtain the Swiss francs.

(b) If the spot rate is higher than 2.6400, sterling's value against the Swiss franc would mean that the **importer** would **pay more** under the forward exchange contract than he would have had to pay if he had obtained the francs at the spot rate on 1 May. He cannot avoid this extra cost, because a forward contract is binding.

Question

Forward exchange contracts

A German exporter is proposing to sell machinery to a UK customer worth £500,000 and is concerned about a change in the value of the Euro against the £. The financial director therefore decides to take out a forward contract. The forward rates quoted are €/£ 1.4500 – 1.4550. How much in Euros will the exporter receive under the contract?

Answer

The exporter in Germany will wish to sell the pounds sterling it anticipates that it will receive. The Finance Director takes out a forward contract maturing at the date of sale. The Euro here is the **term** currency (X units) in the exchange rate quoted, therefore we have to **multiply** by the exchange rate.

Receipts = £500,000 × 1.4500 = €725,000.

5.4 Money market hedges

An exporter who invoices foreign customers in a foreign currency can hedge against the exchange risk by using the money markets

5.4.1 Setting up a money market hedge for a foreign currency payment

Suppose a British company needs to **pay** a Swiss creditor in Swiss francs in three months time. It does not have enough cash to pay now, but will have sufficient in three months time. Instead of negotiating a forward contract, the company could:

Step 1 Borrow the appropriate amount in pounds now

Step 2 Convert the pounds to francs immediately

Step 3 Put the francs on deposit in a Swiss franc bank account

Step 4 When the time comes to pay the company:

(a) Pays the creditor out of the franc bank account
(b) Repays the pound loan account

5.4.2 Setting up a money market hedge for a foreign currency receipt

A similar technique can be used to cover a foreign currency **receipt** from a customer. To manufacture a forward exchange rate, follow the steps below.

Step 1 Borrow an appropriate amount in the foreign currency today

Step 2 Convert it immediately to home currency

Step 3 Place it on deposit in the home currency

Step 4 When the customer's cash is received:

(a) Repay the foreign currency loan
(b) Take the cash from the home currency deposit account

5.5 Derivatives

Derivatives are more complex methods of hedging foreign exchange risk. You only need a basic idea of how these work.

5.5.1 Futures

Futures are similar to forward exchange rate contracts in that they represent an **obligation to buy or sell currency** at a predetermined price at the end of the contract. However unlike forward contracts, futures are **traded on organised exchanges** in contracts of standard size carrying standard terms and conditions. They are only available for a limited number of major currencies.

Futures are often '**closed out'** before they are due to be settled by undertaking a second transaction that reverses the effect of the original commitment. The profit or loss on closing out is set against the company's original requirement to buy or sell currency at whatever the spot rate is on the day that the contract is settled.

5.5.2 Options

Options allow businesses to **benefit from favourable movements** in exchange rates whilst allowing them protection if rates move adversely.

Currency options give the holder the right but not the obligation to buy or sell foreign currency on or before a specified date at a particular price (the exercise price).

(a) If exchange rates move adversely over time, so that buying or selling at the new spot rate is a worse deal than using the option, then the option will be exercised, and the company will deal at the **exercise price**.

(b) On the other hand if exchange rates have moved favourably, so that using the new spot rate is better for the business than using the option, then the option can be allowed to **lapse.**

The main disadvantage with options is that the **premium** that has to be paid to purchase them can be quite expensive. This means that if exchange rates move adversely, it will often be cheaper to have used an alternative method of hedging.

5.5.3 Swaps

In a **currency swap** arrangement, parties agree to swap equivalent amounts of currency for a period, effectively swapping debt between currencies. The interest on the due is also exchanged and at the end of the swap the original amounts are swapped back at an exchange rate agreed at the start of the swap.

Currency swaps can provide a **hedge** against **exchange rate movements** for longer periods than the forward market. If A Ltd gives £1 million to B Inc in return for $1.5 million, and the amounts are repaid after five years, then the effective exchange rate both at the beginning and at the end of the period is $1.50 = £1. Currency swaps can be similarly useful when using currencies for which no forward market is available.

Currency swaps can also be used to **restructure the currency base** of the company's liabilities. This may be important where the company is **trading overseas** and **receiving revenues** in **foreign currencies**, but its borrowings are **denominated** in the **currency of its home country**. Currency swaps therefore provide a means of **reducing exchange risk exposure**.

5.6 Credit risks

FAST FORWARD

Management of **credit risk** is of particular importance to exporters and various instruments and other arrangements are available to assist in this, such as letters of credit, export credit insurance and export credit guarantees.

Key term

Credit risk is the possibility that a loss may occur from the failure of another party to perform according to the terms of a contract.

Credit means allowing customers to pay for their purchases in the future rather than immediately. Most often therefore credit risk means the failure of customers who have been allowed credit to pay for goods within a reasonable time, or even to pay at all.

5.7 Managing credit risk

Whether or not a firm trades overseas, there are certain basic things it can do to reduce the level of credit risk.

(a) Assess the **creditworthiness** of new customers before extending credit, by obtaining trade, bank and credit agency references and making use of information from financial statements and salesmen's reports.

(b) Set **credit limits** and **credit periods** in line with those offered by competitors, but taking account of the status of individual customers.

(c) Set up a system of **credit control** that will ensure that credit checks and terms are being adhered to.

(d) Set out clear **debt collection procedures** to be followed.

(e) **Monitor** the efficiency of the system by the regular production and review of **reports** such as age analysis, credit and bad debt ratios and statistical analyses of incidences and causes of default and bad debts amongst different types of customer and trade.

(f) Consider the use of a **debt factor** to assist in the management, collection and financing of debts where this is cost effective. Debt factors may be employed solely on export sales.

5.8 International credit risk management

Where a company trades overseas, the risk of bad debts is potentially increased by the lack of direct contact with, and knowledge of, the overseas customers and the business environment within which they operate. Whilst the basic methods of minimising foreign credit risk will be as above, there are additional options available to the exporter.

5.8.1 Letters of credit

Letters of credit (documentary credits) provide a method of payment in international trade which gives the exporter a risk-free method of obtaining payment.

At the same time, letters of credit are a method of obtaining **short-term finance** from a bank, for **working capital**. This is because a bank might agree to discount or negotiate a letter of credit.

(a) The exporter receives **immediate payment** of the amount due to him, less the discount, instead of having to wait for payment until the end of the credit period allowed to the buyer.

(b) The buyer is able to get a **period of credit** before having to pay for the imports.

The buyer (a foreign buyer, or a UK importer) and the seller (a UK exporter or a foreign supplier) first of all agree a contract for the sale of the goods, which provides for payment through a documentary credit. The **buyer** then requests a bank in his country to issue a **letter of credit** in favour of the exporter. The issuing bank, by issuing its letter of credit, **guarantees payment** to the exporter. The buyer does not have to pay for the goods until the end of the period specified in the documentary credit.

Documentary credits are slow to arrange, and administratively cumbersome; however, they might be considered essential where the risk of non-payment is high, or when dealing for the first time with an unknown buyer.

5.8.2 Export credit insurance

Key term

Export credit insurance is insurance against the risk of non-payment by foreign customers for export debts.

You might be wondering why export credit insurance should be necessary, when exporters can pursue **non-paying customers** through the courts in order to obtain payment. The answer is that:

(a) If a credit customer defaults on payment, the task of pursuing the case through the courts will be lengthy, and it might be a long time before payment is eventually obtained.

(b) There are various reasons why non-payment might happen (Export credit insurance provides insurance against non-payment for a variety of risks in addition to the buyer's failure to pay on time.)

Not all exporters take out export credit insurance because premiums are very high and the benefits are sometimes not fully appreciated.

5.8.3 Export credit guarantees

Export credit guarantees are aimed at helping to **finance the export of medium-term capital goods**. These exports often involve long credit periods that could adversely affect the exporter's cash flow. In the UK the Export Credit Guarantees Department arranges these facilities.

The export credit guarantee gives **security to banks** providing finance to exporters if that finance is threatened by the overseas customer defaulting. The finance made available to the exporter is for the majority (85% for example) of contract values, often at preferential rates. If the exporter complies with the terms of the loan, then they will not suffer any risk of loss on the amounts financed. The banks are prepared to take the risk because of the security provided by the export credit guarantee

As well as export credit guarantees, the UK's Export Credit Guarantee Department provides a variety of other credit and insurance arrangements.

Chapter roundup

- The **spot rate** is the rate at which currencies are currently quoted on the foreign exchange markets. The **forward rate** is price available now for an agreement to exchange currencies at a set future date.
- Activity in foreign exchange markets partly depends on **currency demands** arising from **international trade**, but much dealing is done between banks.
- If firms want to develop by doing business abroad, they will have to use foreign currency; however their cash flows may be **threatened** by **adverse movements** on the foreign currency markets.
- Longer-term adverse exchange rate movements can threaten a firm's **competitiveness** in world markets.
- Supply and demand for foreign currency are subject to a number of influences.
  - The rate of inflation, compared with the rate of inflation in other countries
  - Interest rates, compared with interest rates in other countries
  - The balance of payments
  - Speculation
  - Government policy on intervention to influence the exchange rate
- Government policies on exchange rates might be **fixed exchange rates** or **floating exchange rates** at two extremes.
- In practice, 'in-between' schemes have included:
  - **Fixed rates**, but with provision for devaluations or revaluations of currencies from time to time ('adjustable pegs') and also some fluctuations ('margins') around the fixed exchange value permitted
  - **Managed floating** within a desired range of values
- **Currency blocs** and **exchange rate systems** enhances currency stability, but limit the ability of governments to pursue independent economic policies.
- If several currencies adopt a **single currency**, then **transactions** between firms in different countries within the currency zone will become **cheaper** (no commission costs on currency dealings), and **financial markets** across the zone will become **more flexible.**
- Basic methods of hedging risk include **matching receipts and payments**, **invoicing in own currency**, and **leading and lagging** the times that cash is received and paid.
- A **forward contract** specifies in advance the rate at which a specified quantity of currency will be bought and sold.
- **Money market hedging** involves borrowing in one currency, converting the money borrowed into another currency and putting the money on deposit until the time the transaction is completed, hoping to take advantage of favourable interest rate movements.
- More complex methods of hedging include use of derivatives such as **futures**, **options** and **swaps.**
- Management of **credit risk** is of particular importance to exporters and various instruments and other arrangements are available to assist in this, such as letters of credit, export credit insurance and export credit guarantees.

Quick quiz

1 A UK trader is due to receive today a sum of $750,000 in settlement of a contract.

The $/£ spot rate is 1.800 – 1.8200.

How much in £ will the UK trader receive?

2 A US firm is due to pay €400,000 for some plant and machinery. The €/$ spot rate is 0.7800 – 0.7850.

How much in $ will the US trader have to pay?

3 A French firm is due to pay an American supplier $600,000. The mid-market price is

€/$ 0.7804. Using this rate, how much in € will the French firm have to pay?

4 A German firm is due to receive £25,000 from a UK customer. The €/£ exchange rate is 1.4650 – 1.4700. How much in € will the German firm receive?

A € 17,007
B € 17,065
C € 36,625
D € 36,750

5 The current mid market spot rate for $/£ is 1.7500. Over the next year inflation is expected to be 2% in the UK, 4% in the US. Assuming that purchasing power parities hold, what would be the $/£ rate in one year's time?

6 The current mid market spot rate for £/€ 0.6800. Over the next year interest rates in the Euro bloc are expected to be 5%, in the UK 3%. If the interest rate parity condition holds, what is the £/€ one-year forward rate?

7 It is 1 May and Growler, a UK company, has undertaken to pay for a major consignment of supplies costing $80,000 from a US supplier on 1 August. Growler has considered ways of reducing its foreign exchange risk and has decided to use a forward contract. The current $/£ spot rate is 1.8200 – 1.8400 and the three month forward rate is quoted at 0.0060 – 00.0050 premium. How much in £ will Growler pay using the forward contract?

A £44,101
B £43,812
C £43,597
D £43,360

8 What is a system where the local currency is backed by a fixed relationship with a major world currency and maintained by holdings of financial assets in that world currency, known as?

A Currency bloc
B Managed floating
C Currency board
D Moveable peg

9 What is foreign currency hedging by means of borrowing the foreign currency converting it to the home currency, and placing the home currency on deposit known as?

A Forward rate hedging
B Money market hedging
C Matching
D Leading and lagging

Answers to quick quiz

1 750,000/1.8200 = £412,088

2 400,000/0.7800 = \$512,821

3 600,000 × 0.7804 = \$468,240. We multiply rather than divide here because we have been given the €/\$ rate.

4 C 25,000 × 1.4650 = €36,625. Note that we are given the €/£ exchange rate. If you chose A you divided rather than multiplied and used the rate that was more favourable to the firm. If you chose B you divided rather than multiplied. If you chose D you used the rate that was more favourable to the firm.

5 Using the purchasing power parity formula

$$\text{Future US\$/£} = \text{Spot US\$/£} \times \frac{1+\text{US inflation rate}}{1+\text{UK inflation rate}}$$

= 1.7500 × 1.04/1.02

= 1.7843

6 Applying the interest rate parity condition

$$\text{Forward rate US\$/£} = \text{Spot US\$/£} \times \frac{1+\text{nominal US interest rate}}{1+\text{nominal UK interest rate}}$$

Amending the formula for the rate given in the question

$$\text{Forward rate £/€} = \text{Spot £/€} \times \frac{1+\text{nominal UK interest rate}}{1+\text{nominal Euro interest rate}}$$

= 0.6800 × 1.03/1.05

= 0.6670

If you got confused over what goes where, remember that the interest rate of the currency on the left hand side of the / (the term currency, the X units currency), goes on the top of the interest rate parity calculation the interest rate of the currency on the right hand side of the / (the base currency, the 1 unit currency), goes on the bottom of the interest rate parity calculation.

7 A 80,000/(1.8200 – 0.0060) = £44,101

If you chose B you added the premium. If you chose C you used the more favourable rate. If you chose D you added the premium and used the more favourable rate.

8 C Currency board

9 B Money market hedging

Now try the questions below from the Exam Question Bank

Question numbers	Page
33 – 35	371

Part D

The macroeconomic context of business

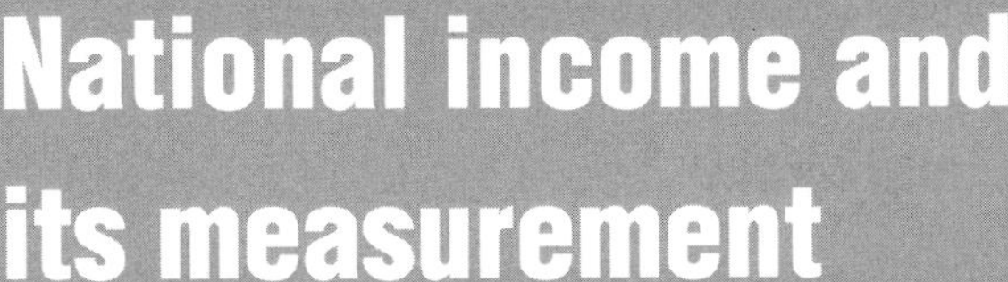

National income and its measurement

12

Introduction

Businesses operate in the economy as a whole and changes in the macroeconomic environment can have major implications for them.

Figures for the level of economic activity and economic growth are monitored closely by economists and by financial institutions because they are indicators of the economic health of a country.

In this chapter we look at how we can measure the total amount of economic activity of a nation.

There are different approaches to measuring economic activity. There are also different measures, with specific definitions. The process of measurement involves some estimates and there are a number of sources of possible inaccuracy in the figures.

This chapter provides a foundation from which to develop the following chapters on the macroeconomic environment.

Topic list	Learning outcomes	Syllabus references	Ability required
1 National income accounting	D (i), D (ii)	D (1)	Comprehension
2 Key measures of national economic output	D (i), D (ii)	D (1), D (2)	Comprehension
3 The circular flow of income in the economy	D (i), D (ii)	D (3)	Comprehension
4 The three approaches to national income accounting	D (i), D (ii)	D (1)	Comprehension
5 Interpretation of national income accounting information	D (i), D (ii)	D (2)	Comprehension

Assessment focus point

For the assessment, you need to develop an understanding of how the economy as a whole functions and the way in which government policy operates. A basic understanding of the concept of the economy as a system and an appreciation of the way the economy performs in terms of employment, output and prices are essential. You should also be aware of the debates within economics about the nature of the macroeconomy, particularly where this affects the conduct of government economic policy.

1 National income accounting

FAST FORWARD

National income accounting is the system through which economic activity on a national scale is measured.

1.1 Measuring economic activity on a national scale

In order to study and understand the economy, we first need to be able to measure it. In the same way that measurement is an essential part of any scientific study, measuring economic activity is essential for studying macroeconomics.

National output is important because of the economic activity in a country:

(a) It is an aggregate of personal incomes. The bigger the aggregate of personal incomes in a country, the more income its individual inhabitants will be earning on average.

(b) More income means more spending on the output of firms, and more spending (ignoring inflation) means that a higher output of goods and services is required to be produced.

(c) Growth is an economic policy objective of most, if not all, governments.

1.2 Aspects of national income accounting

The concept of national income accounting is based on the underlying principle that economic activity in a country can be measured in terms of

(a) The amount of **output** produced in the country
(b) The **income** received by those producing the output
(c) The amount of **expenditure** incurred by those purchasing the output.

National income accounting can be viewed from these three different aspects.

(a) **Output**

The firms (or government departments and corporations) which **produce** the goods or services in the national economy

(b) **Income**

The factors of production, which **earn** factor incomes

(c) **Expenditure**

The people or organisations that **spend money** to buy the goods and services such as consumers (or **households**), the government and foreign buyers (the **overseas sector**)

Factors of production

Before proceeding, recall from an earlier chapter what the factors of production are, and what reward is earned by each.

As we shall see later on in the chapter, the three approaches to the creation of economic wealth give rise to three ways of measuring national economic output.

- The expenditure approach
- The income approach
- The value added approach (also called the output approach)

1.3 National income accounting identity

The national income accounting identity follows from the three approaches to the creation of economic wealth and states that:

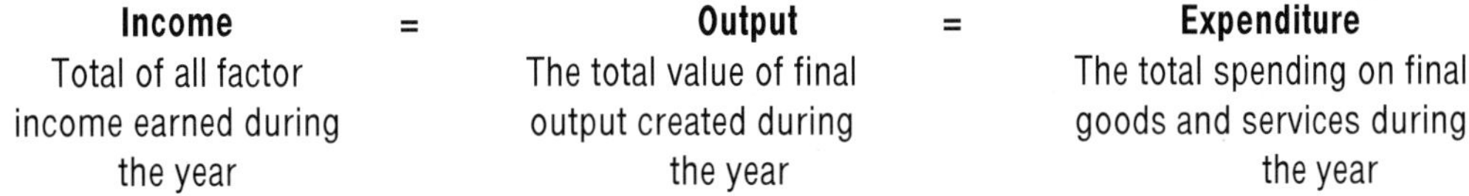

Income	=	**Output**	=	**Expenditure**
Total of all factor income earned during the year		The total value of final output created during the year		The total spending on final goods and services during the year

The identity is illustrated diagrammatically below:

Three approaches to measuring the same thing

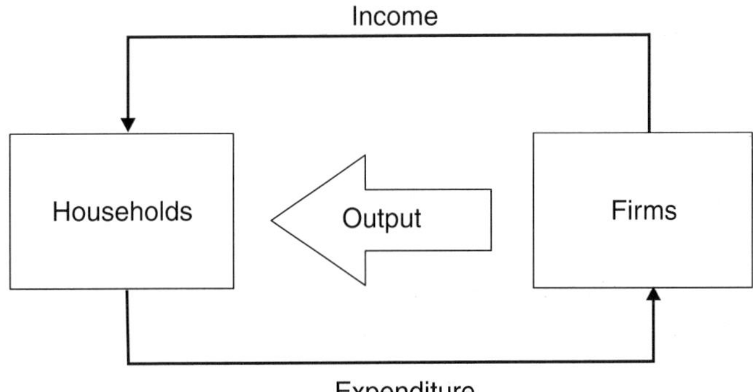

Official national income accounts show each approach to the measurement of economic activity (ie the output account, the income account and the expenditure account) as a separate account.

UK national income is in excess of £1,000bn per year (ie over £ trillion).

1.4 Uses of national income accounting measures

(a) To assess the state of the economy for purposes of constructing economic policy
(b) To monitor the impact of government economic policies
(c) To enable government and business to compare the progress and prospects of different economies
(d) To establish the material standard of living in an economy.

2 Key measures of national economic output

FAST FORWARD

There are three key measures of **national economic output**.

- National income
- Gross national income (GNI)
- Gross domestic product (GDP)

Question **National income**

The three terms above are often encountered in news reports, and yet are often only vaguely understood.

Jot down what you think is the meaning of each, and review what you have written once you come to the end of the chapter.

2.1 Definition of national income

Key term

National income: the sum of all incomes which arise as a result of economic activity, that is from the production of goods and services.

The incomes which make up national income, which include rent, employment income, interest and profit, are known as **factor incomes** because they are earned by the factors of production:

- Land earns rent
- Labour earns wages
- Capital earns interest
- Entrepreneurship earns profit

National income is also called **net national product**.

(a) The terms **income** and **product** are just two different aspects of the same circular flow of income.

(b) The term **net** means 'after deducting an amount for capital consumption or depreciation of fixed assets'. (We shall return to this point later.)

2.2 Gross domestic product (GDP)

Most UK national income is derived from economic activity **within the UK**. Economic activity within the UK is referred to as total **domestic income** or **domestic product**. It is measured **gross** ie before deducting an amount for capital consumption or depreciation of fixed assets and the term **gross domestic product** therefore refers in the UK to **the total value of income/production from economic activity within the UK**.

2.3 Gross national income (GNI)

'Some national income arises from overseas investments while some of the income generated within the UK is earned by non-residents. The difference between these items is **net property income from abroad**'.

Gross national income (GNI) is therefore the gross domestic product (GDP) plus the net property income from abroad – or after subtracting the net property income from abroad, if it is a negative value.

Key term

- **Gross domestic product**: the value of the goods and services produced by an economy in a given period.
- **Gross national income**: GDP **plus** income accruing to domestic residents from investments abroad **less** income accruing to foreign residents from investments in the domestic economy.

2.4 The relationship between GDP, GNI and national income

The relationship between GDP, GNI and national income is therefore this.

	GDP
plus	Net property income from abroad
equals	GNI
minus	Capital consumption
equals	National income (net)

National income is technically GNI **minus** an allowance for depreciation of the nation's capital.

Just as firms calculate depreciation in arriving at accounting profits, so too do economists assess a value for depreciation of the nation's capital (referred to as **capital consumption**) to arrive at net national income.

2.5 Adjustments to GDP at market prices

The GDP, GNP and National income as defined above are expressed at Market prices.

Since the prices of many goods and services are distorted by sales taxes (for example, alcohol and cigarettes) and some are distorted by subsidies (for example, many agricultural products), we often wish to view the situation without these distortions and convert GDP at market prices to **gross value added at basic prices (formerly GDP at factor cost)**.

Thus Gross value added (GVA) at basic prices = GDP at Market prices – Indirect taxes + Subsidies

Question — **Effects on national income**

Which of the following will cause a rise in national income?

A An increase in capital consumption (depreciation)
B A rise in imports
C A rise in subsidies
D A rise in indirect taxes

Answer

D A rise in indirect taxes

2.6 Summary of national income accounting

	Net income from Abroad		Capital consumption
Indirect Taxes – Subsidies			
GVA @ Basic Prices	GDP @ Market Prices	GNI @ Market Prices	National Income @ Market Prices

The first column shows Gross Value Added (GVA) which is the output measure of GDP. Adding indirect taxes and subtracting subsidies produces GDP at market prices. Adding the net income from abroad to GDP (column 2) results in the Gross National Income (column 3). Finally, subtracting capital consumption from the Gross National Income results in the National Income at market prices (column 4).

2.7 Personal Income

Personal income is defined as the total income received by individuals available for consumption, saving and payment of personal taxes. It is calculated as national income less corporate profits and social security taxes (since these are not paid out as income to investors), plus transfer payments, net interest and dividends (since these are paid to investors).

2.8 Disposable Income

Disposable income is defined as income available to individuals after payment of personal taxes. It may be consumed or saved.

3 The circular flow of income in the economy

FAST FORWARD

There is a **circular flow of income** in an economy, which means that expenditure, output and income will all have the same total value.

3.1 Income and expenditure flows

Firms must pay households for the factors of production, and households must pay firms for goods. The income of firms is the sales revenue from the sales of goods and services.

This creates a **circular flow** of income and expenditure, as illustrated in Figure 1. This is a basic **closed economy**, without foreign trade.

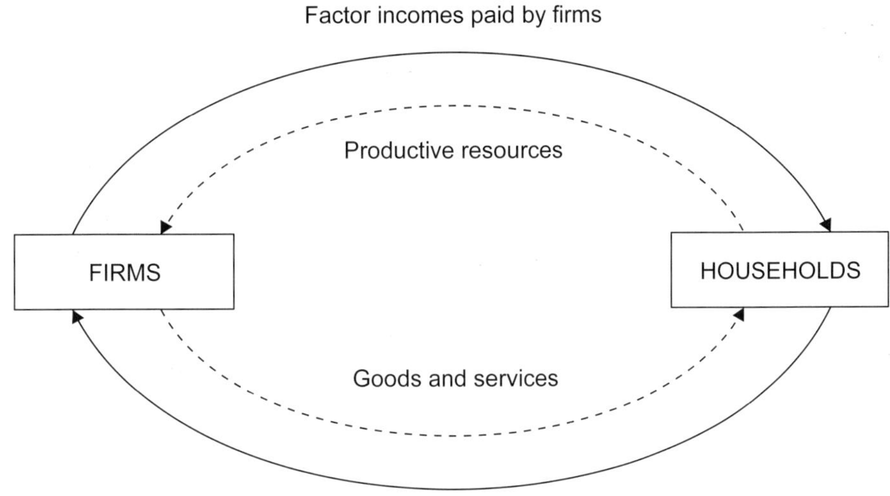

Figure 1 Circular flow of income

Households earn **income** because they have provided the factors of production which enable firms to provide goods and services. The income earned is used as **expenditure** on these goods and services that are made.

(a) The **total sales value** of goods produced should equal the **total expenditure** on goods, assuming that all goods that are produced are also sold.

(b) The amount of **expenditure** should also equal the **total income** of households, because it is households that consume the goods and they must have income to afford to pay for them.

3.2 The government and the circular flow of income

The government has several functions within the national economy, and so plays several different roles in the circular flow of income.

(a) It acts as the **producer** of certain goods and services instead of privately-owned firms, and the production of public administration services, education and health services, the police force, armed forces, fire services and public transport are all aspects of output. The government in this respect acts, like firms, as a producer and must also pay wages to its employees.

(b) It acts as the **purchaser** of final goods and services and adds to total consumption expenditure. National and local government obtain funds from the firms or households of the economy in the form of taxation and then use these funds to buy goods and services from other firms.

(c) It **invests** by purchasing capital goods, for example building roads, schools and hospitals.

(d) It makes **transfer payments** from one section of economy to another, for example by taxing working households and paying pensions, and by paying unemployment benefits and social security benefits.

3.3 Withdrawals and injections into the circular flow of income

FAST FORWARD

There are **withdrawals** from the circular flow of income (**savings, taxation, import expenditure**) and **injections** into the circular flow (**investment, government spending, export income**).

Our simplified diagram of the circular flow of income needs to be amended to allow for two things.

- **Withdrawals** from the circular flow of income
- **Injections** into the circular flow of income

Key terms

- **Withdrawals**: movements of funds out of the cycle of income and expenditure between firms and households.
- **Injections**: movements of funds in the other direction

Withdrawals from the circular flow of income

(a) **Savings (S).** Households do not spend all of their income. They save some, and these savings out of income are withdrawals from the circular flow of income.

(b) **Taxation (T).** Households must pay some of their income to the government, as taxation. Taxes cannot be spent by households.

(c) **Imports (M).** When we consider national income, we are interested in the economic wealth that a particular country is earning.

(i) Spending on imports is expenditure, but on goods made by firms in other countries.

(ii) The payments for imports go to firms in other countries, for output created in other countries.

(iii) Spending on imports therefore withdraws funds out of a country's circular flow of income.

Be aware that **saving** is different from **investment**; saving simply means withdrawing money from circulation. Think of it as cash kept in a money box rather than being put into a bank to earn interest.

Injections into the circular flow of income

(a) **Investment (I).** Investment in capital goods is a form of spending on output, which is additional to expenditure by households. Just as savings are a withdrawal of funds, investment is an injection of funds into the circular flow of income, adding to the total economic wealth that is being created by the country.

(b) **Government spending (G).** Government spending is also an injection into the circular flow of income. In most mixed economies, total spending by the government on goods and services represents a large proportion of total national expenditure. The funds to spend come from either taxation income or government borrowing.

(c) **Exports (X).** Firms produce goods and services for export. Exports earn income from abroad, and therefore provide an injection into a country's circular flow of income.

3.4 The open economy

Figure 2 shows the circular flow of income, taking account of withdrawals and injections. This is an **open economy**, since it participates in foreign trade.

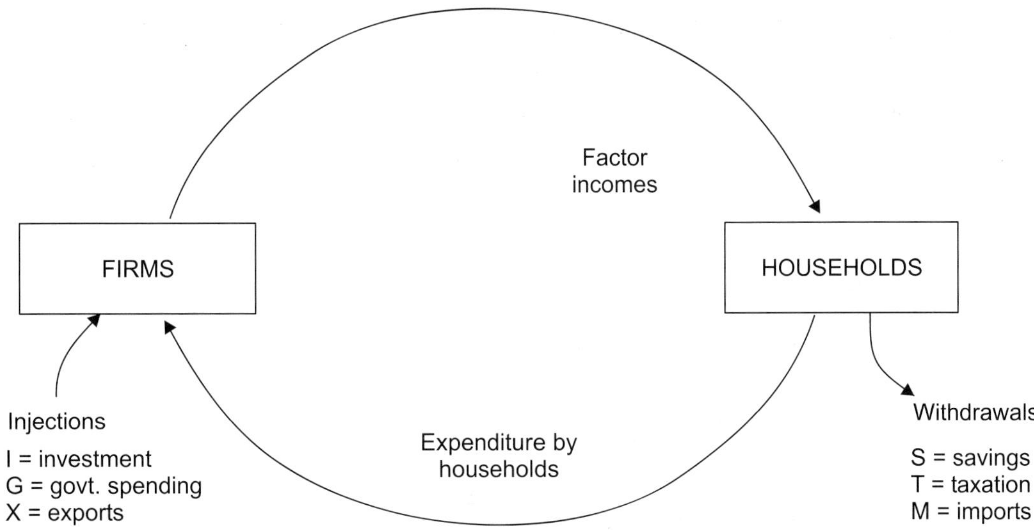

Figure 2 Circular flow of income showing withdrawals and injections

4 The three approaches to national income accounting

FAST FORWARD

Our basic model of circular flow means that **Output** = **Expenditure** = **Income**. GDP can therefore be measured by focusing on output, income or expenditure.

There are three main approaches.

(a) **The expenditure approach**. The economic wealth created in a period can be measured by the amount of expenditure on the goods and services that are produced by the nation's economy.

(i) The expenditures will be incurred by consumers, the government and foreign buyers of exports. Expenditures on **imports** represent wealth created by other countries, and so the value of expenditure on imports must be deducted from the total expenditure figure.

(ii) Expenditures by firms are **excluded**, to avoid double-counting. Firms buy goods and services which become costs of the goods or services that they produce and sell themselves. If we included expenditure by firms, we would be double-counting the value of the wealth created by the suppliers of raw materials and components and the providers of services to other firms.

(b) **The income approach**. This approach measures the income of individuals from employment and from self-employment, the profits of firms and public corporations and rent on property. (Interest earnings will be included within the profits of companies or the income of individuals.)

(c) **The value added or output approach**. This approach is to measure the value added by all activities which produce goods and services, that is their net output in the period.

All three approaches will in theory result in the same total amount for economic wealth created in the period, which we call **national income.** In practice, statistical discrepancies arise which cause differences between the figures.

Measuring national income

We stated above that, in the expenditure approach to measuring national income, expenditures by firms are excluded to avoid double counting.

Think carefully about this and ensure that you understand exactly what is meant. Jot down an explanation.

Answer

Firms buy goods and services which become costs of the goods or services that they produce and sell themselves.

If we included expenditure by firms, we would be double-counting the value of the wealth created by the suppliers of raw materials and components and the providers of services to other firms.

It will be useful to look at some simplified examples which illustrate the three approaches to measuring national income.

4.1 Example: national income

Suppose that a small national economy consists of one firm. During a certain period of time, the firm undertakes certain transactions.

- It imports raw materials from abroad, costing £4,000
- It hires labour, who are paid wages of £9,000
- It sells all its output for £20,000 and so makes a profit of £7,000
- It pays its post-tax profits of £4,000 to shareholders as dividends.

The country's government taxes the labour force £2,000 and the company £3,000.

The firm's sales of £20,000 are to three types of customer.

(a) Domestic consumers spend £11,000. This £11,000 is the post-tax wages earned by the labour force (£7,000) plus the £4,000 in dividends earned by the company's shareholders.

(b) The government spends the £5,000 it has raised in taxes.

(c) Foreign buyers spend £4,000.

Required

Calculate the gross domestic product.

Solution

As we have seen, there are three ways of calculating national income.

(a) **The expenditure approach**

	£
Consumers' expenditure	11,000
Government expenditure	5,000
	16,000
Add exports	4,000
	20,000
Subtract imports	(4,000)
GDP	16,000

(b) **The income approach**

	£
Income from employment (here pre-tax wages)	9,000
Gross (pre-tax) profit of the firm	7,000
GDP	16,000

The income is measured before deducting tax.

(c) **The value added or output approach**

	£
Output of firm at sales value	20,000
Less cost (sales value) of goods or services purchased from outside firms	(4,000)
GDP	16,000

The cost of goods and services purchased from outside firms – here just the imported materials of £4,000 – has to be subtracted so as either to avoid the double-counting of output, or to remove the value of output produced by firms in other countries.

4.2 The expenditure approach to measuring national income

Probably the most widely used measure of national income is the measurement of total spending or expenditure.

The table below shows figures for the UK.

UK national income 2002: expenditure approach

At current market prices	£bn
Households' expenditure	663
Non-profit institutions' consumption	26
General government consumption	209
Gross domestic fixed capital formation	165
Value of increase/(decrease) in stocks and work in progress	(1)
Total domestic expenditure	1,062
Exports of goods and services	269
Imports of goods and services	(288)
Statistical discrepancy	0
Gross domestic product (GDP) at current market prices	1,043
Taxes on expenditure (indirect taxes) *less* subsidies	(118)
Gross value added at basic prices (GDP at factor cost)	925
Net property income from abroad	17
Gross national product (GNP) at current factor cost	932

The expenditure approach

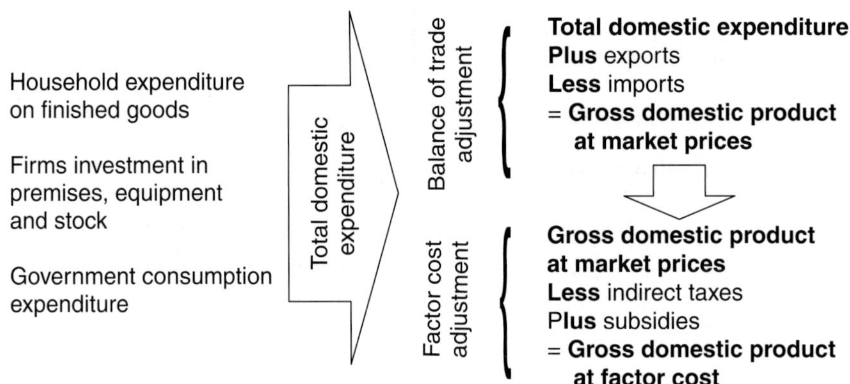

Features of expenditure approach

(a) Accounts broken down by purchaser
(b) Inserts estimated expenditure on non-traded outputs (eg imputed rent) to balance with output approach
(c) Adjusted for **balance of trade** and for **market to factor cost.**

4.3 The income approach to measuring national income

The second method of calculating national income is the income method. Since money spent by an individual or firm must become income to another, except for a residual error the results of the two methods are the same.

The income based approach covers several separate items of income.

(a) **Income from employment** (ie wages and salaries before deducting tax and including employers' national insurance contributions)

(b) **Pre-tax profits of companies**

(c) **Pre-tax profits of public corporations** (including nationalised industries)

(d) The **pre-tax 'surplus'** of other government enterprises

Interest earned by individuals and companies on any investments they hold is included in the first two figures.

These income components do not include two elements.

(a) Income from government pensions or social security payments are **transfer payments**.

(b) Any value for work done by individuals for no monetary reward, such as housework done by housewives or do-it-yourself home improvements are activities for which no money value can be given, and so are not economic activities.

Transfer payments are payments such as state pensions and benefits that are made by government, where the recipient does not make any contribution to output in return. They are payments which involve the transfer of wealth, rather than a reward for creating new economic wealth.

Transfer payments do not lead directly to any increase in marketable output of goods and are therefore excluded from the income figures.

The income approach

Incomes from employment and self-employment

Gross trading profits of companies

Trading surpluses of government

Ignores
- Stock appreciation
- Transfer payments

Includes
- Imputed charges for non-traded items

Features of income approach

(a) Accounts broken down by source of income

(b) Counts all incomes **gross** of tax (ie pre-tax)

(c) Ignores transfer payments (**payments for no productive efforts** eg welfare benefits grants) to avoid double counting (same income to wage earner + claimant)

(d) Adjusted for imputed values (eg rent from owner-occupied houses)

Question **Transfer payments**

Which of the following is or are transfer payments?

(a) Salaries paid to Members of Parliament
(b) Incapacity benefit

Answer

(a) MPs' salaries are *not* transfer payments. MPs are like any other employees – they just happen to be employed by the Government.

(b) This falls within the category of social security payments, which are transfer payments.

4.4 The output or value added method of measuring national income

The third method of calculating national income is the value added or output method.

Since the goods and services we spend our money on must have been produced by some industry or another it is not surprising to find the amount we have all spent is the same as the total value of the output goods and services produced. This total value of output can be calculated by adding up the 'values added' at the various stages of the production and distribution process.

This seeks to measure value of **final products**: ie products of services that are not subsequently used as inputs to other production processes.

Avoids **double counting** by using a value added approach

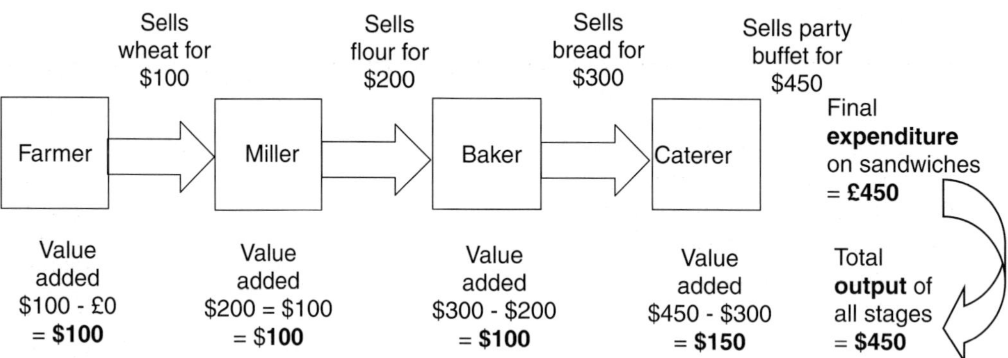

Features of output approach

(a) Accounts broken down by industrial sector

(b) Uses estimates for non-traded outputs (eg services of owner-occupied housing have an imputed rent added in)

(c) No **statistical discrepancy** adjustment. the remaining two accounts made to balance to the output account by having balancing figures inserted.

Question

GDP and GNP

The following data relates to the economy of a country over a one year period.

	£million
Consumers' expenditure	18,400
General government final consumption	4,540
Gross domestic fixed capital formation	4,920
Value of physical decrease in stocks	20
Exports of goods and services	6,450
Imports of goods and services	6,240
Taxes on expenditure	2,760
Subsidies	300
Net income from abroad	210
Capital consumption	1,750

Required

Calculate the following from the above data.

(a) Gross value added at basic prices (GDP at factor cost)
(b) Gross national product (GNP) at factor cost
(c) National income at factor cost

Answer

The calculation below also shows GDP and GNP at market prices, although these are not required in the exercise.

		£million
Consumers' expenditure		18,400
General government final consumption		4,540
Gross domestic fixed capital formation		4,920
Value of physical decrease in stocks		(20)
Total domestic expenditure		27,840
Exports		6,450
Imports		(6,240)
GDP at market prices		28,050
Net property income from abroad		210
GNP at market prices		28,260
GDP at market prices (see above)		28,050
Factor cost adjustment		
Taxes on expenditure		(2,760)
Subsidies		300
Gross value added at basic prices (GDP at factor cost)	(a)	25,590
Net property income from abroad		210
GNP at factor cost	(b)	25,800
Capital consumption		(1,750)
National income at factor cost	(c)	24,050

4.5 Adjustments to all approaches

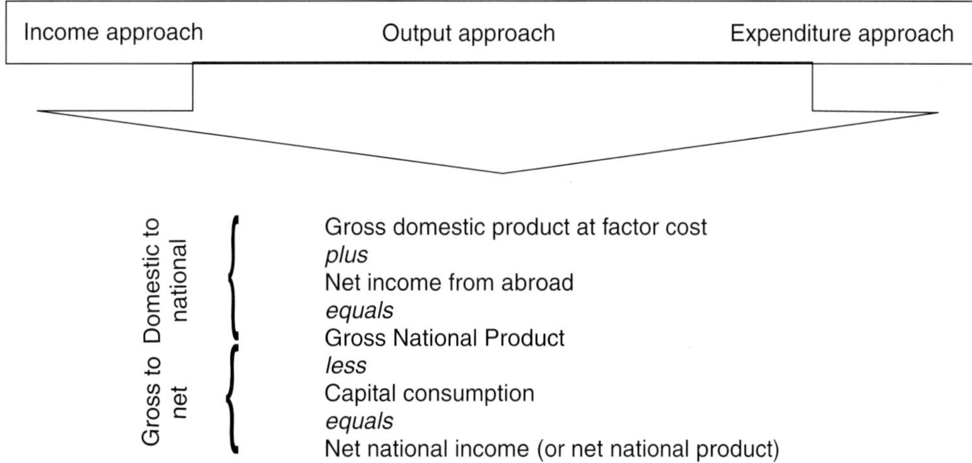

Net income from abroad

Difference between incomes earned by UK nationals from assets overseas and income going overseas due to foreign ownership of assets in the UK.

Capital consumption

Imputed charge for depreciation of nation's capital stock and infrastructure during the year.

5 Interpretation of national income accounting information

5.1 The purposes of calculating national income

Calculating the national income serves several purposes.

(a) It measures the **standard of living** in a country (national income per head).

(b) It allows comparisons between the **wealth** of different countries.

(c) It makes it possible to measure the **improvement** (or deterioration) in national wealth and the standard of living.

(d) It assists central government in its **economic planning**.

National income or GNP per head of the population gives an indication of the **trend over time** in a country's standard of living, because GNP is measured consistently from year to year, whatever the weaknesses of the measurement system that is used.

5.2 National income and inflation

5.2.1 Real and nominal GDP

FAST FORWARD

Nominal (or money) values are expressed in current dollars, meaning that the GDP could increase over time, either due to inflation or due to the underlying real size of the economy.

FAST FORWARD

Real values strip out the impact of any changes due to inflation and, therefore, only reflect changes due to the underlying real size of the economy.

Inflation is a particular problem in using national income as a measure of national wealth. Price inflation increases the **money value** of national income. We should be careful not to interpret this as meaning that there is more economic activity going on in our economy. All that has happened is that the prices of the things we are measuring have increased.

Calculating real GDP

FAST FORWARD

To see if there has been any real change in the level of activity we must deduct any influence due to inflation. The standard method for turning money GDP or GNP into real measures is to use what is called the **GDP deflator** in order to take inflation out of the figures.

In terms of measuring domestic income and comparing it year on year, real GDP is a more relevant measure. The real GDP is calculated by using a price index referred to as the **GDP deflator**. This measures the level of base prices as a proportion of a selected base year, which is measured as 100 on the scale. The real GDP for a year, on the same basis as the base year, can be calculated by adjusting the nominal GDP for inflation over the period, as follows.

$$\text{Real GDP}_{now} = \text{Nominal GDP}_{now} \times \frac{\text{GDP}_{dbase}}{\text{GDP}_{dnow}}$$

where

GDP_{dbase} = GDP deflator in the base year (= 100)

GDP_{dnow} = GDP deflator for current year

Note that the GDP deflator is not the same as the consumer price index (CPI). The CPI focuses only on a relatively narrow basket of consumer goods, whereas the GDP deflator aims to take account of all goods in the economy. Generally, the CPI is more commonly used. It measures the impact of rising prices on the income of consumers. However, the GDP deflator is more used as an economy-wide measure.

5.2.2 Example: Real and nominal GDP

Nominal GDP is $6,000bn. The GDP deflator for the year is 130. What is real GDP?

Solution

$$\text{Real GDP} = 6{,}000 \times \frac{100}{130} = 4{,}615$$

5.3 Problems with the use of GDP

ST FORWARD

National income has serious limitations as a measure of **economic wealth and welfare**. It remains an important indicator nonetheless.

Nonmarket production

Work done where no charge is made will not be included in GDP. This will include, for example, housework, gardening, DIY, picking up family from the station, etc. This makes comparisons of GDP over time less meaningful, particularly since women now do more market production, which is included in GDP, along with the previous household chores. The household chores may take less time with time-saving appliances, the cost of which is again included as part of GDP. In the past, there were more hours of unpaid labor in the house that were not included in GDP.

As a result, GDP tends to overstate the output of developed countries compared to less developed countries.

The underground economy

Transactions in the underground economy are not reported, typically for tax evasion or other illegal purposes, understating GDP.

Leisure and human costs

Increased leisure time and improved safety conditions at work, for example, are not reflected in GDP.

Quality variation and new goods

Improvement in the quality of goods (eg dental treatment) and new goods not previously available (such as CD players replacing record players) are not taken into account. The failure to allow for increased quality tends to result in inflation being overstated.

Economic 'bads'

Harmful side effects, such as pollution, are ignored in GDP. In addition, costs of rebuilding houses in San Francisco after earthquakes, for example, is treated as national income for the year, even though this quite clearly is a cost rather than being a benefit.

5.3.1 Economic welfare

GDP does not measure economic welfare, but rather measures the value of goods and services produced in the year. If consumers spent $1bn on alcohol or on schooling for their children, it would have the same value for GDP.

It is possible to adjust GDP to attempt to reach some measure of economic welfare by deducting the cost of economic bads, deducting expenditure spent on regrettable necessities (e.g. defense) and adding in the value of nonmarket production.

5.4 Using national income figures to compare economies

The main conventions used to make figures more comparable

(a) Uses of real national income per capita (ie national income divided by population) to get a measure of 'average well-offness'

(b) All values equate using exchange rate or expressed in a single currency (eg dollar)

(c) Values converted from **nominal values** (ie measured in the prices at the time) to **real values** or **constant values** by eliminating inflation using a GDP deflator

Chapter roundup

- **National income accounting** is the system through which economic activity on a national scale is measured.
- There are three key measures of **national economic output**.
  - National income
  - Gross national product (GNP)
  - Gross domestic product (GDP)
- There is a **circular flow of income** in an economy, which means that expenditure, output and income will all have the same total value.
- There are **withdrawals** from the circular flow of income (**savings, taxation, import expenditure**) and **injections** into the circular flow (**investment, government spending, export income**).
- Our basic model of circular flow means that **Output** = **Expenditure** = **Income**. GDP can therefore be measured by focusing on output, income or expenditure.
- **Nominal** (or money) values are expressed in current dollars, meaning that the GDP could increase over time, either due to inflation or due to the underlying real size of the economy.
- **Real values** strip out the impact of any changes due to **inflation** and, therefore, only reflect changes due to the underlying real size of the economy.
- To see if there has been any real change in the level of activity we must deduct any influence due to inflation. The standard method for turning money GDP or GNP into real measures is to use what is called the **GDP deflator** in order to take inflation out of the figures.
- National income has serious limitations as a measure of **economic wealth and welfare**. It remains an important indicator nonetheless.

Quick quiz

1 Which of the following are withdrawals from the circular flow of income?

   (a) Exports
   (b) Savings
   (c) Investment
   (d) Government spending

2 Define the income approach to measuring income.

3 What is the gross domestic product?

Answers to quick quiz

1 (b) only. The rest are injections into the circular flow of income.

2 National income is the aggregate of individuals income from employment and self employment, the profits of entities and rent on property.

3 The total value of income/production within the UK without any deduction for capital consumption or depreciation.

Now try the questions below from the Exam Question Bank

Question numbers	Page
36 – 39	372

13

Aggregate demand and supply analysis

Introduction

In macroeconomics we are looking, not at individual spending decisions, investment decisions, pricing decisions, employment decisions, and output decisions but at spending, investment, price levels, employment and output in the economy as a whole and at total income (national income).

In this chapter, we study the basic elements of the Keynesian model for national income determination and equilibrium.

Broadly speaking, macroeconomists divide into the two camps of the Keynesians and the monetarists. These two camps have had differing ideas about how national income can be made to grow, how full employment can be achieved and how booms and slumps of trade cycles can be smoothed out.

The Keynesians and monetarists differ in their views about the causes of inflation, the extent to which inflation creates unemployment and prevents economic growth, and the effectiveness of government measures to stimulate the economy.

Topic list	Learning outcomes	Syllabus references	Ability required
1 The Keynesian approach	D (i)	D (4)	Comprehension
2 Aggregate demand analysis: consumption, savings and investment	D (i)	D (4)	Comprehension
3 The multiplier and the accelerator	D (i)	D (4)	Comprehension
4 Aggregate supply analysis	D (i)	D (4)	Comprehension
5 The determination of national Income	D (i), D (vii)	D (4)	Comprehension
6 The business cycle	D (iii)	D (7), D (8)	Comprehension
7 Inflation and its consequences	D (i), D (vii)	D (6)	Comprehension
8 Unemployment	D (i)	D (6)	Comprehension
9 Unemployment and inflation	D (i), (iv)	D (6)	Comprehension

1 The Keynesian approach

The **Keynesian model** provides a way of explaining how national income is determined, and how national income equilibrium is reached.

1.1 The origin of Keynesianism

Keynesian economics originated with *John Maynard Keynes*, a British economist whose book *The General Theory of Employment, Interest And Money* (1936), revolutionised macroeconomic analysis. Keynes put forward his ideas following a period in which there was an economic boom (after the First World War), followed by the Wall Street Crash in 1929, and the depression in the 1930s when unemployment levels soared.

Pre-Keynesian economists had tried to explain unemployment as a temporary phenomenon. They believed that if there is a surplus of labour available (unemployment) then the forces of demand and supply, through the wages (price) mechanism, would restore equilibrium by bringing down wage levels, thus stimulating demand for labour. Any unemployment would only last as long as the labour market was adjusting to new equilibrium conditions. The pre-Keynesian theory was challenged during the 1930s. If pre-Keynesian theory was right, wages should have fallen and full employment should have been restored. However, this did not happen, and the depression continued for a long time.

It is instructive to note that it was during this economic situation that Keynes put forward his new theory. Its fundamental advance on earlier theory was to explain how **equilibrium could exist in the macroeconomy, but there could still be persistent unemployment and slow growth**.

The term **full employment national income** is used to describe the total national income that a country must earn in order to achieve full employment. By **full employment** we mean that the country's economic resources are fully employed. However, as far as labour is concerned, full employment does not mean that everyone has a job all the time. There will always be some **normal** or **transitional** unemployment as people lose their job or give up one job for another, and so **full** employment might mean, say, that 3-5% of the total working population is unemployed at any time.

Keynes also tried to explain the causes of **trade cycles** which are the continuous cycles of alternating economic boom and slump. Why does an economy not grow at a steady rate, or remain stable, instead of suffering the harmful effects of trade cycles?

1.2 Aggregate demand and aggregate supply

Keynes' basic idea was that demand and supply analysis could be applied to macroeconomic activity as well as microeconomic activity.

Key terms

Aggregate demand (AD) means the total demand in the economy for goods and services.
Aggregate supply (AS) means the total supply of goods and services in the economy.

Aggregate Supply depends on physical production conditions – the availability and cost of factors of production and technical know-how. Keynes was concerned with short-run measures to affect the economy, and he also wrote in a period of high unemployment when there was obviously no constraint on the availability of factors of production. His analysis therefore concentrated on the **demand side**. Supply side economics (discussed in the following chapter) describes the views of economists who do not subscribe to the Keynesian approach to dealing with current problems of national income and employment, and prefer instead to concentrate on the **supply side** – in other words, production factors.

1.3 Aggregate Demand and National income

For Keynesian analysis to have practical value for the management of a national economy, it is necessary to establish how aggregate demand can be shifted.

To understand shifts in AD, we need to turn our attention to expenditure in the economy. A formula for the GNP (= total national expenditure) which was described in the previous chapter is:

E = C + I + G + (X – M)

where E is the total national expenditure (GNP)

C is the total domestic consumption (money spent on consumer goods)

I is the total industrial investment (money spent by private sector firms and the public sector on capital items) *

G is the total government spending (government 'current' or 'consumption' spending)

X is the total exports (including income from property abroad)

M is the total imports (including money paid as income to residents in other countries for property they hold in the country)

* Alternatively, government investment spending on capital items can be included in G leaving I to represent investment by firms only.

Key term

Demand management policies involve the manipulation of E (eg achieving economic growth) by influencing C, I, G or net exports.

If we ignore capital consumption, we can equate E (GNP) with national income. This is what we shall do in our analysis of the Keynesian model.

1.4 Withdrawals and injections

In the previous chapter on national income, the different approaches to calculating national income – the expenditure, income and value added approaches – were explained in terms of the circular flow of income around the economy.

For a national economy, there are certain withdrawals from and injections into this circular flow of income. Withdrawals divert funds out of the circular flow and injections add funds into it.

(a) **Withdrawals** from the circular flow of income (W) consist of imports (M), taxation (T) and savings (S).

(b) **Injections** into the circular flow of income (J) consist of exports (X), government spending (G), and investment spending by firms (I).

Keynes argued that for an equilibrium to be reached in the national income, not only must AD = AS, but also total **planned** withdrawals from the circular flow of funds **must be equal to total planned injections**. Thus, for equilibrium:

W = J, and so M + T + S = X + G + I

In the long term W will always equal J.

(a) The difference between the value of imports M and the value of exports X is the **balance of payments deficit** (or **surplus**). Even in the short term, this difference must be balanced by borrowing (or lending abroad), as we shall see in a later chapter.

(b) The difference between government spending and taxation can only be made up by government borrowing. Loans are eventually repaid.

(c) In the long run, savings will also equal investments, even though the people who save and the firms who invest are not the same. We shall look more closely at savings and investment later.

However, although W and J will be equal retrospectively and in the long run, it does not follow that **planned** J and **planned** W will equal each other **in the short run**, since injections and withdrawals are made by different people.

This frustration of plans in the short run causes national income to change over time. The imbalance between J and W creates factors which can make the level of national income change. Keynes argued that the imbalance between planned withdrawals and planned injections explained **trade cycles** – the fluctuations in national income which give rise to booms and slumps – which prevent an economy from settling down at an equilibrium level.

2 Aggregate demand analysis: consumption, savings and investment

FAST FORWARD

Consumption expenditure depends on income. It might be possible for a government to take measures to boost aggregate demand in the economy, although some price inflation will probably result. When there is inflation in the economy, measures could be taken to suppress aggregate demand.

2.1 Consumption and savings (C and S)

Let us now go into a bit more detail on Keynesian analysis, and concentrate particularly on consumption, savings and investment. To simplify our analysis, we shall ignore government spending, taxation, imports and exports for the time being. By ignoring imports and exports, we are concentrating on a **closed economy** which is not in any way dependent on foreign trade.

If we ignore G, T, X, and M, we can look at a circular flow of income in which households divide all their income between two uses: consumption and saving.

Provided that national income is in equilibrium, we will have:

$$Y \equiv C + S$$

where Y = national income, C = consumption and S = saving.

This should seem logical to you. Income can only be either spent or saved. Since we have a closed economy, consumption must be of goods produced by the economy itself.

2.2 Savings

There are two ways of saving. One is to hold the income as money (banknotes and coin, or in a current bank account). The other way is to put money into some form of interest-bearing investment. In the long run, there is no reason for people to hold banknotes or keep money in a current bank account, unless they intend to spend it fairly soon. If this is so, income that is not spent will be saved and income that is saved will, eventually, be invested. (The people who put their money into interest-bearing savings are not making any investment themselves in capital goods, but the institutions with whom they save will use the deposits to lend to investors and so indirectly there will be a real increase in investment when people save money in this way.)

Question — **Factors influencing savings**

What do you think are the main factors influencing the amount that people will save?

Answer

The amount that people save will depend on:

(a) How much income they are getting, and how much of this they want to spend on consumption

(b) How much income they want to save for precautionary reasons, for the future

(c) Interest rates. If the interest rate goes up we would expect people to consume less of their income, and to be willing to save and invest more.

We can therefore conclude that in **conditions of equilibrium** for national income:

$$Y \equiv C + S$$

and, $Y \equiv C + I$

and so, $I \equiv S$

In the short run, however, savings and investment might not be equal and so there might not be equilibrium.

2.3 The propensities to consume and save

Even when a household has zero income, it will still spend. This spending will be financed by earlier **savings** (and, in the real world, by **welfare receipts**). There is thus a constant, basic level of consumption. This is called **autonomous** consumption. When the household receives an income, some will be spent and some will be saved. The **proportion** which is spent is called the **marginal propensity to consume** (MPC) while the **proportion** which is saved is equal to the **marginal propensity to save** (MPS).

In our analysis (ignoring G, T, X and M) saving and consumption are the only two uses for income, MPC + MPS = 1.

Therefore, we may say that a household's expenditure in a given period is made up of 2 elements.

(a) A fixed amount (a) which is the autonomous consumption.
(b) A further **constant** percentage of its income (b% of Y) representing the MPC.

Similarly, a national economy as a whole will spend a fixed amount £a, plus a constant percentage (b%) of national income Y.

We can then state a consumption function as $C = a + bY$.

Given a consumption function $C = a + bY$:

(a) The marginal propensity to consume is b, where b is the proportion of each extra £1 earned that is spent on consumption.

(b) The average propensity to consume will be the ratio of consumption to income:

$$\frac{C}{Y} = \frac{a + bY}{Y}$$

For example, suppose an individual household has fixed spending of £100 per month, plus extra spending equal to 80% of its monthly income.

(a) When its monthly income is £800, its consumption will be:

£100 + 80% of £800 = £740

(b) When its monthly income is £1,000 its consumption will be:

£100 + 80% of £1,000 = £900

The household's marginal propensity to consume is 80%.

Question

Average propensity to consume

Using the above figures, calculate the household's average propensity to consume:

(a) When its income is £800
(b) When its income is £1,000

Answer

(a) $\text{APC} = \frac{740}{800} = 92.5\%$

(b) $\text{APC} = \frac{900}{1{,}000} = 90\%$

Changes in the marginal propensity to consume and the marginal propensity to save will involve a change of preference by households between current consumption and saving for future benefits. A cause of such a change might be a change in interest rates, which makes the investment of savings more or less attractive than before.

2.4 What factors influence the amount of consumption?

There will always be a minimum fixed amount of total consumption. Total consumption by households, however, is affected by five influences.

(a) **Changes in disposable income, and the marginal propensity to consume**. Changes in disposable income are affected by matters such as pay rises and changes in tax rates. An increase in household wealth may reduce levels of saving thus increasing consumption.

(b) **Changes in the distribution of national income**. Some sections of the population will have a higher marginal propensity to consume than others and so a redistribution of wealth might affect consumption. (A redistribution of wealth might be accomplished by taxing the rich and giving to the poor in the form of more government allowances).

(c) **The development of major new products**. When such developments happen, they can create a significant increase in spending by consumers who want to buy the goods or services.

(d) **Interest rates**. Changes in interest rates will influence the amount of income that households decide to **save**, and also the amount that they might elect to borrow for spending.

(e) **Price expectations**. Expectations of price increases may increase current consumption while expectations of price reductions may have the opposite effect.

Among the determinants of the MPC are **taste and attitude**. If a household believes that saving is a virtue it will save as much as possible and spend as little as possible; and in the economy as a whole, a general belief in the value of thrift may mean that the MPC is low. Nowadays the prestige attached to the possession of consumer goods may have overcome the admiration for thrift, making the MPC higher than it once was.

2.5 Marginal propensity to withdraw

In a model that includes savings (S), taxes (T) and imports (M), the marginal propensity to withdraw (MPW) is given by:

MPW = MPS + MPT + MPM

The MPW is the proportion of national income that is withdrawn from the circular flow of income.

2.6 Investment (I)

The total volume of desired investment in the economy depends on factors similar to those influencing 'micro-level' investment decisions by firms.

- The rate of interest on capital
- The marginal efficiency of capital invested
- Expectations about the future and business confidence
- The strength of consumer demand for goods

A further determinant of MPC is the **attractiveness of savings**. If interest rates are high, households will wish to save more of their income to benefit from the higher rates of interest. The more they save, the less they consume. Conversely some goods are so expensive that they tend to be bought on credit; if interest rates are high there is less incentive to borrow and thus a lower tendency to purchase high-cost goods.

Given C = a + bY, the value of b may also be affected by the value of a. If the cost of essential commodities rises in relation to all other commodities, the value of a will rise. This means that a greater proportion of household consumption becomes fixed and there is less available for variable consumption bY. Thus a rise in a causes a fall in b.

We can show the consumption function in a graph, which shows the relationship between consumption, savings and (disposable) income.

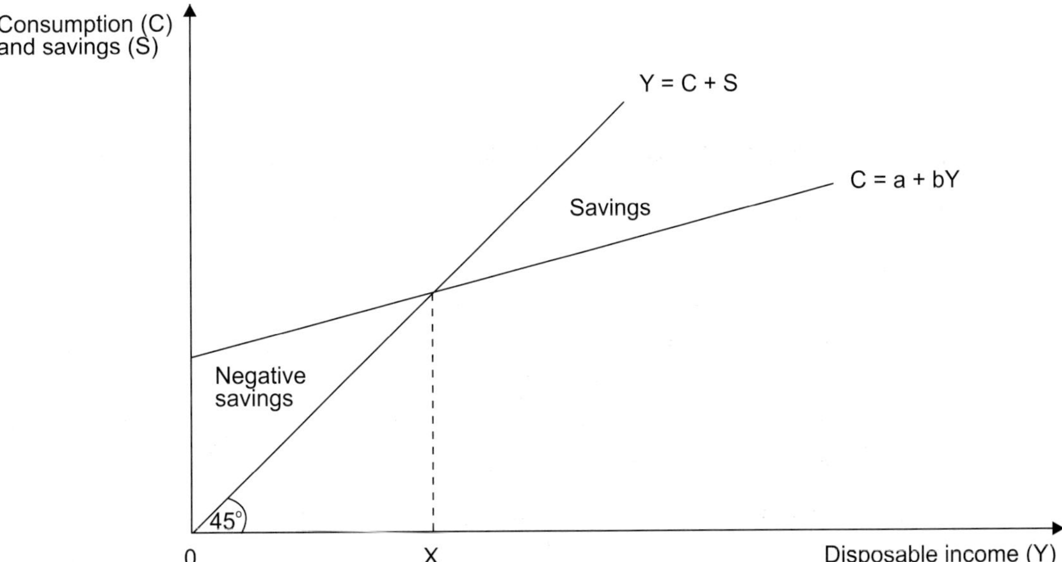

Figure 1 Income, consumption and savings (closed economy)

As we have seen, in a closed economy with no government sector, income must equal the sum of consumption and savings. Consumption will always be a minimum amount, and at lower levels of national income (below X in Figure 1) consumption will exceed national income. This means that households will be using up savings to buy goods.

The demand for funds to invest by firms and the willingness of investors to lend their savings for investment (the supply of funds) should adjust to one another through the price mechanism of the interest rate.

(a) **Higher interest rates** should make firms less willing to invest, because the marginal efficiency of capital will have to be higher to justify the higher interest cost. However, firms cannot always cut their investment plans quickly and at short notice.

Higher interest rates should have two other effects.

(i) They will tempt individuals to consume less of their income and save more, with a view to investing it.

(ii) They will also tempt individuals to invest more of their savings – that is, to hold less cash and more interest-bearing investments.

(b) **Lower interest rates** should have the opposite effect.

An investment involves the acquisition of more buildings, machinery, plant and equipment or stocks of goods and so on. The importance of the interest rate for investment should therefore be apparent in the marginal efficiency of capital. Firms should go on adding to their capital provided that the marginal efficiency of capital exceeds the interest rate, which is its marginal cost.

2.7 New technology and investment

When new technology emerges which changes methods of production (such as robotics) or provides opportunities to produce new types of good, there will be a boost to investment.

(a) New technology which reduces the unit costs of production will increase profitability. The supply curve for the goods that are affected by the new production methods will shift to the right. Firms will invest in the new technology in order to achieve lower costs and remain competitive.

(b) New technology which leads to new types of good will give a stimulus to consumption demand. Firms will invest to make the product and meet the consumer demand.

2.8 Investment and economic recovery

Investment represents one of the major injections in the circular flow of income. Variations in the level of investment can, through the multiplier, affect the level of national income and the level of aggregate demand in the economy. A major conclusion from Keynesian analysis is that in order to achieve economic recovery from a recession, there should be major investment.

Investment can be in either the public or the private sector of the economy, although the money to finance the investment might need to come from different sources.

(a) Private sector investment will come from retained profits, new issues of shares, or borrowing. However, in an economic recession profits might be low, and investors might lack confidence in a recovery, so that new share issues are impossible on a large scale.

(b) Public sector investment might be financed by higher taxation, or by an increased deficit between government income and expenditure, that is, a higher **public sector net cash requirement (PSNCR).**

(c) Public sector spending should have socially valuable spin-off effects, such as improved roads, sewers and public buildings.

(d) However, a high PSBR, meaning large government borrowings, might force up interest rates in the capital markets and **crowd out** private sector investment, by making it too expensive for firms to borrow and invest profitably. (Keynesian economists deny that such crowding out takes place, however.)

There are two additional reasons why investment is very important.

(a) The act of investment represents consumption forgone now in order to increase the capacity to produce, and therefore to consume, in the future. It is through investment (or lack of it) that the future shape and pattern of economic activity is pre-determined.

(b) The growth rate of the economy is determined not only by the technological progress or the increases in the size and quality of the labour force but also by the rate at which the capital stock is increased or replaced. Investment represents an addition to the existing capital stock. If that addition is greater than the amount by which the capital stock depreciates, then the capital stock of the economy is growing and so is the capacity of the economy to produce more goods and services. Hence investment is an important determinant of the long-term growth rate of an economy.

3 The multiplier and the accelerator

ST FORWARD

Changes in national income begin with a small change in expenditure, leading to an even larger eventual change in national income, due to the **multiplier effect**.

3.1 The multiplier

The **multiplier** involves the **process of circulation of income** in the national economy, whereby an injection of a certain size leads to a much larger increase in national income. The firms or households receiving the injection use at least part of the money to increase their own consumption. This provides money for other firms and households to repeat the process and so on.

The level of national income might increase or decrease for a number of reasons; for example, there might be an increase in productivity or an increase in the country's exports. Keynes showed that if there is an **initial** change in expenditure due to an increase in exports, or government spending or investment or consumer spending, a new equilibrium national income level will be reached.

The eventual total increase in national income will be greater in size than the initial increase in expenditure. This is because of the continuing circulation of the funds concerned.

Key term

The ratio of the **total** increase in national income to an initial increase is called the **multiplier**.

$$\text{Multiplier} = \frac{\text{Total increase in national income}}{\text{Initial increase in national income}}$$

The multiplier can be defined as a measure of the effect on total national income of a unit change in a component of aggregate demand: I, G or X.

Multiplier values can therefore be measured specifically for each of these separately.

$$\text{Investment multiplier} = \frac{\text{Eventual change in national income}}{\text{Initial change in investment spending}}$$

$$\text{Government spending multiplier} = \frac{\text{Eventual change in national income}}{\text{Initial change in government spending}}$$

$$\text{Export multiplier} = \frac{\text{Eventual change in national income}}{\text{Initial change in exports}}$$

3.2 Numerical illustration of the multiplier

A numerical illustration of the multiplier might help to explain it more clearly. In this example, we shall again ignore taxes, government spending, exports and imports, and assume a simple closed economy in which all income is either spent on consumption (C) or saved (S). Let us suppose that in this closed economy, marginal propensity to consume (MPC) is 90% or 0.9. Then, out of any addition to household income, 90% is consumed and 10% saved.

(a) If income goes up by £200, £180 would be spent on consumption, and £20 saved.

(b) The £180 spent on consumption increases the income of other people, who spend 90% (£162) and save £18.

(c) The £162 spent on consumption in turn becomes additional income to others, so that a snowball effect on consumption (and income and output) occurs, as follows.

			Increase in expenditure £	*Increase in savings* £
Stage	1	Income rises	200.00	-
	2	90% is consumed	180.00	20.00
	3	A further 90% is consumed	162.00	18.00
	4	"	145.80	16.20
	5	"	131.22	14.58
		etc	...	.....
		Total increase in income	2,000.00	200.00

In this example, an initial increase in income of £200 results in a final increase in national income of £2,000. The multiplier is 10.

3.3 The marginal propensity to save

The multiplier is the reciprocal of the marginal propensity to save. Since MPC = 0.9, MPS = 0.1.

$$\text{Multiplier} = \frac{1}{\text{MPS}} \text{ or } \frac{1}{1\text{-MPC}}$$

$$\text{Increase in national income} = \frac{\text{Initial increase in expenditure}}{\text{MPS}} = \frac{£200}{0.1} = £2,000$$

Note that at the new equilibrium, savings of £200 equal the initial increase in expenditure of £200 but national income has risen £2,000.

If the marginal propensity to consume were 80%, the marginal propensity to save would be 20% and the multiplier would only be 5. Because people save more of their extra income, the total increase in national income through extra consumption will be less.

3.4 The multiplier in the national economy

The multiplier in a national economy works in the same way. **An initial increase in expenditure will have a snowball effect**, leading to further and further expenditures in the economy. Since total expenditure in the economy is one way of measuring national income, it follows that an initial increase in expenditure will cause an even larger increase in national income. The increase in national income will be a multiplier of the initial increase in spending, with the size of the multiple depending on factors which include the marginal propensity to save.

If you find this hard to visualise, think of an increase in government spending on the construction of roads. The government would spend money paying firms of road contractors, who in turn will purchase raw materials from suppliers, and sub-contract other work. All these firms employ workers who will receive wages that they can spend on goods and services of other firms. The new roads in turn might stimulate new economic activity, for example amongst road hauliers, housebuilders and estate agents.

Depending on the size of the multiplier, an increase in investment would therefore have repercussions throughout the economy, increasing the size of the national income by a multiple of the size of the original increase in investment.

If, for example, the national income were £10,000 million and the average and the marginal propensity to consume were both 75%, in equilibrium, ignoring G, T, X and M:

Y = £10,000 million
C = £7,500 million
I = S = £2,500 million

Since MPC = 75%, MPS = 25%, and the multiplier is 4.

An increase in investment of £1,000 million would upset the equilibrium, which would not be restored until the multiplier had taken effect, and national income increased by 4 × £1,000 million = £4,000 million, with:

Y = £14,000 million
C = £10,500 million (75%)
I = S = £3,500 million (25%)

A downward multiplier or **demultiplier** effect also exists. A reduction in investment will have repercussions throughout the economy, so that a small disinvestment (reduction in expenditure/output) will result in a multiplied reduction in national income

3.5 Factors influencing MPC and MPS

You should also be aware of factors which might influence the MPC and MPS in any economy, for example the age distribution of the population, the income distribution of the population, expectations of the future and other socio-economic factors.

3.6 The importance of the multiplier

The importance of the multiplier is that an increase in one of the components of aggregate demand will increase national income by more than the initial increase itself. Therefore if the government takes any action to increase expenditure (for example by raising government current expenditure, or lowering interest rates to raise investment) it will set off a general expansionary process, and the eventual rise in national income will exceed the initial increase in aggregate demand.

This can have important implications for a government when it is planning for growth in national income. By an initial increase in expenditure, a government can 'engineer' an even greater increase in national income, (provided that the country's industries can increase their output capacity), depending on the size of the multiplier.

3.7 The multiplier in an open economy

So far we have been considering a simplified economy in which income is either saved or spent on domestic production. The real world is more complex and we must now consider the effect of taxation and imports. Like savings, these are

withdrawals from the circular flow and they therefore affect the multiplier. Thus, in an open economy, the value of the multiplier depends on three things.

(a) The marginal propensity to save (MPS)

(b) The marginal propensity to import, because imports reduce national income, and if households spend much of their extra income on imports, the snowball increase in total national income will be restricted because imports are a withdrawal out of the circular flow of income. One of the reasons for a low multiplier in the UK is the high marginal propensity to import.

(c) Tax rates, because taxes reduce the ability of people to consume and so are likely to affect the marginal propensity to consume and the marginal propensity to save.

Whereas the multiplier in a closed economy is the reciprocal of the marginal propensity to save, the multiplier in an open economy, taking into account government spending and taxation, and imports and exports, will be less. This is because government taxation and spending on imports reduces the multiplier effect on a country's economy.

For an open economy:

$$\text{Multiplier} = \frac{1}{s+m+t}$$

where s is the marginal propensity to save

m is the marginal propensity to import

t is the marginal propensity to tax – ie the amount of any increase in income that will be paid in taxes.

The multiplier as defined in this way may still be represented as below.

$$\text{Multiplier} = \frac{1}{1\text{-MPC}}$$

since any increase in income is totally accounted for by savings, tax imports and consumption.

For example, if in a country the marginal propensity to save is 10%, the marginal propensity to import is 45% and the marginal propensity to tax is 25%, the size of the multiplier would be:

$$\frac{1}{0.1+0.45+0.25} = \frac{1}{0.80} = 1.25$$

3.8 Changes in equilibrium national income and the multiplier: a graphical representation

It is possible to show the multiplier effect in the form of a diagram.

Assessment focus point

> The multiplier is a vital part of macroeconomic theory. You should understand this diagram clearly.

In Figure 7, the horizontal axis represents national income (Y). The vertical axis represents planned or desired expenditure. The national economy is in equilibrium when actual output (which is the same as national income) is equal to desired expenditure. This occurs at any point along the 45° line Y=E.

On to this basic picture we have superimposed two other lines.

(a) The lower is the consumption function we described in Section 2. This consists of autonomous expenditure (a), which occurs even when income is zero, plus the proportion of income which is spent in accordance with the marginal propensity to consume (bY).

(b) Desired expenditure within the economy is not limited to consumption; we must also consider the **injections**, government spending (G), investment (I), and net exports (X-M). If we assume these are constant, total actual expenditure for any level of national income is shown by the upper line E=C + G + I + (X – M).

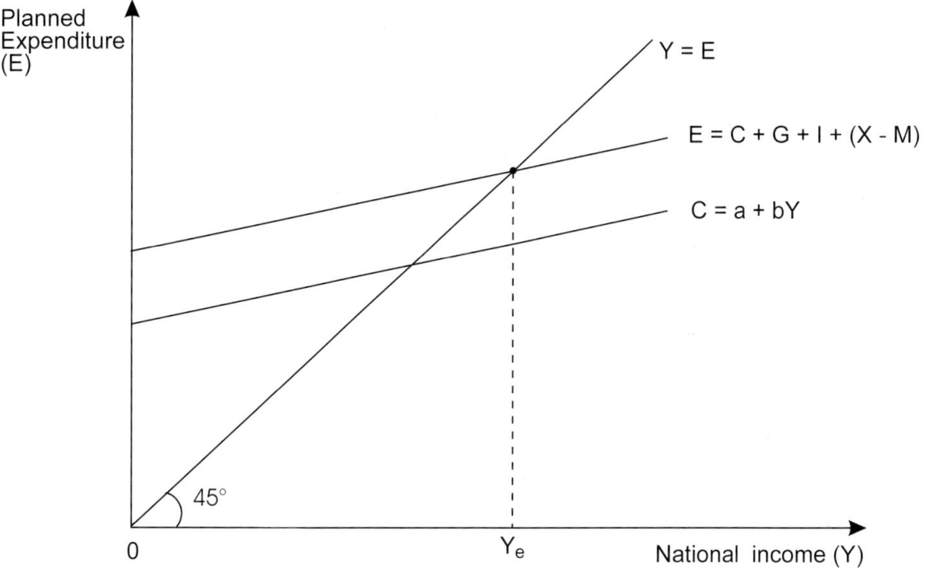

Figure 7 Equilibrium national income

Equilibrium national income in Figure 7 is at Y_e, where Y = E = C + G + I + (X – M).

What will happen if the economy has unemployed resources at national income Y_e, and total expenditure is increased – ie C, G, I or (X – M) increases. By how much will national income increase? This is shown in Figure 8.

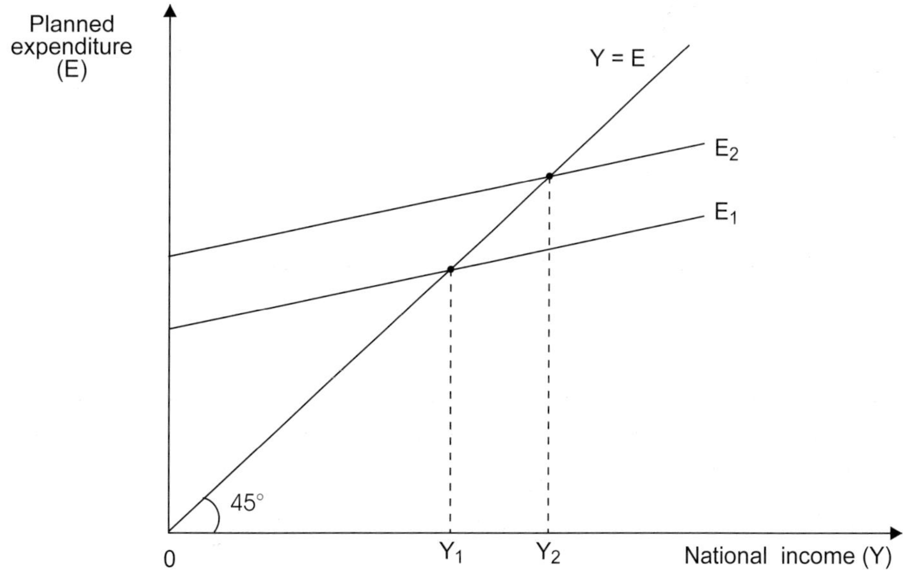

Figure 8 Multiplier effect

If injections were made to increase (for example, an increase in government spending or extra exports) then there would be a shift upwards in the E curve from E_1 to E_2. In Figure 8, the equilibrium level of income has now increased from Y_1 to Y_2. Notice however that the increase in the level of income from Y_1 to Y_2 is **bigger than the increase in injections**. In other words, total national income has increased by more than the amount of the initial increase in expenditure, and this is a portrayal of the multiplier effect.

3.9 Limitations of the multiplier

Keynes developed the concept of the multiplier in order to argue that extra government spending on public works, financed by a budget deficit, would have a pump-priming effect on a demand-deficient economy.

(a) Demand would be increased and national income would increase by more than the amount of the initial injection into the economy of the extra government spending.

(b) Because demand would be increased, unemployment would be reduced.

However, there are several important factors that limit the significance of the multiplier.

(a) It is relevant to a demand-deficient economy with high unemployment of resources. **If there is full employment, any increase in demand will be inflationary**.

(b) The **leakages** from the circular flow of income might make the value of the multiplier very low. This is relevant to the UK, where there is a high marginal propensity to import.

(c) There may be a **long period of adjustment** before the benefits of the multiplier are felt. If a government wants immediate action to improve the economy, relying on demand management and the multiplier could be too slow.

(d) The consumption function in advanced economies is probably more volatile than Keynes believed. If consumption is unpredictable, measures to influence national income through the multiplier will be impossible to predict too.

3.10 The accelerator principle

FAST FORWARD

Changes in national income can be explained partially by the **accelerator principle**, which is the mechanism by which changes in investment spending are proportionally greater than changes in consumption spending, and therefore investment spending is more susceptible to bigger upturns and downturns.

Key term

Accelerator principle: the theory that investment changes disproportionately in response to change in output.

The accelerator principle states that if there is a **small change** in the output of **consumer** goods, there will be a **much greater change** in the output of **capital** equipment required to make those consumer goods. This change in production of capital equipment (investment spending) speeds up the rate of economic growth, or slump.

A numerical example might help to illustrate this principle. Suppose that a firm makes biscuits and has 100 ovens in operation. The life of each oven is 5 years.

(a) If the demand for biscuits is constant, on average, 20 ovens must be replaced each year.

(b) If the demand for biscuits now rises by, say, 10% the firm will need 110 ovens in operation. During the first year of the increase, the demand for ovens will be 30 units. This is made up of replacement of 20 ovens and an extra requirement of 10 ovens to bring the total to 110.

A 10% rise in demand for consumer goods results in a 50% rise in demand for capital goods, in the short term. The accelerator is at work! The accelerator principle indicates how, when the demand for consumer goods rises, there will be an even greater proportional increase in the demand for capital goods. This speeds up growth in national income.

(a) If demand for biscuits now remains constant at the new level, annual replacement of capital equipment will average 22. There is consequently the danger that there will be over-capacity in the oven-making industry because the short-term peak demand of 30 ovens per annum is not maintained.

(b) This means that unless the rate of increase in consumer demand is maintained, over-capacity in capital goods industries is likely to occur.

3.11 The accelerator in reverse

The accelerator also works in reverse. A decline in demand for consumer goods will result in a much sharper decline in demand for the capital goods which make them.

The accelerator implies that investment and hence national income remain high only as long as consumption is rising.

So as income approaches the peak level dictated by available capacity, new investment will fall towards zero, reducing aggregate demand and hence national income. (The sharp fall in investment caused by the fall in consumption, due to the accelerator effect, will be compounded by the 'demultiplier', so that the accelerator and the demultiplier will combine to reduce national income more severely than the initial fall in consumption. The recovery in investment when demand stops falling will stimulate the economy again and cause income and thus demand to rise again.)

Note carefully that the accelerator comes into effect as a consequence of **changes in the rate of consumer demand**.

The extent of the change in investment depends on two things.

(a) The size of the change in consumer demand

(b) The **capital-output ratio**. This is the ratio of capital investment to the volume of output, in other words how much capital investment is needed to produce a quantity of output. For example, if the capital output ratio is 1:3, it would need capital investment of £1 to produce an extra £3 of output pa, and so if demand went up by say, £3 billion, it would need an extra £1 billion of investment to produce the extra output to meet the demand.

Economists at one time believed that the accelerator helped to explain the upswings and downturns of the trade cycle and therefore that the trade cycle was inevitable.

3.12 The paradox of thrift

The **paradox of thrift** is an illustration of the workings of a 'demultiplier' in a situation where savings and investment are temporarily out of balance. The demultiplier operates because households increase savings but there is **not a corresponding increase in investment**.

The paradox of thrift draws attention to the point that the amount of income saved by people is not necessarily invested, because people might choose to hold their savings as money (ie non-interest bearing wealth) rather than to invest the savings, at least in the short term.

Since extra saving does not necessarily result in additional investment (either because people do not want to invest or because entrepreneurs are not prepared to invest), three conclusions follow.

(a) The fall in consumption resulting from a rise in saving adversely affects entrepreneurs' expectations, and therefore they decide to reduce investment.

(b) A reduction in investment, through the multiplier, causes greater reductions in national income.

(c) Since national income falls, households have smaller income and therefore save less.

Thus greater saving without greater investment ends with smaller incomes and smaller savings. This is the paradox of thrift.

4 Aggregate supply analysis

FAST FORWARD

Aggregate supply determines the way aggregate demand influences inflation and unemployment.

The aggregate supply curve shows the amount of goods and services that producers in the economy would supply at a price level. The aggregate supply curve can take a number of shapes.

The aggregate supply curve will be flat, if supply can increase without raising the price level. This could be the case when there are idle resources in the economy. The aggregate supply curve will be **upward sloping**, for the reasons applying to the microeconomic supply curves mentioned in earlier chapters. A higher price means that it is worthwhile for firms to hire more labour and produce more because of the higher revenue-earning capability. So at the macroeconomic level, an increasing price level implies that many firms will be receiving higher prices for their products and will increase their output.

In the economy as a whole, supply will at some point reach a labour constraint, when the entire labour force is employed. When there is full employment, and firms cannot find extra labour to hire, they cannot produce more even when prices rise, unless there is some technical progress in production methods. The aggregate supply curve will therefore rise vertically when the full employment level of output is reached

5 The determination of national income

FAST FORWARD

Equilibrium national income is determined using aggregate supply and aggregate demand analysis

5.1 Aggregate demand and supply equilibrium

AD is total planned or desired consumption demand in the economy for consumer goods and services and also for capital goods, no matter whether the buyers are households, firms or government. AD is a concept of fundamental importance in Keynesian economic analysis. Keynes believed that national economy could be managed by taking measures to influence AD up or down.

The AD curve will be downward sloping because at higher prices, total quantities demanded will be less.

Keynes argued that a national economy will reach equilibrium where the aggregate demand curve and aggregate supply curve intersect.

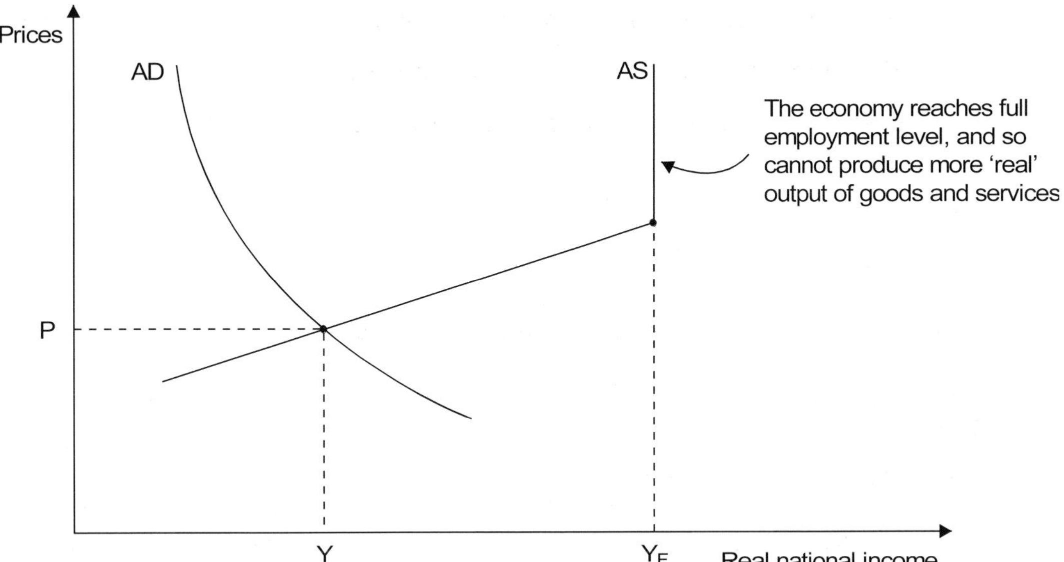

Figure 2 Equilibrium national income, using aggregate supply and aggregate demand analysis

The actual level of national income will be at the intersection of the AD curve and AS curves – ie at Y (Figure 2). The difference between the equilibrium national income Y and the full employment national income Y_F shows how much national income could be increased with the resources at the economy's disposal. Price levels will be at P. Y therefore represents the level of **satisfied** demand in the economy. Note that the aggregate demand function assumes constant prices.

Two points follow on immediately from this initial analysis.

(a) Equilibrium national income Y might be at a level of national income below full employment national income Y_F. This is the situation in Figure 1.

(b) On the other hand, the AD curve might cut the AS curve above the point at which it becomes vertical, in which case the economy will be fully employed, but price levels will be higher than they need to be. There will be inflationary pressures in the economy.

5.2 Full-employment national income

If one aim of a country's economic policy is full employment, then the ideal equilibrium level of national income will be where AD and AS are in balance at the full employment level of national income, without any inflationary gap – in other words, where aggregate demand at current price levels is exactly sufficient to encourage firms to produce at an output capacity where the country's resources are fully employed. This is shown in Figure 3, where equilibrium output will be Y (full employment level) with price level P.

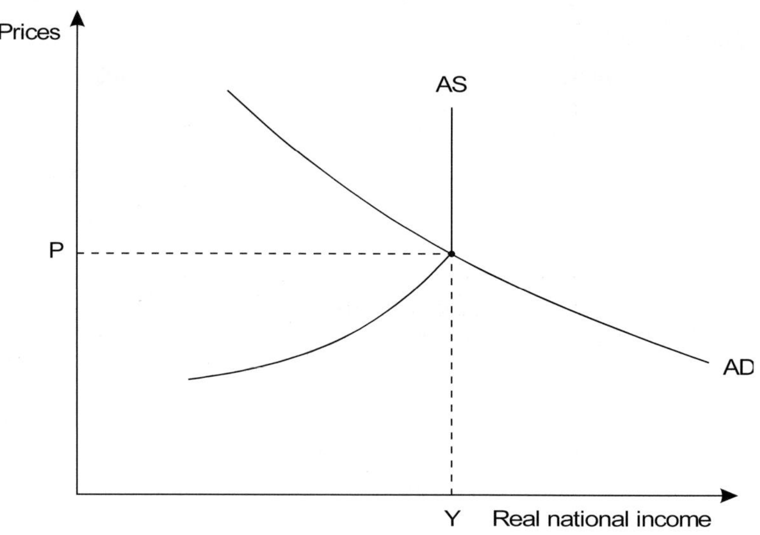

Figure 3 Full Employment Equilibrium national income

(A country will also seek economic growth, but to achieve a real increase in living standards, both AD and AS curves will now have to shift to the right.)

5.3 Inflationary gaps

In a situation where resources are already fully employed, there may be an **inflationary gap** since increases in aggregate demand will cause price changes and not variations in real output. An inflationary gap can be described as the extent to which the aggregate demand function would have to shift downward to produce the full employment level of national income without inflation.

You should also note that a shift in the AD curve or the AS curve will not only change the national income, it will also change price levels (P). In Figure 4, an inflationary gap can be removed by shifting the aggregate demand curve to the left, from AD_1 to AD_2.

If you are not sure about this point, a simple numerical example might help to explain it better. Suppose that in Ruritania there is full employment and all other economic resources are fully employed. The country produces 1,000 units of output with these resources. Total expenditure (that is, aggregate demand) in the economy is 100,000 Ruritanian dollars, or 100 dollars per unit. The country does not have any external trade, and so it cannot obtain extra goods by importing them. Because of pay rises and easier credit terms for consumers, total expenditure now rises to 120,000 Ruritanian dollars. The economy is fully employed, and cannot produce more than 1,000 units. If expenditure rises by 20%, to buy the same number of units, it follows that prices must rise by 20% too. In other words, when an economy is at full employment, any increase in aggregate demand will result in price inflation.

The Keynesian argument is that if a country's economy is going to move from one equilibrium to a different equilibrium, there needs to be a shift in the aggregate demand curve. To achieve equilibrium at the full employment level of national income, it may therefore be necessary to shift the AD curve to the right (upward) or the left (downwards).

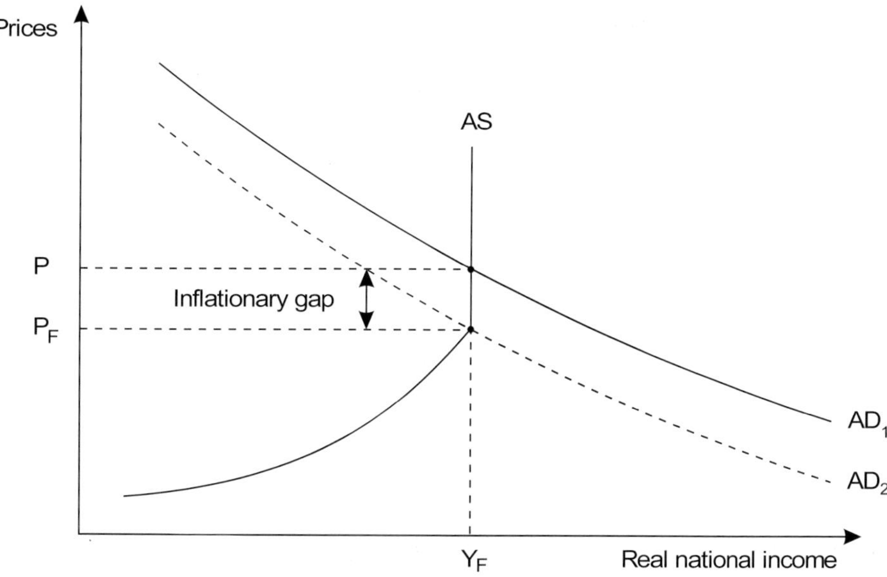

Figure 4 Inflationary gap

Assessment focus point

This diagram and the accompanying ideas are important for your assessment.

5.4 Deflationary gap

In a situation **where there is unemployment of resources** there is said to be a **deflationary gap** (Figure 5). Prices are fairly constant and real output changes as aggregate demand varies. A deflationary gap can be described as the extent to which the aggregate demand function will have to shift upward to produce the full employment level of national income.

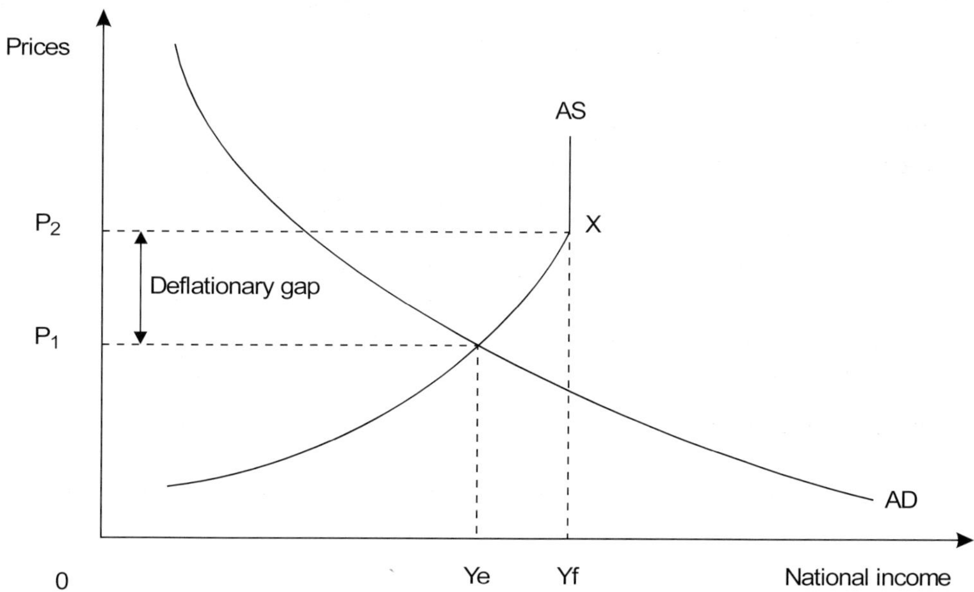

Figure 5 Deflationary gap

5.5 Stagflation

In the 1970s there was a problem with **stagflation**: a combination of unacceptably high unemployment and unacceptably high inflation. One of the causes was diagnosed as the major rises in the price of crude oil that took place. The cost of energy rose and this had the effect of rendering some production unprofitable. The supply curve shifted to the left as a result. The continuing stagnation is illustrated in Figure 6.

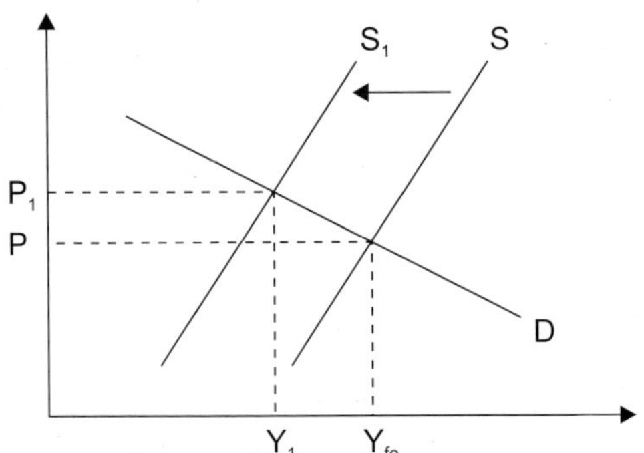

Figure 6 Stagflation

National income falls and both prices and unemployment rise. Any long term major increase in costs (a **price shock**) is likely to have this effect.

5.6 Summary so far

Keynes argued that an equilibrium national income will be reached where aggregate demand equals aggregate supply. There are two possible equilibria.

(a) One is at a level of employment which is below the full employment level of national income. The difference between actual national income and full employment national income is called a **deflationary gap**. To create full employment, the total national income (expenditure) must be increased by the amount of the deflationary gap.

(b) The other is at a level of demand which exceeds the productive capabilities of the economy at full employment, and there is insufficient output capacity in the economy to meet demand at current prices. There is then an **inflationary gap**.

The equilibrium national income will change if there are shifts in the AD curve.

When there is some unemployment in the economy, the aggregate demand curve will be further to the **left** than it could be. In other words, unemployment indicates a lower than necessary aggregate demand, and so a low AD. Although there might be some inflation when there is unemployment, very high levels of inflation are associated with full employment and over-strong aggregate demand.

You should notice that the aggregate supply curve begins to slope upwards before full employment income is reached. This is because the employment of less efficient labour, competition by firms for labour, possibly lower plant efficiency as factories approach capacity output and so on, will raise prices as well as output. In other words, there can be some inflation when there is some unemployment.

6 The business cycle

Trade cycles are explained in Keynesian economics as the combined effect of the **multiplier** and the **accelerator**.

6.1 What is the business cycle?

Business cycles or **trade cycles** are the continual sequence of rapid growth in national income, followed by a slow-down in growth and then a fall in national income. After this recession comes growth again, and when this has reached a peak, the cycle turns into recession once more.

Four main phases of the business cycle can be distinguished.

- Recession
- Depression
- Recovery
- Boom

Recession tends to occur quickly, while recovery is typically a slower process. Figure 7 below can be used to help explain how this is so.

6.2 Diagrammatic explanation

At point A in Figure 7, the economy is entering a recession. In the recession phase, consumer demand falls and many investment projects already undertaken begin to look unprofitable. Orders will be cut, stock levels will be reduced and business failures will occur as firms find themselves unable to sell their goods. Production and employment will fall. The general price level will begin to fall. Business and consumer confidence are diminished and investment remains low, while the economic outlook appears to be poor. Eventually, in the absence of any stimulus to aggregate demand, a period of full **depression** sets in and the economy will reach point B.

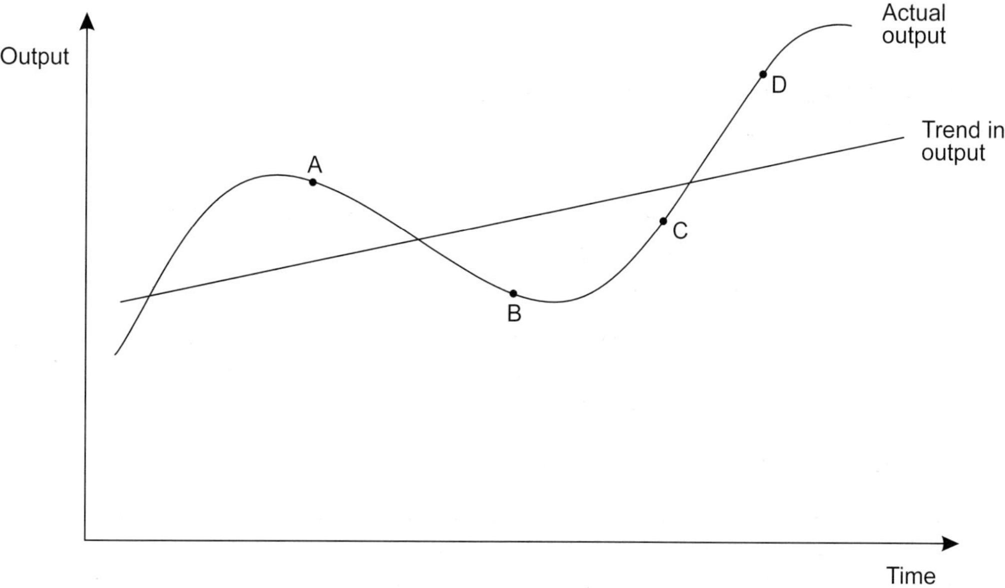

Figure 7 The business cycle

6.3 Analysis of the phases

Recession can begin relatively quickly because of the speed with which the effects of declining demand will be felt by businesses suffering a loss in sales revenue. The knock-on effects of destocking and cutting back on investment exacerbate the situation and add momentum to the recession. Recovery can be slow to begin because of the effect of recession on levels of confidence.

At point C the economy has reached the **recovery** phase of the cycle. Once begun, the phase of recovery is likely to quicken as confidence returns. Output, employment and income will all begin to rise. Rising production, sales and profit levels will lead to optimistic business expectations, and new investment will be more readily undertaken. The rising level of demand can be met through increased production by bringing existing capacity into use and by hiring unemployed labour. The average price level will remain constant or begin to rise slowly.

In the recovery phase, decisions to purchase new materials and machinery may lead to benefits in efficiency from new technology. This can enhance the relative rate of economic growth in the recovery phase once it is under way.

As recovery proceeds, the output level climbs above its trend path, reaching point D, in the **boom** phase of the cycle. During the boom, capacity and labour will become fully utilised. This may cause bottlenecks in some industries which are unable to meet increases in demand, for example because they have no spare capacity or they lack certain categories of skilled labour, or they face shortages of key material inputs. Further rises in demand will, therefore, tend to be met by increases in prices rather than by increases in production. In general, business will be profitable, with few firms facing losses. Expectations of the future may be very optimistic and the level of investment expenditure high.

It can be argued that wide fluctuations in levels of economic activity are damaging to the overall economic well-being of society. The inflation and speculation which accompanies boom periods may be inequitable in their impact on different sections of the population, while the bottom of the trade cycle may bring high unemployment. Governments generally seek to stabilise the economic system, trying to avoid the distortions of a widely fluctuating trade cycle.

6.4 Causes of the business cycle

According to the Keynesian approach to macroeconomics, the trade cycle is caused by fluctuations in aggregate demand and in particular by the interaction between the multiplier and the accelerator.

To see how this can happen suppose that aggregate demand has increased. Because production is increasing, businesses have to invest more to keep up with their orders. But this greater investment also has a multiplier effect, so it causes production to increase further – which requires a still higher rate of investment – which brings about still more increase in production via its multiplier effect – and so on.

Of course, this mutual reinforcement of the multiplier and the accelerator cannot go on forever, but it could explain why booms can go on for several years at a time. It can also explain why a recession occurs when production levels off. With production steady, businessmen only invest to replace their production capacity as it becomes obsolete. This means that investment could drop almost to zero, even though production is stable at a pretty high level.

The fall in investment demand will kick off a reduction in aggregate demand and income. The Keynesian approach assumes that that economic fluctuations could be quite predictable and cyclical. This is where the term 'business cycles' comes from.

7 Inflation and its consequences

FAST FORWARD

High rates of **inflation** are harmful to an economy. Inflation redistributes income and wealth. Uncertainty about the value of money makes business planning more difficult. Constantly changing prices impose extra costs.

7.1 Inflation

Key term

Inflation is the name given to an increase in price levels generally. It is also manifest in the decline in the purchasing power of money.

Historically, there have been very few periods when inflation has not been present. We discuss below why high rates of inflation are considered to be harmful. However, it is important to remember that **deflation** (falling prices) is normally associated with low rates of growth and even recession. It would seem that a healthy economy may require some inflation. This is recognised in the current UK inflation target of 2½%, and the European Central Bank's target of 2%. Certainly, if an economy is to grow, the money supply must expand, and the presence of a low level of inflation will ensure that growth is not hampered by a shortage of liquid funds.

7.2 Why is inflation a problem?

An economic policy objective which now has a central place in the policy approaches of the governments of many developed countries is that of stable prices. Why is a *high* rate of price inflation harmful and undesirable?

7.3 Redistribution of income and wealth

Inflation leads to a redistribution of income and wealth in ways which may be undesirable. Redistribution of wealth might take place from creditors to debtors. This is because debts lose 'real' value with inflation. For example, if you owed £1,000, and prices then doubled, you would still owe £1,000, but the **real value** of your debt would have been halved. In general, in times of inflation those with economic power tend to gain at the expense of the weak, particularly those on fixed incomes.

7.4 Balance of payments effects

If a country has a higher rate of inflation than its major trading partners, its exports will become relatively expensive and imports relatively cheap. As a result, the balance of trade will suffer, affecting employment in exporting industries and in industries producing import-substitutes. Eventually, the exchange rate will be affected.

7.5 Uncertainty of the value of money and prices

If the rate of inflation is imperfectly anticipated, no one has certain knowledge of the true rate of inflation. As a result, no one has certain knowledge of the value of money or of the real meaning of prices. If the rate of inflation becomes excessive, and there is 'hyperinflation', this problem becomes so exaggerated that money becomes worthless, so that people are unwilling to use it and are forced to resort to barter. In less extreme circumstances, the results are less dramatic, but the same problem exists. As prices convey less information, the process of resource allocation is less efficient and rational decision-making is almost impossible.

7.6 Resource costs of changing prices

A fourth reason to aim for stable prices is the resource cost of frequently changing prices. In times of high inflation substantial labour time is spent on planning and implementing price changes. Customers may also have to spend more time making price comparisons if they seek to buy from the lowest cost source.

7.7 Economic growth and investment

It is sometimes claimed that inflation is harmful to a country's economic growth and level of investment. A study by *Robert Barro* (*Bank of England Quarterly Bulletin*, May 1995) examined whether the evidence available supports this view. Barro found from data covering over 100 countries from 1960 to 1990 that, on average, an increase in inflation of ten percentage points per year reduced the growth rate of real GDP per capita by 0.2 to 0.3 percentage points per year, and lowered the ratio of investment to GDP by 0.4 to 0.6 percentage points. Although the adverse influence of inflation on economic growth and investment appears small, some causal effect would appear to exist, which could affect a country's standard of living fairly significantly over the long term.

7.8 Consumer price indices

We have already referred to the way in which inflation erodes the real value of money. In order to measure changes in the real value of money as a single figure, we need to group all goods and services into a single price index.

A consumer price index is based on a chosen 'basket' of items which consumers purchase. A weighting is decided for each item according to the average spending on the item by consumers.

Consumer price indices may be used for several purposes, for example as an indicator of inflationary pressures in the economy, as a benchmark for wage negotiations and to determine annual increases in government benefits payments. Countries commonly have more than one consumer price index because one composite index may be considered too wide a grouping for different purposes.

7.9 The RPI and the CPI

One important measure of the general rate of inflation in the UK used over many years has been the **Retail Prices Index (RPI)**. The RPI measures the percentage changes month by month in the average level of prices of the commodities and services, including housing costs, purchased by the great majority of households in the UK. The items of expenditure within the RPI are intended to be a representative list of items, current prices for which are collected at regular intervals.

In December 2003, it was confirmed that the standardised European measure, sometimes called the Harmonised Index of Consumer Prices (HICP) was now to be used as the basis for the UK's inflation target. The UK HICP is called the **Consumer Prices Index (CPI)**. The CPI excludes most housing costs.

7.10 The underlying rate of inflation

The term **underlying rate of inflation** is usually used to refer to the RPI adjusted to exclude mortgage costs and sometimes other elements as well (such as the local council tax). The effects of interest rate changes on mortgage costs help to make the RPI fluctuate more widely than the underlying rate of inflation.

RPIX is the underlying rate of inflation measured as the increase in the RPI excluding mortgage interest payments. Another measure, called **RPIY**, goes further and excludes the effects of VAT changes as well.

7.11 Causes of inflation

The following can cause inflation:

- Demand pull factors
- Cost push factors
- Import cost factors
- Expectations
- Excessive growth in the money supply

7.12 Demand pull inflation

FAST FORWARD

Demand pull inflation arises from an excess of aggregate demand over the productive capacity of the economy.

Demand pull inflation occurs when the economy is buoyant and there is a high aggregate demand, in excess of the economy's ability to supply.

(a) Because aggregate demand exceeds supply, prices rise.

(b) Since supply needs to be raised to meet the higher demand, there will be an increase in demand for factors of production, and so factor rewards (wages, interest rates, and so on) will also rise.

(c) Since aggregate demand exceeds the output capability of the economy, it should follow that demand pull inflation can only exist when unemployment is low. A feature of inflation in the UK in the 1970s and early 1980s, however, was high inflation coupled with high unemployment.

Key term

Demand pull inflation: inflation resulting from a persistent excess of aggregate demand over aggregate supply. Supply reaches a limit on capacity at the full employment level.

Traditionally Keynesian economists saw inflation as being caused by Demand pull factors. However, they now accept that Cost push factors are involved as well.

7.13 Cost push inflation

FAST FORWARD

Cost push inflation arises from increases in the costs of production.

Cost push inflation occurs where the costs of factors of production rise regardless of whether or not they are in short supply. This appears to be particularly the case with wages.

Key term

Cost push inflation: inflation resulting from an increase in the costs of production of goods and services, e.g. through escalating prices of imported raw materials or from wage increases.

7.14 Import cost factors

Import cost push inflation occurs when the cost of essential imports rise regardless of whether or not they are in short supply. This has occurred in the past with the oil price rises of the 1970s. Additionally, a fall in the value of a country's currency will have import Cost push effects since a weakening currency increases the price of imports.

7.15 Expectations and inflation

A further problem is that once the rate of inflation has begun to increase, a serious danger of **expectational inflation** will occur. This means, regardless of whether the factors that have caused inflation are still persistent or not, there will arise a generally held view of what inflation is likely to be, and so to protect future income, wages and prices will be raised now by the expected amount of future inflation. This can lead to the vicious circle known as the **wage-price spiral**, in which inflation becomes a relatively permanent feature because of people's expectations that it will occur.

7.16 Money supply growth

Monetarists have argued that inflation is caused by **increases in the supply of money**. There is a considerable debate as to whether increases in the money supply are a **cause** of inflation or whether increases in the money supply are a **symptom** of inflation. Monetarists have argued that since inflation is caused by an increase in the money supply, inflation can be brought under control by reducing the rate of growth of the money supply.

8 Unemployment

FAST FORWARD

The monetarist concept of a stable equilibrium implies that with zero price inflation, there is a **natural optimal level of unemployment**, and a rate of economic growth and balance of trade position from which the economy will not deviate. Monetarism focuses on economic stability in the medium to long term, which can only be achieved by abandoning short-term demand management goals.

8.1 The rate of unemployment

The **rate of unemployment** in an economy can be calculated as:

$$\frac{\text{Number of unemployed}}{\text{Total workforce}} \times 100\%$$

The number of unemployed at any time is measured by government statistics. If the flow of workers through unemployment is constant then the size of the unemployed labour force will also be constant.

Flows into unemployment are:

(a) Members of the working labour force **becoming** unemployed

- Redundancies
- Lay-offs
- Voluntary quitting from a job

(b) People **out** of the labour force **joining** the unemployed

- School leavers without a job
- Others (for example, carers) rejoining the workforce but having no job yet

Flows out of unemployment are:

- Unemployed people finding jobs
- Laid-off workers being re-employed
- Unemployed people stopping the search for work

In the UK, the monthly unemployment statistics published by the Office for National Statistics (ONS) count only the jobless who receive benefits.

The ONS also produce figures based on a quarterly survey of the labour force known as the International Labour organisation measure (ILO measure) that provides seasonally adjusted monthly data. This figure is considered to be more useful because it is also an internationally comparable measure.

8.2 Consequences of unemployment

Unemployment results in the following problems.

(a) **Loss of output**. If labour is unemployed, the economy is not producing as much output as it could. Thus, total national income is less than it could be.

(b) **Loss of human capital**. If there is unemployment, the unemployed labour will gradually lose its skills, because skills can only be maintained by working.

(c) **Increasing inequalities in the distribution of income**. Unemployed people earn less than employed people, and so when unemployment is increasing, the poor get poorer.

(d) **Social costs**. Unemployment brings social problems of personal suffering and distress, and possibly also increases in crime such as theft and vandalism.

(e) **Increased burden of welfare payments**. This can have a major impact on government fiscal policy.

8.3 Causes of unemployment

Unemployment may be classified into several categories depending on the underlying causes.

Category	Comments
Real wage unemployment	This type of unemployment is caused when the supply of labour exceeds the demand for labour, but real wages do not fall for the labour market to clear. This type of unemployment is normally caused by strong trade unions which resist a fall in their wages. Another cause of this type of unemployment is the minimum wage rate, when it is set above the market clearing level.
Frictional	It is inevitable that some unemployment is caused not so much because there are not enough jobs to go round, but because of the *friction* in the labour market (difficulty in matching quickly workers with jobs), caused perhaps by a lack of knowledge about job opportunities. In general, it takes time to match prospective employees with employers, and individuals will be unemployed during the search period for a new job. Frictional unemployment is temporary, lasting for the period of transition from one job to the next.
Seasonal	This occurs in certain industries, for example building, tourism and farming, where the demand for labour fluctuates in seasonal patterns throughout the year.
Structural	This occurs where long-term changes occur in the conditions of an industry. A feature of structural unemployment is high regional unemployment in the location of the industry affected.
Technological	This is a form of structural unemployment, which occurs when new technologies are introduced. (a) Old skills are no longer required. (b) There is likely to be a labour saving aspect, with machines doing the job that people used to do. With automation, employment levels in an industry can fall sharply, even when the industry's total output is increasing.
Cyclical or demand-deficient	It has been the experience of the past that domestic and foreign trade go through cycles of boom, decline, recession, recovery, then boom again, and so on. (a) During recovery and boom years, the demand for output and jobs is high, and unemployment is low. (b) During decline and recession years, the demand for output and jobs falls, and unemployment rises to a high level. Cyclical unemployment can be long-term, and a government might try to reduce it by doing what it can to minimise a recession or to encourage faster economic growth.

Seasonal employment and frictional unemployment will be short-term. Structural unemployment, technological unemployment, and cyclical unemployment are all longer term, and more serious.

8.4 Government employment policies

Job creation and reducing unemployment should often mean the same thing, but it is possible to create more jobs without reducing unemployment.

(a) This can happen when there is a greater number of people entering the jobs market than there are new jobs being created. For example, if 500,000 new jobs are created during the course of one year, but 750,000 extra school leavers are looking for jobs, there will be an increase in unemployment of 250,000.

(b) It is also possible to reduce the official unemployment figures without creating jobs. For example, individuals who enrol for a government financed training scheme are taken off the unemployment register, even though they do not have full-time jobs.

A government can try several options to create jobs or reduce unemployment.

(a) **Spending more money directly on job**s (for example hiring more civil servants)

(b) **Encouraging growth** in the private sector of the economy. When aggregate demand is growing, firms will probably want to increase output to meet demand, and so will hire more labour.

(c) **Encouraging training in job skills**. There might be a high level of unemployment amongst unskilled workers, and at the same time a shortage of skilled workers. A government can help to finance training schemes, in order to provide a 'pool' of workers who have the skills that firms need and will pay for.

(d) **Offering grant assistance to employers** in key regional areas

(e) **Encouraging labour mobility** by offering individuals financial assistance with relocation expenses, and improving the flow of information on vacancies

Other policies may be directed at **reducing real wages to market clearing levels**.

(a) Abolishing **closed shop** agreements, which restrict certain jobs to trade union members
(b) Abolishing **minimum wage regulations**, where such regulations exist

Question

Types of unemployment

Match the terms (a), (b) and (c) below with definitions A, B and C.

(a) Structural unemployment
(b) Cyclical unemployment
(c) Frictional unemployment

A Unemployment arising from a difficulty in matching unemployed workers with available jobs
B Unemployment occurring in the downswing of an economy in between two booms
C Unemployment arising from a long-term decline in a particular industry

Answer

The pairings are (a) C, (b) B and (c) A.

9 Unemployment and inflation

FAST FORWARD

There appears to be a connection between the **rate of inflation** and **unemployment**. The **Phillips curve** has been used to show that when there is zero inflation, there will be some unemployment.

9.1 Unemployment and inflation

The problems of unemployment and inflation were very severe for many countries in recent years. It has been found that boosting demand to increase the level of employment can cause a higher rate of inflation. However, **growth in unemployment** can also be associated with a **rising rate of inflation**.

9.2 The meaning of full employment

The term full employment does not mean a situation in which everyone has a job. There will always be at least a certain **natural rate of unemployment**, which is the minimum level of unemployment that an economy can expect to achieve.

An aim of government policy might be to reduce unemployment to this minimum natural rate, and so get as close as possible to the goal of full employment. On the basis that unemployment cannot be kept below its natural rate without causing inflation, the natural rate of unemployment is sometimes called the **non-accelerating inflation rate of unemployment (NAIRU)**. But in order to understand the idea of a natural rate of unemployment more fully, we need to examine in more detail the idea that there is a **trade-off between unemployment and inflation**.

9.3 Inflationary gaps and deflationary gaps

As we saw earlier when looking at the Keynesian model, equilibrium national income can be shown using an aggregate demand curve (AD), where AD is the total demand for all goods in the economy, at different price levels and an aggregate supply curve (AS), where AS is the total supply of all goods in the economy, at different price levels.

According to Keynes, **demand management** by the government could be based on government **spending and taxation policies** (fiscal policy). These could be used for two purposes.

(a) **To eliminate a deflationary gap** and create full employment. A small initial increase in government spending will start off a **multiplier-accelerator** effect, and so the actual government spending required to eliminate a deflationary gap should be less than the size of the gap itself.

(b) **To eliminate an inflationary gap** and take inflation out of the economy. This can be done by reducing government spending, or by increasing total taxation and not spending the taxes raised.

Keynesians accept that reductions in unemployment can only be achieved if prices are allowed to rise: reducing unemployment goes hand in hand with allowing some inflation.

9.4 The Phillips curve

In 1958 *A W Phillips* found a statistical relationship between unemployment and the rate of money wage inflation which implied that, in general, **the rate of inflation falls unemployment rose and vice versa**. A curve, known as a **Phillips curve**, can be drawn linking inflation and unemployment (Figure 8).

Key term

Phillips curve: a graphical illustration of the historic inverse relationship between the rate of wage inflation and the rate of unemployment.

Note the following two points about the Phillips curve.

(a) The curve crosses the horizontal axis at a positive value for the unemployment rate. This means that zero inflation will be associated with some unemployment; it is not possible to achieve zero inflation and zero unemployment at the same time.

(b) The shape of the curve means that the lower the level of unemployment, the higher the **rate of increase** in inflation.

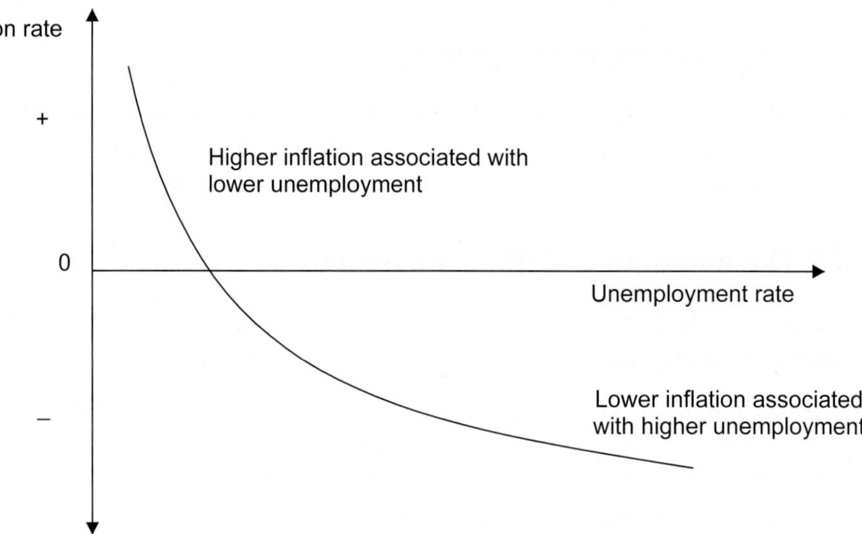

Figure 8 Phillips curve

The existence of a relationship between inflation and unemployment of the type indicated by the Phillips curve suggests that the government should be able to use demand management policies to take the economy to acceptable levels of inflation and unemployment.

This re-emphasises the argument of Keynesian economists that in order to achieve full employment, some inflation is unavoidable. If achieving full employment is an economic policy objective, a government must therefore be prepared to accept a certain level of inflation as a necessary evil.

However, the Phillips curve relationship between inflation and unemployment broke down at the end of the 1960s when Britain began to experience **rising inflation at the same time as rising unemployment.**

Chapter roundup

- The **Keynesian model** provides a way of explaining how national income is determined, and how national income equilibrium is reached.
- **Consumption expenditure** depends on income. It might be possible for a government to take measures to boost aggregate demand in the economy, although some price inflation will probably result. When there is inflation in the economy, measures could be taken to suppress aggregate demand.
- Changes in national income begin with a small change in expenditure, leading to an even larger eventual change in national income, due to the **multiplier effect**.
- Changes in national income can be explained partially by the **accelerator principle**, which is the mechanism by which changes in investment spending are proportionally greater than changes in consumption spending, and therefore investment spending is more susceptible to bigger upturns and downturns.
- **Aggregate supply** determines the way aggregate demand influences inflation and unemployment.
- **Equilibrium national income** is determined using aggregate supply and aggregate demand analysis.
- **Trade cycles** are explained in Keynesian economics as the combined effect of the **multiplier** and the **accelerator.**
- High rates of **inflation** are harmful to an economy. Inflation redistributes income and wealth. Uncertainty about the value of money makes business planning more difficult. Constantly changing prices impose extra costs.
- **Demand pull inflation** arises from an excess of aggregate demand over the productive capacity of the economy.
- **Cost push inflation** arises from increases in the costs of production.
- The monetarist concept of a stable equilibrium implies that with zero price inflation, there is a **natural optimal level of unemployment**, and a rate of economic growth and balance of trade position from which the economy will not deviate. Monetarism focuses on economic stability in the medium to long term, which can only be achieved by abandoning short-term demand management goals.
- There appears to be a connection between the **rate of inflation** and **unemployment**. The **Phillips curve** has been used to show that when there is zero inflation, there will be some unemployment.

Quick quiz

1 For an equilibrium national income level to be reached, withdrawals from and injections into the circular flow of income must be equal. Why are they not always in balance?

2 What are the marginal propensity to consume and the marginal propensity to save?

3 How might a government try to influence the volume of investment by firms?

4 Injections into the economy are:

A Consumption and Investment
B Investment and Government Expenditure
C Investment, Government Expenditure and Export Demand
D Consumption, Investment, Government Expenditure and Export Demand

5 If a consumption function has the formula C = 750 + 0.4Y where is Y the change in national income, and injections are 500, then equilibrium national income will be at:

A 833
B 1,250
C 2,083
D 3,125

6 If the MPC is greater for the poor than the rich then a redistribution of national income in favour of the rich will:

A Raise savings out of a given income
B Increase the multiplier
C Decrease the MPS
D Stimulate import demand

7 A deflationary gap occurs when:

A Aggregate demand is insufficient to buy up all the goods and services the company is capable of producing.
B Aggregate demand is more than sufficient to buy up all the goods and services produced by an economy.
C A government attempts to spend its way out of recession.
D A government is cutting its level of expenditure.

Answers to quick quiz

1 The withdrawals and injections are not made by the same people.

2 When a household receives an increase in income, some will be spent and some will be saved. The proportion which is spent is the marginal propensity to consume, while the proportion which is saved is the marginal propensity to save.

3 Lower interest rates, investment grants and tax incentives may encourage investment. Governments can also stimulate demand by tax cuts or lower interest rates and improve business confidence by business friendly and growth enhancing policies like deregulation and controlling inflation. Policies to encourage technological development may also lead to increased investment.

4 C

5 C Equilibrium occurs when E = Y. E = C + J = 750 + 0.4Y + 500. Therefore 0.6Y = 1,250, therefore Y= 2,083.

6 A The rich will save more, not spend.

7 A

Now try the questions below from the Exam Question Bank

Question numbers	Page
40 – 43	373

14 Fiscal, monetary and supply side policies

Introduction

The previous chapter analysed the main macroeconomic phenomena such as business cycles, unemployment and inflation. In this chapter we present an overview of the goals of macroeconomic policy in relation to this phenomena and concentrate on three broad types of policy, fiscal policy, monetary policy and supply side policies.

First we consider the role of fiscal policy in affecting aggregate demand and examine the types of taxation and the role of taxation in creating incentives.

Secondly we present alternative theories of how the money supply and interest rates affect the aggregate demand and discuss the conduct of monetary policy.

Thirdly we examine the effectiveness of macroeconomic policy in affecting inflation and unemployment.

Monetary and fiscal policy affect aggregate demand. In the final section we discuss supply side policies that affect aggregate supply.

Topic list	Learning outcomes	Syllabus references	Ability required
1 Government policies and objectives	D (iv)	D (5)	Comprehension
2 Fiscal policy	D (iv)	D (9)	Comprehension
3 Monetary theory	D (iv)	D(10)	Comprehension
4 Monetary policy	D (iv)	D(8)	Comprehension
5 Effectiveness of macroeconomic policy	D (iv)	D(10)	Comprehension
6 Supply side policy	D (iv)	D(10)	Comprehension

1 Government policies and objectives

FAST FORWARD

Macroeconomic policy objectives relate to economic growth, inflation, unemployment and the balance of payments.

1.1 Economic policy objectives

All modern governments are expected to manage their national economies to some extent. Electorates generally suppose that government action can support or hinder the growth of prosperity and look to them for serviceable macroeconomic policies. There are four main objective of economic policy, though debate continues about their relative priority.

(a) **To achieve economic growth**, and growth in national income per head of the population. Growth implies an increase in national income in real terms. Increases caused by price inflation are not real increases at all.

(b) **To control price inflation** (to achieve stable prices). This has become a central objective of UK economic policy in recent years.

(c) **To achieve full employment**. Full employment does not mean that everyone who wants a job has one all the time, but it does mean that unemployment levels are low, and involuntary unemployment is short-term.

(d) **To achieve a balance between exports and imports** (on the country's balance of payments accounts) over a period of years. The wealth of a country relative to others, a country's creditworthiness as a borrower, and the goodwill between countries in international relations might all depend on the achievement of an external balance over time.

Key term

Monetary policy: government policy on the money supply, the monetary system, interest rates, exchange rates and the availability of credit.

Fiscal policy: government policy on taxation, public borrowing and public spending.

Monetary and Fiscal policy attempt to attain the macroeconomic policy objectives by influencing aggregate demand.

Supply Side policies on the other hand attempt to the attain the macroeconomic policy objectives by shifting the aggregate supply curve.

2 Fiscal policy

FAST FORWARD

Fiscal policy provides a method of managing **aggregate demand** in the economy.

2.1 Fiscal policy and the Budget

A feature of fiscal policy is that a government must **plan** what it wants to spend, and so how much it needs to raise in income or by borrowing. It needs to make a plan in order to establish how much taxation there should be, what form the taxes should take and so which sectors of the economy (firms or households, high income earners or low income earners) the money should come from. This formal planning of fiscal policy is usually done once a year and is set out in **the Budget**.

The two components of the budget which the government determines and through which it exercises its fiscal policy are:

(a) **Expenditure**. The government, at a national and local level, spends money to provide goods and services, such as a health service, public education, a police force, roads, public buildings and so on, and to pay its administrative work force. It may also, perhaps, provide finance to encourage investment by private industry, for example by means of grants.

(b) **Revenues**. Expenditure must be financed, and the government must have income. Most government income comes from **taxation**, albeit some income is obtained from **direct charges** to users of government services such as National Health Service charges.

A third element of the fiscal policy is:

(c) **Borrowing**. To the extent that a government's expenditure exceeds its income it must borrow to make up the difference. The amount that the government must borrow each year is now known as the **Public Sector Net Cash Requirement (PSNCR)** in the UK Its former name was **Public Sector Borrowing Requirement (PSBR).** Where the government borrows from has an impact on the effectiveness of fiscal policy.

Key term

The **public sector net cash requirement (PSNCR)** is the annual excess of spending over income for the entire sector – not just the central government.

2.2 Budget surplus and budget deficit

If a government decides to use fiscal policy to influence demand in the economy, it can choose either expenditure changes or tax changes as its policy instrument. Suppose, for example, that the government wants to stimulate demand in the economy.

(a) **It can increase demand directly by spending more itself** – eg on the health service or education, and by employing more people itself.

   (i) This extra spending could be financed by higher taxes, but this would reduce spending by the private sector of the economy because the private sector's after-tax income would be lower.

   (ii) The extra government spending could also be financed by extra government borrowing. Just as individuals can borrow money for spending, so too can a government.

(b) **It can increase demand indirectly by reducing taxation** and so allowing firms and individuals more after-tax income to spend (or save).

   (i) Cuts in taxation can be matched by cuts in government spending, in which case total demand in the economy will not be stimulated significantly, if at all.

   (ii) Alternatively, tax cuts can be financed by more government borrowing.

Just as aggregate demand in the economy can be boosted by either more government spending or by tax cuts, financed in either case by a higher PSNCR, so too can demand in the economy be reduced by cutting government spending or by raising taxes, and using the savings or higher income to cut government borrowing.

Expenditure changes and tax changes are not mutually exclusive options, of course. A government has several options.

(a) Increase expenditure and reduce taxes, with these changes financed by a higher PSNCR
(b) Reduce expenditure and increase taxes, with these changes reducing the size of the PSNCR
(c) Increase expenditure and partly or wholly finance this extra spending with higher taxes
(d) Reduce expenditure and use these savings to reduce taxes

When a government's income exceeds its expenditure, and there is a negative PSNCR or **Public Sector Debt Repayment (PSDR),** we say that the government is running a **budget surplus**. When a government's expenditure exceeds its income, so that it must borrow to make up the difference, there is a PSNCR and we say that the government is running a **budget deficit**.

2.3 Functions of taxation

Taxation has several functions.

(a) **To raise revenues for the government** as well as for local authorities and similar public bodies (e.g. the European Union).

(b) **To discourage certain activities regarded as undesirable**. The imposition of Development Land Tax in the United Kingdom in the mid-70s (since abolished) was partially in response to growth in property speculation.

(c) **To cause certain products to be priced to take into account their social costs**. For example, smoking entails certain social costs, including especially the cost of hospital care for those suffering from smoking-related diseases, and the government sees fit to make the price of tobacco reflect these social costs.

(d) **To redistribute income and wealth**. Higher rates of tax on higher incomes will serve to redistribute income. UK inheritance tax goes some way towards redistributing wealth.

(e) **To protect industries from foreign competition.** If the government levies a duty on all imported goods much of the duty will be passed on to the consumer in the form of higher prices, making imported goods more expensive. This has the effect of transferring a certain amount of demand from imported goods to domestically produced goods.

(f) **To provide a stabilising effect on national income**. Taxation reduces the effect of the multiplier, and so can be used to dampen upswings in a trade cycle – ie higher taxation when the economy shows signs of a boom will slow down the growth of money GNP and so take some inflationary pressures out of the economy.

The size of the multiplier, remember, is $\left(\frac{1}{s+m+t}\right)$ where t is the marginal rate of taxation.

2.4 Qualities of a good tax

Adam Smith in his *Wealth of Nations* ascribed **four features to a good tax system.**

(a) **Equity**. Persons should pay according to their ability.

(b) **Certainty**. The tax should be well-defined and easily understood by all concerned.

(c) **Convenience**. The payment of tax should ideally be related to how and when people receive and spend their income (eg PAYE is deducted when wages are paid, and VAT is charged when goods are bought).

(d) **Economy**. The cost of collection should be small relative to the yield (eg by this criterion, the car road tax is an inefficient tax).

Further features of a good tax can be identified.

- **Flexibility**. It should be adjustable so that rates may be altered up or down.
- **Efficiency**. It should not harm initiative, but evasion should be difficult.
- It should attain its purpose **without distorting economic behaviour**.

Note the following distinctions.

(a) A **regressive tax** takes a higher **proportion** of a poor person's salary than of a rich person's. Television licences and road tax are examples of regressive taxes since they are the same for all people. High income earners, even though individual charges can vary from one local authority to another, and in spite of some rebates for the least well-off groups.

(b) A **proportional tax** takes the **same proportion** of income in tax from all levels of income. Schedule E income tax with a basic of tax at 23% is proportional tax, but only within a limited range of income.

(c) A **progressive tax** takes a **higher proportion** of income in tax as income rises. Income tax as a whole is progressive, since the first part of an individual's income is tax-free due to personal allowances and the rate of tax increases in steps from 20p in £1 to 40p in £1 as taxable income rises.

T FORWARD

Direct taxes have the quality of being **progressive** or **proportional**. Income tax is usually progressive, with high rates of tax charged on higher bands of taxable income. **Indirect taxes** can be **regressive**, when the taxes are placed on essential commodities or commodities consumed by poorer people in greater quantities.

2.5 Advantages and disadvantages of progressive taxation

Arguments in favour of progressive direct taxes

(a) **They are levied according to the ability of individuals to pay**. Individuals with a higher income are more able to afford to give up more of their income in tax than low income earners, who need a greater proportion of their earnings for the basic necessities of life. If taxes are to be raised according to the ability of people to pay (which is one of the features of a good tax suggested by Adam Smith) then there must be some progressiveness in them.

(b) **Progressive taxes enable a government to redistribute wealth from the rich to the poor in society**. Such a redistribution of wealth will alter the consumption patterns in society since the poorer members of society will spend their earnings and social security benefits on different types of goods than if the income had remained in the hands of the richer people.

(c) **Indirect taxes tend to be regressive and progressive taxes are needed as a counter-balance** to make the tax system as a whole more fair.

Arguments against progressive taxes

(a) **In an affluent society, there is less need for progressive taxes than in a poorer society**. Fewer people will live in poverty in such a society if taxes are not progressive than in a poorer society.

(b) **Higher taxes on extra corporate profits might deter entrepreneurs** from developing new companies because the potential increase in after-tax profits would not be worth the risks involved in undertaking new investments.

(c) **Individuals and firms that suffer from high taxes might try to avoid or evade paying tax** by transferring their wealth to other countries, or by setting up companies in tax havens where corporate tax rates are low. However, tax avoidance and evasion are practised whether tax rates are high or low. High taxes will simply raise the relative gains which can be made from avoidance or evasion.

(d) When progressive taxes are harsh, and either tax high income earners at very high marginal rates or tax the wealthy at high rates on their wealth, **they could act as a deterrent to initiative**. Skilled workers might leave the country and look for employment in countries where they can earn more money.

2.6 The 'poverty trap'

If one considers the effects of state benefits on income as a form of 'negative taxation', then the highest marginal rates of taxation/loss of benefit in past years in the UK have fallen on low income earners receiving state benefits. For example where the benefit rules state than an individual loses £1 of benefit for each £1 of extra part-time earnings, then the individual is suffering a marginal rate of taxation/loss of benefit of 100% and there is no financial incentive for him to work at all. This is sometimes called a **poverty trap**.

2.7 Proportional and regressive taxes

It is often argued that tax burdens should be **proportional** to income in order to be fair, although a proportional tax has the following disadvantages.

(a) A large administrative system is needed to calculate personal tax liabilities on a proportional basis. The costs of collecting income tax relative to tax revenues earned can be high, particularly in the case of lower income taxpayers.

(b) Such a tax does not contribute towards a redistribution of wealth among the population.

In the case of a **regressive** tax, a greater proportionate tax burden falls on those least able to afford it. The main disadvantage of a regressive tax is that it is not fair or equitable. The main advantage of a regressive tax is that it is often relatively easy to administer and collect. This is the case with motor vehicle tax, for example. However, a regressive tax might also be expensive to collect.

Question — Taxation types

Below are details of three taxation systems, one of which is regressive, one proportional and one progressive. Which is which?

	Income before tax	*Income after tax*
	£	£
System 1	10,000	8,000
	20,000	15,000
System 2	10,000	7,000
	20,000	14,000
System 3	10,000	9,000
	20,000	19,000

Answer

	Tax paid on low income	*Tax paid on high income*	*Nature of tax*
System 1	20%	25%	Progressive
System 2	30%	30%	Proportional
System 3	10%	5%	Regressive

2.8 Direct and indirect taxes

T FORWARD

A government must decide how it intends to raise tax revenues, from **direct or indirect taxes**, and in what proportions tax revenues will be raised from each source.

A **direct tax** is paid direct by a person to the Revenue authority. Examples of direct taxes in the UK are income tax, corporation tax, capital gains tax and inheritance tax. A direct tax can be levied on income and profits, or on wealth. Direct taxes tend to be progressive or proportional taxes. They are also usually unavoidable, which means that they must be paid by everyone.

An **indirect tax** is collected by the Revenue authority from an intermediary (a supplier) who then attempts to pass on the tax to consumers in the price of goods they sell. Indirect taxes are of two types.

Key term

A **specific tax** is charged as a *fixed sum* per unit sold.

An **ad valorem tax** is charged as a *fixed percentage* of the price of the good.

2.9 Direct taxation on income: advantages and disadvantages

The main advantages of direct taxes on income are that they can be made fair and equitable by being designed as progressive or proportional to the degree desired. Because of their generally progressive nature they also tend to stabilise the economy, automatically taking more money out of the system during a boom and less during depression. Moreover, because they are more difficult to pass on, they are less inflationary than indirect taxes. Finally, taxpayers know what their tax liability is.

When income tax is levied at a high rate, it could **discourage** the geographical and the occupational mobility of labour.

(a) There might be higher gross income levels in one region of the country where jobs are in plentiful supply than in an area of high unemployment. High income tax rates, however, might make the after-tax increase in income an insufficient incentive to move. High marginal rates of taxation might also cause a migration of highly skilled and therefore highly paid workers to countries with a more favourable tax regime.

(b) High marginal tax rates, by narrowing the differentials in the after-tax pay of skilled and unskilled labour, may reduce the incentive to train and thereby cause a shortage of skilled labour.

High marginal rates of tax could **encourage tax avoidance** (finding legal loopholes in the tax rules so as to avoid paying tax). In Britain, high tax rates led to a growth of making income payments-in-kind by way of fringe benefits, for example, free medical and life insurance, preferential loans and favourable pension rights. The tax authorities responded to this by bringing an increasing number of fringe benefits into the tax net – for example, the private use of a company car.

In some cases individuals and companies may resort to **tax evasion**, which is the illegal non-payment of tax. Employed people have limited scope for tax evasion, because of the **pay as you earn** (PAYE) tax system in the UK. Undoubtedly, the self-employed have a greater ability to evade tax by failing to declare earnings. If evasion becomes widespread the cost of enforcing the tax laws may become very expensive.

2.10 Incentive effects

A direct tax on **profits might act as a disincentive to risk-taking and enterprise**. The tax will reduce the net return from a new investment and any disincentive effects will be greater when the tax is progressive. In addition, a tax on profits will reduce the ability to invest. A considerable part of the finance for new investment comes from retained profits so any tax on corporate profits will reduce the ability of firms to save and therefore limit the sources of funds for investment.

High taxation acts as a disincentive to work because if marginal tax rates (ie the proportion of additional income taken as tax) are high, individuals are likely to behave in one of two ways.

(a) They may forgo opportunities to increase income through additional effort on the basis that the increase in net income does not adequately reward the effort or risk.

(b) They may resort to working in the parallel 'black' economy to avoid paying the tax.

2.11 The Laffer curve

The **Laffer curve** (named after Professor Arthur Laffer) illustrates the effect of tax rates upon government revenue and national income.

In the hypothetical economy depicted in Figure 1 a tax rate of 0% results in the government receiving no tax revenue irrespective of the level of national income. If the rate is 100% then nobody will work because they keep none of their earnings and so once again total tax revenue is zero. At 25% tax rates the government will achieve a total tax take of £30bn; the same as the revenue they enjoy at rates of 75%. By deduction the level of national income when taxes are 25% must be £120bn compared with only £40bn if taxes are 75%. High taxation appears to operate as a disincentive and reduce national income.

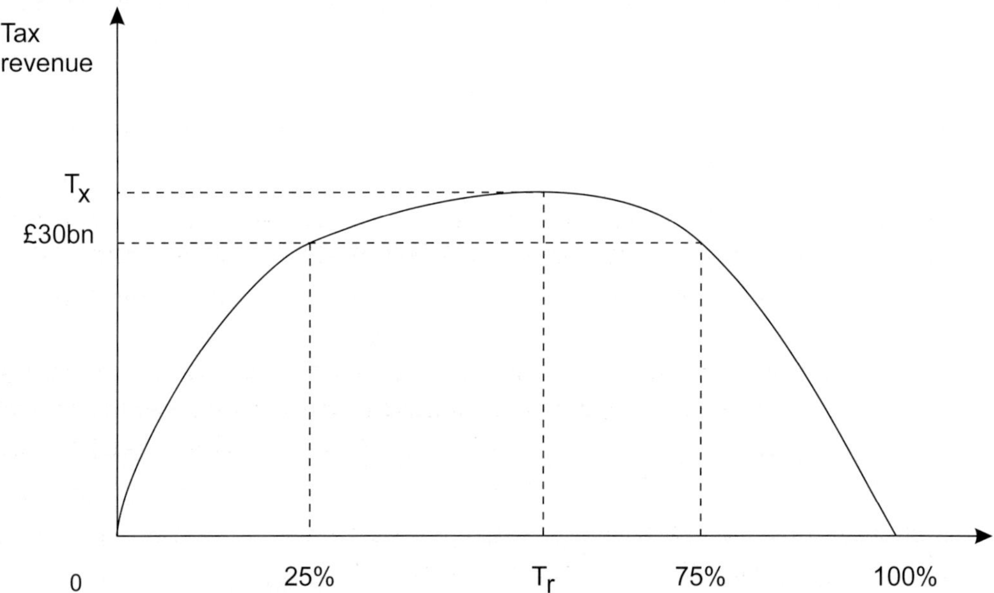

Figure 1 Laffer curve for a hypothetical economy

Three consequences flow from this Laffer curve analysis.

(a) High rates of taxation act as a disincentive to work and accordingly reduce output and employment.

(b) Governments cannot always expect to increase tax revenue by increasing tax rates. There appears to be a crucial tax rate beyond which the fall in national income resulting from the erosion of incentives and effort outweighs the increased tax rate. In Figure 3 the maximum tax revenue is T_X, at average tax rate T_r. If tax rates are above T_r, the government can increase tax revenues by cutting tax rates.

(c) There will always be two tax rates available which can yield the same total tax revenue: one associated with a high level of national income and another associated with a lower level. In consequence, governments committed to high government expenditure need not necessarily be associated with high rates of tax.

Key term

Laffer curve a curve depicting the relationship between tax revenue and the average tax rate, designed to illustrate the thesis that there is an optimal tax rate at which tax revenues are maximised.

2.12 Indirect taxation: advantages and disadvantages

Indirect taxes are hidden in the sense that the taxpayer is frequently unaware of the amount of tax he is paying, so that it is almost painlessly extracted (eg the high rate of tax on beer and spirits). This has considerable advantages from the government's point of view.

Indirect taxation can be used to encourage or discourage the production or consumption of particular goods and services and hence affect the allocation of resources. For example, the production of goods that produce environmental pollution may be taxed as a means of raising the price in order to reduce demand and output. Similarly, the consumption of cigarettes can be discouraged by high indirect taxation.

Question **Indirect tax**

The burden of an indirect tax must either be borne by the producer or passed on by the producer to consumers. If a producer feels able to pass on the whole of the burden, what can you deduce about the elasticity of demand for his product?

Answer

Demand for the product must presumably be inelastic, at least in the opinion of the producer. Otherwise he would fear to pass on the tax burden by increasing his prices as this would lead to a fall in demand.

Indirect taxation is a relatively **flexible instrument of economic policy**. The rates of indirect taxes may be changed to take effect immediately. For example, if the Chancellor wished to boost aggregate demand in the economy he could reduce rates of indirect taxation and this would have an immediate effect on private consumption. In the case of direct taxes, more notice must be given to the taxpayer.

Indirect taxes can be **cheap to collect**. Traders and companies are required to act as collectors of value added tax in the UK, thus reducing the administrative burden on government.

Indirect taxes do have disadvantages however.

(a) **They can be inflationary**. In the UK, a switch from direct tax to indirect tax in the budget of 1979, when VAT rates were increased, resulted in a large increase in the reported rate of inflation. When prices are rising the burden of *ad valorem* indirect taxes will naturally rise also. However, a specific indirect tax will only be inflationary if the rate at which it is applied is changed.

(b) **Indirect taxes also tend to be regressive**. A broadly levied indirect tax like VAT is likely to be quite regressive because the poorer members of the community spend a very much larger fraction of their income than very rich people. A system of indirect taxes on luxury goods would not be regressive, however.

(c) **Indirect taxes are not completely impartial in their application in other ways**. For example, someone who seeks to relax with a cigarette in a pub is going to be much more heavily hit by indirect taxes than someone who likes walking. The differential taxes, moreover, prevent resources from being distributed

optimally according to consumer preference. Unlike an income tax, indirect taxes change the relative price of goods. This means that consumers have to arrange their patterns of expenditure accordingly. This substitution may involve loss of satisfaction.

(d) Like taxes on incomes, **indirect taxes may be evaded by some**. The so-called 'black economy', in which cash payments are made and income is not declared for tax purposes, is undoubtedly large and widespread in the UK, particularly in the self-employed sector.

2.13 Fiscal policy and aggregate demand

Fiscal policy is concerned with **government spending** (an injection into the circular flow of income) and **taxation** (a withdrawal).

(a) If government spending is increased, there will be an increase in the amount of injections, expenditure in the economy will rise and so national income will rise (either in real terms, or in terms of price levels only; i.e. the increase in national income might be real or inflationary).

(b) If government taxation is increased, there will be an increase in withdrawals from the economy, and expenditure and national income will fall. A government might deliberately raise taxation to take inflationary pressures out of the economy.

A government's **'fiscal stance'** may be **neutral, expansionary** or **contractionary,** according to its effect on national income.

(a) **Spending more money** and financing this expenditure by borrowing would indicate an expansionary fiscal stance.

(b) **Collecting more in taxes** without increasing spending would indicate a contractionary fiscal stance.

(c) Collecting more in taxes in order to **increase spending**, thus diverting income from one part of the economy to another would indicate a broadly neutral fiscal stance.

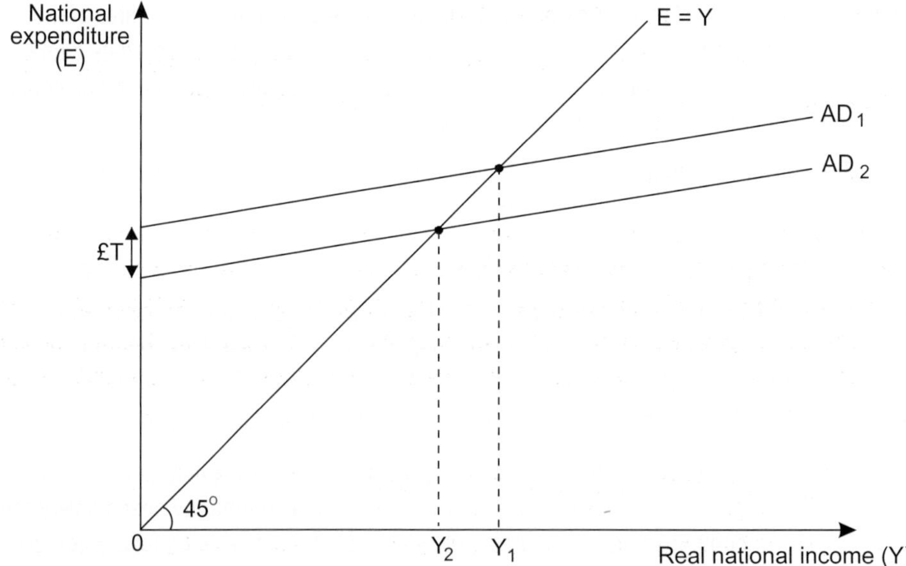

Figure 2 Increase in taxation

An increase in taxation by £T in Figure 2, without any matching increase in government expenditure, would **reduce** the aggregate expenditure in the economy from AD_1 to AD_2 and so the money value of national income would fall from Y_1 to Y_2. This would result in either a fall in real output or it would dampen inflationary pressures.

Similarly, a reduction in taxation without any reduction in government spending would **increase** the money value of national income. This would either cause real output to increase, or it would give a boost to price rises and inflation.

2.14 Fiscal policy and unemployment

Fiscal policy can be used to reduce unemployment and provide jobs.

(a) More government spending on capital projects would create jobs in the construction industries.

(b) Government-funded training schemes are a means of spending by government to improve training, so as to make people more qualified for jobs in private industry.

(c) A government might tax companies on the basis of the numbers and pay levels of people they employ (as with employers' national insurance contributions). Lower employment taxes would possibly make employers more willing to take on extra numbers of employees.

If government raises taxes and spending by the same amount, so that the budget remains in balance, there will be an **increase in aggregate monetary demand**. This is because tax payers would have saved some of the money they pay in increased tax and the government spends all of it within the economy. This effect is called the **balanced budget multiplier**.

Government spending, however, might create inflationary pressures, and inflation tends to create more unemployment. Fiscal policy must therefore be used with care, even to create new jobs.

2.15 Other effects

Since government spending or tax reductions might be inflationary, and higher domestic prices make imports relatively cheaper and exports less competitive in foreign markets, fiscal policy has possible implications for the **balance of payments** (discussed later in this Study Text).

The impact of changes in fiscal policy is not always certain, and fiscal policy to pursue one aim (eg lower inflation) might for a while create barriers to the pursuit of other aims (eg employment).

2.16 Crowding out

Deficit budgets have been criticised on the grounds that they 'crowd out' private sector activity; that is, the government spending merely replaces private spending with no net increase in AD. In particular, it is suggested that increased government borrowing to finance government expenditure, inevitably leads to higher interest rates, which, in turn, lead to a reduction in private borrowing for both consumption and investment. The Keynesian response to this criticism is to say that crowding out will not occur when there are **idle resources** within the economy, such as a large number of unemployed.

2.17 The success of fiscal policy as a method of demand management

The success of fiscal policy as a means of influencing the economy sufficiently has been called into question.

(a) At the end of the 1970s, *Lewis and Ormerod* concluded that the multiplier effect of various fiscal policies is quite small (perhaps less than 1.0 after the first year). The implication of this conclusion is that to increase government spending by borrowing more might have a disappointingly small effect on demand and employment in the UK.

(b) Expansion and contraction of the economy are both subject to the effect of **automatic stabilisers**. There are two types.

  (i) Tax revenues that *rise* as national income *rises*. Nearly all taxes fall into this category.

  (ii) Government expenditures that *fall* as national income *rises*. Welfare payments associated with unemployment and low incomes make up the bulk of this category.

The effect of automatic stabilisers is to reduce the value of the **multiplier**, thus dampening the rate of both expansion and contraction. When the economy is in the process of recovering from a recession the effect of the automatic stabilisers is called **fiscal drag**.

2.18 The National Debt

Key term

> The **National Debt** is the amount of debt owed by the **central** government of a country to its various creditors.

Creditors of the government may be nationals of the country (eg investors in government loan stock) or foreign nationals (perhaps foreign banks or even the International Monetary Fund).

When the National Debt is high, interest repayments will account for a large proportion of central government expenditure. It is therefore important that when a government borrows money, it should be invested or spent in such a way as to ensure that sufficient income is eventually generated to repay the interest and debt capital. If a government is unable to do this (as in the case of many developing and less developed countries at the moment) it will lose its creditworthiness and find future loans much harder to come by.

The National Debt exists in the form of debt instruments of two types.

(a) **Marketable debt**

- Short-term debt, which consists of **Treasury bills**. This is a very small amount.
- Long-term debt, which consists of **gilt-edged securities**.

(b) **Non-marketable debt**

- National Savings & Investments (NS&I)
- Any non-marketable loans raised by the government

2.19 Servicing the National Debt and the burden on society

To service the National Debt, a government must pay interest on the debt and make capital repayments when they fall due. However, the problem of making capital repayments can be overcome, if required, by taking out new loans when old loans mature (eg to repay a loan of £100 million, a government can borrow a further £100 million).

If the loan is obtained from the private sector of the country's economy, the National Debt and servicing the debt involve the transfer of funds between different sections of society. When the government borrows, it takes money from one group and spends it on other sections of society. When the government pays interest, it will raise money in taxes from the rest of society and pay this money to its creditors. Once again, this involves a transfer of the funds.

Servicing the National Debt thus involves two processes.

(a) A redistribution of funds within society, through government borrowing and spending, or through taxation to pay debt interest.

(b) Borrowing to spend now and only repaying the debt with interest later. In other words, society benefits now, and the payment burden falls on society in later years, perhaps in some cases as long as a generation or so later.

When money is borrowed from abroad, the flow of funds in obtaining the money and in repaying the debt crosses national boundaries, and so there are implications for the balance of payments and the exchange rate of the domestic currency. Repaying a debt to foreign debtors also places a burden on society, because the money raised from taxes to service the debt must be paid abroad.

2.20 Public expenditure control

FAST FORWARD

If the government kept its own spending at the same level, but **reduced levels of taxation**, it would also **stimulate demand** in the economy because firms and households would have more of their own money after tax for consumption or saving/investing.

If the entire public sector had a balanced budget, the PSNCR would be nil. When there is an annual excess of income over expenditure, some of the National Debt can be repaid and so there is a Public Sector Debt Repayment.

To reduce the size of the PSNCR, a government must either reduce its expenditure or raise its income from taxation. The sale of nationalised industries to the private sector is another source of funds.

Keynesian economists argue the need for **more government spending in a recession** to boost demand in the economy and create jobs. An argument put forward is that it makes sound financial sense to use current revenues from taxation to meet current expenditures and interest payments on debt, but to use borrowing for capital expenditure needs. Since taxation revenue exceeds current spending, the argument concludes that the government should borrow more for capital spending. The UK government has rejected this argument, and believes that the upward spiral of public expenditure of earlier years made the burden of taxation on companies and individuals intolerable.

Question — Government budget

Why might a government's budget vary from time to time, sometimes being in balance, sometimes in surplus and sometimes in deficit?

Answer

A budget deficit occurs where expenditure exceeds income and a budget surplus occurs where expenditure is less than income.

In a mixed economy like that of the United Kingdom, the level of economic activity fluctuates depending upon where we are in the trade cycle. During the upturn in the trade cycle production is rising, firms and individuals earn more profits and wages so the government should collect more revenue. Unemployment should also fall during this period, and so government expenditure should fall. At this stage of the cycle, the budget may be in surplus.

During the downturn of a trade cycle, the reverse applies. Profits and incomes fall and government revenue falls, but unemployment rises and government expenditure on unemployment benefit rises. There is then more likely to be a budget deficit.

Keynes suggested that budget deficits should be used to help an economy out of recession. According to Keynes, unemployment was caused by a lack of aggregate demand in the economy. So if the government increased its expenditure, this would raise aggregate demand.

Using Keynesian policies, a government may plan a budget deficit to boost aggregate monetary demand. Increased government expenditure might be on infrastructure such as roads, schools or the health service. Alternatively, taxes could be cut to increase consumers' disposable incomes. The objective would be to close the 'deflationary gap' that is seen to be preventing the economy reaching a level of full employment. Thus, variations in the budget balance can be the result of deliberate government budgetary policy.

3 Monetary theory

FAST FORWARD

Monetary theory deals with the way changes in monetary variables affect the aggregate demand in the economy and its ultimate impact on **prices** and **output**. There are three theories of how the changes in the money supply are transmitted to the real economy. The quantity theory, the Keynesian theory, and the monetarist theory.

3.1 The classical quantity theory of money

The **classical quantity theory of money**, goes back many years. It is associated with *Irving Fisher's* book *The Purchasing Power of Money*, which was published in 1911. The classical quantity theory is based on the view that money is used only as a **medium of exchange** and people require it only in order to settle transactions in good and services.

However, Keynesian economists argue that there are other reasons for wanting to hold money, as we shall see later.

If the number of transactions in the economy is fixed, and independent of the amount of the money supply, then the total money value of transactions will be PT, where

P is the price level of goods and services bought and sold
T is the number or quantity of transactions.

The amount of money needed to pay for these transactions will depend on the **velocity of circulation**. Money changes hands. A person receiving money can use it to make his own purchases. For example, if A pays B £2 for transaction X, B can use the £2 to pay C for transaction Y and C can use the same £2 to pay D for transaction Z. If the three transactions X, Y, and Z all occur within a given period of time then the money value of the transactions is:

£2 price level × 3 transactions = £6.

The total amount of money is the same £2 in circulation for all three transactions but this money has exchanged hands three times. The velocity of circulation is 3 and MV = 6, where M is the money supply and V is the velocity of circulation.

The quantity theory of money is summarised by this identity, known as the **Fisher equation.**

$$MV \equiv PT$$

MV **must** be equivalent to PT because they are two different ways of measuring the same transactions. In practice, the velocity of circulation V is calculated as the balancing figure in the equation below.

$$V = \frac{PT}{M}$$

Question

Velocity of circulation

Which of the following definitions correctly describes the velocity of circulation?

(a) The money stock in a given time period divided by the level of prices
(b) The number of times in a given period that a unit of money is used to purchase final output
(c) The total value of transactions in a given time period divided by the average price level

Answer

According to the quantity theory, $V = \frac{PT}{M}$. This is described by (b), which is therefore the correct answer.

Answer (a) implies that $V = \frac{M}{P}$, and answer (c) implies that $V = \frac{PT}{P}$, both of which are incorrect.

Key term

Quantity theory of money: the theory which holds that changes in the level of prices are caused predominantly by changes in the supply of money. This derives from the Fisher equation, MV = PT, assuming that the velocity of circulation V and the number of transactions T are stable.

The quantity theory of money makes three further **assumptions**.

(a) **V has a roughly constant value**. The velocity of circulation of money remains the same at all times, or at least only changes very slowly over time.

(b) **T is either given or it is independent of the amount of money, M**. The reason why T should be a given total was that the supporters of the quantity theory argued that full employment of resources is the norm and if all resources are fully utilised, the volume of transactions T must be a constant value.

(c) **The amount of M is determined by other factors and is independent of V, T or (most significantly) P.** The money supply could be controlled by government authorities, including the central bank.

Given these assumptions, the quantity theory of money becomes a theory of **price levels** because, since MV = PT, then:

$$P = \frac{V}{T}M$$

If V and T are roughly constant values, P will vary directly with increases or decreases in the amount of M: changes in the money supply M cause prices P to change. In other words, inflation is **directly related to** the money supply, and a 10% increase in the money supply, say, would result in 10% inflation.

There is a logic behind the algebra of the classical quantity theory and it relates to the basic assumption that money is used only for transactions relating to goods and services. If this is true, it follows that an excess of money will lead to increased attempts to spend it. Similarly, a shortage of money will have the effect of reducing demand. If the economy is utilising its productive resources to the full (that is, if there is full employment) it will not be possible to increase output. Any increase in demand will therefore cause prices to rise by the action of market forces. Similarly, any reduction in demand will cause prices to fall.

This theory is very satisfactory in explaining past experience of price rises and falls over long periods, as during the nineteenth century. In the first half of the nineteenth century there was large scale economic expansion, but the money supply was based on the gold standard and expanded only slowly: prices generally fell. In the second half of the century there were extensive increases in the supply of gold as a result of mining in Australia and America. The growth of economic activity, and hence output, did not match the growth in the gold supply and prices rose.

Important conclusions from the quantity theory of money equation.

(a) If the velocity of circulation of money, V, is more or less constant, then any **growth in the money supply**, M, over and above the potential in the economy to increase T, will cause **inflation**.

(b) If **the number of transaction or the output in the economy, T, is** growing and if the velocity of circulation, V, is constant, then a **matching growth in the money supply,** M, is needed to avoid deflation.

(c) Government's monetary policy should be to allow some growth in the money supply **if the economy is growing**, but not to let the growth in the money supply get out of hand.

The extent to which these conclusions are valid depends largely on whether the velocity of circulation of money is roughly constant or not. For example, if the money supply increases by 10%, and real growth in the economy (the increase in the volume of transactions) is 3%, we could predict that inflation will be about 7% – but only if the velocity of circulation is constant.

The quantity theory of money relates the money supply directly to the general level of prices. It has no close connection to the classical theory of interest rates. This was simply a supply and demand equilibrium price model for liquid funds. The rate of interest is effectively the price of borrowing and the reward of lending. This model was discussed in the chapter on markets for factors of production.

3.2 The Keynesian demand for money

Keynes identified three reasons why people hold wealth as money rather than as interest-bearing securities.

Key term

The **transactions motive.** Households need money to pay for their day-to-day purchases. The level of transactions demand for money depends on household incomes.

The **precautionary motive.** People choose to keep money on hand or in the bank as a precaution for when it might suddenly be needed.

The **speculative motive.** Some people choose to keep ready money to take advantage of a profitable opportunity to invest in bonds which may arise (or they may sell bonds for money when they fear a fall in the market prices of bonds).

There is an important contrast here with the classical quantity theory of money. The **quantity theory** assumes that the demand for money is governed by **transactions** only. By proposing two further reasons, Keynes strikes out into new territory.

The precautionary motive is really just an extension of the transactions motive. However, the **speculative motive** for holding money needs explaining a bit further.

(a) If individuals hold money for speculative purposes, this means that they are not using the money to invest in bonds. They are holding on to their savings for speculative reasons. Hence, savings and investment might not be in equilibrium, with consequences for changes in national income.

(b) The reason for holding money instead of investing in bonds is that **interest rates are expected to go up**. If interest rates go up, bond prices will fall. For example, if the current *market price* of bonds which pay 5% interest on face value is £100, and interest rates doubled to 10%, the market value of the bonds would fall, perhaps to £50. This is because the interest paid on a bond is fixed at a percentage of *face value*. The ratio between the income paid and the *market value* adjusts to the current prevailing interest rate by means of

changes in the market value. So if interest rates are expected to go up, any bonds held now will be expected to lose value, and bond holders would make a capital loss. Thus, it makes sense to hold on to money, for investing in bonds later, *after* interest rates have gone up. Keynes called such money holdings **idle balances**.

(c) What causes individuals to have expectations about interest rate changes in the future? Keynes argued that each individual has some expectation of a **normal rate of interest**. This concept of a normal interest rate reflects past levels and movements in the interest rate, and expectations of the future rate level, obtained from available market information.

Question

Interest rates

Following this Keynesian analysis, how would you expect an individual to act if:

(a) He thinks that the current level of interest is below the 'normal' rate?
(b) He thinks that the current level of interest is above the 'normal' rate?

Answer

(a) If someone believes that the normal rate of interest is above the current level, he will expect the interest rate to rise and will therefore expect bond prices to fall. To avoid a capital loss the individual will sell bonds and hold money.

(b) Conversely, if an individual believes that the normal rate of interest is below the current market interest rate, he will expect the market interest rate to fall and bond prices to rise. Hence he will buy bonds, and run down speculative money holdings, in order to make a capital gain.

Key term

Liquidity preference is the preference of people to hold on to their savings as money (in liquid form) rather than investing it.

Keynes argued further that people will need money to satisfy the transactions motive and precautionary motive regardless of the level of interest. It is only the speculative motive which alters the demand for money as a result of interest rate changes.

(a) If interest rates are high, people will expect them to fall and will expect the price of bonds to rise. They will therefore purchase bonds in anticipation of a capital gain and will therefore have **low liquidity preference**.

(b) If interest rates are low but are expected to rise, this implies that bond prices are likely to fall. People will therefore hold liquid funds in order to be able to invest in bonds later on. Their **liquidity preference will be high**.

The conclusion is that the demand for money will be high (liquidity preference will be high) when interest rates are low. This is because the speculative demand for money will be high. Similarly, the demand for money will be low when interest rates are high, because the speculative demand for money will be low.

There is thus a **minimum fixed demand** for money (transactions and precautionary motives) and **some demand** for money that varies with interest rates (speculative motive). This can be shown as a liquidity preference curve (Figure 3). A minimum quantity of money is needed, regardless of interest rate, to satisfy the minimum demand arising from the transactions and precautionary motives for holding money.

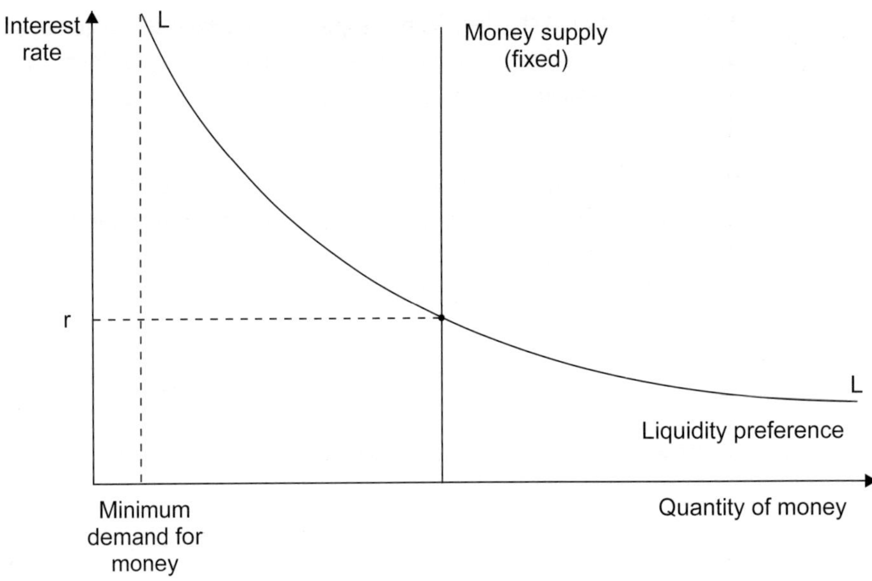

Figure 3 Interest rates, money demand and the money supply

Keynes' view on the determination of interest rates is, like the classical view, a market model. He argued that the level of interest rates is determined by the interaction of demand for and supply of money. While the liquidity preference curve may be thought of as a normal demand curve, with the rate of interest being the price of money, Keynes suggested that the money supply was fixed by government and therefore inelastic: a vertical supply curve, in other words, as shown in Figure 3.

The **quantity theory** assumes that an increase in the money supply will automatically lead to an increase in AD. Since the economy is assumed to be operating at full employment and therefore not able to produce more goods and services, this increase in AD will cause a rise in the level of prices generally. **Keynes took a different view**. He said that an increase in the money supply would lead to a fall in interest rates.

It is an important aspect of this theory, and a contrast with the quantity theory, that an increase in the money supply would not lead directly to an increase in AD.

If there is an increase in the money supply, from MS_1 to MS_2 in Figure 4, not surprisingly, it will become cheaper and interest rates will fall from r_1 to r_2. There will be some increase in the level of investment spending, since it now becomes more profitable for firms to invest in new capital because of the fall in the cost of borrowing. The increase in investment, being an injection into the circular flow of income, causes some increase in the level of national income through the multiplier process. According to the Keynesians, therefore, a change in the money supply only indirectly affects the demand for goods and services, and hence the level of income, via a change in the rate of interest. This is called an **indirect transmission mechanism**.

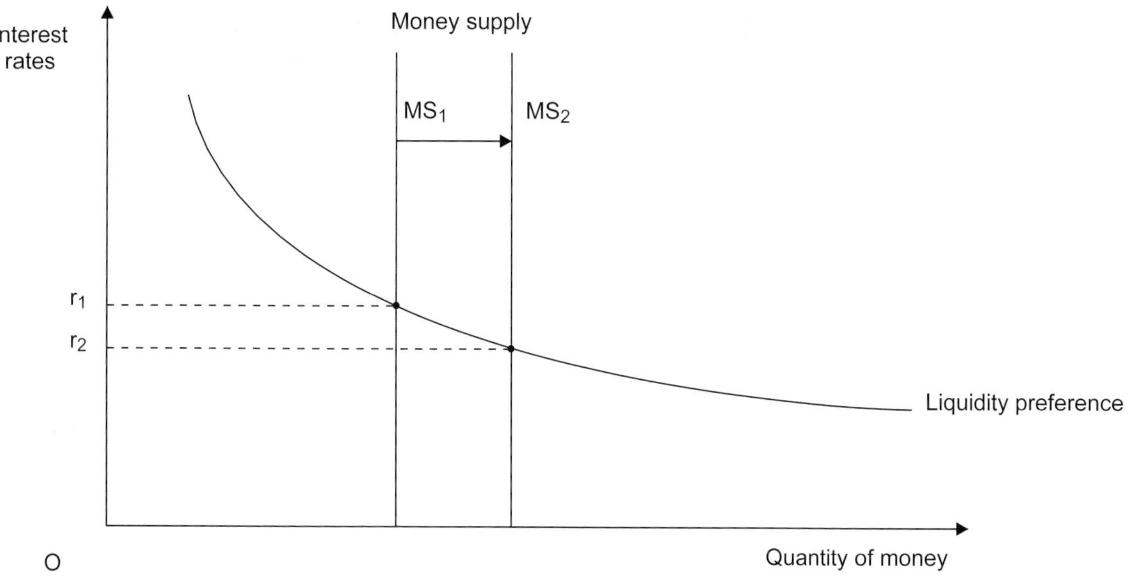

Figure 4 Consequence of an increase in the money supply

The impact on the economy of the increase in the money supply therefore depends on the effect that the fall in interest rates produces. According to the Keynesian view, both investment demand and consumer spending are **relatively insensitive** to interest rate changes, that is, they are relatively interest-inelastic. The **volume of investment** depends heavily, Keynes argued, on **technological changes** and **business confidence and expectations** too. It follows that the increase in the money supply will have only a limited effect on aggregate demand and consequently relatively little effect on output and employment or on price levels. This view implies that the velocity of circulation, V, is **not fixed**, since a varying amount of money is held as investment in bonds.

Keynesians therefore argue that monetary policy to control the money supply would have an effect on interest rates and changes in interest rates might in the longer term affect investment. In other respects, however, monetary policy would not really affect the economy and national income, because increases in the money supply would be neutralised by reductions in the velocity of circulation, leaving PT unaffected.

3.3 The new quantity theory of money

Friedman re-stated the quantity theory of money, as follows.

$$MV \equiv PQ$$

where M is the **money supply**
V is the **velocity of circulation** of money
P is the **average price level**
Q is the physical quantity of **national output per period** (ie the real volume of economic output)

Thus, PQ is the **money value of national output** (ie national income Y at current prices). Remember that in Fisher's version of this equation P was the **general level** of prices rather than a numerical average and T was the number of transactions. PT was therefore the money value of transactions and **proportional** to national income, **not equal** to it.

Monetarists argue that V and Q are independent of M. Therefore, an increase in money supply M will tend to raise prices P, via the direct transmission mechanism.

(a) Individuals will have more money than they want.

(b) They will spend this excess money, buying not just 'bonds' (as Keynes believed) but also equities and physical goods.

(c) The greater demand for physical goods will boost expenditure in the economy (and so the money value of national income).

(d) However, a rapid increase in the money supply will increase spending at a faster rate than the economy will be able to produce more physical output.

(e) A rapid increase in the money supply will therefore inevitably be inflationary.

In conclusion, for monetarists, changes in the money supply cause changes in the money value of national income. Remember that Keynes believed there was only a weak link between changes in the money supply and changes in aggregate demand.

Question

Money supply increases

According to monetarist economics, which of the following consequences will result from an increase in the money supply?

1 Households will have excess money.
2 Households will use this money to buy more bonds, equities and physical goods.
3 Interest rates will rise.
4 The demand for money will respond to the change in interest rates.
5 Expenditure in the economy will increase.

Answer

Consequences 1, 2 and 5 (but not 3 and 4) will result. According to monetarists, an increase in the money supply creates excess supply over demand. Households use the excess money to buy bonds (and so interest rates *fall*), equities and physical goods (and so expenditure in the economy rises). The demand for money is interest-rate inelastic, according to monetarists (but not according to Keynesians) and so this does not increase in response to any interest rate fall.

3.4 The monetarist view of money supply and inflation in the economy

Whereas Keynes argued that an increase in the money supply would merely result in lower interest rates, with no immediate effect on national income, Friedman and other monetarists argue that an increase in the money supply will lead directly and quickly to changes in national income and PT, with the velocity of circulation V remaining fairly constant.

In his analysis of the demand for money, Friedman argued that money is just one of five broad ways of holding wealth.

- **Money**
- **Bonds**
- **Equities**
- **Physical goods**
- **Human wealth**

(Human wealth here is a special concept and may be ignored for the purpose of our analysis.)

Each method of holding wealth brings some form of return or yield to the holder.

(a) The main yield from money is the **convenience** of having it when it is needed. This cannot be measured in money terms.

(b) The return on **bonds** is the interest plus any capital gain (or loss).

(c) **Equities** should provide dividends and capital growth which keep ahead of the rate of inflation.

(d) **Physical assets in this analysis,** do not waste away through use, because assets which are consumed cannot be a store of wealth. There might be an increase in their capital value but the yield also includes the non-monetary return, such as the use of furniture, the enjoyment from paintings and so on.

Friedman argued that the demand for money is related to the demand for holding wealth in its other forms. While Keynes believed that if people did not want to hold money, they would invest it to earn interest, monetarists believe that they might also use it instead to buy equities or physical assets.

Friedman argued that money gives a convenience yield but it is not an asset which is held for its own sake. It is a 'temporary abode of purchasing power' waiting to be spent on other types of financial or physical asset. The **demand for money** is therefore a function of the yield on money and the yield on other forms of holding wealth. **Yield** as defined here includes non-monetary yield such as convenience and enjoyment.

Monetarists would argue, further, that the demand for money is fairly interest-inelastic. The demand for money is related to a transactions motive, but not to any speculative motive. An expected rise in interest rates might persuade individuals to sell bonds and buy other assets, but not to hold speculative money.

Monetarists argue that since money is a direct substitute for all other assets, an increase in the money supply, given a fairly stable velocity of circulation, will have a direct effect on demand for other assets because there will be more money to spend on those assets. If the total output of the economy is fixed, then an increase in the money supply will lead directly to higher prices.

Monetarists therefore reach the same basic conclusion as the old quantity theory of money. A rise in the money supply will lead to a rise in prices and probably also to a rise in money incomes. (It is also assumed by monetarists that the velocity of circulation remains fairly constant, again taking a view similar to the old quantity theory.) In the short run, monetarists argue that an increase in the money supply might cause some increase in real output and so an increase in employment. In the long run, however, all increases in the money supply will be reflected in higher prices unless there is longer term growth in the economy.

3.5 Weaknesses in monetarist theory

There are certain **complications with the monetarist views**, for example the following.

(a) The velocity of circulation is known to fluctuate up and down by small amounts.

(b) Increases in prices will not affect all goods equally. Some goods will rise in price more than others and so the relative price of goods will change. For example, the price of houses might exceed the average rate of inflation but the price of electronic goods might rise more slowly.

(c) A higher rate of inflation in one country than another might affect the country's balance of payments and currency value, thereby introducing complications for the economy from international trade movements.

(d) Prices in the economy might take some time to adjust to an increase in the money supply.

3.6 What makes the money supply grow?

We have looked at the demand for and supply of money without yet asking what it is that makes the money supply grow in the first place. If we define money broadly, to include bank deposits, **four main factors contribute to money supply growth.**

(a) Government short term borrowing has a direct effect on the money supply since the banks can use the Treasury bills they receive as part of their liquid reserves. Government borrowing thus releases cash into circulation that would otherwise be tied up in bank reserves.

(b) Who the government borrows from, banks or non-banks, since only banks have the ability to create money by lending

(c) Bank lending generally

(d) Flows of money between the country and foreign traders/investors

3.7 Approaches to controlling the growth of the broad money supply

A government might take any of four broad approaches to controlling the growth of the money supply.

(a) To reduce or control government borrowing

(b) To finance as much government borrowing as possible by borrowing from the UK non-bank private sector, for example by encouraging National Savings in preference to issuing gilts

(c) To control the increase in bank lending

(d) To control external and foreign currency items, for example by keeping the balance of payments under control

Question — **Functions of money and Keynesian analysis**

In an earlier chapter we identified four functions of money: a means of exchange, a unit of account, a standard of deferred payment and a store of value. Which one of these is central to the Keynesian analysis of the demand for money?

Answer

It is the function of money as a liquid store of value or wealth which is central to the concept of liquidity preference.

3.8 The loanable funds theory of interest rates

According to Keynesians, the level of interest rates is determined by the interaction of the speculative demand for money and the money supply.

Monetarists hold the traditional view that the reasons for demanding money are for transactions only, not speculation about future investment. Monetarists argue instead that interest rates are determined by the demand and supply of **loanable funds**. An increase in the money supply, without any increase in demand for money (investment), will increase the amount of loanable funds available (savings). Interest rates will fall, and investment will rise.

3.9 The transmission mechanism and imbalances between money supply and demand

Monetarists say that the connection between the demand for money, the money supply and national income can be explained by **a direct transmission mechanism**.

Starting from a position of equilibrium holding of assets of all kinds, **an increase in the money supply** would leave individuals holding an excess of money balances. In order to restore the level of money holdings to its desired level, individuals will substitute **assets of all kinds** for money: the demand for goods and services will increase, not just demand for financial assets.

(a) The increase in the quantity of money means a fall in the rate of interest. This will not lead to an increase in the demand for money, according to the monetarists, because they believe that the **demand for money is interest-inelastic**.

(b) The increase in direct spending on goods and services will, however, lead to a **rise in the level of money national income**.

By assuming that money is a substitute for all assets, the monetarists conclude that variations in the money supply have a great influence on the level of national income. In terms of the classical quantity theory of money, if M goes up, and MV = PT, there will be an increase in PT, but this could mean an increase in either real output (T) or in prices and inflation (P).

Suppose that the demand for money goes up, but the authorities stop the money supply from increasing, so that there is an **excess demand** for money. The transmission mechanism will work the other way. Households will sell bonds and equities and reduce consumption on other goods in order to acquire more money. Interest rates will go up. There will be a decline in total spending in the economy until money supply and demand are again in equilibrium. Since MV = PT, a decline in PT will have one of two effects.

(a) If the economy is operating below its full employment national income level, there will be a decline in T leading to even less output and so more unemployment.

(b) If the economy has an inflationary gap, there will be a decline in P, and inflation will be brought under control.

3.10 Comparison of theories

	Classical Quantity Theory	Keynesian Theory	New Quantity Theory
Name	Fisher	Keynes	Friedman
Keyword/equation	MV≡PT	'liquidity preference'	MV≡PQ
Use for money	Transactions	Transaction motive Precautionary motive Speculative motive	Cash Bonds Equities Physical goods Human wealth
Assumptions	T, V constant M independently determined	Only speculative demand varies Money supply usually fixed	Demand for money is interest-inelastic
Effect if rise in money supply when economy at full employment	AD up, price rises	Price of bonds up, interest rate falls, small rise in AD and prices	Spending on assets of all kinds up, AD up, prices up
Transmission mechanism	Direct	Indirect, via interest rate	Direct
Determination of interest rate	Supply and demand for money	Since money supply fixed, depends on speculative demand for bonds	Supply and demand of loanable funds

Question

Counter-inflation policies

(a) A government can help to counter demand pull inflation by reducing interest rates. True or false?

(b) A government can help to counter demand pull inflation by increasing value added tax. True or false?

(c) A government can help to counter cost push inflation by increasing income tax rates. True or false?

(d) A government can help to counter cost push inflation by linking wage increases to productivity improvements. True or false?

Answer

(a) *False*. On the contrary, this would increase consumer borrowing and hence stimulate Demand pull inflation.

(b) *True*. This might increase total spending on goods and services *inclusive* of the tax, but spending *net* of tax will probably fall.

(c) *False*. Increasing direct taxation will reduce consumers' disposable income, and is therefore a measure aimed at countering Demand pull inflation, not Cost push inflation.

(d) *True*. This will reduce the unit costs of production.

3.11 Expectations and money supply growth

If the government controls the money supply without telling anyone what its planned targets of growth are, then people's **expectations** of inflation will run ahead of the growth in the money supply. Wage demands will remain at levels in keeping with these expectations and so the rate of increase in P will exceed the rate of increase in M. If the government succeeds in its aim of limiting the growth of the money supply, but wages rise at a faster rate, then higher wages will mean less real income (Y) and less real output (T). In other words, the economy will slump even further.

It is for this reason that the government must announce its targets for growth in the money supply.

(a) Most monetarists argue that the government must give a clear announcement of its targets for monetary growth so as to influence people's expectations of inflation.

(b) Some economists might argue that an **incomes policy** should be imposed by the government to prevent wage rises in excess of government targets.

Monetarists pointed to the high inflation of the mid-1970s as evidence in support of their views since very rapid monetary growth preceded the price inflation. However, later research suggested that soaring oil and commodity prices were the culprits. Falling commodity prices helped subsequently to reduce inflation.

4 Monetary policy

ST FORWARD

Monetary policy uses money supply, interest rates or credit controls to influence aggregate demand.

4.1 Objectives of monetary policy

sessment cus point

Questions on monetary policy will often focus on its impact on the business sector.

Monetary policy can be used as a means towards achieving ultimate economic objectives for inflation, the balance of trade, full employment and real economic growth. To achieve these **ultimate objectives**, the authorities will set **intermediate objectives** for monetary policy.

In the UK, the ultimate objective of monetary policy in recent years has been principally to reduce the rate of inflation to a sustainable low level. The intermediate objectives of monetary policy have related to the level of interest rates, growth in the money supply, the exchange rate for sterling, the expansion of credit and the growth of national income.

4.2 The money supply as a target of monetary policy

To monetarist economists, the **money supply** is an obvious intermediate target of economic policy. This is because they claim that an increase in the money supply will raise prices and incomes and this in turn will raise the demand for money to spend.

When such a policy is first introduced, the short-term effect would be unpredictable for three reasons.

(a) The effect on interest rates might be erratic.

(b) There might be a time lag before anything can be done. For example, it takes time to cut government spending and hence to use reduction in government borrowing as an instrument of monetary policy to control the growth in M0 or M4.

(c) There might be a time lag before control of the money supply alters expectations about inflation and wage demands.

Growth in the money supply, if it is a monetary policy target, should therefore be a **medium-term target**. When the UK government set targets for the growth of the money supply as a main feature of its economic policy strategy from 1980, it was consequently prepared to wait for some years to see any benefits from its policies and therefore set out its policy targets in a **medium-term** financial strategy.

There are other problems with using growth in the money supply as an intermediate policy target.

(a) There will be difficulty in selecting a suitable monetary aggregate, whose growth rate will either affect or reflect changes in economic conditions. For example, if the aim of controlling the money supply is to control inflation, but if M4 increases by 20% per annum when the rate of inflation is just 5% per annum, targets for M4 growth would be an unsuitable monetary policy objective.

(b) It is debatable whether controlling the growth in the money supply will result in control over the rate of inflation. In the UK, the fall in the velocity of circulation of the broad money supply aggregates through the 1980s has meant that the broad money supply has risen at a much faster rate than inflation.

4.3 Interest rates as a target for monetary policy

The authorities might decide that **interest rates** – the price of money – should be a target of monetary policy. This would be appropriate if it is considered that there is a direct relationship between interest rates and the level of expenditure in the economy, or between interest rates and the rate of inflation.

A rise in interest rates will raise the price of borrowing in the internal economy for both companies and individuals. If companies see the rise as relatively permanent, rates of return on investments will become less attractive and **investment plans may be curtailed**. Corporate profits will fall as a result of higher interest payments. Companies will reduce stock levels as the cost of having money tied up in stocks rises. Individuals should be expected to reduce or postpone consumption in order to reduce borrowings, and should become less willing to borrow for house purchase.

Although it is generally accepted that there is likely to be a connection between interest rates and investment (by companies) and consumer expenditure**, the connection is not a stable and predictable one**, and interest rate changes are only likely to affect the level of expenditure after a **considerable time lag**.

Other effects of raising interest rates

(a) High interest rates will keep the value of sterling higher than it would otherwise be. This will keep the cost of exports high, and so discourage the purchase of exports. This may be necessary to protect the balance of payments and to prevent 'import-cost-push' inflation. UK manufacturers have complained bitterly about this effect in recent years and BMW cited it as one of the reasons for disposing of Rover.

(b) High interest rates will attract foreign investors into sterling investments, and so provide capital inflows which help to finance the large UK balance of payments deficit.

An important reason for pursuing an interest rate policy is that the authorities are able to influence interest rates much more effectively and rapidly than they can influence other policy targets, such as the money supply or the volume of credit. As we have already seen, in 1997 the new Labour Government of the UK placed responsibility for interest rate decisions with the Bank of England, which sets rates with the objective of meeting the government's inflation target.

4.4 The exchange rate as a target of monetary policy

Why the exchange rate is a target

(a) If the exchange rate falls, exports become cheaper to overseas buyers and so more competitive in export markets. Imports will become more expensive and so less competitive against goods produced by manufacturers at home. A fall in the exchange rate might therefore be good for a domestic economy, by giving a **stimulus to exports** and **reducing demand for imports**.

(b) An increase in the exchange rate will have the opposite effect, with dearer exports and cheaper imports. If the exchange rate rises and imports become cheaper, there should be a reduction in the rate of domestic inflation. A fall in the exchange rate, on the other hand, tends to increase the cost of imports and adds to the rate of domestic inflation.

When a country's economy is heavily dependent on overseas trade, as the UK economy is, it might be appropriate for government policy to establish a target exchange value for the domestic currency. However, the exchange rate is dependent on both the domestic rate of inflation and the level of interest rates. Targets for the exchange rate cannot be achieved unless the rate of inflation at home is first brought under control.

4.5 Growth in money national income as a target of monetary policy

The authorities might set targets for the level of national income in the economy. For example, the policy might be for the growth in the national income (or GNP or GDP) to be X% per annum for Y years. However, it takes time to collect information about national income whereas targets of monetary policy should be items for which statistical data can be collected regularly and easily.

For this reason, although a target growth rate in national income itself is, in theory, probably the most suitable target of monetary policy, it is the least practical because the authorities would always be working with out-of-date information.

4.6 Targets and indicators

An economic indicator provides information about economic conditions and might be used as a way of judging the performance of government.

(a) A **leading indicator** is one which gives an advance indication of what will happen to the economy in the future. It can therefore be used to predict future conditions. For example, a fall in the value of sterling by, say, 2% might be used to predict what will happen to the balance of payments and to the rate of inflation.

(b) A **coincident indicator** is one which gives an indication of changes in economic conditions **at the same time** that these changes are occurring. For example, if the narrow money supply rises by 5%, this might 'confirm' that the rate of increase in GDP over the same period of time has been about the same, 5% in 'money' terms.

(c) A **lagging indicator**, you will have guessed, is one which 'lags behind' the economic cycle. Unemployment, to take an example, often continues to rise until after a recession has ended and only starts to fall again after recovery has begun.

Items which are selected as monetary targets will also be indicators, but not all indicators are selected by the authorities as targets. There are a number of monetary indicators.

(a) The size of the money stock

(b) Interest rates such as the banks' base rate of interest, the Treasury bill rate and the yield on long-dated government securities

(c) The exchange rate against the US dollar, or the trade-weighted exchange rate index

(d) The size of the government's borrowing

(e) Government borrowing as a percentage of Gross Domestic Product

4.7 The interrelationship between targets: the money supply and interest rate targets

The authorities can set intermediate targets for the growth of the money supply, but to achieve their targets of growth it will be necessary to allow interest rates to adjust to a level at which the demand for money matches the size of the money supply. For example, a policy to cut the growth of the money supply might result in higher real interest rates.

On the other hand, the authorities might set targets for the level of interest rates. If they do so, they must allow whatever demand for money there is to be met at that rate of interest by allowing the money supply to meet the demand. If they did not, interest rates would then rise above or fall below the target level.

This means that the authorities can set a target for the money supply or a target for interest rates, but **they cannot set independent targets for both at the same time**.

4.8 Instruments of monetary policy

There are a number of **techniques** or **instruments** which are available to the authorities to achieve their targets for monetary policies.

- Changing the level and/or structure of **interest rates** through **open market operations**
- **Reserve requirements**
- **Direct controls**, which might be either quantitative or qualitative
- **Intervention to influence the exchange rate**

4.9 Control over the level and structure of interest rates

When a government uses interest rates as an instrument of policy, it can try to influence either the general level of interest rates or the term structure of interest rates. It could do this by influencing either short-term interest rates or long-term interest rates. In the UK since 1997, the Bank of England has had responsibility for setting short-term interest rates. Long-term rates could possibly be influenced by increasing or reducing the PSBR.

4.10 Reserve requirements on banks as a means of controlling the money supply

As another technique for controlling money supply growth, the government might impose **reserve requirements** on banks. A reserve requirement might be a compulsory minimum cash reserve ratio (ie ratio of cash to total assets) or a minimum liquid asset ratio.

You will recall that any initial increase in bank deposits or building society deposits will result in a much greater eventual increase in deposits, because of the credit multiplier.

Ignoring leakages, the formula for the credit multiplier is:

$$D = \frac{C}{r}$$

where C is the initial increase in deposits
r is the liquid assets ratio or reserve assets ratio
D is the eventual total increase in deposits

If the authorities wished to control the rate of increase in bank lending and building society lending, they could impose minimum reserve requirements – ie a minimum value for r. **The bigger the value or r, the lower size of the credit multiplier would be**.

There are drawbacks to reserve requirements as a monetary policy instrument.

(a) Unless the same requirements apply to all financial institutions in the country, some institutions will simply take business from others. For example, reserve requirements on UK banks but not on building societies would give the building societies a competitive advantage over the banks, without having any effect on the control of total credit/money supply growth.

(b) Similarly, restrictions on domestic financial institutions which do not apply to foreign banks would put the domestic financial institutions at a competitive disadvantage in international markets. This is one reason why international co-operation on the capital adequacy of banks (the Basle agreement) is an important step towards better regulation of financial markets.

4.11 Direct controls as a technique of monetary control

Another way of controlling the growth of the money supply is to impose direct controls on bank lending. Direct controls may be either quantitative or qualitative.

(a) **Quantitative controls** might be imposed on either bank lending (assets), for example a 'lending ceiling' limiting annual lending growth, or bank deposits (liabilities). The purpose of quantitative controls might be seen as a means of keeping bank lending in check without having to resort to higher interest rates.

(b) **Qualitative controls** might be used to alter the type of lending by banks. For example, the government (via the Bank) can ask the banks to limit their lending to the personal sector, and lend more to industry, or to lend less to a particular type of firm (such as, for example, property companies) and more to manufacturing businesses.

4.12 Quantitative controls

Controls might be temporary, in which case, in time, interest rates would still tend to rise if the money supply growth is to be kept under control. However, the advantage of a temporary scheme of direct quantitative controls is that it gives the authorities time to implement longer term policy. Quantitative controls are therefore a way of bridging the time-lag before these other policies take effect.

Quantitative controls might be more permanent. If they are, they will probably be unsuccessful because there will be financial institutions that manage to escape the control regulations, and so thrive at the expense of controlled institutions.

Direct controls on banks, for example, might succeed in reducing bank deposits but they will not succeed in controlling the level of demand and expenditure in the economy if lending is re-directed into other non-controlled financial instruments of non-controlled financial institutions. For example, large companies might use their own bank deposits to set up a scheme of lending themselves.

Direct controls are therefore rarely effective in dealing with the source rather than the symptom of the problem. Direct controls tend to divert financial flows into other, often less efficient, channels, rather than to stop the financial flows altogether, ie 'leakages' are inevitable.

4.13 Qualitative controls

Qualitative controls might be **mandatory** or they might be applied through **moral suasion**. Mandatory directives of a qualitative nature are unlikely in practice, because they are difficult to enforce without the co-operation of banks and other financial institutions. Moral suasion, on the other hand, might be used frequently. This is a process whereby the Central Bank appeals to the banks to do one or more things.

- To restrain lending
- To give priority to certain types of lending such as finance for exports or for investment
- Refuse other types of lending such as loans to private individuals

Moral suasion might therefore be a temporary form of control. As just one example, in 1989, the governor of the Bank of England 'advised' the banks to be wary of lending in such large amounts to property companies, thereby trying to influence banks' lending decisions without giving them directives or instructions.

4.14 Exchange rate control as an instrument of monetary policy

The exchange rate and changes in the exchange rate, have implications for the balance of payments, inflation and economic growth. The government might therefore seek to achieve a target exchange rate for its currency. More will be said about exchange rates later.

4.15 Monetary policy and fiscal policy

Monetary policy can be made to act as a subsidiary support to fiscal policy and demand management. Since budgets are once-a-year events, a government must use non-fiscal measures in between budgets to make adjustments to its control of the economy.

(a) A policy of **low interest rates** or the absence of any form of credit control might stimulate bank lending, which in turn would increase expenditure (demand) in the economy.

(b) **High interest rates might** act as a deterrent to borrowing and so reduce spending in the economy.

(c) Strict **credit controls** (for example restrictions on bank lending) might be introduced to reduce lending and so reduce demand in the economy.

Alternatively, monetary policy might be given prominence over fiscal policy as the most effective approach by a government to achieving its main economic policy objectives. This might not however be possible: from 1990 to 1992, for example, monetary policy in the UK was heavily constrained by the need to set interest rates at levels which maintained sterling's position in the European exchange rate mechanism (ERM). From 1997, the Government has given the Bank of England the role of setting interest rates, although it is still the government which sets an inflation target. If the UK joined a single European currency, interest rates would largely be determined at the European level.

4.16 Monetary policy, inflation control and economic growth

Monetarists argue that monetary control will put the brake on inflation, but how does this help the economy? We have already noted *Robert Barro's* finding that inflation seems to hinder economic growth. We might argue like this.

(a) High inflation increases **economic uncertainty**. Bringing inflation under control will restore business confidence and help international trade by stabilising the exchange rate.

(b) A resurgence of business confidence through lower interest rates (due to less uncertainty and lower inflation) will **stimulate investment** and real output.

(c) A **controlled growth in the money supply** will provide higher incomes for individuals to purchase the higher output.

5 Effectiveness of macroeconomic policy

T FORWARD

The effectiveness of monetary policy in influencing aggregate demand and unemployment is limited in the long-run.

Having discussed the way fiscal and monetary policies operate on aggregate demand we review here their role in controlling inflation and affecting the level on unemployment.

5.1 The control of inflation

The best way of controlling inflation will depend on the causes of it. In practice, it may be difficult to know which cause is most significant. The table below sets out various policies designed to control inflation.

Cause of inflation	Policy to control inflation
Demand pull (high consumer demand)	Take steps to reduce demand in the economy • Higher taxation, to cut consumer spending • Lower government expenditure (and lower government borrowing to finance its expenditure) • Higher interest rates
Cost push factors (higher wage costs and other costs working through to higher prices)	Take steps to reduce production costs and price rises • De-regulate labour markets • Encourage greater productivity in industry • Apply controls over wage and price rises (prices and incomes policy)
Import cost push factors	Take steps to reduce the quantities or the price of imports. Such a policy might involve trying to achieve either an appreciation or depreciation of the domestic currency
Excessively fast growth in the money supply	Take steps to try to reduce the rate of money supply growth • Reduced government borrowing and borrow from the non-bank private sector • Try to control or reduce bank lending • Try to achieve a balance of trade surplus • Maintain interest rates at a level that might deter money supply growth
Expectations of inflation	Pursue clear policies which indicate the government's determination to reduce the rate of inflation

5.2 High interest rates and inflation

A government may adopt a policy of raising **interest rates** as a means of trying to reduce the rate of inflation, when inflation is being caused by a boom in consumer demand (with demand rising faster than the ability of industry to increase its output to meet the demand). In the UK however, as already mentioned, the Government has transferred the power to set interest rates to the Bank of England from 1997.

(a) When interest rates go up, there will be an initial increase in the rate of inflation. (As we have seen, mortgage interest payments are included in the retail prices index in the UK.)

(b) If interest rates are high enough, there should eventually be a reduction in the rate of growth in consumer spending.

(i) People who borrow must pay more in interest out of their income. This will leave them less income, after paying the interest, to spend on other things. (The government would not want wages to rise, though, because if people build up their income again with high wage settlements, the consumer spending boom could continue.)

(ii) High interest rates might deter people from borrowing, and so there would be less spending with borrowed funds.

(iii) High interest rates should encourage more saving, with individuals therefore spending less of their income on consumption.

(iv) High interest rates will tend to depress the values of non-monetary assets, such as houses, and the reduction in people's perceived wealth may make people feel 'poorer' and consequently reduce the amounts they spend on consumer goods.

5.3 Prices and incomes policy

Control of prices and incomes by government regulation (or voluntary agreement) is a further approach to keeping inflation down. In Britain, this was last tried in the 'social contract' of the Labour government of James Callaghan in the late 1970s. A prices and incomes policy is likely to be treated as a temporary policy. Such policies have been used in the past as a last resort when other policies to govern the economy have failed.

Problems with wage controls

- Non-comparable wages between work groups and erosion of pay differentials
- The problem of rewarding productivity improvements
- Evasion of the controls
- Trade union resistance

A policy for controlling prices also has particular problems to overcome.

- Administrative difficulty of imposing control
- Rising prices of imports which should be passed on
- Special cases needing price rises to avoid insolvency

There is also the enormous practical problem of establishing a policing agency or agencies to monitor, control and approve increases in prices and incomes. If this agency has to vet every individual price rise and wages settlement, it would need a very large staff, and might easily become a slow-working bureaucracy, denounced by firms and employees for its delayed decisions. If price controls are too rigid, the government might face the problem that a black market economy might develop in certain goods, with prices on the black market rising to levels that are far in excess of the government's limits.

5.4 Inflationary expectations

An explanation of rising inflation rates combined with rising unemployment was put forward, based on **inflationary expectations**. This **natural rate hypothesis** is supported by monetarist economists.

Inflationary expectations reflect the rates of inflation that are **expected** in the future. The inflationary expectations of the work force will be reflected in the level of wage rises that is demanded in the annual round of pay negotiations between employers and workers.

(a) If the work force expects inflation next year to be 3%, they will demand a 3% wage increase in order to maintain the real value of their wages.

(b) If we now accept that any increase in wages will result in price inflation then a 3% pay rise to cover expected inflation will result in an actual rate of inflation of 3%.

(c) The work force might also try to achieve some increase in the real value of wages. If inflation next year is expected to be 3%, the work force might demand a pay rise of say, 4%. According to monetarist economists, a pay rise of 4% would simply mean inflation of 4%. If workers wish to achieve a 1% increase in real wages each year, then during each successive period the rate of inflation will begin to accelerate from 5% to 6% to 7% and so on, and the real increases in wages will not happen.

(d) To compound the problem of inflation still further, it is argued that if mistakes are made over expectations, then money wages will be adjusted upwards next period in order to rectify the mistake made last period.

   (i) For example, in one year the work force might expect inflation to be 3%, and so demand a 3% increase in wages. If this is achieved, but the actual rate of inflation during the year is 5%, the work force will try to put things right. They will demand a 2% pay increase, just to cover the 'lost ground' last year, as well as an increase to cover expected inflation next year.

   (ii) It follows that if expected inflation next year is 5%, the pay demand will be 7% (plus any demand for an increase in the value of wages). If a 7% pay rise is granted, inflation will go up to 7% pa.

(e) Any 'external' factor (such as increases in the prices of imported goods, or higher indirect taxes) which may lead wage earners to expect higher prices in the near future will of course result in even higher wage claims.

The example used here is simplified because expectations change and adapt. However, many economists believe that events in the UK from about 1967 well into the 1970s followed a sequence of events not unlike that described above.

Question — **Philips curve**

Which of the following conclusions is supported by the Phillips curve?

(a) Higher inflation causes unemployment
(b) Higher unemployment causes inflation
(c) Full employment and low inflation cannot be achieved together

Answer

The answer is (c). The Phillips curve expresses an assumed relationship between unemployment and inflation. It does not purport to offer a causal explanation of the link.

5.5 The natural rate hypothesis

The **natural rate hypothesis** incorporates these views on inflationary expectations, to produce a refinement of the Phillips curve.

Suppose that the economy is characterised by the Phillips curve PC_1 in Figure 5. Initially, say, that is at an unemployment rate of 5% and zero price and wage inflation.

(a) Suppose now that the government expands aggregate demand so as to reduce unemployment to, say, 3% of the labour force. There is a movement along the Phillips curve, and the new unemployment level turns out to be associated with 4% inflation.

(b) As employers realise that they are paying higher wages as well as higher prices, they cut their costs by laying workers off and the unemployment rate rises to 5% again.

(c) But in the meantime the period of positive inflation has generated inflationary expectations and 5% unemployment is now associated with 4% inflation, because the Phillips curve has shifted from PC_1 to PC_2.

In effect, the **short-run** Phillips curve has shifted outwards from PC_1 to PC_2 in Figure 5.

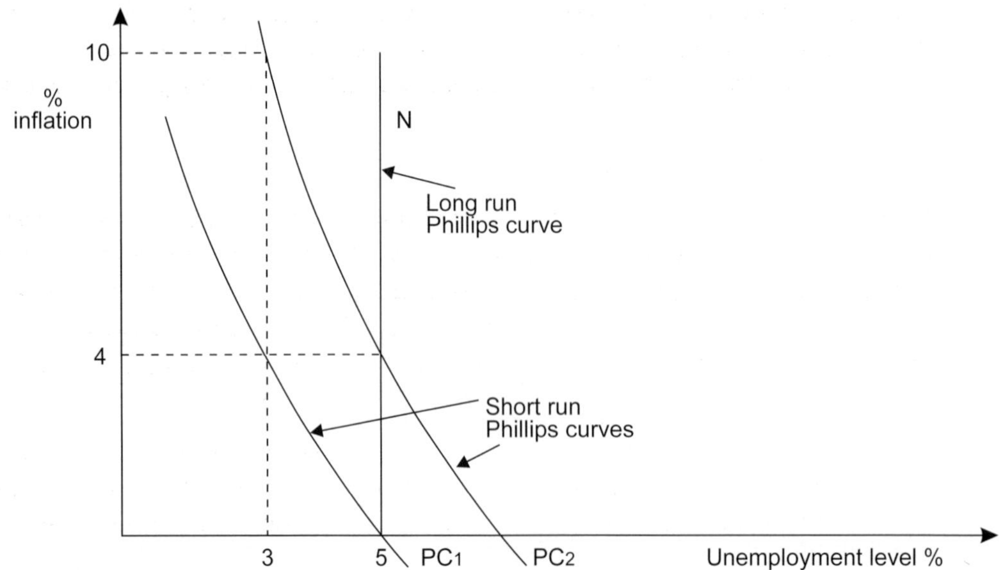

Figure 5 Natural rate hypothesis

Moderate monetarist economists state that the **long-run Phillips curve is vertical at the natural rate of unemployment**. In our example, monetarists would claim that the long-run Phillips curve is line N in Figure 5 so that there is a natural unemployment rate of 5% (but note that this figure of 5% is simply being used as an example here). This rate of unemployment is sometimes called the non-accelerating inflation rate of unemployment and referred to as the NAIRU.

In the long run, unemployment will revert towards its natural level. The rate of inflation, however, will be determined by the short-run Phillips curve, which will shift upwards as inflationary expectations increase. The distinction between short and long-run Phillips curves can help explain the observation that in the UK unemployment and inflation have often both risen at the same time.

Key term

The **natural rate hypothesis** says that the expansion of AD to reduce unemployment below its natural rate will only produce inflation. The natural rate is also called the **non-accelerating inflation rate of unemployment (NAIRU)**.

Question

Short-run Phillips curve

To check whether you understand this point, suppose that the short-run Phillips curve is now PC_2 in Figure 5, with unemployment at 5% and annual inflation at 4%. What would happen if the government now took measures to reduce unemployment to 3%?

Answer

Inflation would rise to about 10%, which is the rate of inflation on PC_2 associated with 3% unemployment. However, according to the natural rate hypothesis, in the longer run, unemployment would move back to 5%. A new short-run Phillips curve would be established, according to which an unemployment rate of 5% would be associated with 10% inflation.

Monetarist economists argue that the only way to reduce the rate of inflation is to get inflationary expectations out of the system. In doing so, excessive demands for wage rises should be resisted by employers. However a firm approach to reducing the rate of inflation could mean having to accept high levels of unemployment for a while.

5.6 New classical school

The **new classical school** of monetarist believes that the aggregate supply and Phillips curves are **vertical in the short run**. Therefore, they condemn any policy to expand demand as leading only to increased inflation. They suggest that human behaviour is governed by **rational expectations**; that is, by a rational assessment of all the information currently available. The implication is that the public will recognise inflation-producing policies as soon as they are introduced and adjust their expectations of inflation **immediately**. This will lead to increased wage demands and the expected inflation will ensue.

The new classical school sees unemployment as unrelated to inflation. They suggest that unemployment should be tackled by supply-side measures designed to reduce the NAIRU, while the sole aim of monetary policy should be to control inflation. Governments should announce clear monetary rules and then stick to them.

6 Supply side policy

Supply Side policies provide a method of managing **aggregate supply** in the economy.

6.1 The supply side approach

The Keynesian policy of demand management relies upon the proposition that the level of aggregate demand determines the level of national income and prices, since demand creates supply. The **supply side approach** advocated by monetarists, on the other hand, focuses policy upon the **conditions of aggregate supply**, taking the view that the availability, quality and cost of resources are the long term determinants of national income and prices. Supply side economists argue that by putting resources to work, an economy will automatically generate the additional incomes necessary to purchase the higher outputs.

Key term

Supply side economics can be defined as an approach to economic policymaking which advocates measures to improve the supply of goods and services (eg through deregulation) rather than measures to affect aggregate demand.

Supply side economics is characterised by the following propositions.

(a) The predominant long-term influences upon output, prices, and employment are the conditions of aggregate supply.

(b) Left to itself, the **free market** will automatically generate the highest level of national income and employment available to the economy.

(c) **Inflexibility in the labour market** through the existence of trade unions and other restrictive practices retain wages at uncompetitively high levels. This creates unemployment and restricts aggregate supply.

(d) The rates of **direct taxation** have a major influence upon aggregate supply through their effects upon the **incentive** to work.

(e) There is only a **limited role for government** in the economic system. Demand management can only influence output and employment 'artificially' in the short run, whilst in the long run creating inflation and hampering growth. Similarly state owned industries are likely to be uncompetitive and accordingly restrict aggregate supply.

6.2 Supply side economic policies

Supply side economists advise **against government intervention** in the economy at both the microeconomic and macroeconomic levels. **Microeconomic intervention** by government is disliked by supply side economists for a number of reasons.

(a) **Price regulation** distorts the signalling function essential for markets to reach optimal equilibrium.

(b) **Wage regulation** distorts the labour market's ability to ensure full employment.

(c) **Public ownership** blunts the incentive effects of the profit motive and leads to inefficiency.

(d) **Government grants and subsidies** encourage inefficient and 'lame duck' industries.

(e) **Public provision of services** may not encourage efficiency and can limit the discipline of consumer choice.

(f) **Employment legislation** such as employment protection limits market flexibility through discouraging recruitment and encouraging over-manning.

Macroeconomic intervention by government is regarded by supply side economists as harmful for several reasons.

(a) **Demand management** will be inflationary in the long run.

(b) High taxes will act as a **disincentive**.

(c) The possibility of **politically motivated policy changes** will create damaging uncertainty in the economy. This will discourage long-term investment.

Although most would accept the need for **expansion of the money stock** by government to accommodate increases in aggregate demand, some supply-siders have denied even this role to the government.

The main supply side policies are:

(a) **Reduction in government expenditure** and greater involvement of the private sector in the provision of services.

(b) **Reduction in taxes** in order to increase incentives.

(c) **Increasing flexibility** in the labour market by curbing the power of trade unions.

(d) **Increasing competition** through deregulation and privatisation of utilities.

(e) **Abolition of exchange controls** and allowing the free movement of capital.

6.3 The role of aggregate supply

The **central role of aggregate supply** is demonstrated in Figures 6(a) and (b).

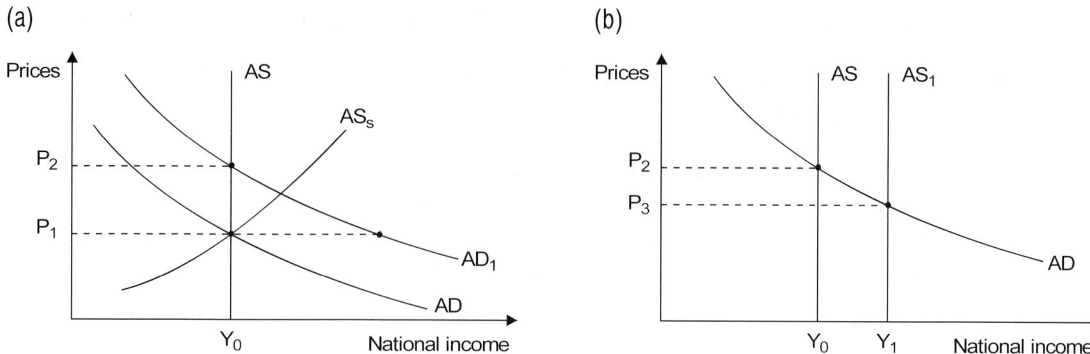

Figure 6 The importance of aggregate supply

Figure 6(a) shows the effect of a rise in aggregate demand, perhaps as the result of expansionary demand management policies, as a shift in the aggregate demand schedule from AD to AD_1, but in the long run national income remains at Y_0. AS_S is the short run supply schedule. In the long run, aggregate supply is inelastic, represented by AS. The effect of the rise in aggregate demand is due to increased prices from P_1 to P_2. Supply side theorists accept that in the short run, national income may rise along the short-run aggregate supply curve AS_S but contend that ultimately national income will fall to its long-run level of Y_0 because supply cannot be maintained above its long run level. Consequently aggregate demand is powerless to increase long-run output or employment.

Figure 6(b) illustrates a rise in aggregate supply from AS to AS_1. The income generated from the higher employment causes aggregate demand to extend and consequently national income rises from Y_0 to Y_1. This demonstrates the supply side view that **only changes in the conditions of aggregate supply can lead to a sustained increase in output and employment**. The vertical aggregate supply curve suggests that changes in aggregate demand do not affect output but rather only influence prices.

The economy will self-regulate through the action of the price mechanism in each market. Flexible prices in goods and factor markets will ensure that at the microeconomic level each market tends towards a market-clearing equilibrium. At the macroeconomic level the maximum attainable level of national income is at the level of full employment. The exponent of supply side economics argues that **flexible wages** will ensure the economy reaches this point.

6.4 Flexible wages

The importance of flexible wages is shown in Figure 7. When the wage rate is at W_0 the demand for labour is Q_d whilst the total supply of labour stands at Q_S. This creates involuntary unemployment of $(Q_S - Q_d)$ at the prevailing wage rate. By accepting lower wages workers can 'price themselves back into jobs' and consequently unemployment falls. If wages were perfectly flexible downwards then the market would restore full employment at wage rate W_1. This would leave unemployment at its natural rate.

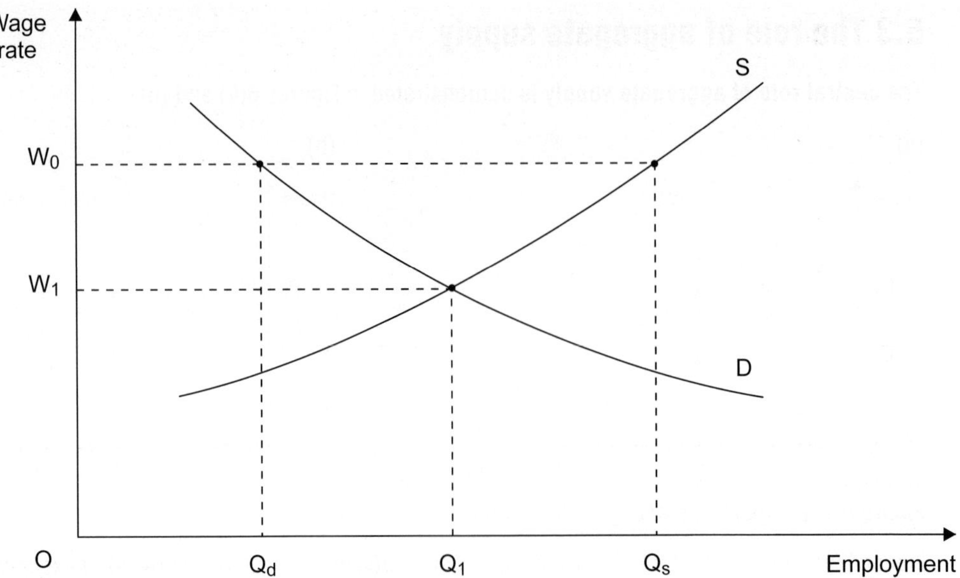

Figure 7 The labour market

Chapter roundup

- **Macroeconomic policy objectives** relate to economic growth, inflation, unemployment and the balance of payments.
- **Fiscal policy** provides a method of managing **aggregate demand** in the economy.
- **Direct taxes** have the quality of being **progressive** or **proportional**. Income tax is usually progressive, with high rates of tax charged on higher bands of taxable income. **Indirect taxes** can be **regressive**, when the taxes are placed on essential commodities or commodities consumed by poorer people in greater quantities.
- A government must decide how it intends to raise tax revenues, from **direct or indirect taxes**, and in what proportions tax revenues will be raised from each source.
- If the government kept its own spending at the same level, but **reduced levels of taxation**, it would also **stimulate demand** in the economy because firms and households would have more of their own money after tax for consumption or saving/investing.
- Monetary theory deals with the way changes in monetary variables affect the aggregate demand in the economy and its ultimate impact on prices and output. There are three theories of how the changes in the money supply are transmitted to the real economy: the quantity theory, the Keynesian theory, and the monetarist theory.
- **Monetary policy** uses money supply, interest rates or credit controls to influence aggregate demand.
- **The effectiveness of monetary policy** in influencing aggregate demand and unemployment is limited in the long-run.
- **Supply Side policies** provide a method of managing **aggregate supply** in the economy.

Quick quiz

1. What is the difference between fiscal policy and monetary policy?
2. What are the components of the UK National Debt?
3. Outline how the government may use fiscal policy to influence aggregate demand.
4. What is:

   (a) A regressive tax?
   (b) A proportional tax?
   (c) A progressive tax?

5. Distinguish between direct taxation and indirect taxation.
6. The government of a certain country decides to introduce a poll tax, which will involve a flat rate levy of £200 on every adult member of the population. This new tax could be described as:

   A Regressive
   B Proportional
   C Progressive
   D Ad valorem

7 High rates of personal income tax are thought to have a disincentive effect. This refers to the likelihood that the high rates of tax will:

A Encourage illegal tax evasion by individuals
B Lead to a reduction in the supply of labour
C Lead to a reduction in savings by individuals
D Discourage consumer spending and company investments

8 The total yield from an indirect tax levied on a good is likely to be greatest when:

A Demand is inelastic, supply is elastic
B Demand is inelastic, supply is inelastic
C Demand in elastic, supply is elastic
D Demand is elastic, supply is inelastic

9 Which of the following will *not* be the immediate purpose of a tax measure by the government?

A To discourage an activity regarded as socially undesirable.
B To influence interest rates.
C To protect a domestic industry from foreign competition.
D To price certain products so as to take into account their social cost.

10 Which of the following government aims might be achieved by means of fiscal policy? 1. A redistribution of income between firms and households. 2. A reduction in aggregate monetary demand. 3. A change in the pattern of consumer demand.

A Objectives 1 and 2 only
B Objectives 1 and 3 only
C Objectives 2 and 3 only
D Objectives 1, 2 and 3

11 Write the equation for the classical quantity theory of money.

12 According to Keynes, what are the three motives for wanting to hold money?

13 What will be the consequence for bond prices of an increase in interest rates?

14 What are the two main types of inflation?

15 What effect does an increase in interest rates have on the exchange rate?

16 For the Quantity Theory of Money identity $MV \equiv PT$ to explain short-run price behaviour, it is necessary that:

A P varies inversely with M
B Interest rates remain unchanged
C Changes in V in the short run are predictable
D T remains unchanged

17 According to Keynes, which one of the following is very sensitive to changes in interest rates?

A The money supply
B The speculative demand for money
C The precautionary demand for money
D Transactions demand for money

18 Other things remaining the same, according to Keynes, an increase in the money supply will tend to reduce:

A Interest rates
B Liquidity preference
C The volume of bank overdrafts
D Prices and incomes

19 According to monetarist economists, which of the following consequences will result from an increase in the money supply? 1. Households will have excess money. 2. Households will use this money to buy more bonds, equities and physical goods. 3. Interest rates will rise. 4. The demand for money will respond to the change in interest rates. 5. Expenditure in the economy will increase.

A 1, 2 and 5 only will happen
B 3 and 5 only will happen
C 1, 2, 4 and 5 only will happen
D 3, 4 and 5 will all happen

20 How do supply side policies affect inflation and unemployment?

Answer in terms of the effect on the aggregate supply curve.

Answers to quick quiz

1 A government's fiscal policy is concerned with taxation, borrowing and spending; and their effects upon the economy. Monetary policy is concerned with money, the money supply, interest rates, inflation and the exchange rate.

2 The UK National Debt has two main parts: marketable instruments (Treasury bills and gilt-edged securities) and non marketable debt, which chiefly comprises National Savings & Investments.

3 A government can increase demand by spending more itself or by reducing taxation so that firms and households have more after-tax income to spend.

4 A regressive tax takes a higher proportion of a poor person's income than a rich person's. A progressive tax takes a higher proportion of a rich person's income and a lower proportion of a poor person's. A proportional tax takes the same proportion of all incomes.

5 Direct taxes are levied on income while indirect taxes are levied on expenditure. Indirect taxes are regressive. Direct taxes can be progressive.

6 A A flat-rate poll tax, with no concession for the lower-paid, would take a higher proportion of the income of lower-income earners than of higher income earners. This is a regressive tax system.

7 B The disincentive effect refers specifically to the disincentive of individuals to work.

8 B The total yield from an indirect tax is likely to be greatest when (a) demand for the good is relatively unaffected by the addition of a tax on to the price and (b) supply is relatively unaffected, even though suppliers will be receiving the price net of the tax.

9 B The main purpose of taxation will be to raise revenue for the government. Other aims might be to redistribute wealth or affect demand in the economy. Changes in rate of tax do not have a direct influence on interest rates, which can be influenced by a government's *monetary* policies.

10 D Objective 1 could be achieved by raising (or lowering) taxes on firms and lowering (or raising) taxes on households. Objective 2 could be achieved by raising taxation in order to reduce consumers' disposable income and so to reduce aggregate expenditure in the economy: these consequences should lead to a fall in the demand for money. Objective 3 can be achieved either by taxing income or by means of selective indirect taxes on certain goods.

11 $MV \equiv PT$

12 The transactions, precautionary and speculative motives.

13 Bond prices will fall until the fixed income they provide equates to the rate of interest.

14 Demand pull and Cost push

15 It attracts foreign investment, thus increasing the demand for the currency. The currency typically strengthens as a result.

16 D T has to be unchanged for $MV \equiv PT$ to be a predictor of price behaviour. Any increase in M, given no change in V in the short run, would result in a matching percentage increase in prices P.

17 B According to Keynes the money supply would be fixed by the authorities. The demand for money depends on three motives (transactions, precautionary and speculative) but it is the speculative demand for money that is sensitive to changes in interest rates, and this explains the liquidity preference schedule.

18 A Lower interest rates should be a consequence of an increase in the money supply, with a movement along the liquidity preference curve rather than a shift in the liquidity preference curve.

19 A The question describes the transmission mechanism, which is the link between an excess of money supply over demand (or money demand over supply) and changes in expenditure in the economy. According to monetarists, an increase in the money supply creates excess supply over demand. Households use the excess money to buy bonds (and so interest rates *fall*), equities and physical goods (and so expenditure in the economy rises). The demand for money is interest-rate inelastic, according to monetarists (but not according to Keynesians) and so this does not increase in response to any interest rate fall.

20 By shifting to the right the supply curve.

Now try the questions below from the Exam Question Bank

Question numbers	Page
44 – 47	375

International Trade

Introduction

In this final chapter, we examine three things.

- The balance of payments and the economic policies affecting it
- Arguments for and against free trade
- Globalisation

The balance of payments is a statistical 'accounting' record of a country's international trade transactions (the purchase and sale of goods and services) and capital transactions (the acquisition and disposal of assets and liabilities) with other countries during a period of time.

If a country imports more than it exports, the resulting current account deficit may present a problem. The country must attract capital inflows (for example, new investment) in order to offset its payments for high levels of imports. By 2006 the USA had been running a trade deficit for many years..

Topic list	Learning outcomes	Syllabus references	Ability required
1 The balance of payments	D (v)	D (6), D (11)	Comprehension
2 The terms of trade	D (vi)	D (12)	Comprehension
3 International trade and its economic advantages	D (vi)	D (13)	Comprehension
4 Free trade agreements	D (ix)	D(13)	Comprehension
5 Globalisation of markets	D (viii)	D(14) & D(15)	Analysis
6 Global institutions	D (ix)	D (16)	Comprehension

1 The balance of payments

FAST FORWARD

The **balance of payments accounts** consist of a current account with visibles and invisibles sections and transactions in capital (external assets and liabilities including official financing). The sum of the balances on these accounts must be zero, although in practice there is a balancing figure for measurement errors.

1.1 The nature of the balance of payments

Assessment focus point

Confusion of the balance of payments with the government budget is common. Make sure that the distinction is clear in *your* mind.

Under the current method of presentation of the UK balance of payments statistics, **current account** transactions are sub-divided into four parts.

- Trade in goods
- Trade in services
- Income
- Transfers

Before 1996, the term **visibles** was used in official statistics for trade in goods and the term **invisibles** was used for the rest. These terms have now been dropped in order to give more emphasis to the balances for trade in goods and services, although you may still find them mentioned.

Income is divided into two parts.

(a) Income from employment of UK residents by overseas firms
(b) Income from capital investment overseas

Transfers are also divided into two parts:

(a) Public sector payments to and receipts from overseas bodies such as the EU. Typically these are interest payments

(b) Non-government sector payments to and receipts from bodies such as the EU

The **capital account** balance is made up of public sector flows of **capital** into and out of the country, such as government loans to other countries.

The balance on the **financial account** is made up of flows of capital to and from the non-government sector, such as direct investment in overseas facilities; portfolio investment (in shares, bonds and so on); and speculative flows of currency. Movements on government foreign currency reserves are also included under this heading.

1.2 Net errors and omissions

A balancing item appears in the balance of payments accounts because of errors and omissions in collecting statistics for the accounts (for example, sampling errors for items such as foreign investment and tourist expenditure and omissions from the data gathered about exports or imports).

The sum of the balance of payments accounts must always be zero (ignoring statistical errors in collecting the figures). This is for the same reason that a balance sheet must always balance: for every debit there must be a credit.

1.3 The UK balance of payments accounts

A UK balance of payment account at a particular point in time is summarised below.

UK balance of payments accounts

	£ billions
Current account	
Trade in goods	–26,767
Trade in services	11,538
Income	8,332
Transfers	–4,084
Current balance	–10,981
Capital account	776
Financial account	5,853
Net errors and omissions	4,352
	0

Given that the balance of payments in principle sums to zero, you may wonder what is meant by a surplus or deficit on the balance of payments. When journalists or economists speak of the balance of payments they are usually referring to the deficit or surplus on the **current account**, or possibly to the surplus or deficit on trade in goods only (this is also known as the **balance of trade**).

Question **Balance of payments**

'If the balance of payments always balances why do we hear about deficits and surpluses?'

Answer

The sum of the three balance of payments accounts must always be zero because every transaction in international trade has a double aspect. Just as accounting transactions are recorded by matching debit and credit entries, so too are international trade and financing transactions recorded by means of matching plus and minus transactions.

If a UK exporter sells goods to a foreign buyer:

(a) The value of the export is a plus in the current account of the balance of payments

(b) The payment for the export results in a reduction in the deposits held by foreigners in UK banks (a minus in the assets and liabilities section)

When we use the phrases 'deficit' or 'surplus on the balance of payments' what we actually mean is a deficit or surplus on the current account. If there is a surplus (+) on the current account we would expect this to be matched by a similar negative amount on the assets and liabilities section. This will take the form of:

(a) Additional claims on non-residents (for example, overseas loans)
(b) Decreased liabilities to non-residents (paying off our loans abroad)

This will involve not only banks and other firms but it may also involve the government too, since it is responsible for the 'reserves'.

If there is a deficit (-) on the current account the result will be a similar positive amount on the assets and liabilities section. This will consist of inward investment and/or increased overseas indebtedness, representing how the deficit has been 'financed'. This means that banks and other firms will owe more money abroad and the government may also be borrowing from abroad.

Assessment focus point

Do not, as some students do, equate a trade surplus or deficit with a 'profit' or 'loss' for the country. 'A country is not like a company and the trade balance has nothing to do with profits and losses', commented the Examiner for the old syllabus.

1.4 Foreign currency and international trade

With international trade, there is often a need for foreign currency for at least one of the parties to the transaction.

(a) If a UK exporter sells goods to a US buyer, and charges the buyer £20,000, the US buyer must somehow obtain the sterling in order to pay the UK supplier. The US buyer will do this by using some of his US dollars to buy the £20,000 sterling, probably from a bank in the USA.

(b) If a UK importer buys goods from Germany, he might be invoiced in euros, say €100,000. He must obtain this foreign currency to pay his debt, and he will do so by purchasing the euros from a UK bank in exchange for sterling.

(c) If a UK investor wishes to invest in US capital bonds, he would have to pay for them in US dollars, and so he would have to sell sterling to obtain the dollars.

Thus **capital outflows**, such as investing overseas, not just payments for imports, cause a demand to sell the domestic currency and buy foreign currencies. On the other hand, exports and capital inflows to a country cause a demand to buy the domestic currency in exchange for foreign currencies.

Exporters might want to sell foreign currency earnings to a bank in exchange for domestic currency, and importers may want to buy foreign currency from a bank in order to pay a foreign supplier.

1.5 Exchange rates and the UK balance of payments

As in any other market, the market for foreign exchange is a market in which buyers and suppliers come into contact, and 'prices' (exchange rates) are set by supply and demand. Exchange rates change continually. Significant movements in the exchange rate for a country's currency can have important implications for the country's balance of payments.

1.6 Equilibrium in the balance of payments

A balance of payments is in equilibrium if, over a period of years, the exchange rate remains stable and autonomous credits and debits are equal in value (the annual trade in goods and services is in overall balance). However, equilibrium will not exist if these things require the government to introduce measures which create unemployment or higher prices, sacrifice economic growth or impose trade barriers (eg import tariffs and import quotas).

1.7 Surplus or deficit in the current account

FAST FORWARD

A surplus or deficit on the balance of payments usually means a **surplus or deficit on the current account**.

A problem arises for a country's balance of payments when the country has a deficit on current account year after year, although there can be problems too for a country which enjoys a continual current account **surplus**.

The problems of a **deficit** on the current account are probably the more obvious. When a country is continually in deficit, it is importing more goods and services that it is exporting. This leads to two possible consequences.

(a) It may borrow more and more from abroad, to build up external liabilities which match the deficit on current account, for example encouraging foreign investors to lend more by purchasing the government's gilt-edged securities.

(b) It may sell more and more of its assets. This has been happening recently in the USA, for example, where a large deficit on the US current account has resulted in large purchases of shares in US companies by foreign firms.

Even so, the demand to buy the country's currency in the foreign exchange markets will be weaker than the supply of the country's currency for sale. As a consequence, there will be pressure on the exchange rate to depreciate in value.

If a country has a **surplus** on current account year after year, it might invest the surplus abroad or add it to official reserves. The balance of payments position would be strong. There is the problem, however, that if one country which is a major trading nation (such as Japan) has a continuous surplus on its balance of payments current account, other countries must be in continual deficit. These other countries can run down their official reserves, perhaps to nothing, and borrow as much as they can to meet the payments overseas, but eventually, they will run out of money entirely and be unable even to pay their debts. Political pressure might therefore build up within the importing countries to impose tariffs or import quotas.

1.8 How can a government rectify a current account deficit?

The government of a country with a balance of payments deficit will usually be expected to take measures to reduce or eliminate the deficit. A deficit on current account may be rectified by one or more of the following measures.

(a) A depreciation of the currency (called **devaluation** when deliberately instigated by the government, for example by changing the value of the currency within a controlled exchange rate system).

(b) Direct measures to restrict imports, such as tariffs or import quotas or exchange control regulations.

(c) Domestic deflation to reduce aggregate demand in the domestic economy.

The first two are **expenditure switching** policies, which transfer resources and expenditure away from imports and towards domestic products while the last is an **expenditure reducing** policy.

1.9 Depreciation/devaluation of the currency

A rising (ie appreciating) exchange rate may reflect relatively low inflation and strong trade and general economic performance. Conversely, poor economic performance and high inflation will result in **currency depreciation**. As a result of a fall in the value of the currency, exports would be relatively cheaper to foreign buyers, and so the demand for exports would rise.

The extent of the increase in export revenue would depend on several factors.

(a) The price elasticity of demand for the goods in export markets.

(b) The extent to which industry is able to respond to the export opportunities by either producing more goods, or switching from domestic to export markets.

(c) Perhaps also the price elasticity of supply. With greater demand for their goods, producers should be able to achieve some increase in prices (according to the law of supply and demand), and the willingness of suppliers to produce more would then depend on the price elasticity of supply.

(Appreciation of a currency will have converse effects to those of a depreciation.)

The cost of imports would rise as a result of **currency depreciation** because more domestic currency would be needed to obtain the foreign currency to pay for imported goods. The volume of imports would fall, although whether or not the total value of imports fell too would depend on the elasticity of demand for imports.

(a) If demand for imports is inelastic, the volume of demand would fall by less than their cost goes up, so that the total value of imports would rise.

(b) If demand for imports is elastic, the total value of imports would fall since the fall in volume would outweigh the increase in unit costs.

If a country imports raw materials and exports manufactured goods which are made with those materials, the cost of imported raw materials will rise, and so producers will have to put up their prices to cover their higher costs. There will be a net fall in export prices, as explained above, but perhaps not by much.

1.10 Effects of a fall in exchange rate on the balance of payments

The effects of a fall in the exchange rate (for example, due to a government policy of devaluation) are likely to vary in the short term and the long term. The immediate effects will depend on the elasticity of demand for imports. Demand is likely to be fairly inelastic in the short term and so total expenditure on imports will rise. Exports will be cheaper in overseas markets (in foreign currency) but in the short term exporters might be unable to increase their output to meet the higher demand.

Until domestic industry adjusts to the change and increases its output of exported goods and home produced substitutes for imported goods, there will be a deterioration in the current account of the balance of payments.

After a time lag, production of exports and import substitutes can be expected to rise, so that the volume of exports will rise, thereby increasing the sterling value of exports (regardless of sterling's lower exchange rate) and the volume of imports will fall further. This will improve the current account balance.

The improvement in the balance of payments will have some limit, and the current balance should eventually level off. The effect of the falling exchange rate on the current balance through time has been portrayed in the form of the so-called **J curve** (Figure 1).

Key term

J curve effect: the effect on the balance of payments of a falling exchange rate. Inelasticity of both supply and demand means that the current account will deteriorate at first but then improve.

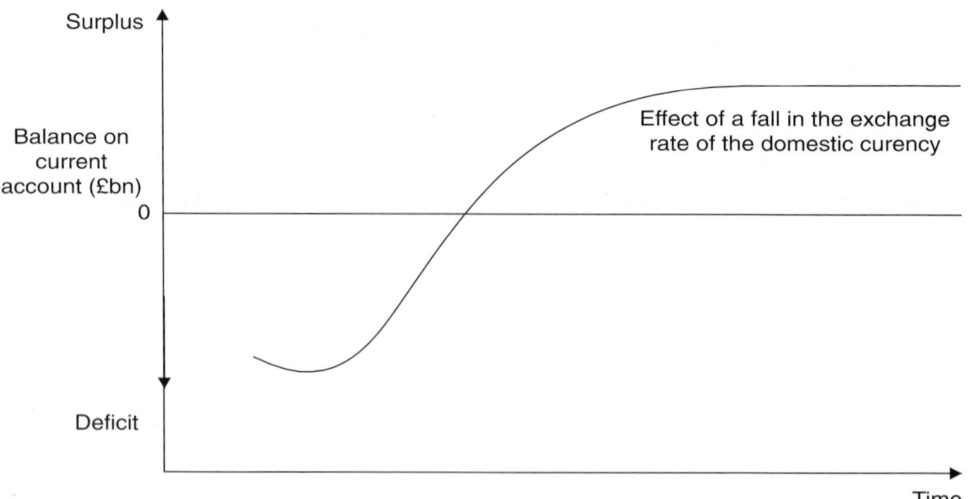

Figure 1 J curve

1.11 Effects of currency appreciation

As noted above, an **appreciating exchange rate** may reflect relatively low inflation and strong trade and general economic performance, as in the case of Japan in the 1970s and 80s. (Conversely, poor economic performance and high inflation will result in currency depreciation.) To consider the implications for an economy such as Japan's of a rise in the value of the currency in more detail, we may look first at the effects on exports and then on imports required to buy 100 yen rises.

As the yen rises in value, so other currencies weaken relatively. Over the years, the number of dollars, pounds, marks and so on required to buy 100 yen rises. **The result is to increase the effective price of Japanese goods abroad, so that with price elasticity of demand the volume of exports would be depressed**. The diminished volume of exports would have domestic consequences.

- Stocks would gradually build up, leading to a curtailment of production.
- In turn, this could result in higher unit costs as fixed costs are less effectively spread.
- Short-time working and possibly labour redundancies might follow.
- Some investment decisions might be deferred or even cancelled altogether.

These reductions in the level of economic activity would have negative multiplier effects.

A strong currency means that imports become cheaper. Therefore costs of imported raw materials and foodstuffs fall. Input costs for industry therefore fall and any rises in retail prices are restrained. Inflationary pressures in the system are thus lessened. This may be used to advantage on exports to offset partially the effect of the rising currency: firms may be able to hold down their ex-factory price and so enable the net price overseas to rise very little. Any advantage on the import side of a stronger currency would depend on the relative importance of imports: a country having to import much of its raw materials and fuel could find this a useful advantage.

With a strong currency, there will also be an increased attraction in buying foreign consumer goods. Invisible imports may begin to rise: more Japanese residents might venture abroad on holiday, so increasing the supply of yen in currency markets and raising the demand for other currencies. This would exert some downward pressure on the yen. Any recessionary effects on industry would, of course, tend to lessen these import pressures.

The overall effect would depend on the balance between export and import effects – some unfavourable, some favourable. Any significant decline in the net inflow of capital as economic expansion slows could have a de-stabilising effect. The overall effect would also depend upon the ability of the economy to adjust to the changed conditions, for example through improved efficiency, so enabling ex-factory prices to be reduced. It would also depend upon economic conditions in the rest of the world.

1.12 Protectionist measures

Another way of attempting to rectify a balance of payments deficit is to take direct protectionist measures like those we have already described to reduce the volume of imports. These measures might include these below.

(a) Import tariffs

(b) Import quotas

(c) A total ban or embargo on imports from a certain country

(d) Placing administrative burdens on importers (for example increasing the documentation required or safety standards that imported goods must comply with)

(e) Exchange control regulations which make it difficult for importers to obtain foreign currency to buy goods from abroad

(f) Providing export subsidies to encourage exports, and other measures of financial support to exporters

Import restrictions and export subsidies give rise to counter-measures by other countries. They are therefore potentially dangerous measures for a country whose economy relies heavily on external trade. Exchange control regulations might be essential, however, for a country with a balance of payments deficit, low official reserves and one which has great difficulty in borrowing capital from abroad.

1.13 Domestic deflation

Deflation can be used to adjust a balance of trade deficit. When the total volume of expenditure and demand for goods in a country's economy is too high, the government can take steps to reduce it, by reducing its own expenditure, raising interest rates to deter borrowing, and cutting private consumption by raising taxes. This fall in demand should lead to a fall in prices or at least to a reduction in the rate of domestic inflation. Unfortunately, it might also lead, in the short term at least, to a reduction in industrial output and a loss of jobs in the country's economy. Certainly, the country must accept a lowering of its standard of living if severe deflationary measures are taken. The effect of deflation is not only to dampen domestic inflation rates, but to force domestic manufacturers, who will be faced with lower domestic demand for their goods, to switch more effort into selling to export markets.

Deflationary measures include cutting government spending, increasing taxation and raising interest rates. They have three purposes.

(a) To reduce the demand for goods and services at home, and so to reduce imports

(b) To encourage industry to switch to export markets, because of the fall in domestic demand

(c) To tackle domestic inflation, which might be undermining the beneficial effect for exports of a depreciating domestic currency by raising the prices of exported goods in terms of the domestic currency

Sometimes, a government's domestic economic policies are not deflationary, despite a balance of payments deficit, and on the contrary, the government's economic policies might encourage increasing demand, which will both boost demand for imports, and cause more inflation and a falling exchange rate. Economic policies which boost demand in the economy in spite of a balance of payments deficit will worsen, rather than improve, the deficit.

1.14 The balance of payments and the domestic economy

You should try to view any country's balance of payments position in the context of its domestic economy.

(a) When a country's exports exceed its imports, or *vice versa*, there may be a lack of equilibrium between withdrawals from the circular flow of income in the domestic economy (remember that these withdrawals include imports) and injections into the circular flow of income (which include exports). Equilibrium in the balance of payments (external equilibrium) will also help a country to achieve equilibrium in its circular flow of income (internal equilibrium).

(b) If a country's international trade is only small in size compared with its domestic economy, problems with any balance of payments deficit will be much less than for a country which relies heavily on international trade.

1.15 Interest rates and the balance of payments

Comparative interest rates between one country and another, and changes in interest rates, affect the balance of payments in two ways.

(a) Directly, by stimulating or discouraging foreign investment, and so inflows and outflows of capital.

(b) Indirectly, through the exchange rate. Foreign investment creates a demand for the currency and keeps the exchange rate at a high level.

Is a high interest rate policy a good solution to the problem of a deficit on the balance of payments current account?

(a) If a country relies on inflows of capital to finance a continuing balance of trade deficit, the country's balance of payments will never get into equilibrium. High interest rates will keep the exchange rate high for the country's currency, and this will make it more difficult to export (high export prices to foreign buyers) and encourage imports (cheaper prices). The country might therefore be unable to rectify its balance of trade deficit.

(b) If there is a continuing balance of trade deficit, there will always be a threat that the country's currency will eventually depreciate in value. This will deter investors. The UK is in this position at the time of writing.

Investors will only put money into capital investments abroad if they have satisfactory expectations about what the exchange rate for the foreign currency will be. Interest rates alone are not the only factor on which to base an investment decision. After all, what is the value to an investor of high interest rates from investments in a foreign currency when the exchange value of the currency is falling?

1.16 External debt

A country's external debt is the total amount that the country owes to foreign creditors. It can include several elements.

(a) Loans from specialist international lending organisations, in particular the International Monetary Fund (IMF) and the World Bank

(b) Loans from foreign governments

(c) Loans from private foreign investors, in particular foreign banks

Question

External debt

See if you can think through what the effect of a balance of payments current account deficit will be on a country's external debt.

Answer

A country's external debt increases whenever it has a balance of payments deficit on current account.

(a) A deficit on current account must be balanced (that is, equalled) by a matching surplus in transactions in external assets and liabilities, in other words, by:

  (i) Borrowing from abroad
  (ii) Selling assets that are owned abroad

(b) If a country's balance of trade deficit is very high, it must borrow heavily from abroad. Borrowing could be:

  (i) Borrowing by the government

  (ii) Borrowing by the private sector

  (iii) Increasing investments in the country's private sector by foreign firms, eg takeovers of domestic companies by foreign companies

(c) There would be fears of a depreciation in the exchange rate of the country's currency, as a consequence of the balance of trade deficit. How can a country succeed in attracting foreign investors if they fear that the value of their investment might fall because of a currency depreciation?

Interest rates will probably have to remain high to compensate foreign investors for this risk.

(d) If the country's external debt becomes very high, the cost of servicing the debt by meeting interest payment schedules could become a severe burden on the country's economy.

2 The terms of trade

The balance of trade depends not only on the volumes of goods traded, but on the **relative prices** of exports and imports (ie on the **terms of trade**).

2.1 What are the terms of trade?

The **balance of trade** for any country depends on two things.

- The volume of goods exported and imported
- The relative prices of exports and imports

Key term

Terms of trade: the quantities of domestic goods that a country must give up to obtain a unit of imported goods.

In effect, the **terms of trade** are an export: import price ratio, which measures the relative prices of a country's exports and imports. The terms of trade for a country continually change as export prices and import prices change.

The terms of trade determine the volume of exports necessary to pay for a given volume of imports or, meaning the same thing, the volume of imports that can be purchased with the proceeds of a given volume of exports.

Other things being equal, if the price of exports falls relative to that of imports (a fall in the terms of trade) the trade balance will deteriorate, or *vice versa*.

Note that trade balance depends not just on the physical volume of exports and imports, but on the prices at which they are traded.

Question — **Trade effects**

A country's electronics industry, which is its major export industry, switches from the production of mass low cost, low profit margin microchips to the production of more high powered, high cost, high profit margin custom-built microchips. Which one of the following effects would you expect to occur?

A An improvement in the balance of trade
B A deterioration in the balance of trade
C An improvement in the terms of trade
D A worsening in the terms of trade

Answer

The answer is C. This is one example of how a country's terms of trade might improve. By switching from low priced to high priced products in a major export industry, unit export prices will go up and the terms of trade will improve. The change in the *balance* of trade depends on changes in the *volume* of exports and imports *as well as changes in export and import prices.*

2.2 Measuring the terms of trade

The terms of trade are measured as:

$$\frac{\text{Unit value of exports}}{\text{Unit value of imports}}$$

In practice economists are usually concerned not with a measurable value for the terms of trade but with a measure of *changes* in the terms of trade, (eg from one year to the next).

Using indices for the average prices of imports and exports, the movement in the terms of trade between 2003 and 2004 would be computed as:

$$\frac{\text{Price of exports in 2004/price of exports 2003}}{\text{Price of imports 2004/price of imports 2003}}$$

2.3 Changes in the terms of trade

Change in a country's terms of trade occur for two reasons.

(a) A change in the composition of exports or imports; in the UK, two main things have improved the UK's terms: lower oil imports and manufacturers trading up to higher-price products for export.

(b) Lower or higher prices of imports/exports – such as the oil price collapse in 1985, which worsened the terms of trade for the UK.

A government has limited powers to influence its country's terms of trade, since it cannot directly influence the composition nor the prices of imports and exports – although it *can* affect the terms of trade through a revaluation or devaluation of the currency which would alter relative import/export prices.

(a) If a country's terms of trade **worsen**, the unit value of its imports will rise by a bigger percentage than the unit value of its exports. The terms of trade will worsen when the exchange rate of the currency depreciates in value against other currencies.

(b) If a country's terms of trade **improve**, the unit value of its exports will rise by a bigger percentage than the unit value of its imports. The terms of trade will improve when the exchange rate of the country's currency appreciates in value against other currencies.

It would seem logical to assume that an improving terms of trade is good for a country and a worsening terms of trade is bad for it. But **this is not necessarily the case**.

2.4 Terms of trade and the balance of payments

The effect of a change in the terms of trade should be considered in the context of the country's balance of payments. If the terms of trade worsen for a country, the country will be unable to afford the same volume of imports, or else its balance of payment position will deteriorate. In contrast, a country with improving terms of trade will be able to afford more imports or will improve its balance of payments.

Changes in the terms of trade affect a country's balance of payments via the price elasticity of demand for the goods traded. If a country's terms of trade improve, so that the price of its exported goods rises relative to the price of its imported goods, there will be a relative fall in the volume of goods exported and a rise in the volume of imports. The size of this fall in exports and increase in imports will depend on the price elasticities of demand for exported goods in foreign markets and imported goods in the country's domestic markets.

Question

Terms of trade and balance trade

From your knowledge of the theory of elasticity of demand, analyse what will happen to the current balance of trade when the terms of trade improve, on the assumptions:

(a) That demand for exported goods and demand for imported goods are both *inelastic*
(b) That both demands are *elastic*

Answer

(a) If the demand for exported goods is inelastic the total value of exports will rise if their price goes up.
(b) If the demand for imported goods is inelastic the total value of imports will fall if their price falls.

Provided that price elasticity of demand for both exports and imports is inelastic, an improvement in the terms of trade will result in an improvement in the current balance of trade.

On the other hand if the price elasticity of demand for both exports and imports is elastic, an improvement in the terms of trade will lead to a worsening current balance of trade, because:

(a) A rise in export prices would reduce total export revenue
(b) A fall in import prices would increase total payments for imports

An improvement in the terms of trade might therefore result in a better or a worse balance of payments position. The same applies to worsening terms of trade.

3 International trade and its economic advantages

FAST FORWARD

World output of goods and services will increase if countries **specialise** in the production of goods/ services in which they have a **comparative advantage**. Just how this total wealth is shared out between countries depends on circumstances.

3.1 International trade in goods and services

Economists distinguish the concepts of **comparative advantage** and **absolute advantage** in international trade. Our explanation of this distinction makes the following assumptions.

- There are only two countries, country X and country Y
- Only two goods are produced, lorries and wheat
- There are no transport costs and no barriers to trade
- Resources within each country are easily transferred from one industry to another

3.2 Absolute advantage

A country is said to have an absolute advantage in the production of a good when it is more efficient than another country in the production of that good, ie when it can produce more of a particular good with a given amount of resources than another country. It is a fairly common situation for one country to be more efficient than another in the production of a particular good.

Assuming that Y produces wheat more efficiently than country X, while country X has an absolute advantage in producing lorries, a simple arithmetical example can illustrate the potential gains from trade. The table below shows the amounts of lorries and wheat that each country can produce in year 0, assuming that each country has an equal quantity of resources and devotes half of its resources to lorry production and half to wheat production.

Year 0

	Lorries	*Wheat (tons)*
Country X	20	100
Country Y	10	150
World total	30	250

The relative cost of lorry production is lower in country X than in country Y, but the situation is reversed in the case of wheat production. Country X has an absolute advantage in lorry production and country Y has an absolute advantage in wheat production. Greater specialisation will, however, increase total output.

Question — **Absolute advantage**

Suppose that each country devotes its entire production resources to the product for which it enjoys an absolute advantage. What will be the total output of lorries and wheat?

Answer

Total world output will be 40 lorries (produced by country X) and 300 tons of wheat (produced by country Y).

By specialising, total world output is now (see Exercise 1 solution) greater with ten more lorries and 50 tons more wheat now available for consumption. In order to obtain the benefits of specialisation these countries can exchange some part of their individual outputs. It is not possible to specify the exact rate of exchange but the limits of the exchange rate must be somewhere between the domestic opportunity cost ratios of the two countries. These are: for country X, 5 tons of wheat per lorry; for country Y, 15 tons of wheat per lorry. One country will not benefit from international trade if the 'exchange rate' is not between these ratios.

3.3 Comparative advantage

Key term

The law of **comparative advantage** (or comparative costs) states that two countries can gain from trade when each specialises in the industries in which it has lowest opportunity costs.

The theory of **comparative advantage** is based on the idea of **opportunity cost** and the **production possibility frontier**. Within a country, opportunity cost for any category of product may be established in terms of the next most advantageous use of national resources. If two countries produce different goods most efficiently and can exchange them at an advantageous rate in terms of the comparative opportunity costs of importing and home production, then it will be beneficial for them to specialise and trade. Total production of each good will be higher than if they each produce both goods. This is true even if one country has an absolute advantage in both goods.

3.4 Illustrative example

The principle of comparative costs can be shown by an arithmetical example. It is now assumed that in year 10 country X is more efficient in the production of both lorries and wheat. If each country devotes half its resources to each industry the assumed daily production totals are as shown below.

Year 10

	Lorries	*Wheat (tons)*
Country X	20	200
Country Y	10	150
World total	30	350

In terms of resources used, the costs of production in both industries are lower in country X. If we consider the opportunity costs, however, the picture is rather different. In country X the cost of one lorry is ten tons of wheat: in devoting resources to the production of one lorry in country X there is a sacrifice in terms of ten tons of wheat forgone. The opportunity cost of one lorry in country Y is fifteen tons of wheat. Country X therefore has a comparative advantage in the production of lorries.

In country X the opportunity cost of a ton of wheat is now $^1/_{10}$ of a lorry, while in country Y the opportunity cost is $^1/_{15}$ of a lorry. In terms of the output of lorries forgone, wheat is cheaper in country Y than in country X. Country Y has a comparative advantage in wheat. It would now be possible for country Y to buy 10 lorries from country X in exchange for 200 tons of wheat. Country X would transfer some of its resources from the production of wheat to the production of lorries, while country Y would put all of its resources into the production of Wheat. Total production would now look like this.

	Lorries	*Wheat* (tons)
Country X	30	100
Country Y	0	300
World total	30	400

There is an increase in the world output of wheat.

Alternatively, country X might buy 150 tons of wheat form country Y in exchange for 15 lorries. Country X would transfer even more resources to the production of lorries and the total production figures would change again.

	Lorries	*Wheat* (tons)
Country X	35	50
Country Y	0	300
	35	350

There has now been an increase in the world output of lorries.

Clearly, the two countries could adjust their trade between these extremes, achieving overall increases in **both** types of good.

3.5 Other advantages of free international trade

Other advantages of free international trade are as follows.

(a) Some countries have a surplus of **raw materials**, and others have a deficit. A country with a surplus can take advantage of its resources to export them. A country with a deficit of a raw material must either import it, or accept restrictions on its economic prosperity and standard of living.

(b) International trade increases **competition** among suppliers in the world's markets. Greater competition reduces the likelihood of a market for a good in a country being dominated by a monopolist. The greater competition will force firms to be competitive and so will increase the pressures on them to be efficient, and also perhaps to produce goods of a high quality.

(c) International trade creates **larger markets** for a firm's output, and so some firms can benefit from **economies of scale** by engaging in export activities. Economies of scale improve the efficiency of the use of resources, reduce the output costs and also increase the likelihood of output being sold to the consumer at lower prices than if international trade did not exist.

(d) There may be **political advantages** to international trade, because the development of trading links provides a foundation for closer political links. An example of the development of political links based on trade is the European Union.

sessment cus point

Make sure that you are clear about the concept of comparative advantage. Fundamentally, the comparative advantage model explains trade in terms of the benefits of international specialisation. Note that it is trade that leads to specialisation and not the other way round.

3.6 Transport costs

In the earlier example, we assumed that transport costs in international trade are negligible. High transport costs, however, can negate the advantages of specialisation and international trade.

3.7 Free movement of capital

Free trade is associated with the free movement of goods (and services) between countries. Another important aspect of international trade is the free movement of capital.

(a) If a UK company (or investor) wishes to set up a business in a different country, or to take over a company in another country, how easily can it transfer capital from the UK to the country in question, to pay for the investment?

(b) Similarly, if a Japanese company wishes to invest in the UK, how easily can it transfer funds out of Japan and into the UK to pay for the investment?

Some countries (including the UK, since the abolition of exchange controls in 1979) have allowed a fairly free flow of capital into and out of the country. Other countries have been more cautious, mainly for one of the following two reasons.

(a) The free inflow of foreign capital will make it easier for foreign companies to take over domestic companies. There is often a belief that certain key industries should be owned by residents of the country. Even in the UK, for example, there have been restrictions on the total foreign ownership of shares in companies such as British Aerospace and Rolls Royce.

(b) Less developed countries especially, but other more advanced economies too, are reluctant to allow the free flow of capital out of the country. After all, they need capital to come into the country to develop the domestic economy.

For countries with a large and continuing balance of trade deficit, such as the UK and the USA, it is **essential** that capital should flow into the country to finance the deficit. The deficit country's currency may need to decline in value to attract funds in. The balance of payments is discussed in detail in the next chapter.

3.8 Barriers to free international trade

In practice many barriers to free trade exist because governments try to protect home industries against foreign competition.

Protectionism can be practised by a government in several ways.

- Tariffs or customs duties
- Import quotas
- Embargoes
- Hidden subsidies for exporters and domestic producers
- Import restrictions

3.9 Tariffs or customs duties

Tariffs or customs duties are taxes on imported goods. The effect of a tariff is to raise the price paid for the imported goods by domestic consumers, while leaving the price paid to foreign producers the same, or even lower. The difference is transferred to the government sector.

3.10 Import quotas

Import quotas are restrictions on the **quantity** of a product that is allowed to be imported into the country. The quota has a similar effect on consumer welfare to that of import tariffs, but the overall effects are more complicated.

(a) Both domestic and foreign suppliers enjoy a higher price, while consumers buy less at the higher price.
(b) Domestic producers supply more.
(c) There are fewer imports (in volume).
(d) The government collects no revenue.

An **embargo** on imports from one particular country is a total ban, ie effectively a zero quota.

3.11 Hidden export subsidies and import restrictions

There has been an enormous range of government subsidies and assistance for exports and deterrents against imports. Some examples are given below.

(a) **For exports** – export credit guarantees (insurance against bad debts for overseas sales), financial help (such as government grants to the aircraft or shipbuilding industry) and state assistance via the Foreign Office;

(b) **For imports** – complex import regulations and documentation, or special safety standards demanded from imported goods and so on.

When a government gives grants to its domestic producers, for example regional development grants for new investments in certain areas of the country or grants to investments in new industries, the effect of these grants is to make unit production costs lower. These give the domestic producer a cost advantage over foreign producers in export markets as well as domestic markets.

3.12 Arguments in favour of protection

Protectionist measures may be taken against imports of cheap goods that compete with higher-priced domestically produced goods, and so **preserve output and employment** in domestic industries. In the UK, advocates of protection have argued that UK industries are declining because of competition from overseas, and the advantages of more employment at a reasonably high wage for UK labour are greater than the disadvantages that protectionist measures would bring.

(a) Measures might be necessary to **counter dumping of surplus production** by other countries at an uneconomically low price. For example, if the European Union (EU) were to over-produce, it might decide to dump the surpluses on other countries. The losses from overproduction would be subsidised by the EU governments, and the domestic industries of countries receiving dumped goods would be facing unfair competition from abroad. Although dumping has short-term benefits for the countries receiving the cheap goods, the longer term consequences would be a reduction in domestic output and employment, even when domestic industries in the longer term might be more efficient.

(b) Protectionist measures by one country are often implemented in **retaliation** against measures taken by another country that are thought to be unfair. This is why protection tends to spiral once it has begun. Any country that does not take protectionist measures when other countries are doing so is likely to find that it suffers all of the disadvantages and none of the advantages of protection.

(c) There is an argument that protectionism is necessary, at least in the short term, to protect a country's **infant industries** that have not yet developed to the size where they can compete in international markets. Less developed countries in particular might need to protect industries against competition from advanced or developing countries.

(d) Protection might also help a country in the short term to deal with the problems of a **declining industry**. Without protection, the industry might quickly collapse and there would be severe problems of sudden mass unemployment. By imposing some protectionist measures, the decline in the industry might be slowed down, and the task of switching resources to new industries could be undertaken over a longer period of time.

(e) Protection is often seen as a means for a country to **reduce its balance of trade deficit**, by imposing tariffs or quotas on imports. However, because of retaliation by other countries, the success of such measures by one country would depend on the demand by other countries for its exports being inelastic with regard to price and its demand for imports being fairly elastic.

3.13 Undesirable effects of protection

As well as reducing the benefits brought by trade, protection can have direct disadvantageous effects on a country's businesses.

Higher costs. Protection is likely to raise costs to domestic business for three reasons.

(a) Imports of raw materials, components, fuel and so on will be more expensive.
(b) Domestic producers of inputs will take advantage of the reduction in competition to raise their prices.
(c) Rising prices of both imports and domestic goods will lead to increased wage demands.

Reduced demand. Domestic producers will face reduced demand for two reasons.

(a) Foreign trading partners are likely to retaliate with protective measures of their own, thus reducing export demand.

(b) Home consumers will find their real income declines as costs rise (see above) and thus domestic demand will decline.

4 Free trade agreements

FAST FORWARD

Free trade agreements include the WTO and the European Union.

4.1 The World Trade Organisation

The world Trade Organisation (WTO) was formed in 1995 as a successor to the General Agreement on Tariffs and Trade (GATT). In 2005 WTO had 148 countries as members. The main objective of WTO is to encourage free trade by policies such as the reciprocal dropping of tariffs between trading countries and the elimination of other forms of protectionism. WTO has not made much progress with these objectives. In 1999 WTO talks terminated after rioters protested against the policies of some of the wealthier member nations. Recession in some economies has encouraged an increase in protectionism. The recent 2001 'interim' agreement to liberalise trade in agricultural products had yet to materialise in international trade.

4.2 The European Union

The European Union (EU) (formerly the European Community) is one of several international economic associations. It was formed in 1957 by the Treaty of Rome and now consists of 25 nations, and there are ten more countries waiting to join.

The European Union has a **common market** combining different aspects, including **a free trade area** and a **customs union**.

(a) A **free trade area** exists when there is no restriction on the movement of goods and services between countries. This may be extended into a **customs union** when there is a free trade area between all member countries of the union, and in addition, there are common external tariffs applying to imports from non-member countries into any part of the union. In other words, the union promotes free trade among its members but acts as a protectionist bloc against the rest of the world.

(b) A **common market** encompasses the idea of a customs union but has a number of additional features. In addition to free trade among member countries there are also free markets in each of the **factors of production**. A British citizen has the freedom to work in any other country of the European Union, for example. A common market will also aim to achieve stronger links between member countries, for example by harmonising government economic policies and by establishing a closer political confederation.

4.3 The single European market

The EU set the end of 1992 as the target date for the removal of all existing physical, technical and fiscal barriers among member states, thus creating a large multinational European Single Market. This objective was embodied in the Single European Act of 1985. In practice, these changes have not occurred overnight, and many of them are still in progress.

Elimination of trade restrictions covers the following areas.

(a) **Physical barriers** (eg customs inspection) on good and services have been removed for most products. Companies have had to adjust to a new VAT regime as a consequence.

(b) **Technical standards** (eg for quality and safety) should be harmonised.

(c) Governments should not discriminate between EU companies in awarding **public works contracts**.

(d) **Telecommunications** should be subject to greater competition.

(e) It should be possible to provide **financial services** in any country.

(f) There should be **free movement of capital** within the community.

(g) **Professional qualifications** awarded in one member state should be recognised in the others.

(h) The EU is taking a co-ordinated stand on matters related to **consumer protection.**

At the same time, you should not assume that there will be a completely 'level playing field'. There are many areas where harmonisation is a long way from being achieved. Here are some examples.

(a) **Company taxation**. Tax rates, which can affect the viability of investment plans, vary from country to country within the EU.

(b) **Indirect taxation** *(*eg Value Added Tax or VAT*)*. Whilst there have been moves to harmonisation, there are still differences between rates imposed by member states.

(c) **Differences in prosperity**. There are considerable differences in prosperity between the wealthiest EU economy (Germany), and the poorest (eg some of the newly enrolled Eastern European members).

(d) **Differences in workforce skills**. Again, this can have a significant effect on investment decisions. The workforce in Germany is perhaps the most highly trained, but also the most highly paid, and so might be suitable for products of a high added value.

(e) **Infrastructure**. Some countries are better provided with road and rail than others. Where accessibility to a market is an important issue, infrastructure can mean significant variations in distribution costs.

4.4 The European Free Trade Association (EFTA)

The European Free Trade Association (EFTA) was established in 1959, with seven member countries, one of which was the UK. The UK, Denmark and Portugal have since transferred to the EU, while Finland and Iceland joined the other original member states, Sweden, Norway, Austria and Switzerland. More recently, Finland, Sweden and Austria have also joined the EU. There is free trade between EFTA member countries but there is no harmonisation of tariffs with non-EFTA countries.

4.5 The European Economic Area (EEA)

On 1 January 1993, EFTA forged a link with the EU to create a European Economic Area (EEA) with a population of 465 million, so extending the benefits of the EU single market to the EFTA member countries (excluding Switzerland, which stayed out of the EEA). The membership of the EEA now comprises the EU countries plus Norway, Liechtenstein and Iceland.

4.6 The North American Free Trade Agreement (NAFTA)

Canada, the USA and Mexico formed the North American Free Trade Agreement (NAFTA) in 1993. This free trade area covering a population of 414 million is similar in size to the European Economic Area.

5 Globalisation of markets

FAST FORWARD

The growth of **multinational enterprises** has taken place in an environment of increasing **globalisation of markets**.

5.1 The size and significance of multinational enterprises

A multinational company is one that has production or service facilities in more than one country. Multinational enterprises range from medium-sized companies having only a few facilities (or subsidiaries or 'affiliates') abroad to giant companies having an annual turnover larger than the gross national product (GNP) of some smaller countries of the world. Indeed the largest – the US multinationals Ford, General Motors and Exxon have each been reported to have a turnover larger than the GNPs of all but 14 countries of the world.

The size and significance of multinationals is increasing. Many companies in middle-income countries such as Singapore are now becoming multinationals, and the annual growth in output of existing multinationals is in the range 10-15%.

5.2 Globalisation of production

Transitional companies are tending more and more to take a global view of production. Production facilities may be located in particular countries for a variety of reasons.

- To give access to markets protected by tariffs
- To reduce transport costs
- To exploit national or regional differences in demand for goods
- To take advantage of low labour costs

Centralisation of manufacturing can bring important **economies of scale**. These must be balanced against transport costs and barriers to trade.

5.3 Globalisation of capital markets

Globalisation describes the process by which the capital markets of each country have become internationally integrated. The process of integration is facilitated by improved telecommunications and the deregulation of markets in many countries (for example, the UK stock market's so-called Big Bang of 1986). Securities issued in one country can now be traded in capital markets around the world. This trend can only increase as stock exchanges are linked electronically as has happened with the London and Frankfurt markets.

For companies planning international investment activities (also known as foreign direct investment (FDI)), easy access to large amounts of funds denominated in foreign currencies can be very useful. Such funds are available in the

eurocurrency markets. The eurocurrency markets can also help to bypass official constraints on international business activities.

5.4 Problems in managing international operations

Although multinationals can exploit a number of advantages over smaller firms (for example economies of scale, access to capital markets worldwide, and the ability to manufacture and produce in countries where material and labour resources are cheap), they also suffer from a number of **specific managerial problems**.

Problem	Comment
Planning	The environmental variables within which an organisation operates make planning difficult even in local terms. But a multinational faces problems of forecasting environmental variables over many countries. Plans which look promising in the local environment may founder abroad.
Organising	The possible structures of an organisation have been discussed in earlier chapters. Multinationals face the problem that no one structure can meet the needs of the many different environments in which they operate.
Staffing	The basic problem here is whether managers should be chosen from the home country or selected locally. Home-grown managers may be familiar with headquarters philosophy, but may find it difficult to get on with local staff from a different background. On the other hand, use of locally selected managers may lead to a lack of homogeneity in the multinational's trading efforts.
Leading	In some countries a participative style of management is practised. But this may be difficult to transfer to other countries where there is a tradition of autocratic rule.
Controlling	Effective controlling depends on accurate measurement of performance. When many aspects of performance are measured in monetary terms this means that currency differences are a serious obstacle to control. In addition, accounting practices, financial reporting and taxation may all vary from country to country. Inflation rates may be different, and exchange rates will exacerbate the problem. The sheer size and geographical dispersion of multinationals mean that delays elapse between the measurement of performance and the taking of corrective action.

5.5 Forms of foreign investment

FDI provides an alternative to growth restricted to a firm's domestic market. A firm might develop horizontally in different countries, replicating its existing operations on a global basis (**horizontal integration**). **Vertical integration** might have an international dimension through FDI to acquire raw material or component sources overseas (backwards integration) or to establish final production and distribution in other countries (forward integration). Diversification might alternatively provide the impetus to developing international interests.

AST FORWARD

The principal institutions of the global economy include the **World Bank** and the **International Monetary Fund**

5.6 Globalisation

Globalisation may be defined as the interdependence of different national economies. It reflects the tendency of markets to become global rather than national and for it to be difficult to view any national economy as a stand-alone entity.

Factors driving globalisation

(a) Improved communications, for example the speed of access to the internet
(b) Reduction of transport costs
(c) Political realignments, for example the collapse of the soviet block
(d) Growth of global industries and institutions
(e) Break down of some trade barriers by free trade organisations and treaties

5.7 Global institutions

A number of Institutions are central to the process of globalisation including the World Bank (WB), International Monetary Fund (IMF) and the European Central Bank. WB and IMF were both established after the Second World War and are based in Washington DC. WB has developed from its original function to provide finance and other aid in the form of commercial loans to developing countries to become much more involved in controlling the economic policy of those countries. Similarly the IMF has moved from a concern with supervision of the fixed rate exchange rate regime established after the war to becoming much more involved in the economic policy decisions of a number of countries with regard to government budgets, monetary policy, overall borrowing and trade. The IMF acts as a central bank to individual countries when in need of emergency funding to avoid a collapse of their currency and to ensure the smooth running of international trade. Recent examples where the IMF has provided emergency loans to countries in difficulties include Russia, Argentina and Turkey.

5.8 Impacts of globalisation

Globalisation used to be the unquestioned model for economic growth and stability but there are now many critics of the phenomena.

For globalisation

(a) Emergence of new growth markets, for example in the less developed countries
(b) Enhanced competitiveness as more producers and customers make up the global marketplace
(c) Growth of previously poor economies, such as China
(d) Cross-national business alliance and mergers
(e) International support for poorer nations and assistance provided in development of their economies
(f) World economic equalisation

Criticisms of globalisation

(a) The main institutions of globalisation follow the collective will of the G7 countries (USA, Japan, Germany, Canada, Italy, France and the UK and G8 when Russia is included) and are more concerned therefore in aiding the economic wealth of these countries.

(b) IMF, WB and ECB along with powerful multinational organisations dictate economic policy in countries but do not include real representation of these countries within their organisations. This lack of accountability has been called 'global governance without global government' (Joseph Stiglitz, Globalisation and its Discontents

(c) World poverty is still an issue and many fear that the policies adopted by WB, IMF and others, for example in restricting subsidy in Africa and opening up their markets for Western imports that are produced under subsidy, actually makes some nations poorer.

(d) There is no enduring political and economic stability in the world and the collapse of one part of the economy, for example in South America, could have disastrous knock on effects for the rest of the world.

(e) Not all countries are included in global activity Instead there is an increasing tendency for groups of counties, usually located in the same region to become involved in each others economies, for example the countries in the Eurozone.

Chapter roundup

- The **balance of payments accounts** consist of a current account with visibles and invisibles sections and transactions in capital (external assets and liabilities including official financing). The sum of the balances on these accounts must be zero, although in practice there is a balancing figure for measurement errors.
- A surplus or deficit on the balance of payments usually means a **surplus or deficit on the current account**.
- The balance of trade depends not only on the volumes of goods traded, but on the **relative prices** of exports and imports (ie on the **terms of trade**).
- World output of goods and services will increase if countries **specialise** in the production of goods/ services in which they have a **comparative advantage**. Just how this total wealth is shared out between countries depends on circumstances.
- **Free trade agreements** include the WTO and the European Union.
- The growth of **multinational enterprises** has taken place in an environment of increasing **globalisation of markets**.
- The principal institutions of the global economy include the World Bank and the International Monetary Fund

Quick quiz

1 What does the J curve describe?

2 How do deflationary measures help to eliminate a balance of payments deficit?

3 What is meant by the terms of trade?

4 What does the theory of purchasing power parity say?

5 How may the government intervene in the foreign exchange markets?

6 What is the balance of trade?

A The balance of payments on current account
B Net visible trade
C Net visible and invisible trade
D The theory of gains from trade

7 Which of the following statements concerning international trade are true? (1) The J curve effect will work in reverse if there is a depreciation when the current account is in deficit. (2) Protectionism could reduce exports. (3) Devaluation of the domestic currency will reverse a current account deficit.

A (1) and (3) only
B (1), (2) and (3)
C (1) and (2) only
D (2) and (3) only

8 From a given base year, a country's export prices rise by 8% and import prices rise by 20%. During this period, the terms of trade will have:

A Risen from 100 to 111.1
B Risen from 100 to 112
C Fallen from 100 to 90
D Fallen from 100 to 88

9 A devaluation will only benefit the UK balance of payments if:

A The sum of the price elasticities of demand for imports and exports is less than 1
B The sum of the price elasticities of demand for imports and exports is greater than 1
C The sum of the price elasticities of demand for imports and exports is less than 0
D The sum of the price elasticities of demand for imports and exports is greater than 0

10 What is meant by the law of comparative advantage?

11 What is meant by:

(a) A free trade area
(b) A customs union
(c) A common market?

12 Assume that two small countries, X and Y, produce two commodities P and Q, and that there are no transport costs. One unit of resource in Country X produces 4 units of P or 8 units of Q. One unit of resource in Country Y produces 1 unit of P or 3 units of Q. which of the following statements is true?

A Country X has an absolute advantage over Country Y in producing P and Q, and so will not trade.
B Country X does not have an absolute advantage over Country Y in producing P and Q.
C Country Y has a comparative advantage over Country X in producing Q.
D Country X has a comparative advantage over Country Y in producing both P and Q.

13 Define a multinational enterprise.

14 Outline the main problems encountered in managing international business operations.

15 What are the main factors driving globalisation?

Answers to quick quiz

1 The J curve shows the effect on the balance of payments of a falling exchange rate. A falling exchange rate will eventually reduce demand for imports and increase demand for exports. However, in the short term, both domestic and export demand are likely to be inelastic and the ability of domestic industry to meet any increase in export demand will be limited. The volume of goods and services traded is therefore unlikely to change in the short term, but imports will cost more in foreign currency and exports will sell for less. It is therefore likely that there will be a deterioration in the balance of payments in the short term.

2 Domestic deflation cuts demand, including demand for imports. Industry is therefore encouraged to switch to export markets.

3 The terms of trade are the ratio of export prices to import prices. This ratio determines the volume of exports necessary to pay for a given volume of imports.

4 Purchasing power parity theory suggests that exchange rates are determined by relative inflation rates. The currency of the country with high inflation will tend to weaken against those of countries with lower inflation rates, since more of its currency will be required to buy any given good.

5 Governments may intervene directly by buying and selling currency. They may also influence exchange rates by adjusting their interest rates and by direct currency controls such as limiting the amount of foreign currency which individuals are allowed to buy.

6 B Learn this definition.

7 D The J curve would work in reverse if there were a surplus and the currency appreciated.

8 C $108/120 \times 100 = 90$.

9 B In order to benefit, internal demand must react to a rise in the price of imports and external demand must react to a fall in the price of UK exported goods.

10 The law of comparative advantage or comparative costs states that two countries can gain from trade when each specialises in the industries in which it has the lowest opportunity costs.

11 A free trade area exists when there is no restriction on trade between countries. This is extended into a customs union when common external tariffs are levied on imports from non-member countries. A common market adds free movement of the factors of production, including labour and may harmonise economic policy.

12 C Country X has an *absolute* advantage over Country Y in making P and Q, because 1 unit of resource in Country X will make more of either P or Q than one unit of resource in Country Y. However, international trade should still take place because of *comparative* advantage in producing P and Q. The opportunity costs of producing a unit of P is 2 units of Q in Country X and 3 units of Q in Country Y. Similarly, the opportunity cost of producing a unit of Q is $\frac{1}{2}$ a unit of P in Country X and $\frac{1}{3}$ of a unit of P in Country Y. Country X has a comparative advantage in producing P and Country Y has a comparative advantage in the production of Q. International trade should be beneficial for both countries, with country X exporting P and Country Y exporting Q.

13 A multinational enterprise is one which has a physical presence or property interests in more than one country.

14
- Planning is complicated by the wide variation in conditions between countries.
- It is difficult to structure an organisation to meet the demands of operations in different countries.
- Multinationals have to achieve a balance between local and ex-patriate staff
- Successful management styles vary from country to country.
- Control by reference to monetary measures is complicated by varying inflation rates, exchange rates, taxation rates and financial reporting practices.

15 The main factors affecting globalisation are:

(a) Reduced transport costs
(b) Improved communications
(c) Emergence of multinational organisations
(d) Breakdown of barriers to trade

Now try the questions below from the Exam Question Bank

Question numbers	Page
48 – 50	375

Question Bank

1 In economics, the central economic problem means:

A Consumers do not have as much money as they would wish
B There will always be a certain level of unemployment
C Resources are not always allocated in an optimum way
D Output is restricted by the limited availability of resources

2 Which of the following would cause the production possibility frontier for an economy to shift outwards?

(i) A reduction in the level of unemployment
(ii) A rise in the rate of investment
(iii) A fall in the price of one factor of production
(iv) A rise in output per worker

A (i) and (ii) only
B (i), (ii) and (iii) only
C (i), (iii) and (iv) only
D (ii) and (iv) only

3 Write alongside each of the following industries the sector of the economy to which it belongs – primary, secondary or tertiary.

(a) Processing of fish to produce cod-liver oil
(b) Sale of chipped wood bark from sawmills as garden mulch
(c) Insurance of fishing vessels
(d) A water supply company
(e) Provision of capital for the purchase of mature woodland

4 With whom is the sales maximisation model associated?

A Keynes
B Cyert
C Baumol
D Adam Smith

5 The 'divorce of ownership from control' in a modern economy describes:

A The growth of government regulation

B Management of companies by salaried personnel who do not have significant shareholding in their company

C Enhancement of employee rights over conditions of work

D Expansion of share ownership through privatisation

6 The table below shows a firm's total cost (TC), average cost (AC) and marginal cost (MC) for certain levels of output. Which is which?

Units of output	*1* £	*2* £	*3* £
1	1.10	1.10	1.10
2	0.80	0.50	1.60
3	0.58	0.15	1.75
4	0.50	0.25	2.00
5	0.50	0.50	2.50
6	0.52	0.62	3.12

A 1 = AC, 2 = TC, 3 = MC
B 1 = AC, 2 = MC, 3 = TC
C 1 = MC, 2 = AC, 3 = TC
D 1 = TC, 2 = AC, 3 = MC

7 Put the correct labels in the boxes on this diagram of short run costs.

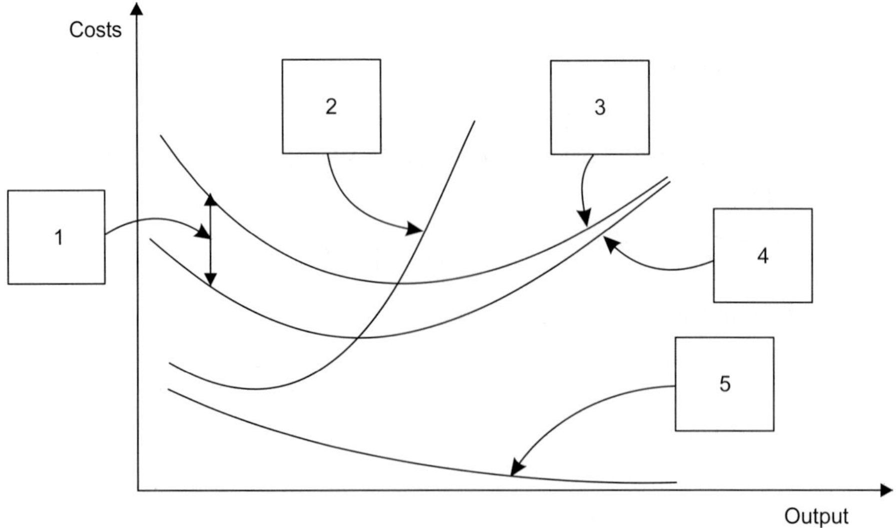

A Marginal cost
B Average fixed cost at this output
C Average total cost
D Average fixed cost curve
E Average variable cost

8 Which of the following statements is true when constant returns to scale apply?

A Marginal cost remains constant but average cost falls
B Average cost remains constant but marginal cost falls
C Average fixed cost falls
D Average cost and marginal cost remain constant

9 In the diagram below, point 5 represents equilibrium. If the government starts to pay a cash subsidy to producers of the commodity, what will the new equilibrium be?

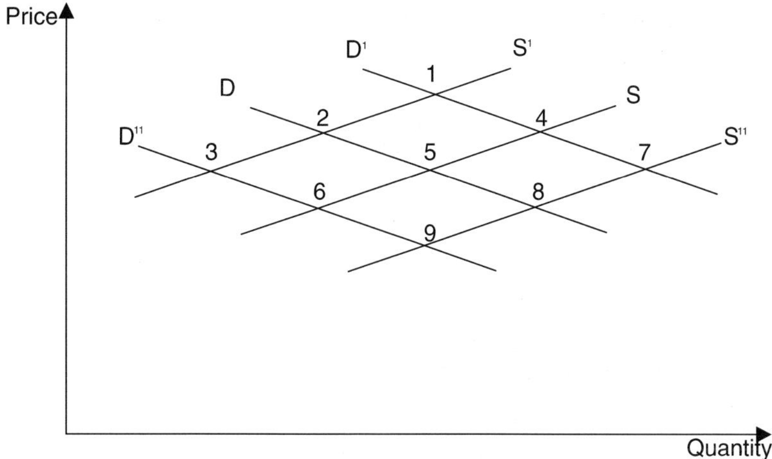

A Point 2
B Point 4
C Point 6
D Point 8

10 Surpluses will be enjoyed by some suppliers and some consumers even when the market clears under perfect competition.

Match the correct labels to the boxes on this diagram.

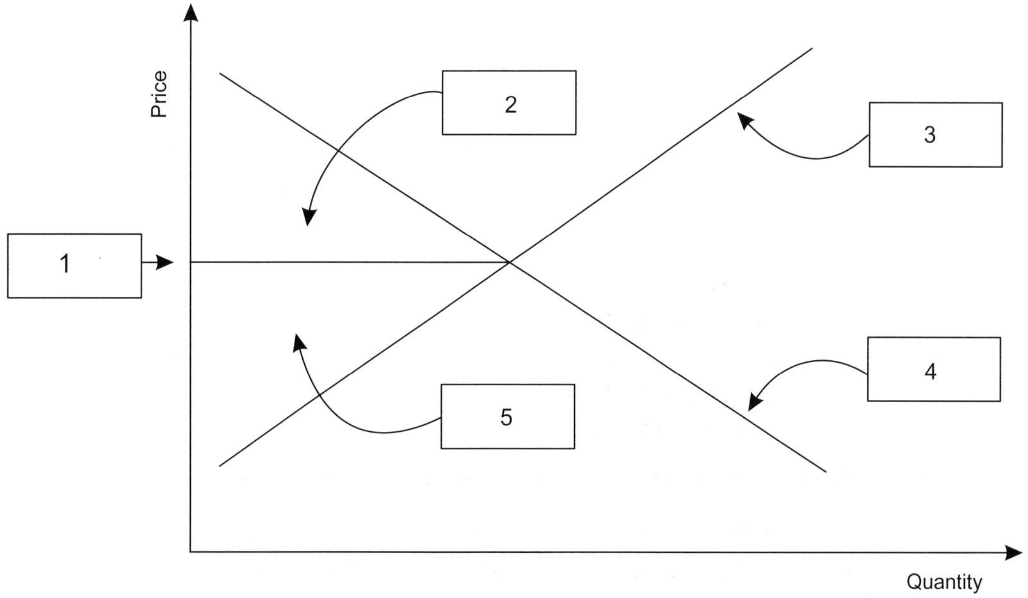

Labels:

A Equilibrium price
B Consumer surplus
C Market supply
D Market demand
E Producer surplus

11 If the cost of milk rises, and milk is a major ingredient in yoghurt, then the yoghurt:

A Demand curve shifts to the left
B Supply curve shifts to the left
C Supply curve shifts to the right
D Demand and supply curves both shift to the right

12 Which of the following is *not* one of the roles performed by prices in a market economy?

A A signal to consumers
B A signal to producers
C A way of allocating resources between competing uses
D A way of ensuring a fair distribution of incomes

13 The price elasticity of demand (PED) of good A is negative, its income elasticity of demand (IED) is positive and its cross elasticity of demand (XED) with respect to good X is negative. What is the nature of good A?

A A good bought for purposes of ostentation, complementary to X
B An inferior good, substitute for X
C A normal good, complementary to X
D A Giffen good, substitute for X

14 There are three special cases of elasticity of supply.

Put correct labels in the boxes on this diagram.

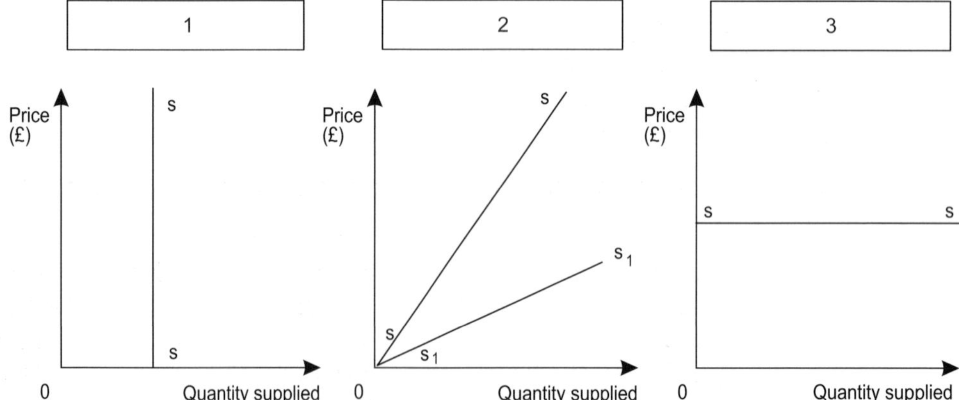

A Unit elastic supply
B Perfectly elastic supply
C Perfectly inelastic supply

15 The income elasticity of demand for a product is high. This means that:

A Sales will increase sharply if the price is reduced
B Sales will fall only slightly when incomes of households fall
C Sales will rise sharply when incomes of households rise
D The good is inferior good

16 A selective indirect tax will have predictable effects.

In this diagram, an indirect tax has been imposed and supply has shifted from S_0 to S_1.

Put the correct labels in the boxes on the diagram.

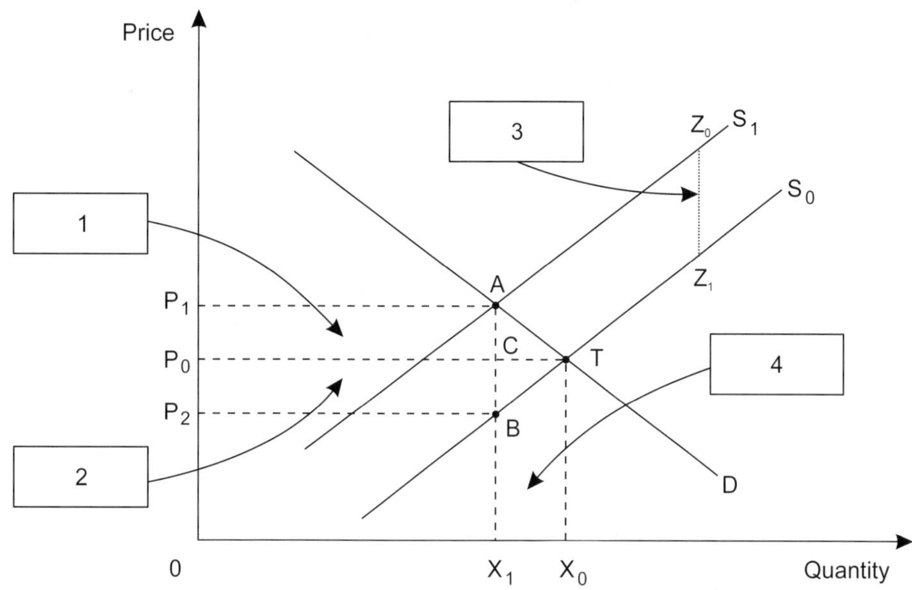

A Fall in output
B Tax borne by supplier
C Tax borne by customer
D Supernormal profit
E Tax imposed per unit

17 The table below shows a market demand schedule and a market supply schedule for beans.

Price per tonne £	*Quantity demanded per month* ('000 tonnes)	*Quantity supplied per month* ('000 tonnes)
280	4,000	9,200
260	5,000	8,800
240	6,400	8,200
220	7,400	7,400
200	8,200	6,600
180	9,000	5,800
160	9,800	4,800

What would be the consequences of the introduction by the government of a maximum price for beans of £200 per tonne? Assume that supply quantities can be readily adjusted to any new market conditions.

1 There would be a need for rationing of beans
2 There would be a 'bean mountain'
3 There would be a shortage of 1,600,000 tonnes per month
4 There would be a surplus of 1,600,000 tonnes per month
5 The price for beans would be unchanged

A Consequences 1 and 3 only
B Consequences 2 and 4 only
C Consequence 5 only
D Consequence 4 only

18 Which of the following statements about externalities is true?

(i) Externalities are the differences between the private and social costs or benefits of a transaction
(ii) Externalities are the benefits provided by merit goods
(iii) Monopolistic market transactions are characterised by the absence of positive externalities

A (i) and (iii) only
B (ii) only
C (i), (ii) and (iii)
D (i) only

19 Which diagram shows marginal cost and marginal revenue under perfect competition?

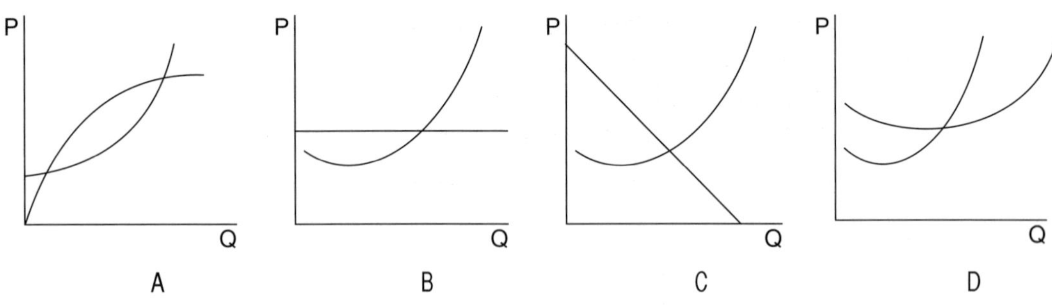

20 This diagram shows equilibrium under monopoly.

Label the diagram.

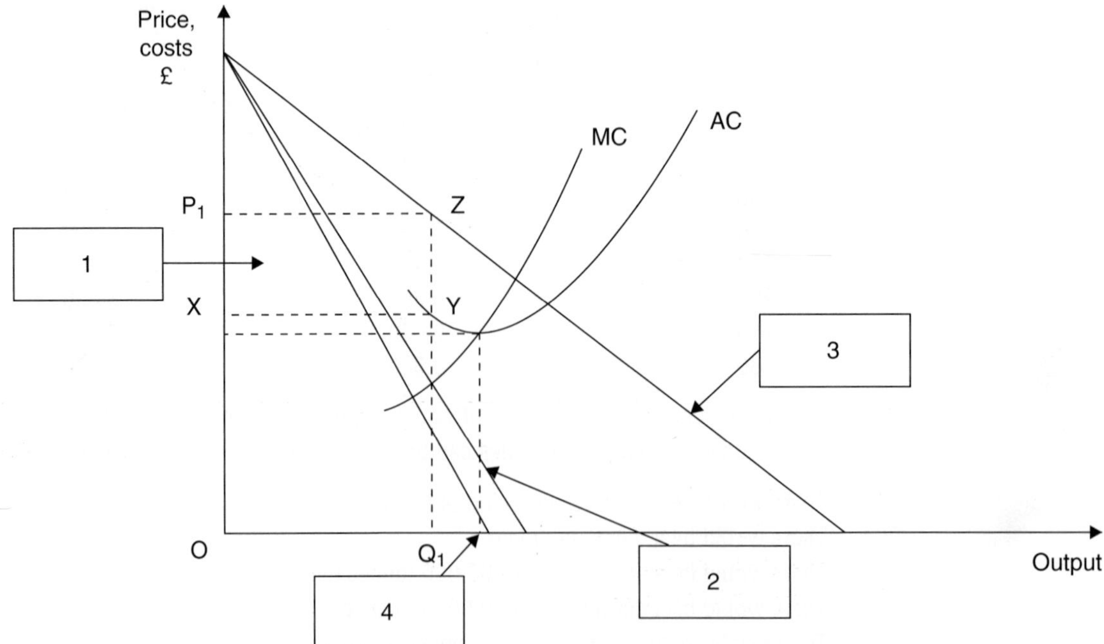

A Supernormal profit
B Marginal revenue
C Transfer earnings
D Profit maximising output
E Average revenue
F Most efficient level of output

21 Discounts are offered on the price of standby tickets on scheduled air flights because:

A Marginal revenue is increased by price discrimination
B Marginal cost exceeds average cost for standby seats
C Up to full occupancy, the marginal cost of seats is low
D Demand for seats is always price elastic

22 In what way does monopolistic competition differ from monopoly?

Under monopolistic competition:

A There is no possibility of supernormal profit
B There are no barriers to entry
C The excess capacity theorem does not apply
D The average revenue curve slopes downwards

23 Oligopoly markets usually show little price competition.

Label the diagram.

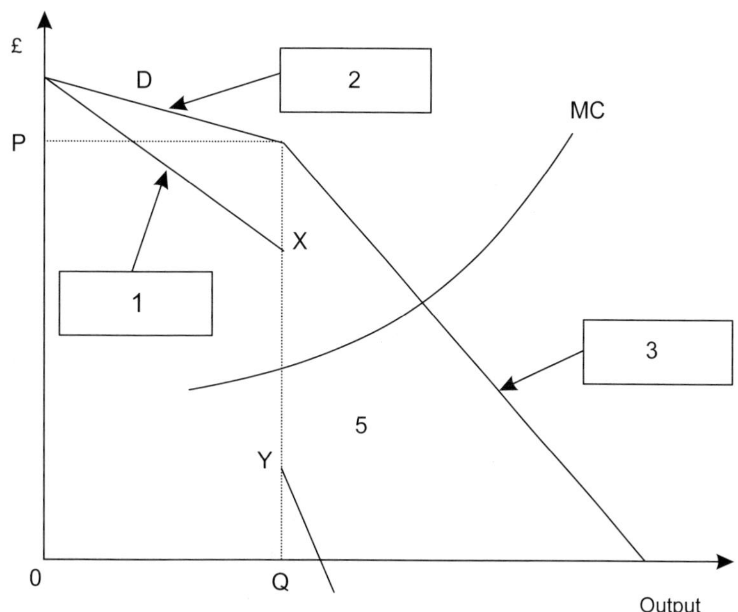

A Average cost
B Very inelastic demand
C Marginal revenue
D Very elastic demand

24 Which of the following statements about market concentration is correct?

A A straight line Lorenz curve at forty five degrees from the origin and a Herfindahl index of 10,000 both indicate perfect competition
B A Gini coefficient of zero and a Herfindahl index of 10,000 both indicate perfect competition
C A straight line Lorenz curve at forty five degrees from the origin and a Gini coefficient of unity both indicate perfect competition
D A Gini coefficient of zero and a Herfindahl index of zero both indicate perfect competition

25 Which of the following is not generally regarded as tending to justify government regulation of markets?

A Imperfect competition
B Externalities
C Regulatory capture
D Imperfect information

26 Which one of the following statements is *incorrect*?

A If the effect of privatisation is to increase competition, the effect might be to reduce or eliminate allocative inefficiency

B Privatisation means selling off nationalised industries by the government to the private sector

C The effect of denationalisation could be to make firms more cost-conscious, because they will be under the scrutiny of stock market investors

D The government may appoint consumer watchdogs to regulate privatised industries

27 The money market is most closely described as:

A The market for short-term capital, enabling businesses and government to maintain liquidity
B The market for trading unquoted company shares
C The market for mortgages, enabling individuals to buy their own homes
D A government agency for raising finance

28 What is a deficit unit?

A A kind of financial security
B A bank specialising in venture capital
C A 'blue chip' investment
D A firm or household that needs to borrow

29 What is maturity transformation?

A The rolling-over of government debt at its maturity date into new long-term bonds
B The packaging up of small investor deposits into large loans
C The conversion of short-term capital into long-term capital
D The banking practice of allowing depositors to withdraw funds at short notice while making long-term loans

30 The slope of a normal yield curve is:

A Upwards because of government monetary policy
B Upwards because of uncertainty about the future
C Downwards because of price inflation
D Downwards because of reducing demand

31 The relationship between the inflation rate (i), the money rate of interest (m) and the real rate of interest (r) is:

A $(1 + m) \times (1 + i) = (1 + r)$

B $\frac{(1+m)}{(1+i)} = (1 + r)$

C $(1 + m) \times (1 + r) = (1 + i)$

D $\frac{(1+r)}{(1+i)} = (1 + m)$

32 Which of the following is the most liquid asset of a commercial bank?

A Money at call
B Government Bonds
C Cash
D Operational balances with the Bank of England

33 Suppose that the US dollar - £ sterling exchange rate is initially $1.50 = £1. During the subsequent period of time, inflation in the USA is 2% and in the UK it is 12%. If the only movement in the exchange rate during this period could be explained by purchasing power parity theory, the exchange rate at the end of the time period would be:

A $1.3500 = £1
B $1.3660 = £1
C $1.6470 = £1
D $1.6500 = £1

34 Which of the following statements about exchange rates is correct?

(i) If Country A has 8% inflation and Country B has 12% inflation, Country A's currency will tend to weaken against that of Country B.
(ii) A country that has a persistent large deficit on its balance of trade cannot have a stable exchange rate in the short-term.
(iii) Foreign currency reserves are necessary when the exchange rate is fixed.

A (i) and (iii)
B (ii) only
C (ii) and (iii)
D (iii) only

35 IRR plc, a UK company, needs to pay a German supplier €550,000 in three months' time. It will have sufficient sterling to market the payment when it falls due, but not now. IRR borrows sufficient sterling to purchase €550,000 now, makes the currency exchange and puts the euros on deposit for three months in Germany, planning to use them to pay the supplier's invoice when it falls due and to repay its sterling loan with its own expected positive cash flow.

This technique is known as:

A A forward contract
B A leading payment
C A currency swap
D A money market hedge

36 Here are some entries from the national accounts of Psychomania. All entries are in millions of Psychomanian groats. 'Firms' includes public corporations.

Income of individuals before tax	9,000
Output of firms at sales value	20,000
Government expenditure	2,000
Firms' pre-tax profit	7,000
Firms' investment	3,000
Consumers' expenditure	11,000
Exports	4,000

What is the value of imports?

A 2,000
B 8,000
C 4,000
D 9,000

37 There is a circular flow of value around the macroeconomy

Label the diagram.

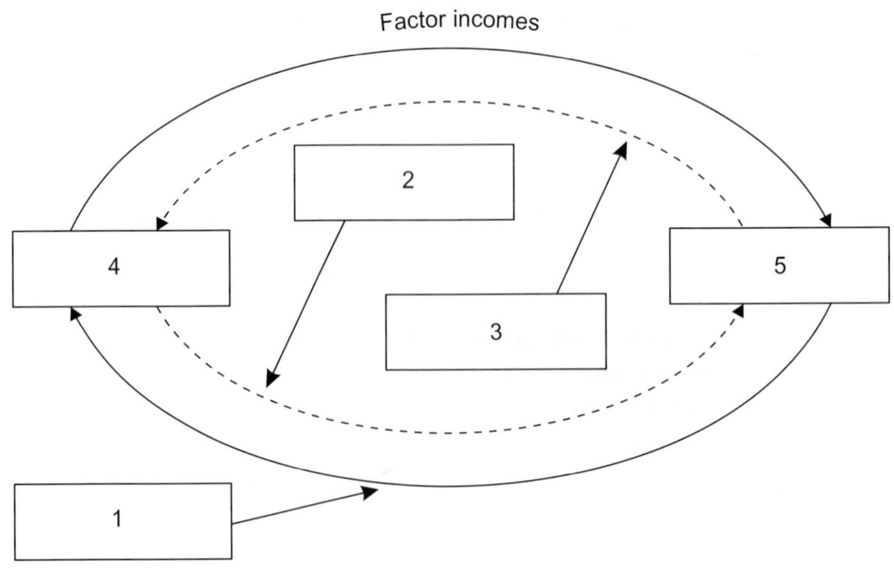

A Households
B Expenditure on goods and services
C Factors of production
D Firms
E Goods and services produced and sold

38 In the country of Petrovia, the nominal gross domestic product grew by 9% and real gross domestic product grew by 4%. Inflation for the year is:

A –5%
B 5%
C 9%
D 13%

39 Withdrawals from the circular flow of income in an economy are:

A Savings, investments and exports
B Investment, taxation and imports
C Investment, government spending and exports minus imports
D Savings, taxation and imports

40 Keynes applied the idea of supply and demand to the macroeconomy.

Label the diagram.

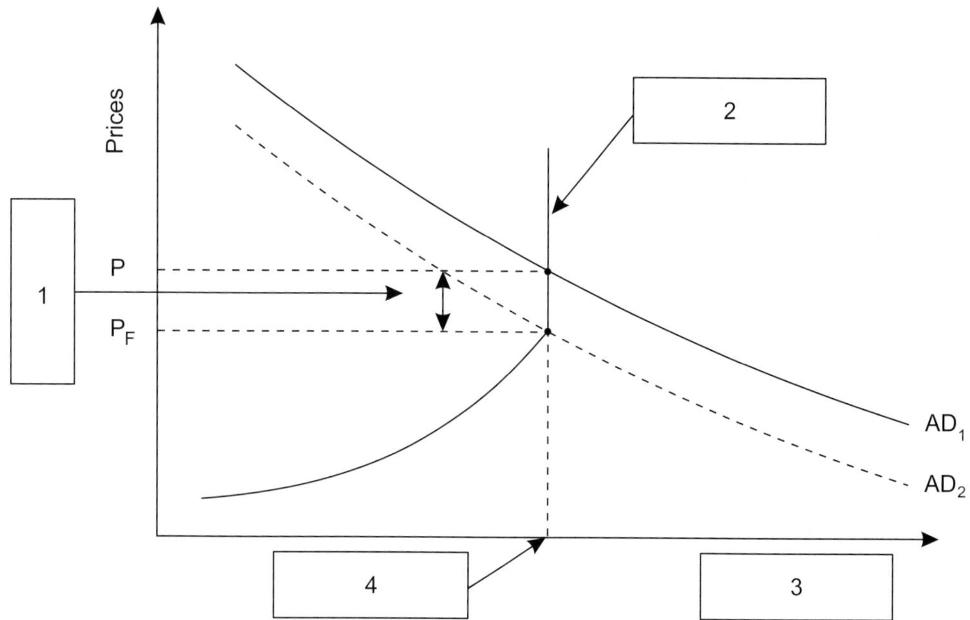

A Full employment level of output
B Real national income
C Inflationary gap
D Aggregate supply

41 The Phillips curve was at first seen as describing a method for the government to control the economy.

Label the diagram.

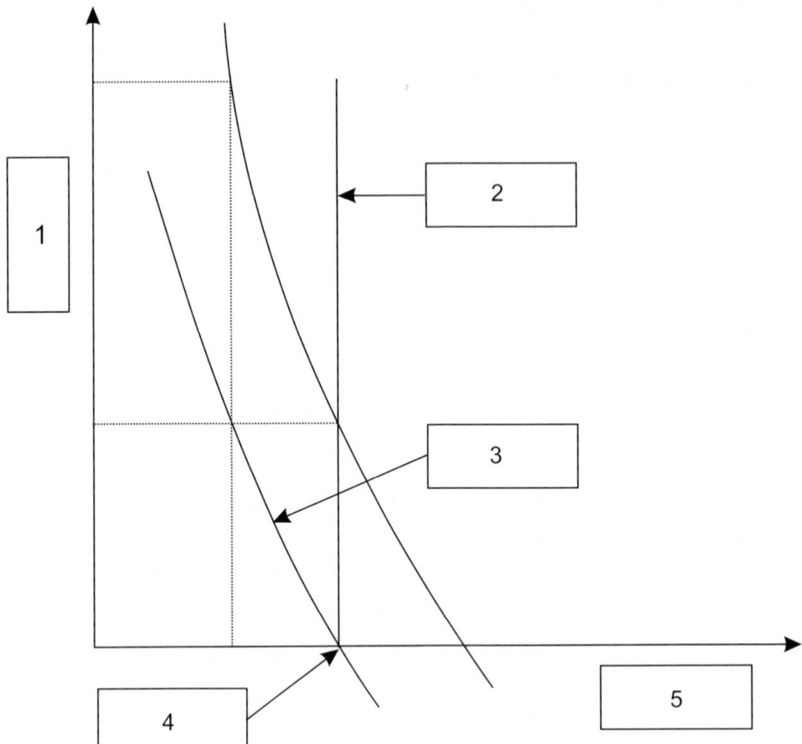

A Short run Phillips curve
B Unemployment
C Inflation
D Long run Phillips curve
E NAIRU

42 Which of the following diagrams shows an inflationary gap?

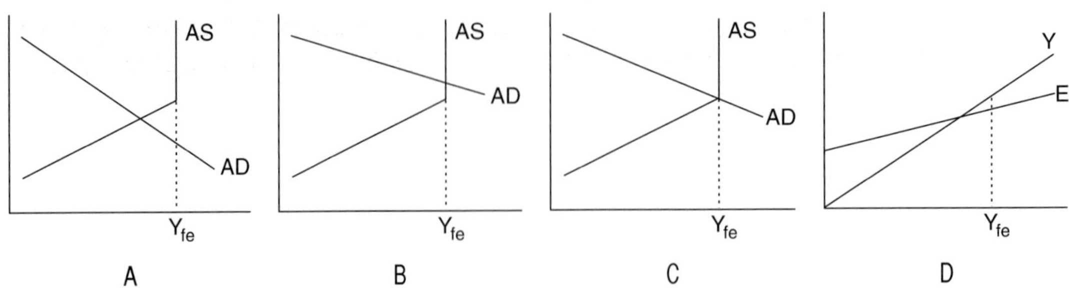

43 Which of the following is an example of structural unemployment?

A A computer programmer leaves his job and moves abroad
B A car worker is replaced by a robot
C A worker loses her job during a recession
D A construction worker is always unemployed during the winter months

44 Fixed interest securities that pay £1.50 every six months are trading at a price of £40 each, though their face value is £50 each. What is the current rate of annual interest available on investments of this type?

A 6%
B 3¾%
C 7½%
D 3%

45 The relationship between money supply and prices can be expressed in the quantity theory of money identity as follows.

A M/V = P/T
B MV = PT
C MP = VT
D MT = VP

46 A government wishes to continue to combine an expansionary fiscal stance with anti-inflationary monetary policy. What combination of policy instruments should it choose?

A Taxation up, borrowing down, interest rates up
B Spending down, taxation down, interest rates down
C Interest rates stable, taxation greater than spending
D Spending greater than taxation, interest rates up

47 The most likely effect of a cut in the basic rate of UK income tax is:

A A rise in the value of the pound
B A fall in the value of the pound
C A fall in the PSBR
D A fall in the amount of VAT receipts

48 According to the law of comparative advantage, the consequences of protectionism in international trade are that protectionist measures will prevent:

A Each country of the world from maximising its economic wealth
B Each country of the world from maximising the value of its exports
C The countries of the world from maximising their total output with their economic resources
D Each country of the world from achieving equilibrium in its balance of payments

49

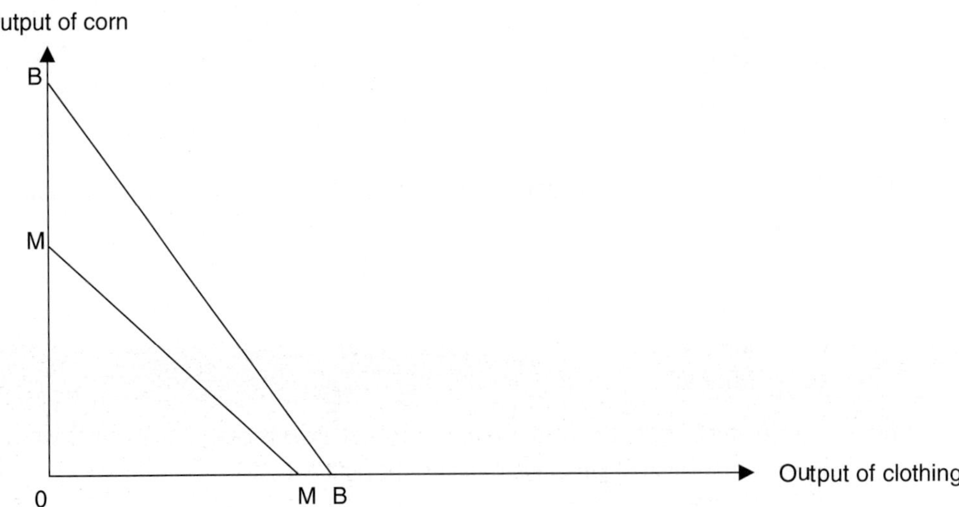

MM and BB represent production possibility boundaries of two countries, Mula and Burra respectively. Each country produces just two goods, corn and clothing. From the diagram, it can be seen that:

A Mula has a comparative advantage in the production of clothing

B Burra has an absolute advantage in the production of both corn and clothing

C In the absence of international trade, Burra has a higher national income per head of the population than Mula

D Burra has a comparative advantage in the production of clothing

50 A country has a comparative advantage over the other in producing coffee beans when:

A It has more coffee beans than the other country
B It can produce coffee beans at a lower opportunity cost than the other country
C It does not need to import coffee beans
D It wants to export as much coffee beans as possible

Answer Bank

1 D Scarce resources are the fundamental problem of economics

2 D These items will increase the economy's productive potential. A fall in employment does not increase productive potential, it merely makes better use of existing potential. Similarly, a fall in the price of a factor of production does not increase the amount of the factor that is available overall, though it may lead to the utilisation of a greater quantity of it.

3
(a) Secondary: this is manufacture, using a primary sector output
(b) Tertiary: this is distribution of a secondary sector by-product
(c) Tertiary: insurance of primary sector capital equipment
(d) Secondary: by definition
(e) Tertiary: finance for a primary sector asset

4 C Baumol is a name worth remembering. You will come across him again in other subjects.

5 B Smaller companies are often 'owner-managed', but larger public companies generally use hired managers to serve shareholders.

6 B 3 must be TC as it is the largest of any level of output greater than one unit. 2 is MC since it shows the increase in TC for each extra unit of production. Therefore 1 must be AC. Also 1 is equal to 3 divided by the units of output.

7
1 B Fixed costs plus variable costs equals total costs.
2 A Marginal cost crosses the average cost lines at their lowest points.
3 C Average total cost equals average fixed cost plus average variable cost.
4 E Average costs fall while marginal costs are lower and rise when they are higher.
5 D Fixed costs are spread over more units as output increases.

8 D The essence of constant returns to scale is that costs per unit do not change

9 D The effect of a cash subsidy is to shift the supply curve to the right. Producers are willing to supply bigger quantities at the same market price, because they will get a cash subsidy from the government in addition to the market price. The new supply curve goes through points 7, 8 and 9, and so the new equilibrium, given no change in demand, is at point 8.

10
1 A The market clears at the equilibrium price – there is neither surplus nor shortage.
2 B Some consumers would have paid a higher price.
3 C The higher the price, the more attractive it is to suppliers.
4 D The demand curve usually slopes downwards.
5 E Some suppliers would have sold at lower price.

11 B Demand conditions, and therefore the demand curve, are unchanged, Less will be supplied at a given price and so the supply curve will move to the left.

12 D A government may intervene, for example through progressive taxation, to make the distribution of income fairer.

13 C Ostentation goods and Giffen goods have positive PED. Inferior goods have negative IED. Substitutes have positive XED.

14
1 C Quantity available to purchase remains the same no matter what price is offered.
2 A Any straight line passing through the origin shows unit elasticity.
3 B Any desired quantity is available at the prevailing price, none at a lower price.

15 C The income elasticity of demand measures the responsiveness of demand to changes in consumers' incomes. An 'inferior' good has a negative income elasticity: as incomes fall, more is bought.

16
1 C Customer now pays P_1 instead of P_0
2 B Supplier receives P_2 net of tax instead of P_0
3 E The supply curve shifts vertically by the amount of the tax
4 A Demand is lower at the higher price

Supernormal profit does not appear in the diagram.

17 A Before the maximum price regulations were introduced, the equilibrium price was £220, with 7,400,000 tonnes demanded and supplied each month. With a maximum price of £200, demand will be 8,200,000 tonnes per month and supply only 6,600,000 tonnes per month. With demand exceeding supply, there wil be a bean shortage and a need for rationing - since prices cannot be raised to eliminate the excess demand.

18 D This is a point of definition. It is true to say that merit goods have merit because of the extensive positive externalities their provision creates, but this is not a definition of externalities. Monopolies are just as likely to generate externalities, both positive and negative, as any other market form.

19 B A shows total cost and total revenue and C shows marginal cost and marginal revenue, both where perfect competition does not exist. D shows marginal cost and average cost for a typical firm.

20
1 A Profits are maximised at output Q_1; revenues exceed opportunity costs.
2 B Marginal and average revenue must both fall if sales are to increase.
3 E
4 F Efficiency is highest when average costs are lowest, which is where MC cuts AC.

There is no label for profit maximising output.

Transfer earnings do not appear on the diagram.

21 C The marginal cost of vacant seats is low. Only a little more fuel and food cost is incurred, plus taxes.

22 B However, firms attempt to differentiate their products. Supernormal profits can be made, but they are likely to be competed away in the longer term. The excess capacity theorem applies. The AR curve slopes downwards in all market models except perfect competition.

23
1 C

2 D Customers will desert an oligopolist who increases prices

3 B A price cut will be matched by the other oligopolists, with little eventual change in market share.

Average cost is not shown on this diagram

24 D A straight line Lorenz curve at forty five degrees from the origin, a Gini coefficient of zero and a Herfindahl index of zero all indicate perfect competition. A Herfindahl index of 10,000 indicates monopoly.

25 C The others are types of market failure. Regulatory capture occurs when the regulator becomes unduly influenced by the regulated firms.

26 B Privatisation *could* mean selling off nationalised industries, but it can also refer to deregulation of industries to allow private firms to compete with state-run business (eg private bus companies) and contracting out work previously done by government employees to private firms (eg refuse collection).

Statement C is correct, and refers to the influence of stock market competition on newly-privatised monopolies. Statement D is correct: an example in the UK is the regulatory body Oftel for BT (formerly British Telecom).

27 A The money market meets short term capital requirements of companies and government.

28 D A deficit unit is an economic entity that needs more cash than it has.

29 D Maturity transformation is undertaken by banks. They can borrow short and lend long because they are confident that new depositors will continue to provide funds as time goes by.

30 B The interest charged on a long term loan is likely, *ceteris paribus*, to be higher than that charged on a short term loan because of the greater risk involved in committing money for the longer term.

31 B This is a definition.

32 C Cash is the most liquid asset of all.

33 B Purchasing power parity theory predicts that changes in exchange rates between two currencies are attributable to the different rates of price inflation in each country.

$$\text{New exchange rate (\$/£)} = \text{Old exchange rate} \times \frac{1 + \text{inflation rate in USA (\$)}}{1 + \text{inflation rate in UK (£)}}$$

The inflation rate is a proportion, and so 10% = 0.10 etc.

Therefore we have a new US dollar/pound sterling exchange rate of:

$$\$1.50 \times \left(\frac{1.02}{1.12}\right) = \$1.3660.$$

The dollar has strengthened in value against sterling because the rate of inflation has been lower in the USA than in the UK.

34 D If Country A has 8% inflation and Country B has 12% inflation, Country A's currency will tend to strengthen against Country B's. A large deficit on the balance of trade can persist for many years if there are adequate inward capital flows. A fixed exchange rate makes foreign currency reserves essential.

35 D This is a typical money market hedge.

36 C

National income	=	Income of individuals and profit of firms (income approach) = 9,000 + 7,000 = 16,000.
Also, national income	=	Total expenditure + exports – imports (expenditure approach)
⇒ 16,000	=	3,000 + 2,000 + 11,000 + 4,000 – imports
⇒ imports	=	5,000 + 11,000 + 4,000 – 16,000
	=	4,000

37

1	B	Expenditure is financed by factor incomes
2	E	Goods and services are produced by firms and consumed by households
3	C	Productive resources are land, labour, capital and enterprise
4	D	Firms produce for consumption by households
5	A	Households supply factors of production to firms

38 B Nominal gross domestic product is a measure of national output using current prices. Real gross domestic product measures national output using a constant set of prices. Real gross domestic product thus takes account of the changes in the price level and measures only the changes in real output. The difference in the growth rates of the two measures is attributable to changes in the price level. Inflation for the year must be 9% – 4% = 5%.

39 D This is a point of definition.

40 1 C With the economy at full employment, there is no spare capacity so an increase in aggregate demand produces inflation.

2 D Aggregate supply cannot increase once full employment is reached.

3 B National income and national output are the same thing.

4 A Full employment places an upper limit on output.

41 1 C

2 D Once NAIRU is reached, increases in aggregate demand only produce inflation.

3 A

4 E

5 B

42 B A and D show a deflationary gap. C shows an economy at ideal equilibrium.

43 B Structural unemployment is where long-term changes such as automation occur.

44 C A £40 investment produces an annual return of £3. This is equivalent to 7½%.

45 B The quantity theory of money identity states that MV = PT.

46 D B would reduce the size of the state sector, which would be contractionary; the reduction in interest rates might lead to sufficient private sector demand for the economy to expand overall, or it may not. The effect of such a policy combination on inflation is impossible to say.

A would control inflation by making a public sector debt repayment possible, as well as via interest rate control. However, this is not an expansionary fiscal stance.

C is a contractionary fiscal stance and a neutral policy on inflation.

47 B Consumption of all goods will increase, including imports. This will increase the supply of sterling on the currency markets and the price of sterling will therefore fall.

48 C A conclusion from the law of comparative advantage is that if free trade is allowed, countries will specialise in the production of goods and services in which they have a comparative advantage over other countries. As a result, the world's economic resources will be put to their most productive uses, and total output will be maximised. It does not follow that each country of the world will maximise its own national income or economic wealth (statement A), because the distribution of wealth between the individual countries in the world could be uneven, with some countries earning much more than others from their output and their exports.

49 A A production possibility boundary shows the possible combinations of two goods that a country can produce with its resources. The slope of the line for each country indicates the opportunity cost of producing corn in terms of lost production of clothing, and the opportunity cost of producing clothing in terms of lost production of corn. In Burra, the opportunity cost of producing corn is a lot less than it is in Mula. (If it were the *same* in both countries, the slopes of the production possibility boundaries would be parallel to each other.) This means that Burra has a comparative advantage in the production of corn. By the same analysis, we can conclude that Mula has a comparative advantage in the production of clothing.

Statement B cannot be proved or disproved. *Absolute* advantage cannot be ascertained from the diagram. Burra might be a country with *many more resources* than Mula, and absolute advantage refers to the production capabilities of each country *per unit of resource*.

Statement C cannot be proved or disproved either, because although Burra can produce more output in total than Mula, its national income per head of population depends on *population size*, for which we do not have any information.

50 B The other statements may be true but they do not describe comparative advantage.

Index and key terms

Note: Key Terms and their references are given in **bold**.

Review Form & Free Prize Draw – Paper C4 Fundamentals Of Business Economics (6/06)

All original review forms from the entire BPP range, completed with genuine comments, will be entered into one of two draws on 31 July 2006 and 31 January 2007. The names on the first four forms picked out on each occasion will be sent a cheque for £50.

Name: ______________________ **Address:** ______________________

____

____

How have you used this Interactive Text?
(Tick one box only)

☐ Home study (book only)
☐ On a course: college ______________
☐ With 'correspondence' package
☐ Other ______________

Why did you decide to purchase this Interactive Text? *(Tick one box only)*

☐ Have used BPP Texts in the past
☐ Recommendation by friend/colleague
☐ Recommendation by a lecturer at college
☐ Saw information on BPP website
☐ Saw advertising
☐ Other ______________

During the past six months do you recall seeing/receiving any of the following?
(Tick as many boxes as are relevant)

☐ Our advertisement in *Financial Management*
☐ Our advertisement in *Pass*
☐ Our advertisement in *PQ*
☐ Our brochure with a letter through the post
☐ Our website www.bpp.com

Which (if any) aspects of our advertising do you find useful?
(Tick as many boxes as are relevant)

☐ Prices and publication dates of new editions
☐ Information on Text content
☐ Facility to order books off-the-page
☐ None of the above

Which BPP products have you used?

Text	☑	*Success CD*	☐	*Learn Online*	☐
Kit	☐	*i-Learn*	☐	*Home Study Package*	☐
Passcard	☐	*i-Pass*	☐	*Home Study PLUS*	☐
MCQ cards	☐				

Your ratings, comments and suggestions would be appreciated on the following areas.

	Very useful	*Useful*	*Not useful*
Introductory section (Key study steps, personal study)	☐	☐	☐
Chapter introductions	☐	☐	☐
Key terms	☐	☐	☐
Quality of explanations	☐	☐	☐
Case studies and other examples	☐	☐	☐
Assessment focus points	☐	☐	☐
Questions and answers in each chapter	☐	☐	☐
Fast forwards and chapter roundups	☐	☐	☐
Quick quizzes	☐	☐	☐
Question Bank	☐	☐	☐
Answer Bank	☐	☐	☐
Index	☐	☐	☐
Icons	☐	☐	☐

Overall opinion of this Study Text *Excellent* ☐ *Good* ☐ *Adequate* ☐ *Poor* ☐

Do you intend to continue using BPP products? *Yes* ☐ *No* ☐

On the reverse of this page are noted particular areas of the text about which we would welcome your feedback.

The BPP author of this edition can be e-mailed at: steveosbourne@bpp.com

Please return this form to: Janice Ross, CIMA Certificate Publishing Manager, BPP Professional Education, FREEPOST, London, W12 8BR

Review Form & Free Prize Draw (continued)

TELL US WHAT YOU THINK

Please note any further comments and suggestions/errors below

Free Prize Draw Rules

1 Closing date for 31 January 2007 draw is 31 December 2006. Closing date for 31 July 2007 draw is 30 June 2007.

2 Restricted to entries with UK and Eire addresses only. BPP employees, their families and business associates are excluded.

3 No purchase necessary. Entry forms are available upon request from BPP Professional Education. No more than one entry per title, per person. Draw restricted to persons aged 16 and over.

4 Winners will be notified by post and receive their cheques not later than 6 weeks after the relevant draw date.

5 The decision of the promoter in all matters is final and binding. No correspondence will be entered into.

how banks create credit + prosperity.

Role of central bank + how it influences F.S

How to calc. the real rate of int.

Yields of instruments that trade in the F.M

Relationship btw risk + interest rates.

- Bank/credit multiplier.